LONGMAN LINGUISTICS LIBRARY

GENERATIVE AND NON-LINEAR PHONOLOGY

Generative and Non-Linear Phonology

Jacques Durand

LONGMAN

LONDON AND NEW YORK

Longman Group UK Limited
Longman House, Burnt Mill, Harlow,
Essex CM20 2JE, England
and Associated Companies throughout the world.

Published in the United States of America
by Longman Inc., New York

First published 1990
Third impression 1994

British Library Cataloguing in Publication Data
Durand, Jacques, 1947–
Generative and non-linear phonology.
(Longman linguistics library).
1. Generative phonology
I. Title
414

ISBN 0-582-00329-6 PPR
ISBN 0-582-05303-X CSD

Library of Congress Cataloging in Publication Data
Durand, Jacques, 1947 –
Generative and non-linear phonology.

(Longman linguistics library)
Bibliography: p.
Includes index.
1. Grammar, Comparative and general – Phonology.
2. Generative grammar. I. Title. II. Series.
P217.3.D87   1989   414   88-27203

Set in 10/11 pt Linotron 202 Times

Produced by Longman Singapore Publishers (Pte) Ltd.
Printed in Singapore

Contents

Preface

Phonology, to be judged by the number of monographs and articles on the subject, is a well-charted field. On close inspection, however, advanced syntheses of a kind which have become familiar in syntax are few and far between. The motivation of this book has been an attempt to provide such a synthesis – a book which would help fellow-linguists, students of linguistics, colleagues from neighbouring disciplines, and perhaps even fellow-phonologists, to take a global view of the field of modern phonology. Of course, I do not claim to have surveyed here all current ramifications of phonological theory. There are many strands (Natural Morphology, Two-level Morphology, Charm and Government Phonology to name but a few) which deserve treatment but are unfortunately not dealt with here. On the other hand, the space accorded, for instance, to a 'minority model' such as Dependency Phonology reflects my own theoretical prejudices. But it is my conviction that Dependency Phonology has given innovative answers to many problems and that phonological theory is only slowly rediscovering some of the solutions tentatively proffered in this framework.

I have chosen to embed this book in the paradigm defined by Chomsky and Halle in the *Sound Pattern of English* (1968) and then to depart from this paradigm in various directions. The amount of space devoted to classical issues in what follows will be seen by some as a distraction from the preoccupations of the moment. But it is my conviction that current approaches still feed off SPE and most articles presuppose a solid understanding of classical generative concepts, not to mention a good knowledge of the pre-generative literature. A reconfiguration of the field which makes Chomsky and Halle's work obsolete has not yet taken place, even though many current proposals point to directions far removed from this classical paradigm. In any case, it seems to me that there is a way of reasoning about phonological generalizations and underlying systems inherited from SPE and precursors like Sapir and Bloomfield which is still shared by modern generative phonologists and is worth exploring in some detail.

A great number of people have helped me in the preparation of this volume, either in discussion or in reading chapters of the manuscript. Among the people who provided me with useful and stimulating feedback on portions of the book, may I, in particular, thank Gillian Brown, Keith Brown, Monik Charette, Fran Colman, Heinz Giegerich, Richard Hogg, Harry van der Hulst, Erik Koning, Bernard Laks, Ken Lodge, Chris McCully, Tina Tan Stok Mei, Kim Plested, Andy Spencer and Peter Trudgill. While their advice has been precious to me, they are not to be held responsible for any of the errors or wrong-headed ideas promoted in this book.

Two Essex colleagues, Ian Crookston and Jane Shelton, deserve a special mention as they undertook to read the last version of the manuscript and tracked down a number of inconsistencies and errors. More generally, I am greatly indebted to the whole Department of Language and Linguistics at Essex University for providing over the years such a fine environment for doing linguistics.

I would like to take this opportunity of thanking the Longman series editors, Professor Martin Harris and Professor R. H. Robins for their encouragements and constructive criticisms. Indeed, I found the whole editorial staff at Longman most helpful at all stages of the preparation of this book.

I would also like to record a special debt of gratitude to John Anderson for stimulating collaboration within the framework of Dependency Phonology. May this association and our friendship long continue!

I would also like to thank Emmanuel Flipo of Pezenas, France for providing the cover painting for this book.

Last but not least, I wish to thank my wife, Jane, and my children, Marianne and Sophie, for all the support, warmth and love they gave me during the writing of this book.

List of Main Abbreviations

U   Utterance
UG   Universal grammar
UPSID   UCLA Phonological Segment Inventory Database
UT   Underspecification Theory
V   Vowel
VS   Vowel Shift
WFRs   word-formation rules

Chapter 1

Introduction

1.1 Scope of this book

In 1968, Chomsky and Halle's monumental book *The Sound Pattern of English*, was published. While work in generative phonology stretched back to the late 1950s, *The Sound Pattern of English* (hereafter *SPE*) defined a paradigm that is often referred to as 'standard' or 'classical generative phonology'. Since *SPE* offered *inter alia* a theory of the internal structure of sound-segments, a theory of levels and derivation, a theory of the link-up between syntax and phonology, much work since 1968 has been devoted to upholding or rejecting some fundamental thesis or other of this work.

Initially, the major body of assumptions made by Chomsky and Halle remained fairly stable and most researchers were content, as it were, to nibble at the *SPE* edifice. More recently, however, many of the *SPE* theses have been much more fundamentally questioned within a variety of frameworks including Autosegmental Phonology, Metrical Phonology, CV Phonology, Dependency Phonology, Three-dimensional Phonology, Grid-only Phonology, etc. All these models can be described as **non-linear** by opposition to standard generative phonology where, as will be detailed in this book, a phonological representation is simply depicted as a **linear** arrangement of sound-segments (even though each segment is composed of simultaneously occurring features) and where phonological rules operate on such strings (they delete, insert or permute segments, or change their feature-values).

Despite undeniable differences in outlook between the current alternative frameworks, there are many lines of convergence between them and a fair measure of agreement on what a theory of phonology should account for. In particular, they all share the belief that phonological representations need to be much more articulated than traditionally assumed and that a number of phenomena (particularly, but not exclusively, stress and tone contours) cannot be appropriately accounted for if phonological representations are limited to string-like arrangements of segments and boundaries. Chapters 6, 7 and 8 are devoted to non-linear issues and it will be shown that the insights of various independent frameworks can be combined in 'multidimensional' representations. Whether the label 'non-linear' is always appropriate in connection with current proposals is not a question with which I will be concerned here (see J. M. Anderson 1987b). I shall use it as a cover term for a set of hypotheses concerning phonological structure which I will in turn subsume under the umbrella term 'generative phonology'.

There are good reasons to retain the label 'generative phonology'. Firstly, even if many current insights had been anticipated in other schools, the 'non-linear' models described here have clearly arisen from the practice of generative phonologists confronted with phenomena which were difficult to handle within the *SPE* notation. Secondly, portions of the standard theory (*eg* distinctive features) are often preserved in 'non-linear' accounts. Thirdly, the 'non-linear' frameworks do not exhaust the set of new proposals concerning phonological structure. Two important developments, presented in Chapter 5, Underspecification Theory and Lexical Phonology, address questions which are partially orthogonal to the linear–non-linear dimension. Finally, *SPE*-based analyses often form the backdrop to current work (*cf eg* Mohanan 1986; Kenstowicz and Rubach 1987) or are even recast, with minor changes, into new theoretical frameworks (*cf* Halle and Mohanan 1985 and Chs. 4–5). In other words, while there are many local changes, there is no sharp overall discontinuity with the past. In fact, many of the issues still debated in phonology – *eg* the role played by levels – go back to the practice of seminal thinkers such as Bloomfield or Sapir. Readers of recent technical articles certainly need to be as familiar with the conceptual and notational apparatus of *SPE* as with the tools devised within more recent frameworks.

I have therefore chosen to offer a broad view of the field and hope that this book will give the reader a good perspective on current developments while preserving a modicum of historical depth. I have presupposed very little knowledge of phonology on the part of the reader but assume a basic knowledge of phonetics of the sort which is available in Ladefoged's *A Course in Phonetics* (1982). The rest of this chapter sketches an introduction to standard generative phonology by relating it to classical structuralist assumptions. However, no attempt is made at a real historical reconstruction and the reader is asked to exercise some charity in this connection. There are excellent discussions of past schools of phonology in S. R. Anderson (1985), Fischer-Jørgensen (1975), Lass (1984) and Sommerstein (1977), among others. Chapters 2 and 3 are devoted to the theory of distinctive features and related topics and sketch much of the background required to present recent technical developments. In Chapter 4, 'The derivational issue: aspects of the abstractness–concreteness debate', I broach questions which, while not currently fashionable, confront any phonologist in his or her practice: What distance is allowed between underlying representations and surface representations? Should underlying representations be constrained? Should rules be ordered? While the framework of Natural Generative Phonology devised in the 1970s in reaction against *SPE* abstractness will be found wanting, it forces phonologists to think hard about their constructs and seems to me to deserve a place in the survey offered here. In addition, without a good understanding of the classical analysis of English segmental phonology presented in 4.2, frameworks such as Lexical Phonology would be difficult to present and discuss. Most of the chapters can be read in relative independence of one another but, of course, examples recur and there are many cross-references.

1.2 From classical phonemics to generative phonology

At the root of writings on sound structure from a classical or structuralist perspective is the assumption that, behind the diversity of sounds as physical units, there is in each language a small set of sounds whose function is to distinguish words from one another. For instance, the difference between the spoken realizations of *lack* and *rack* is made possible by the fact that /l/ and /r/ are two distinctive sounds of English, or **phonemes**, conventionally enclosed between diagonals. Phonemes can be sequenced according to rules, often referred to as **phonotactic** rules, which vary from language to language. English allows /s/ + consonant word-initially (*cf spirit*), whereas Spanish forbids such sequences unless a vowel precedes (*espíritu*).[1] One way of coining new words is to take advantage of unexploited gaps in the distribution of phonemes as in Lewis Carroll's Jabberwocky: 'Twas brillig, and the slithy toves, Did gyre and gimble in the wabe: All mimsy were the borogoves, And the mome raths outgrabe.'

These two criteria – distinctive function and combinatorial possibilities – set phonemes apart from other sounds that play a role in a communication event. Take the example of clicks in English – *ie* sounds such as the awkwardly transcribed *tut(-tut)* (IPA [ʇ]) which is used to express mild disapproval or the *gee-up* used as a command to horses. While these sounds are relevant for the purpose of communication, they are quite different from phonemes: in English, they do not combine with other sounds and do not differentiate words from one another. In fact, *tut(-tut)* functions as a whole 'word' very much like the signs used by children at an early stage of language acquisition. There is, however, no natural reason preventing clicks from combining with other sounds and playing a distinctive role in a language. In some African languages like Zulu, clicks are contrastive units and combine with vowels to make up words. So the clicks are phonemes in Zulu but not in English.

Following the above, we can define **phonology**, from a classical perspective, as the component of language that deals with phonemes and their possible combinations (**phonotactics**). While the ability to produce and understand clicks, for instance, is undeniably part of the overall communicative competence of speakers of English, ideophones, as such sounds are called, will not be considered part of the **phonology** of the language. They constitute an example of what Abercrombie (1968) defines as paralanguage: *ie* the set of features (whether phonic or gestural) which modulate spoken language. Jakobson and Waugh (1979: 28–35) argue that the differences in linguistic status that we establish between sounds is grounded in neurology. Some split-brain patients retain the ability to produce paralinguistic sounds while suffering from global aphasia, suggesting that a different part of the brain is responsible for paralinguistic sounds from that responsible for language (see 2.4).

1.2.1 Phonemes and allophones

In positing phonemes, we operate at a fair degree of abstraction from real sounds by thinking of contrasting units at a given position within words. Observation of speech-events reveals, however, that sounds which we consider as tokens of identical phonemes can in fact be noticeably different according to their position within words or sentences. Let us take a familiar example from English. If we consider two words such as *train*

and *rain*, transcribed in this book as /trejn/ and /rejn/, we find
that the /r/ in *train* is auditorily different from the /r/ in *rain*.
Under the influence of /t/ which is voiceless and aspirated in this
position, the /r/ is partially devoiced and some friction is audible.
We can indicate the distinction between these two *r*'s by phonetic
transcriptions (within square brackets) such as [rejn] vs. [tr̥ejn].
The reason why speakers of English do not normally attend to
this phonetic distinction, and cope well with a writing system
which uses only one *r* symbol, is that no two words of English
are differentiated by [r] vs. [r̥]. These two *r*'s are contextual
realizations, technically called **allophones**, of the phoneme /r/.
Following classical assumptions, we can say that there are two
fundamental levels of representation of sounds: the level of
phonemes (phonemic level) and the level of allophones (phonetic
level). Two further examples of this distinction are given in [1]:

[1] phonemic level   /pepə/ pepper   /lɪlt/ lilt
    phonetic level   [pʰepə]   [lɪɫt]

In the case of *pepper*, the first /p/, but not the second, is aspirated since it occurs in a stressed position. (But note that in the
context of a preceding /s/, as in *spin* [spɪn], no aspiration occurs.)
In *lilt*, the first /l/ is 'clear' (*ie* has front vowel resonance)
whereas the second /l/ is 'dark' or 'velarized' (*ie* involves a
raising of the back of the tongue towards the soft palate).

One piece of evidence that aspiration is automatically determined is provided by slips of the tongue. In errors of the type
petid for *tepid*, we observe [pʰetɪd]. Now, if the shifting of the
/p/ had taken place at the phonetic level we would expect
[petʰɪd] from [tʰepɪd]. On the other hand, if the substitution is
made at a processing level corresponding to the phonemic representation, we can assume that /tepɪd/ → /petɪd/ and that
aspiration is determined after the substitution.

1.2.2 Mappings and rules

In classical phonemics, the question of the mapping between the
two levels of representation was not usually considered a burning
issue. Most structuralist works simply give lists of allophones
beside each phoneme or non-symbolic descriptions of the realizations of phonemes. Generative phonology, by contrast, is
committed to a programme where the primitive terms and the
rules for their combination and transformation must be couched
in symbolic notation and formally defined. Thereby, an important
step is taken towards making the system easier to fault, or to

refute, and our descriptions should be highly valued according to a common view of what defines a scientific enterprise.

The standard way of expressing the relationship between phonemes and realizations adopted in generative phonology is by means of rules on the format of [2]:

[2] $/r/ \rightarrow \text{ɹ} / \begin{bmatrix} -\text{voice} \\ -\text{continuant} \end{bmatrix}$ _____

This is to be read as: the phoneme $/r/$ is realized as voiceless in the context of a preceding voiceless stop, where '/' indicates the beginning of the context, and _____ marks the position of the segment undergoing the transformation. Here [2] uses classificatory features which can have a positive or a negative value allowing us to identify the set of segments providing a context for the rule (*eg* [−continuant] is to be read as 'minus continuant' = stop). A level-oriented presentation of the same rule is given below:

[3] phonemic level $\begin{bmatrix} -\text{voice} \\ -\text{continuant} \end{bmatrix} \begin{matrix} /r/ \\ \downarrow \end{matrix}$

   phonetic level $\qquad\qquad\qquad [\text{ɹ}]$

To obtain [2] from [3], isolate the two segments undergoing the change by writing them horizontally ($r \rightarrow \text{ɹ}$), leave a dash instead of the top $/r/$ and write this modified top line to the right of '/' which marks the environment of the rule.

In more abstract terms, phonological rules reduce to [4]:

[4] $A \rightarrow B / X \_\_Y$

which says that an element of type A is to be rewritten as an element of type B when A appears in the context $X \_\_Y$ (that is, with X to its left and Y to its right, where X and Y may be empty).

One of the central tenets of generative phonology is that the rules of a language interact in complex ways. Many structuralist writings seem to assume that the mapping is simple and one-shot – that is, a whole level is translated into another level by rules applying simultaneously to the input. But this does not account for even simple examples of allophonic statements to be found in standard structuralist expositions. For example, following Jones (1964) and Gimson (1980), it seems reasonable to analyse Received Pronunciation (RP) $/l/$ at the phonemic level as an alveolar lateral unspecified for 'frontness' or 'backness' since the clear and dark allophones of $/l/$ can be determined by the following rule:

[5] L-realization

$$/l/ \rightarrow \begin{cases} [ł] / \underline{\hspace{1cm}} \begin{Bmatrix} \# \\ C_I \end{Bmatrix} & \text{[5a]} \\ [l] \text{ elsewhere} & \text{[5b]} \end{cases}$$

In rule [5], we are collapsing two (or more) rules into one schema by factoring out common elements and enclosing the differences inside braces. Here, the outside braces abbreviate two sub-rules. Case [5a] makes /l/ velarized in two contexts themselves collapsed within braces: (i) at the end of a word, marked here by a # boundary (*hell, sill, canal*); (ii) when it is followed by one or more consonants (*help, silky, paltry*). Case [5b] applies if case [5a] does not apply. Following Kiparsky (1973a), we could leave the word 'elsewhere' out, if we agreed that in rules of this form, the braces indicate that the rules are **disjunctively** ordered. In other words, if [5a] applies then [5b] is skipped, but if [5a] does not apply, then [5b], which is the most general case, automatically comes into force.

Now, in dealing with /e/, Jones (1964: 71) notes the existence of 'an opener and retracted variety when 'dark' *l* follows' – which we will transcribe as [ë]. This allophonic statement can be formulated as

[6] E-retraction
$$/e/ \rightarrow [ë] / - [ł]$$

It should be clear that [5] and [6] cannot apply simultaneously since the environment of [6] is supplied by [5]. In other words, [5] and [6] must apply in a linear order with rule [5] 'feeding' rule [6]. The relationship between rules is therefore well worth examining and various types of rule ordering will be considered below.

1.2.3 Classical tests for the identification of phonemes
In classical phonemics, the identification of phonemes was usually done according to a battery of tests. Here, we can content ourselves with four central criteria: opposition, complementary distribution, phonetic similarity and free variation. The term 'phone' will be used for a sound-unit whose status is still in the balance.

1.2.3.1 *Opposition*
Given two phones, if replacing one by the other yields a different lexical item, they can tentatively be considered as different phonemes. To make this test operational, one takes what are called **minimal pairs**: that is, two words which are identical except at one place in the sequence. Thus, in English, [set], [bet],

[let], [net] are minimal pairs and give us ground for positing phonemes such as /s/, /b/, /l/ and /n/.

1.2.3.2 Complementary distribution

If two phones always occur in mutually exclusive environments, they can tentatively be considered as allophones of the same phoneme. The two variants of *r* ([r], [ɹ]) mentioned above occur in complementary environments and can be tentatively considered as realizations of the phoneme /r/.

1.2.3.3 Phonetic similarity

The above criteria are not watertight enough as they stand. While aspirated [pʰ] and non-aspirated [p] would correctly be grouped together as allophones of the phoneme /p/, it is equally true that aspirated [tʰ] and non-aspirated [p], for instance, also occur in complementary distribution. In grouping [pʰ] and [p] together, but not [tʰ] and [p], a tacit appeal is usually made to the notion of phonetic similarity. Without phonetic similarity, the most absurd groupings could become possible. For instance, it has often been pointed out that [h] and [ŋ] could be analysed as realizations of one phoneme on the grounds that [h] always occurs at the beginning of a syllable, whereas [ŋ] always occurs at the end of a syllable. The reason why this grouping has never been seriously entertained is that phonetically [h] and [ŋ] share very little apart from the fact that they are consonants. The notion of 'phonetic similarity' is, of course, vague but can be made more precise by reference to distinctive features (*cf* Ch. 2).

1.2.3.4 Free variation

If two phones can be substituted for each other in the same environment without destroying the identity of the lexical item under consideration, they can be said to be free variants of the same phoneme. For instance, in English final stops can be released with explosive noise or unreleased, and often reinforced with a glottal stop (as in *eg cat* [kætʰ] or [kætº] or [kæʔt]), whereas in some languages like French they must be released explosively. The various types of final [t] in English would be said to be free variants of the phoneme /t/. It is often pointed out by sociolinguists that so-called 'free variants' are, in fact, controlled by sociolinguistic variables and not freely interchangeable as suggested by the traditional labelling. While this may be correct, it is still useful to distinguish non-distinctive variation at one point of the phonic chain from variation due to the position of allophones within lexical units.

In structuralist writings the above tests were supplemented by notions such as 'pattern congruity', 'economy' and 'completeness'. But, the most striking characteristic of the approach taken by a number of influential American linguists in the 1940s and 1950s, often referred to as the post-Bloomfieldians, was the construing of these tests as **discovery procedures**. For a variety of methodological and philosophical reasons that we need not go into here (cf eg Hyman 1975: Ch. 3, Lyons, 1977: Ch. 3, Sommerstein, 1977: Ch. 2), it was believed that the phonemic structure of a language could be unlocked by the mechanical application of criteria such as 'opposition', 'complementary distribution', etc. Moreover, the description of the sound-system had to be done without reference to the grammatical system. As Hockett (1942: 20–1) put it: 'There must be no circularity; phonological analysis is assumed for grammatical analysis, and so must not assume any part of the latter.' The description, in other words, had to be bottom-up (from sounds to grammatical structure) and inductive.

The programme of early generative phonology was very much a reaction against classical phonemics. Chomsky (1964), in particular, offered a devastating critique of the methodological stances of the post-Bloomfieldians. He showed that if we formalize the conditions on phonological representations of types 1.2.3. 1–4 above, they are either unclear or impose conditions on phonological representations which are far too strong. Section 1.2.4 offers an example of the kind of argumentation used by Chomsky. This is not to say that criteria 1.2.3.1–4 are worthless. They are part of the arsenal of heuristic procedures that linguists use when describing a language. But they do not yield an analysis as such. How a linguist reaches his/her analysis is not crucial. What is important is how theoretical constructs correspond to 'facts', what consequences flow from them, etc. In that sense, modern phonology is resolutely hypothetico-deductive.

However, it is also fair to point out that a number of the key concepts of classical phonemics were preserved in generative phonology (eg 'junctures' under the guise of boundaries). Crucially, the idea that phonological representations were essentially sequences of segments following one another like beads on a string was inherited from previous work. Other schools (like the Firthians) were more or less ignored and it is only in more recent work (cf Ch. 7) that this 'oversight' has been corrected.

1.2.4 On the insufficiency of surface contrast
As reported in Chomsky (1964), there are accents of American

English where the words *writer* and *rider* are respectively pronounced [rajɾər] and [ra:jɾər], where [ɾ] is a (voiced) 'flap', and the final sequence [ər] is often a single retroflexed vowel [ɚ], and diphthongs are transcribed as sequences of vowel + semi-vowel. Given that the phonetic distinction between [a:] and [a] encodes a difference in meaning, if we applied the principles of phonemicization mechanically, we would set up a phonemic opposition between /a/ and /a:/ (or /aj/ and /a:j/ for clarity). But this is unsatisfactory on various grounds.

First of all, the length distinction between [aj] and [a:j] is clearly predictable in all other contexts. That is, we observe [aj] before voiceless consonants ([sajt] *sight*, [rajt] *write*) and [a:j] before voiced consonants ([sa:jd] *side*, [ra:jd] *ride*). Generalizing, there is, in fact, an independently motivated rule of lengthening, which, ignoring complexities involving the precise degree of lengthening, can be formulated as

[7] Lengthening
$$V \rightarrow [+\text{long}] / \text{_____} \text{ (j) } \begin{bmatrix} C \\ +\text{voice} \end{bmatrix}$$

In other words, a vowel (V) is lengthened in the context of a following voiced consonant (C), with an optional /j/ intervening between the two. (Optionality, here and throughout, is indicated by parentheses.)

The flap is also normally the result of a neutralization of the /t/ − /d/ contrast in examples like [bɪɾər] *bitter* vs. [bɪɾər] *bidder*. That is, there is a rule of the form [8] operative in American English:

[8] Flapping
$$\begin{Bmatrix} t \\ d \end{Bmatrix} \rightarrow ɾ / \begin{bmatrix} V \\ \text{stressed} \end{bmatrix} \text{\_\_\_\_} \begin{bmatrix} V \\ \text{unstressed} \end{bmatrix}$$

American speakers are usually able to recover the underlying consonant in slow speech. But, even if, for some words, there is uncertainty, the rule of flapping is clearly active. If a speaker forms a new word by adding a suffix such as *-er* or *-ing* to a base ending in /t, d/, a flap automatically appears instead of /t, d/: *eg kit* [kɪt] would give rise to [kɪɾər] *kitter*. If we recognize the relevance of the morphological make-up of words, the underlying representations that suggest themselves for *writer* and *rider* are respectively /rajtər/ and /rajdər/.

If this is correct, how can we account for the surface realizations? All we need to do is assume that the two rules just described apply to these underlying representations in the fixed order lengthening–flapping as shown below:[2]

[9]

Underlying form	/rajtər/ 'writer'	/rajdər/ 'rider'
Lengthening	——	raːjdər
Flapping	rajɾər	raːjɾər
Phonetic form	[rajɾər]	[raːjɾər]

If, on the other hand, we made the notion of surface phonetic contrast central, and postulated a phonemic opposition /aj/-/aːj/, we would have to restrict this opposition to one environment (before a flap). At the same time, we would leave unexpressed the relation of *writer* to *write* and *rider* to *ride*, and we would fail to resort to two general and independently motivated rules of the phonology. It is therefore no accident that structuralists such as Harris (1951: 70–1) when faced with these dire consequences drew away from applying the methodological principles they were advocating and accepted underlying forms such as the above.

In addition to the situation summarized by [9], there are speakers of American English who pronounce *writer* and *rider* identically as [raːjɾər]. Do we need to assume that their underlying forms are different from the ones given in [9]? Given that the grammatical system used by these speakers contains the same rules and the same morphological relations, we can account quite straightforwardly for the observed pronunciations, if we simply posit that the rules of flapping and lengthening apply in the opposite order from [9] as in [10]:

[10]

Underlying form	/rajtər/ 'writer'	/rajdər/ 'rider'
Flapping	rajɾər	rajɾər
Lengthening	raːjɾər	raːjɾər
Phonetic form	[raːjɾər]	[raːjɾər]

Since the flap is a voiced sound the application of flapping in [10] feeds lengthening and, as a result, the latter now applies to more inputs than in [9]. We observe here a situation where two accents have the same underlying forms and rules but differ in rule application. We will see later in Chapter 4, that within the standard generative tradition, the observable differences between modern accents of English are argued to conceal striking similarities at the underlying level and in the set of core rules of the language.

On the basis of examples such as the above, Chomsky (1964) argued that the structuralist ideal of a one-to-one correspondence between underlying forms and surface realizations can be systematically flouted. An underlying distinction at point X in the phonemic chain may be neutralized or coded at a non-corresponding point Y of the phonetic chain. Surface representations mirror only indirectly underlying representations (as detailed at various points of this book).

1.2.5 Rule ordering
If all rule orderings were of the type exemplified in [5] and [6], where L-realization feeds E-retraction, no ordering statement would need to be made in the grammar. Here E-retraction cannot be ordered before L- realization since it would never apply. We could therefore resort to a general principle that rules must apply whenever their structural description is met or that rules must be ordered in a way so as to maximize feeding relations. The situation here is similar to the one in syntax where given two rules: (i) S → NP VP, (ii) NP → DET N, the application of (ii) requires (i) to have applied. The ordering of (i) and (ii) follows from the content of the rules and is technically called **intrinsic**. By contrast, we have seen that in [9] and [10], two grammars could differ in terms of the ordering relationships between two (or more) rules. The ordering in such cases does not follow from general principles and is said to be **extrinsic**. The position advocated in standard generative phonology and much work derived from it is that rules are **linearly ordered** (that is, not simultaneous) and that **extrinsic orderings** are required. This issue is taken up again in Chapter 4 which exemplifies much more involved orderings than the above.

1.3 Phonemes or features?

So far we have operated with a mixture of symbols representing either phonemes or fairly *ad hoc* features. One question that we have deliberately left aside is the following: what are the primitive building blocks of sound structure? A traditional answer to this question is that **phonemes** are the ultimate units of phonological structure, *ie* the elements that keep morphemes apart from one another. Jakobson and Waugh (1979) claim that, as far back as' in the Greek philosophical literature, the sound units which were the basis of meaningful strings, termed **stocheia**, were viewed as indivisible primes of sounds and letters. They point out that 'This concept proved to be so persuasive that Democritus . . . and his adherent Lucretius, in searching for an analogy which might confirm their theory of the atomic structure of the physical world, cited **stocheia** as the minimal components of

speech' (Jakobson and Waugh 1979: 10). Earlier, Bloomfield in
'A set of postulates for phonemic analysis' (1926) defined the
phoneme as 'a minimum same of vocal feature'. And in *Language*
(1933: 79) he tells us:

> Further experiment fails to reveal any more replaceable parts in
> the word *pin*: we conclude that the distinctive features of this
> word are three indivisible units. Each of these units occurs also
> in other combinations, but cannot be further analysed by partial
> resemblances: each of the three is a *minimum unit of distinctive
> sound-feature, a phoneme* [the emphasis is Bloomfield's – JD].
> Thus we say that the word *pin* consists of three phonemes: the
> first of these occurs also in *pet, pack, push* and many other
> words; the second also in *fig, hit, miss*, and many other words;
> the third also in *tan, run, hen* and many other words.

Now, if we take the view that phonemes are the ultimate
indivisible units of phonological structure as a strong theoretical
claim, it can be shown to be unsatisfactory. Suppose we wished
to state, as a first approximation, the generalization that, in
English, **all and only voiceless plosives** are aspirated when they
occur initially in a stressed syllable. If we want our notation to
mirror the theoretical claim that phonemes are 'uncuttable' we
will have to mention all the phonemes affected in a step-by-step
fashion. In other words, the following symbolization will be
forced on us:

[11a] /p/ $\rightarrow$ [p^h] / initially in a stressed syllable
[11b] /t/ $\rightarrow$ [t^h] / initially in a stressed syllable
[11c] /k/ $\rightarrow$ [k^h] / initially in a stressed syllable

or, at best, if we take advantage of a notation which allows the
factoring out of the common right-hand context:

$$
\begin{matrix} [12a] \\ [12b] \\ [12c] \end{matrix}
\begin{bmatrix} /p/ \\ /t/ \\ /k/ \end{bmatrix} \rightarrow
\begin{bmatrix} [p^h] \\ [t^h] \\ [k^h] \end{bmatrix} / \text{ initially in stressed syll.}
$$

(where by convention, the bracket notation indicates that the
segments are matched along the same horizontal row).

By contrast, if we assume that phonemes are decomposable
into features, the statement of this generalization is expressible
in a simple and natural way:

$$
[13] \begin{bmatrix} -\text{continuant} \\ -\text{nasal} \\ -\text{voice} \end{bmatrix} \rightarrow [+\text{aspirated}] / \text{ init. in stressed syll.}^3
$$

In other words, every time a process makes reference to a
property common to a group of phonemes, the whole list has to

be provided if we go on assuming that phonemes cannot be split into constituents. While the point may not seem to be crucial when we deal with a small set such as /p, t, k/, consider the very real problem of characterizing – as we constantly have to do – the class of vowels within the phonologies of languages. Full commitment to the atomic theory of phonemes entails that every vowel should be listed. As the generality of the class increases the notation should be simpler. The reverse is true if phonemes are assumed to be indivisible. This point seems so obvious that one wonders why it was not noted and taken care of. In fact, examples like the one we have just considered were often taken to imply not that phonemes should be systematically and exhaustively decomposed into distinctive features, but rather that the segments of a language enter into a variety of phonetic classes. Thus, Daniel Jones, who in practice treats the phoneme as the basic unit of phonological structure, tells us (1964: 42): 'the fact is that most consonants fall naturally into well-defined classes, classes which are clearly separated from the neighbouring classes by essential differences in place and manner'. And Bloomfield himself was not always consistent. When he says in *Language* (1933) 'the distinctive features occur in lumps and bundles each one of which we call a phoneme', he is seemingly using the notion of distinctive feature in its modern sense. Yet, distinctive features do not appear to be part of what he calls 'a structural description'.

The primary phonological unit in many classical writings is the **phoneme** and when reference is made to features it is on an *ad hoc* basis and not centrally as **distinctive, discriminative** units but rather as phonetic properties allowing convenient reference to groups of phonemes. So long as the metalanguage of phonology is everyday language, this may not appear to make an important difference. But, as soon as we start symbolizing and formalizing our descriptive vocabulary, the defects of a mixed notation soon become apparent. Throughout this book, the basic units of phonology will be features, and phonemes will be conceived as sets of distinctive features. The implications of shifting the emphasis away from phonemes will become more and more apparent as our arguments unfold.

1.3.1 Phonetic vs. phonological features

The idea that phonological segments are bundles of co-occurrent features is, in one sense, intuitively obvious if we think of the production of speech. One well-known, but by no means uncontroversial, view of the act of speaking is that it involves the simultaneous co-ordination of a variety of components in order to attain a series of states or target configurations which follow one another along the axis of time. For instance, a typical French [ɛ] (as in *mer* [mɛr] 'sea') involves at the same time an egressive airstream, vibrations of the vocal folds, a raised velum shutting off the nasal cavity, a specific tongue position on the anterior–posterior axis (*ie* front) and the close–open axis (*ie* mid-low) and a lip gesture (spread lips). But all these components are independent of one another. The lips could have been rounded resulting instead in an [œ] sound as in *mœurs* [mœr(s)] 'habits', the tongue could have been retracted (*cf mort* [mɔr] 'death'), the velum could have been lowered giving the sound a nasal quality (*cf main* [mɛ̃] 'hand') and so on. This componential aspect of speech production does, of course, provide support for distinctive features but it should not lead us into thinking that every parameter of speech production is phonologically relevant. As will be argued presently, it is crucial to establish a fundamental distinction between **phonological** and **phonetic** features.

If features are thought of as oppositive or contrastive units keeping successive slots (or phonemes) apart from one another, it will be clear that not every phonetic characteristic of a segment will be relevant to differentiate it from the other segments of the language. Thus, it is common in descriptive studies of the pronunciation of English to set up a class of **bilabial** consonants /p, b, m, w/ separate from the class of **labio-dental** consonants /f, v/. But, the phonetic difference between **bilabiality** and **labio-dentality** in English is not used distinctively: it does not separate two segments which are otherwise identical. Note that while [p] and [f] are both voiceless, [p] is a plosive whereas [f] is a fricative. What is needed to show that bilabiality is truly opposed to labio-dentality is the existence of pairs of segments which differ only along this dimension. This is, for instance, the case in the West African language Ewe where we have minimal pairs of the following type:

[14] Bilabial vs. labio-dental contrasts in Ewe (Ladefoged, 1968: 53):

/ɸ/	éɸá	'he polished'	/f/	éfá	'he was cold'[4]
/β/	èβɛ̀	'the Ewe language'	/v/	èvɛ̀	'two'

A maximally simple description of English which respects the patterning of the English consonant system should therefore group these segments as [+labial] at the phonological level leaving [bilabiality] and [labio-dentality] to the phonetic level.

Now, one question which is often raised in connection with the procedure we have just outlined is: 'Do we gain anything apart from the greater simplicity of the statement?' The answer is that we do since features like [labial] are independently needed for other areas of the phonology of English as we show in 1.3.2.1.

1.3.2 The evidence for distinctive features

In this section, we consider what counts as evidence in favour of distinctive features. For convenience, a distinction is often made between internal and external evidence. Internal evidence is provided by the structure and functioning of synchronic grammars: see 1.3.2.1–2. External evidence is derived from a variety of other sources such as slips of the tongue, historical linguistics, language acquisition, psycholinguistic experiments and the like: see 1.3.2.3.

1.3.2.1 Phonotactic statements

One dimension of the phonology of all languages which must be accounted for is the statement of sequences of phonemes which are allowed within words. This falls under the technical label 'phonotactics'. In this section, we examine an interesting portion of the phonotactics of English. Words in English can start with zero, one, two or three consonants (*cf ant, cant, plain, spruce*). If we consider words which start with three consonants a simple generalization can be made. The first one must be /s/, the second one must be one of /p, t, k/, the third one must be one of /l, r, j, w/. Symbolically, the generalization can be expressed by the following if–then statement:

[15] if: #   C   C   C
     then: s   p   l
                        t   r
                        k   j
                             w

Thus, attested words of English conforming to this template are: *spleen, strut, sclerosis, spring, string, screw, stew, squirm*, and well-formed potential words of English are *spleak, strit, scruse*. What is interesting about [15] is that once again we encounter the grouping /p, t, k/ which was used for the statement of aspiration earlier on. In other words, the set of voiceless plosives functions **recurrently** within the phonology of English. A notation in terms of atomic phonemes such as /p, t, k/ simply does not account for this since it does not make explicit what it is that brings these sounds together.

Let us now turn to the structure of initial CC clusters in English. Gimson (1980: 241) lists the following combinations as the only permissible ones:

[16] INITIAL CC CLUSTERS

```
p  +  l, r, j
t  +     r, j, w
k  +  l, r, j, w
b  +  l, r, j
d  +     r, j, w
g  +  l, r, j, w
m  +        j
n  +        j
f  +  l, r, j
v  +        j
θ  +     r, j, w
s  +  l,  j, w, p, t, k, m, n, f
š  +     r
h  +        j
```

The listing of these patterns does not constitute a phonological analysis but is only a first step towards such. First of all, let us note that [š][5] and [s] occur in complementary distribution and, given that [s] allows a wide set of consonants to follow it, we could treat [š] as a realization of /s/ before /r/. Leaving this problem aside, it can be observed that all the consonants above can occur before [j]. But the vowel which can follow [j] in such #CCV combinations is always [u:] (*cf. cue, few, beauty, view*) with the exception of a few foreign borrowings such as *fjord*. This contrasts strikingly with the range of vowels allowed after single [j] word-initially (*cf yield, yet, yard, yawn, young, yearn*, etc.). Various compelling analyses of English have suggested that this discrepancy is best accounted for by treating [ju:] either as the reflex of a single vocalic unit (*eg* a long unrounded back vowel which is converted to [ju:] on the surface: see *SPE*: 192ff, Halle and Mohanan 1985 and 4.2.3) or as a rising diphthong /iu:/ (Anderson 1986b). In either analysis we are dealing with a unit which is not part of the consonantal (CC) margin of a syllable but part of its vocalic core. If we make this assumption, another odd distributional fact can be explained: [m, n, l, v, h] do not appear in word-initial clusters – with the exception of words like *music, nuisance, lieu, view, hue*. But since we treat [ju:] as a type of vocalic nucleus, the exception is only apparent. Note that our analysis should also be extended to the /j/ which we have listed as a possible third C slot in [15] since it only occurs before /u:/.

The following negative generalization forbidding /j/ as second or third element of English initial clusters emerges:[6]

[17] * # (C) C C V
                  |
                  j

The question which we now want to ask is why the following sequences /tw, dw, kw, gw, sw, θw/ should be allowed initially, even if their lexical distribution is sometimes restricted, but not /pw, bw, fw, vw/. Whereas the following examples are well entrenched in the native lexicon of English:

[18] /tw/   twaddle, twelve, twin
     /dw/   dwell, dwarf, dwindle
     /kw/   queen, quite, quest
     /gw/   Gwent, Gwyn, Gwyned, Gwyniad (only proper names
            of Welsh origin)
     /sw/   sweat, swat, swine
     /θw/   thwack, thwart

the only attested cases of initial /pw, bw, fw, vw/ are foreign borrowings such as (*petits*) *pois, poilu, Puerto Rico, Buenos Aires, bwana, foie* (*gras*), (*Tierra del*) *Fuego, voyeur*, and it has been pointed out that they tend to be anglicized by some speakers (*eg Puerto* pronounced as [pɔrtə] and *Buenos* pronounced as [bjunɔs], *cf* Hawkins 1984: 53–4).

This discrepancy in distribution is odd until we notice that the initial consonants in /pw, bw, fw, vw/ are all labial and so is /w/, whereas in [18] the first consonant is not labial. The phonotactics of English include therefore another restriction on initial CC clusters: they cannot both be labial:[7]

[19] * #   C   C   V
                    | |
                 +labial   +labial

The use of [labial] in [19] supports our earlier contention that this phonological feature does not just provide us with a means of simplifying our specification of English segments, but has wider implications for the phonology of this language.

1.3.2.2 *The statement of rules*
Consider the phonological expression of the plural of English nouns.[8] Clearly, the selection of the allomorphs of the plural morpheme in English is not random. If we leave aside the closed class plural that we find in forms such as *ox–oxen, child–children, leaf–leaves, sheep–sheep*, etc. all the other nouns

already in the language and the near-totality of newcomers undergo the following rule (as described in many reference works on English):

[20a] add /ız/ after /s, z, š, ž, č, ǰ/ (*eg ass–asses, bush–bushes, judge–judges*)

[20b] add /s/ after /p, t, k, f, θ/ (*eg cap–caps, bluff–bluffs*)

[20c] add /z/ after /b, d, g, v, ð, m,n, l/ and all the vowels of English (*eg cub–cubs, slave–slaves, ball–balls, sea–seas*).

While formulating the plural rule as in [20] may be of some use in a pedagogical grammar of English, the **linguistic** value of this statement does not stand up to close scrutiny. In terms of symbols, the subparts of [20] are not any better than random rules such as:

[21] add /iz/ after p, i, r, l, s, and all the diphthongs

Yet the segments listed in the environments of [20] will appear far from random to anybody with a basic grounding in phonetics. For instance, the sounds given in [20a] are all fricatives and affricates traditionally classified as sibilants. In terms of the feature system defined in Chapter 2, since /s, z, š, ž, č, ǰ/ all involve a raising of the blade of the tongue in the direction of the alveolar or palato-alveolar region, they are classified as [+cor(onal)]. And the special articulatory–acoustic property which sets them apart from other fricatives such as /θ, ð/ is [+str(ident)]. The consonants listed in [20b] are all the remaining voiceless consonants of English, and those in [20c] are all the voiced sounds of English apart from those covered in [20a]. The rule can therefore already be reformulated as in [22]:

[22a] add /ız/ after all [+coronal, +strident] segments

[22b] add /z/ after all remaining [−voice] segments

[22c] add /s/ after all remaining [+voice] segments

Notice, however, that by not giving the feature composition of /z/ and /s/ we are not bringing out the fact that we get the voiced allomorph /z/ after voiced segments and the voiceless allomorph /s/ after voiceless segments. But, we also know that /z/ and /s/ differ only in terms of voicing. Traditionally, they are both classified as alveolar fricatives and, once again, in terms of the features in Chapter 2 they are both [+coronal, +strident]. Rule [22] can be reformulated as [23] below where we now take advantage of the notation briefly defined above and assume that the ordering of rules is disjunctive (that is, if [23a] is applicable skip [23b] and [23c], otherwise move to [23b]; and if [23b] is applicable skip, [23c] otherwise apply [23c]).

$$[23] \quad plur \rightarrow \left\{ \begin{array}{ll} /\text{ız}/ & / \left[\begin{array}{l} +\text{coronal} \\ +\text{strident} \end{array} \right] \underline{\quad} \quad [23a] \\[2mm] \left[\begin{array}{l} +\text{cor} \\ +\text{str} \\ -\text{voice} \end{array} \right] & / [-\text{voice}] \quad \underline{\quad} \quad [23b] \\[3mm] \left[\begin{array}{l} +\text{cor} \\ +\text{str} \\ +\text{voice} \end{array} \right] & / [+\text{voice}]\text{-} \underline{\quad} \quad [23c] \end{array} \right\}$$

Formulating the rule as in [23] brings out the fact that the selection of /s/ vs. /z/ for the segments not covered by [23a] is a question of feature agreement. But, ideally, the notation should allow us to show the agreement explicitly and should eliminate unwanted redundancies such as are present in [23b, c]. To this effect, we introduce the notion of variable. Let us assume that every phonetic feature has two possible values: + and −, where [+X] indicates that a segment possesses the property X and [−X] that it lacks X. A variable (α, β, γ, etc.) in a phonological rule ranges over the two values (+ or −) and once a value is chosen for a given variable all occurrences of that variable must be replaced by this value. As a result, [23b] and [23c] can now be replaced by a single statement:

$$[24] \quad plur \rightarrow \left[\begin{array}{l} +\text{cor} \\ +\text{strid} \\ \alpha\text{voice} \end{array} \right] / [\alpha\text{voice}] \underline{\quad}$$

Two important queries can, however, be made regarding our formulation. Firstly, it still retains two independent portions: *plural* is /ız/ in some contexts and /z~s/ in others. Yet these allomorphs are clearly related. Secondly, we have treated the voicing agreement observed in *cats* [kæts] vs. *cads* [kədz] as the result of a special subpart of the rule. Yet, voicing agreement in obstruents (ie stops, fricatives and affricates) in English, and perhaps universally, is general at the beginning and end of words. Thus, no word can end in */pz, ds, fz, vs, etc./. If we assumed that such a constraint applied dynamically we would not need to posit a language-specific rule. The realization /z/~/s/ would be the result of the rule Obstruent Voicing Agreement (OVA) given below and where [−son(orant)] picks out the class of obstruents:

[25] Obstruent Voicing Agreement
     (a) word-final   (b) word-initial

$$\begin{array}{cccc} \text{C} & \text{C} \# & \# \text{C} & \text{C} \\ | & | & | & | \\ \left[\begin{array}{l} -\text{son} \\ \alpha\text{voice} \end{array} \right] & \left[\begin{array}{l} -\text{son} \\ \alpha\text{voice} \end{array} \right] & \left[\begin{array}{l} -\text{son} \\ \alpha\text{voice} \end{array} \right] & \left[\begin{array}{l} -\text{son} \\ \alpha\text{voice} \end{array} \right] \end{array}$$

Suppose we now treated the /ɪ/ in /ɪz/ as the result of a rule of epenthesis such as [26]:

[26] I-insertion (I-INS)

$$\emptyset \rightarrow \iota \; / \begin{bmatrix} +\text{strident} \\ +\text{coronal} \end{bmatrix} \; \# \_\_ z \; \#$$

whose function is to break up clusters of obstruents which, while pronounceable, would be highly marked. In that case, we could reduce all the allomorphs of the plural to an abstract underlying form /z/. The surface forms of the plural would be derived as in the examples of [26] where I-INS applies before Obstruent voicing agreement:

[27]

	'misses'	'cats'	'cads'
	mɪs # z	kæt # z	kæd # z
I-INS	mɪsɪ z		
OVA		kæt s	
OUTPUT	[mɪsɪz]	[kæts]	[kædz]

The above paragraphs show how recourse to distinctive features allows us to capture generalizations in a compact and elegant way. But, if the features were merely an ink-saving device, there would not be much point in devoting time and energy to studying them. The motivation for our approach, however, is that we take features as making **real claims about the structure of language**. One piece of evidence in favour of this assertion is that features have a predictive value. Consider the following test suggested by L. Menn (quoted in Halle 1981). English speakers are asked to form the plural of nouns which end in sounds not occurring in English. One example might be *Bach* which ends in /x/. If English speakers operate in terms of lists such as in [20a–c], the answer ought to be arbitrary given that /x/ is not explicitly mentioned. If, on the other hand, speakers operate in terms of distinctive features then our feature-theory should make some prediction as to the classification of /x/. In terms of the consonantal structure of English and the features offered in Chapter 2, /x/ would be [−coronal, −strident, −voiced, . . .]. Therefore, I-insertion would not operate and the feature-value [−voice] of /x/ would trigger an [s] realization of *plural* by voicing agreement – *ie* [baxs]. This is indeed the response that the majority of English speakers produce. The conclusion is that the statement of plural formation in terms of features is a more adequate representation of the knowledge of English speakers than an alternative formulation based on indivisible speech sounds.

1.3.2.3 External evidence

Whereas the reasoning used above in favour of distinctive features was based on the language-data itself, it is also possible to appeal to evidence from various types of linguistic behaviour which can only be explained by relating it to the speakers' knowledge of their language. In this category are commonly included data from first and second language acquisition, speech errors (*eg* slips of the tongue), language games, pathological data and so on. Only one illustrative example will be briefly mentioned here – that of speech errors (see Kenstowicz and Kisseberth 1979: Ch. 5, for further discussion of corpus-external evidence).

Speech errors – a category which includes 'slips of the tongue' and 'spoonerisms' are not solely of interest for amateurs of wit and Freudian explanation in terms of psychological repression. They also give important evidence as to the nature and functioning of linguistic systems (see Fromkin 1971, 1973, from which all the following examples are borrowed). From our point of view here, it is interesting to note that a number of speech errors can only be explained if we go below the level of the segment. This is not to say that units like the segment have necessarily no reality. If we consider slips of the tongue like:

[28a] fish and tackle → fash and tickle
[28b] split pea soup → plit spea soup

what seems to be happening in [28a] is that the two segments /i/ and /æ/ are interchanged, whereas in [28b] a segment is simply moved forward. Consider, however, [29]:

[29] pedestrian → tebestrian

This example is easily explicable if we start from the feature make-up of /p/ and /d/: /p/ is a voiceless labial stop ([+labial, −coronal, −voice, −continuant, . . .]) and /d/ is a voiced alveolar stop ([−labial, +coronal, +voice, −continuant, . . .]). All that we need to assume is that, in traditional terms, there is a labial–alveolar interchange between /p/ and /d/, other features remaining constant. A /p/ which loses its labiality and acquires alveolarity becomes a /t/ (voiceless alveolar stop), and a /d/ which loses alveolarity and acquires labiality becomes a /b/ (voiced labial stop).

1.4 Levels of representation

In 1.3.2.2, we envisaged the possibility of a representation such as /z/ for the plural morpheme to capture the similarities

between the three allomorphs: /ɪz/, /z/ and /s/. The possibility
of a single underlying representation for morphemes was indeed
envisaged by linguists such as Bloomfield and his followers (*eg*
Hockett) who spoke of 'underlying form' or 'theoretical base
form' or 'basic alternant'. The framework that was, by and large,
adopted in structuralist writings was a division between three
levels of representation: morphophonemic, phonemic and
phonetic. The plural morpheme would be said to be represented
as //z// morphophonemically (sometimes represented by
doubled diagonals) and this underlying form would be converted
by ordered descriptive statements to the phonemic forms /ɪz, z,
s/, which in turn would be converted to allophonic realizations
as in [30]:

[30] Structuralist levels of representation

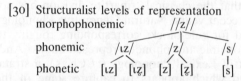

For linguists like Bloomfield and Hockett, among others, it is,
however, clear that morphophonemic representations were set up
simply for convenience and, unlike phonemic representations,
had a purely conventional status. As for the order of rules,
Bloomfield (1933: 13) says of it: 'The terms "before, after, first,
then" and so on in such statements, tell the *descriptive order* [the
emphasis is Bloomfield's – JD]. The actual sequence of constituents, and their structural order are a part of the language, but
the descriptive order of grammatical features is a fiction and
results simply from our method of describing the forms.'

Standard generative phonology starts from the position that the
kind of argumentation which leads to the postulation of, say,
//z// as the underlying form for the plural is of the same type
as that which guides the 'ascent' from allophones to phonemes.
All representations and rules have the same status of 'theoretical
constructs', not in the weak 'conventionalist' interpretation
adopted by Bloomfield, but as descriptive statements tentatively
offered as true of a given domain. But, in an interesting twist,
the privileged position of the phonemic level was rejected in all
early generative work. Halle (1959) argued, on the basis of
Russian, that by postulating an intermediate level (corresponding
to classical phonemes) between underlying forms and surface
representations a general rule of voicing assimilation had to be
arbitrarily split into two rules (a morphophonemic one and an
allophonic one), thus forgoing the generalization that assimilation

applies uniformly to all obstruents. Halle's demonstration will not
be repeated here. It has been widely discussed in the literature
and similar arguments can be constructed from different
languages (*cf* Sommerstein, 1977: 122–3, who gives an example
from Latin borrowed from Matthews 1972). For this reason, we
will not adopt a notational convention separating morphopho-
nemes from phonemes. Underlying forms will be usually
represented within single diagonals and surface forms within
square brackets, but I will not adhere to this convention rigidly.
In a grammar where underlying representations and surface
representations are related by sequences of ordered rules, it is
difficult to maintain conventions which were devised for two
levels of representation related by unordered taxonomic rules.

This is not to say that the classical tripartite division has not
had its supporters in recent years. Natural Generative Phonology
(*cf* Ch. 4) has argued for rule-blocks corresponding roughly to
morphophonemic, phonemic and phonetic representations. And,
within the framework of Lexical Phonology (*cf* Ch. 5), a stratal
view is also defended which appears to capture some of the
traditional intuitions. Until we turn to these developments, we
shall posit only two levels of representation (underlying and
surface) connected by linearly ordered rules. The next section
will exemplify the standard generative paradigm with reference
to a small portion of Southern French phonology.

1.5 Aspects of a standard generative analysis of Midi French

The phonemic system of standard French is usually argued to
include the following vowels: /i, e, ɛ, a, ɑ, ɔ, o, u, y, ø, œ/ and
/ə/ (schwa). In the Languedoc variety of Midi French spoken by
the author (*cf* Durand 1976; Durand, Slater and Wise 1987),
which is close to the Bordeaux French variety described in
Rochet (1982), there is no contrastive distinction between
/ø/–/œ/, /e/–/ɛ/, and /o/–/ɔ/, nor between /a/ and /ɑ/. The
following examples (where only one possible translation has been
arbitrarily selected), which constitute minimal pairs for standard
French, are pronounced in the same way:

[31] jeune   [žœnə] été   [ete] côte   [kɔtə] pâte   [patə]
     'young'   'summer'   'hill'   'pastry'
     jeûne   [žœnə] étais   [ete] cote   [kɔtə] patte   [patə]
     'fast'   'was'   'rating'   'leg'

Note that final schwas are usually pronounced in this accent.
Schwa behaves differently from the other vowels and can be left

out of the discussion for the moment (see 1.5.1). In the light of [31], the contrastive vowel system of Midi French can be characterized as a seven-phoneme inventory as in [32]:

[32] i   y   u
        e   ø   o
               a

At the phonetic level, however, [ø] and [œ], [e] and [ɛ], and [o] and [ɔ] appear but they are in complementary distribution as shown by the following representative examples:

[33] [e]   [ɛ]
      ses   'his'   [se]   sec   'dry'   [sɛk]
      mettra   'will put'   [metra]   mettre   'to put'   [mɛtrə]
      séchait   'will dry'   [seše]   sceptique   'sceptical' [sɛptikə]
      [ø]   [œ]
      peu   'little'   [pø]   peur   'fear'   [pœr]
      heureux   'happy'   [ørø]   heurter   'to hit'   [œrte]
      aveugler   'to blind'   [avøgle]   aveugle   'blind'   [avœglə]
      [o]   [ɔ]
      beau   'handsome'   [bo]   bord   'side'   [bɔr]
      poser   'to put'   [poze]   poster   'to post'   [pɔste]
      rosier   'rosebush   [rozje]   rose   'rose'   [rɔzə]

As [33] shows, the distribution of the mid-high and mid-low variants is governed by a variant of what has been called the 'loi de position': a mid-vowel phoneme is realized as mid-high in an open syllable and as mid-low in closed syllables and whenever the next syllable contains schwa /ə/. As the *SPE* framework, within which we shall operate in the first part of this book, did not make directly available a concept of syllable or syllable boundary, the rule will have to be specified with reference to sequences of segments. In the system of vowel features offered in *SPE*, which will be explained fully in Chapter 2, the Midi French contrastive system might be characterized as in [34].

[34]

| | −back || +back ||
	−round	+round	−round	+round
+high −low	i	y		u
−high −low	e	ø		o
−high +low			a	

Although /a/ would traditionally be said to be 'central', in this system, it would be classified as phonologically 'back'. What [34] does is provide us with a 'default' value for the mid vowels. That is, they will appear as [e, ø, o] if they do not undergo any modification. This leaves us with the simpler task of predicting the [ɛ, œ, ɔ] variants which will be classified as [−high, +low] within this scheme and fill in the empty slots at the bottom of [34]. This is done by [35] which is directly explained:

[35] Mid-Vowel Lowering (MVLOW)

$$\begin{bmatrix} V \\ -\text{high} \\ -\text{low} \end{bmatrix} \rightarrow [+\text{low}] \ / \ \underline{\quad} \ C \begin{Bmatrix} C_0 \ \vartheta \\ C \\ \# \end{Bmatrix} \quad \begin{matrix} [35a] \\ [35b] \end{matrix}$$

condition: C C in [35b] is not obstruent + liquid

[35a] tells us that lowering takes place if a consonant (C) is followed by a schwa from which it can be separated by a string of zero or more consonants (C_0) as in [36]:

[36]   __ C C_0 ə
rose	/rozə/	→	r ɔ z ə	'rose'
mettre	/metrə/	→	m ɛ t r ə	'to put'
meurtre	/mørtrə/	→	m œ r tr ə	'murder'

Then the general case [35b] indicates that MVLOW occurs before two consonants (CC) or a consonant followed by a word-boundary (C#) as in [37]:

[37a]   __ C C
| heurter | /ørte/ | → | œ r t e |

[37b]   C #
| sec | /sek/ | → | s ɛ k |

But the condition indicates that MVLOW can only apply if the two consonants following the mid vowel are not of the type obstruent + liquid: cf aveugler [avøgle] (not *[avœgle]).

At various points of this book, this rather elaborate rule will be reconsidered and ultimately reduced to a simple statement (cf 5.1.2, 6.1.6, 6.1.9). For the moment, we will examine some apparent exceptions to MVLOW. Consider the words in [38] below:

[38] déstabiliser [destabilize] not *[dɛstabilize]
'destabilize'
préscolaire [preskɔlɛrə] not *[prɛskɔlɛrə]
'preschool'
prostalinien [prostalinjɛ̃] not *[prɔstalinjɛ̃]
'prostalinist'

The mid vowel in the first syllable of each of these words should become mid low since it precedes two consonants. But these 'exceptions' belong to an obvious pattern: the vowel that should be lowered is part of a prefix. It has often been observed that prefixes behave as if they were separated from the base by a strong boundary. One standardly advocated treatment would consist in analysing these words as:

[39]   /#de#stabilize#/
       /#pre#skolerə#/
       /#pro#stalinjɛ̃#/

If we specify that MVLOW must operate within a domain flanked by two word-boundaries: # . . . # (eg Basbøll 1978), all the potential counter-examples disappear. Let us now examine the vowel /ə/ which has been left aside so far.

1.5.1 On schwa

The vowel usually transcribed /ə/ is often referred to as 'mute e' in standard French but we shall refer to it by the more neutral term schwa since it is typically pronounced in this accent. Thus, the words *foc* 'jib' and *phoque* 'seal' are homophonous – both pronounced [fɔk] – in standard French, whereas they are usually pronounced [fɔk] and [fɔkə] in Midi French. However, probably under the influence of the prestigious Northern varieties of French, some speakers do delete schwas in a variety of environments. The question of the overall distribution of schwas within words is quite complex, but for our purposes we can limit the discussion to two environments.

(a) At the end of polysyllabic words (cf. *bête, phoque*): in this context, schwa can be realized as a phonetic schwa (that is, a central unrounded lax vowel) as portrayed above for ease of description but, more often than not, its realization is identical to [œ]. The syllable that contains it is phonetically unstressed in relation to the preceding syllable. A typical phonetic realization of /betə/ might therefore be [bɛ́tœ].

(b) In monosyllables (*cf le, je, ce, ne, . . ., me*): here the realization of schwa in the accent under description is always [ø] so that sequences such as *je dis* 'I say' and *jeudi* 'Thursday' are pronounced identically [ʒødi]. Some of these monosyllables, but not all, can be attached as clitics to a previous word (*eg est-ce* 'is it' *mets-je* 'do I put') in which case they fall under (a) in terms of realization. That is, although the pronunciation of *ce* ('this') in isolation is [sø], it is pronounced as [sœ] when cliticized. Moreover, the addition of *ce* to *est*, pronounced [e] by itself, gives rise to [ɛ] ([ɛsə]) in accord with MVLOW.

If we compare the behaviour of *ce* described above with the suffixation of *-eux* [ø] to *peur* [pœr] 'fear', which gives rise to *peureux* [pørø] 'fearful', we can see why we want to treat schwa differently from other vowels from a **phonological** point of view. Phonetically, however, schwa can merge with [ø] as mentioned in (b).

Suppose, however, that playing devil's advocate, somebody were to suggest that since a word like *ne* is pronounced like *nœud* [nø] and can never be cliticized and realized, say, as [nœ], there is no reason to depart from phonetic reality and transcribe it as /nə/. The reason why we do indeed want to depart from phonetic reality is that schwa is obligatorily deleted before a vowel within close-knit syntactic phrases. Thus, while *Je ne vois ni Pierre ni Marie* 'I can see neither Pierre nor Marie' is pronounced [žənøvwanipjɛrənimari], we observe that *ne* is pronounced [n] before a vowel as in *Je n'ai pas vu Pierre avec Marie* 'I didn't see Pierre with Marie' [žønepavupjɛravɛkmari]. (Note that, in this example, the deletion of the schwa in *ne* is reflected in the spelling by the presence of an apostrophe. French orthography, on the other hand, does not reflect the deletion of schwa in polysyllables such as *Pierre* in the same example.) By contrast with schwa, the vowel /ø/ never deletes before another vowel. Thus, *Fais un nœud à ton mouchoir!* 'Tie a knot in your hanky!' is always pronounced [feɛ̃nøatɔ̃mušwar].[9] Such behaviour is easily accounted for if *ne* has a schwa (/nə/) whereas *nœud* has /ø/ at the underlying level. We are therefore led to the postulation of a rule of obligatory schwa-deletion in front of a vowel (traditionally called elision) as in [40]:

[40] Elision (domain: phrases)
$$/ə/ \rightarrow \emptyset / \underline{\hspace{2cm}} \#_1 V$$

The subscripted hash symbol indicates that elision can take place across one or more word-boundaries. Examples of elision across phrasal boundaries are provided by *Je n'ai-pas vu Pierr∉ avec Marie* or *Pierr∉ arrive demain* 'Pierre arrives tomorrow where schwa deletion operates across a strong subject–predicate division (NP##VP). In the following discussions, we will just assume that boundaries are not arbitrarily assigned but distributed by rules. The assignment of boundaries is, in fact, the result of universal conventions in *SPE*. These conventions are outlined in Chapter 5 and discussed there in the light of more recent work (see especially 5.2 and 5.2.8).

Elision, however, also applies obligatorily within words. Compare, in this respect, [41a, b] and [41c, d]:

[41a]	reprendre	'to take again'	[røprãdrə]
[41b]	resortir	'to go out again'	[røsɔrtir]
[41c]	rallumer	'to light up again'	[ralyme]
[41d]	rajouter	'to add again'	[ražute]

In [41a, b] the prefix re-appears as [rø], whereas in [41c, d], where the stems allumer and ajouter are vowel-initial, we observe [r], suggesting the underlying form [rə[for the prefix re-. Since, earlier on, it was proposed that prefixes should be separated from the base by a word-boundary it is tempting to assume that the examples of [41] are the result of elision in the form [40]. Underlying /rə#ažute/ for rajouter provides an environment for [40] and the schwa would be deleted as required. But, if we compare [42a, b] with [42c, d]:

[42a]	bête	'stupid'	[bɛtə]
[42b]	rouge	'red'	[ružə]
[42c]	bêtise	'stupidity'	[betizə]
[42d]	rougir	'to go red'	[ružir]

we can see that the suffixation of a vowel-initial suffix to a stem ending in a schwa also results in the deletion of the stem-final /ə/: /betə+izə/ → [betizə] (where a derivational suffix is separated from the base by the weaker morpheme boundary '+'). Since, furthermore, schwa is never attested before a vowel morpheme-internally, we can make the presence of a boundary optional· and formulate a process of word-internal elision as follows:

[43] Intra-word elision[10]

$$\text{ə} \rightarrow \emptyset \,/ \underline{\hspace{2cm}} \left(\left\{ \begin{array}{c} + \\ \# \end{array} \right\} \right) \; V$$

The problem is whether [43] and [40], given their striking similarity, are two rules or one. If we believe in maximizing rule-simplicity – a strategy we have been advocating so far and will continue defending – we should collapse them as in (44) below where [−segment]$_0$ refers to zero or an indefinite number of boundaries:

[44] Generalized elision
$$\text{ə} \rightarrow \emptyset \,/ \underline{\hspace{2cm}} \; [-\text{segment}]_0 \; V$$

But, then, we face a so-called ordering paradox in relating MVLOW and elision. Since the world *bête* in isolation would be pronounced [bɛtə], the pronunciation [betizə] of *bêtise* from underlying /betə+izə/ shows that intra-word elision applies first and 'bleeds' MVLOW (*ie* deprives it of a possible input). On the other hand, within phrases, elision must follow MVLOW, as shown by the pronunciation of *Pierre* in *Pierre avec Marie* [pjɛravɛkmari]. Compare the derivations in [45]:

[45] Underlying form /pjerəavekmari/   /pjerəavekmari/
     Elision   pjeravekmari   MVLOW   pjɛrəavɛkmari
     MVLOW   *pjeravɛkmari   elision pjɛravɛkmari

Two practically identical rules of elision must therefore be postulated to account for the facts – one ordered before MVLOW, the other one after. The duplication of a rule is rather unexpected within the *SPE* paradigm where a single block of rules projects underlying representations on to surface phonetic forms. But we shall see in Chapter 5 that, within the framework of Lexical Phonology, a fundamental distinction should be established between **lexical** rules, which apply within words, and **post-lexical** rules, which apply at utterance-level, with the possibility that the same rule might span these two domains. In such a framework, MVLOW is a lexical rule and elision both a lexical and an utterance rule.

The various data that we have just considered in this section suggest that the notion of word, often alleged to play no role in French phonology, is, in fact, crucial to an account of this accent. Moreover, the analysis of schwa has shown that phonology was under-determined by phonetic data (since phonetic [ø] can correspond either to /ə/ or to /ø/) – a thesis we will go on maintaining throughout this book. We are now in a position to turn to liaison and related topics and depart more radically from surface forms than we have done so far.

1.5.2 The phonology of liaison, flexion and derivation

In Midi French, as in the northern varieties, there is a type of phonological adjustment, called **liaison**, which takes place between words: a consonant which is normally mute can appear between two closely related words if the second word begins with a vowel. Consider the following examples of liaison [46] and non-liaison [47] involving the words *les* [le], *vous* [vu], *petit* [pøti], *dans* [dã]:

[46] les amis [lezami] 'the friends'; vous avez [vuzave]; petit
     anneau [pətitano] 'small ring'; mauvais élève [movezelɛvə]
     'bad pupil'; dans un jour [dãzœ̃ʒur] 'in a day'

[47] les chats [leša] 'the cats'; vous voyez [vuvwaje] 'you see'; c'est petit [sepəti] 'it is small'; mauvais père [movepɛrə] 'bad father'; dans Paris [dãpari] 'in Paris'

Other words like *joli* [žoli] 'pretty' never participate in liaison: *cf joli anneau* [žoliano] 'pretty ring'.

The stylistic and grammatical conditioning of liaison will be left aside until later: see 5.2.8 for further discussion. We will only assume here that liaison takes place between words which are separated by one word-boundary: *eg vous#avez, petit#anneau*. What will concern us is the status of the liaison consonant. Is it inserted by a rule of epenthesis? Or is it, on the contrary, a latent consonant which is part of the phonological representation of a liaison word but is only preserved when followed by a vowel? We will take this second option here and assume that the underlying form of our sample words is as in [48]:

[48]
les	/lez/ – [le]		vous	/vuz/ – [vu]
petit	/pətit/ – [pəti]		dans	/dãz/ – [dã]
mauvais	/movez/ – [move]			

On this assumption, we can account for the non-surfacing of the latent consonant by positing a rule of truncation which deletes a final obstruent when the next word begins with a consonant, or at the end of a phrase:

[49] Truncation

$$[\text{-sonorant}] \rightarrow \emptyset / \underline{\hspace{1cm}} \# \begin{Bmatrix} C \\ \# \end{Bmatrix} \begin{matrix} (a) \\ (b) \end{matrix}$$

Two examples of the context of application of [49] are given in [50] below:

[50] $\underline{\hspace{1cm}}$# C [50a]
vu z # vwaje 'vous voyez'
         ↓
         Ø

         $\underline{\hspace{1cm}}$## [50b]
(c'est) pəti t ## 'c'est petit'
         ↓
         Ø

Words in their citation form, as in [48], form minimal utterances: each word can therefore be considered to be bounded by phrase boundaries ## ... ## which would trigger deletion under [49b]. Within the perspective adopted here liaison is therefore non-truncation. Given the formulation of [49], words whose final consonant is never deleted (*eg sac* 'bag', *cap* 'cape') have to be marked as exceptions to truncation.

One immediate objection might be that we are being led astray by the spelling of French which gives a unique form to each word including the liaison consonant. But, it may also be the case that French orthography, despite its inconsistencies, is supported by mental representations of words which include latent consonants. We are reminded here of Sapir's famous article on 'The psychological reality of phonemes' (1933) where he points out that English speakers (conservative RP), despite the objective identity of pronunciation of *soared* and *sawed* as [sɔ:d], can feel in their bones a distinction between these words. The first one should be transcribed as /sɔ:r-d/ and the second one as /sɔ:-d/ as can be shown by adding -*ing* to each of the stems: *soaring* [sɔ:rɪŋ] vs *sawing* [sɔ:ɪŋ] (see 4.2.4–5). We shall not get entangled here in the controversial issue of the relationship between spelling and phonology in literate societies. We will simply assume that phonological accounts should not depend on the knowledge by speakers of the spelling conventions of their own language (but see 4.3). Studies of modern societies have sadly revealed greater numbers of illiterates than were suspected. But, to our knowledge, no evidence has been offered showing that, from a phonological standpoint, these speakers behaved differently from other speakers. However that may be, let us see whether any further light can be shed on this matter by widening the data.

The main type of support for underlying consonants as in [48] comes from patterns of inflection and derivation in French. Thus, given that the feminine of adjectives is typically formed by suffixation of a schwa, we see a surfacing of the liaison consonant as in [51]:

		MASC		FEM	
[51]	petit	[pəti]	petite	[pətitə]	'small'
	mauvais	[move]	mauvaise	[movɛzə]	'bad'
	étonnant	[etonã]	étonnante	[etonãtə]	'surprising'

And, if we look at various forms of a verb like *mettre* as in [51], we can observe alternations between zero and a consonant before a vowel:

[52]	met	[me]	'wear 3-sg-indic-pres'
	met-il?	[metil]	'does he wear?'
	mettons	[metɔ̃]	'wear 1-pl-indic- pres'
	mettable	[metablə]	'wearable'

The parallelism between liaison, inflection and derivation is not total: thus, the liaison consonant for *gros* is /z/ (*gros anneau*

[grozano] 'big ring') while /s/ is observed in derivation and inflection (*grossir* [grosir], *grosse* [grɔsə]). Nevertheless, literally
hundreds of alternations exist between zero and a given consonant across liaison, flexion and derivation and this needs
accounting for within the phonology of French. By adopting
unique underlying forms as in [48], we pave the way for a
straightforward treatment: an underlying final consonant is saved
by suffixation of a vowel or in the context of a vowel in the next
word but doomed otherwise.

The above summarizes the essence of a standard generative
treatment of Midi French. The same arguments have been
mounted for standard French (see Schane 1968; Dell 1973) but
with the difference that the feminine schwa in [51] has to be
obligatorily deleted on the surface, whereas they are normally
pronounced in the variety of French discussed here (see Durand,
Slater and Wise 1987). This postulation of a 'fictitious' segment
has been one important part of the abstractness–concreteness
debate in French phonology (see Durand 1986b; Encrevé, 1988:
Ch. 3; Love 1981; Morin and Kaye 1982 and Tranel 1981). The
most prominent 'concrete' alternative has involved the postulation of a rule of insertion of a consonant as in [53]:

[53] Insertion: $\emptyset \rightarrow C / V \underline{\quad} \# V$

(a rule exemplified in [51] below). But this rule cannot quite be
correct as it stands because it does not tell us which consonant
to insert. To be fully explicit, we would need to mark individual
words with a diacritic telling us which consonant will appear and
split [53] into a number of unrelated rules inserting sometimes
a /t/, sometimes a /z/, sometimes a /p/, etc. By contrast [49]
expresses a single generalization and will be preferred here on
simplicity grounds.

There is, unfortunately, one outstanding difficulty with the
treatment sketched above. MVLOW should apply to underlying
forms where a mid vowel is followed bv a liaison consonant. For
instance, the word *les* /lez/ in [54] should give rise to *[lɛ(z)]
on the surface. But the liaison consonant never triggers mid-
vowel lowering in this accent. As a result, one can observe
surface contrasts such as

[54] ses amis   [sezami]   'his/her friends'
      seize amis   [sɛzami]   'sixteen friends'

This might, of course, be taken as an argument in favour of an epenthesis of the liaison consonant within phrases with sample derivations as in [55]:

[55]	ses amis	/se#ami/	seize amis	/sezə#ami/
Intra-word elision [43]		———		———
MVLOW [35]		———		sɛzə#ami
Elision [40]		———		sɛz #ami
Insertion [53]		sez#ami		———
output		[sezami]		[sɛzami]

In 6.1.7, we shall see, however, that independently motivated assumptions concerning syllable structure in Midi French allow us to capture the generalizations embedded in the deletion account, while avoiding an incorrect application of MVLOW. Whichever solution to liaison is adopted, it is, in any case, interesting to observe that in this accent [e] and [ɛ] can contrast within utterances (see [54]), while being clear variants of a single underlying unit from a lexical point of view (note that the [ɛ] in *seize* is derived from /e/). This shows, if further demonstration were necessary, that the post-Bloomfieldian dream of building the phonology upwards from utterances without any grammatical information could only be doomed to failure.

Much more would need to be said to articulate a full treatment of the Midi French phonological system and, in particular, the way the rules posited so far are ordered and interact with other rules should be explored in greater depth. But this fragment should suffice to show readers how a generative treatment would proceed and place us in a position to consider much more complex examples from Chapter 3 onwards.

1.6 Phonology within the model of grammar

At the end of this chapter, a few words should be said concerning the place of phonology within the overall system of grammar, in the Chomskyan sense. In the paradigm corresponding to Chomsky's *Aspects of the Theory of Syntax* (1965) and Chomsky and Halle's *The Sound Pattern of English* (1968), phonology is an interpretive device which projects surface syntactic representations on to phonetic forms. The overall structure of this model of grammar is outlined in [56]. Given a surface bracketing, and a theory of boundaries (see 5.2), surface phonetic forms are derived from underlying representations (where typically each morpheme has an invariant abstract shape) by a battery of linearly ordered rules.

Although, so far, we have concentrated on issues of descriptive adequacy, phonology in this perspective must be seen as part of

The classical *aspects–SPE* model of grammar

[56] Phrase structure rules   Lexicon

      Deep structure → Semantic representations
      ↓ transformations
      Surface structure
      ↓ Readjustment rules
      Phonological representation
      ↓ Phonological rules
      Phonetic representation

the enterprise of Universal Grammar – *ie* the attempt 'to develop
an account of linguistic universals that, on the one hand, will not
be falsified by the actual diversity of languages, and, on the other
hand, will be sufficiently rich to account for the rapidity and
uniformity of language learning, and the remarkable complexity
and range of the generative grammars which are the product of
language learning' (Chomsky 1965: 28). In this respect, phonology makes a double contribution. First of all, a number of
formal universals are proposed concerning the kinds of rules
which can appear in a grammar, the structures on which they
operate and the ordering conditions under which they apply.
Secondly, a set of substantive universals in the shape of distinctive features are offered as part of the overall alphabet of
linguistic theory: see Chapter 2. While the assumptions embodied
in [55] have been challenged from various angles (see *eg* Bresnan
1971, 1972), the overall picture has remained identical. A
common way of presenting the model of grammar in the tradition
of Chomsky (1981) is given in [57] (adapted from van Riemsdijk
and Williams 1986: 173).

The details of [57] need not preoccupy us. What should nevertheless be obvious is that the role of phonology as an interpretive
component remains very much the same in this picture of the

[57] The Government and Binding model of grammar

      X-bar theory of
      phrase structure rules   Lexicon
            ↘ D-structure ↙
             ↓ 'Move-α'
          S-structure

[57a]	Deletion rules	[57d]	Rules of anaphora
[57b]	Filters	[57e]	Rules of quantification
[57c]	Phonological rules	[57f]	Rules of concord
	↓		↓
	Phonetic form		Logical form

grammatical system. This assumption will be maintained in this book. But we shall present a different model of the link-up between morphology and phonology in Chapter 5 from the one delineated above, and the relationship between syntax and phonology will occupy us again at other points in this work. As our presentation progresses, we shall see that the Spartan theory of phonology embodied in *SPE* has had to be enriched in a variety of directions. But, in compensation for this, we will also show how, in more recent work, much of the emphasis has shifted away from language-specific rules to universal conventions and default operations.

Notes

1. Throughout this work, stresses are marked by accents over the vowel of the affected syllable: v́ indicates a primary stress, v̀ a secondary stress, v̌ a tertiary stress and v a lack of stress. See the Appendix for help with phonetic symbols.
2. To be precise the assignment of stress to the first syllable of *writer* and *rider* also ought to be specified.
3. In traditional terms, [-continuant] = stop, [-nasal] = oral, [-voice] = voiceless, [+aspirated] = aspirated.
4. The gloss 'he was cold', according to one of my Ewe informants, is an error for 'it is cold'.
5. In this book š, ž, č, ǰ are respectively used for IPA ʃ, ʒ, tʃ, dʒ as in *sh*in, lei*s*ure, *ch*in, *g*in. See the Appendix for help with phonetic symbols.
6. The asterisk (*) indicates that the structure in question is ungrammatical (that is, violates the rules of the language).
7. This restriction appears to reflect a general tendency which is acoustically motivated (see Ohala 1985: 226–7).
8. For a thorough discussion of the phonology of inflectional endings in English, *cf* Zwicky (1975).
9. The transcriptions of Midi French adopted here include nasal vowels for convenience. In fact, in this accent, nasal vowels compete with oral vowel + nasal consonant (VN) on the surface: *bon* can be pronounced [bɔ̃] or [bɔn]. Underlyingly, the nasal vowels in this accent are best treated as VN clusters (see Durand 1988).
10. In *SPE*, the + boundary has a special status. Chomsky and Halle (1968: 67) say: 'We assume that the presence of + can be marked in a rule, but the absence of + cannot be marked in a rule.' In other words, a rule such as $X \rightarrow Y / A \underline{\quad} B$ abbreviates all the following rules: (a) $X \rightarrow Y / A + \underline{\quad} + B$, (b) $X \rightarrow Y / A + \underline{\quad} B$, (c) $X \rightarrow Y / A \underline{\quad} + B$, and (d) $X \rightarrow Y / A \underline{\quad} B$. This convention means that an optional + boundary does not actually have to be indicated in a formulation of rule [42].

Chapter 2

The theory of Distinctive Features

2.1 Preliminaries

In Chapter 1, it was argued that the basic units of phonology should be features and not segmental units such as the phoneme. A segment is a set of simultaneous Distinctive Features (DFs) as in the partial specification of [1]:

[1]	æ	t
syllabic	+	−
consonantal	−	+
nasal	−	−
coronal	−	+
sonorant	+	−
. . .		

In [1], the information concerning the representation of the morpheme *at* is organized in a two-dimensional matrix where the rows are associated with features and the columns correspond to segments. A specification + or − for each feature, at successive locations of the speech chain, indicates whether or not each segment belongs to the category in question. But, in presenting DFs in this manner, we appear to be positing two primitives: features and a higher level construct the phoneme (as a set of DFs). In that case, how different is our position from the classical one where phonemes were taken as the primitive units of phonological structure, albeit units which enter into a variety of relationships with other units? This, for instance, would have been the position of Trubetzkoy (1969) for whom distinctive features are specifications of the networks of relationships along which phonemes are structured, rather than autonomous units with ontological status as claimed here. Is not the distinction between these two positions 'more a matter of philosophical rather than linguistic significance' as S. R. Anderson (1985: 118) asks. But, as he points out, there are fundamental differences in the range of issues addressed within both frames of reference.

To begin with, if phonemes are basic units, given that phonemic inventories vary from language to language, there will be a strong expectation that features will be language-specific, as they were indeed for Trubetzkoy. By contrast, in the wake of Jakobson's work, generative phonology has assumed that the set of features provides a **universal** inventory. Secondly, taking features as the basic discriminative units, even if coupled with a bead-like conception of phonological sequences, does not imply belief in full-blown phonemes as necessary units. There is nothing preventing the analyst from positing the presence of a single feature at a particular place in phonological structure. For instance, in a language where the onset of syllables is either a single consonant or the sequence [s] + consonant, one might well defend the position that a single feature – say [+continuant] – is enough to specify the initial [s] **phonologically**. Thirdly, and more crucially, making features basic leaves open the specification of the domain of a feature. If phonemes are basic, then each feature is, as it were, locked within the unidimensional matrix characterizing phonemes one at a time. But there are cases such as tone spreading or vowel harmony (see Ch. 7 in particular) where the domain of a feature should be seen as simultaneously spanning a whole sequence. If features are parasitic upon phonemes, the existence of features tied to sequences is odd. If, on the other hand, features are primitive elements, it is a matter of empirical adequacy of our theory whether or not there are higher-order derivative units comparable to the classical phoneme. The classical position with its emphasis on phonemes is by no means equivalent to modern theories which emphasize the distinctive feature as the phonological primitive.

In Chapter 1, some justification was offered in favour of DFs, but a number of fundamental questions concerning them were left aside or summarily answered. Do the DFs characterizing a language form part of a universal inventory? Are the correlates of DFs primarily articulatory, acoustic or both? Should DFs be binary or not? These are questions which we shall examine in this chapter and at various points of this book. The basis of the presentation adopted here (see 2.3) is the set of DFs put forward by Chomsky and Halle (1968) in *The Sound Pattern of English* (*SPE*) as revised by Halle and Clements (1983). As the *SPE* inventory forms the cornerstone of most developments in distinctive feature theory and still underlies much descriptive and theoretical work in phonology, there are a number of advantages in starting from a set which departs only marginally from that of the *SPE*. In any event, alternative proposals and their significance will emerge from the discussion of DFs in this chapter and in the rest of the book.

2.2 Some general assumptions

As was briefly pointed out earlier, the set of DFs offered in 2.3 is conceived as a universal inventory capable of describing the phonology of any human language. The assumption of universalism is one that has systematically been made in the generative tradition, in the wake of Jakobson, Fant and Halle (1952). This position contrasts with previous approaches like Trubetzkoy's – and that of his heirs such as Martinet in France (*eg* Martinet 1955) – for whom distinctive features are established piecemeal, language by language. It should be noted that what is adopted here is what is sometimes called a 'weak' version of universalism (each language draws a subset of features from the overall inventory) by opposition to a 'strong' version of universalism (all languages have features 'x', 'y' and 'z').

One standard argument in favour of universalism is the **recurrent** and **finite** nature of the dimensions that phonologists refer to in the analysis of phonological systems, whether in terms of rules, phonotactic statements or in system inventories. Even phoneticians like Catford (1977: 14) who 'refrain from positing a specific set of positive, fixed, parametric values that constitute *the* universal set of distinctive phonetic features' admit that 'in descriptive linguistic phonetics we seem to have reached a point of diminishing returns: it is only occasionally that some totally new and unknown phonetic phenomenon turns up.' And in practice, Catford ends by putting forward a set of 'prime features' which do constitute a hypothesis as to what dimensions are relevant for the phonic analysis of languages. The issue of universalism is once again broached in 2.4.

In the mainstream generative tradition, although DFs are more abstract than their implementations, they are grounded in phonetics. Over the years, within radically different frameworks, some linguists (*eg* Foley 1977; Fudge 1967; Hjelmslev 1953) have advocated the position that underlying phonological entities should be completely abstract markers devoid of phonetic content. This position, which was effectively destroyed by Postal

(1968), is unsatisfactory since the mapping between phonological features and phonetic realizations becomes akin to the patently arbitrary relation between morphological features (*eg* first/second conjugation, singular/plural) and phonological forms. Moreover, if phonological units are characterized in terms of arbitrary diacritics, the fact that many languages use the same parameters (*eg* labiality, nasality) to distinguish lexical items becomes a matter of coincidence (see Coates 1979; Kiparsky 1968a: 5–8; Chomsky and Halle 1968: 169–70, 295). A more controversial question is whether the DFs should have an articulatory basis or an auditory basis or be neutral between the two. Although Chomsky and Halle (1968) in *SPE* mention the relevance of acoustic and perceptual correlates, their system is biased towards articulation. In 2.3, the DFs will be defined in articulatory terms but this whole issue will occupy us in the closing sections of this chapter.

Finally, the features will be assumed here to be binary at the **phonological** level. In current technical parlance familiar from syntax, features are attribute-value pairs where the attribute is a given property (say [labial]) and the values are plus or minus. The normal way of writing this in phonology is by prefixing the attribute with the value given to it: [+labial], [−labial]. When reference is made to a feature X as a classificatory dimension without specifying a value, we will write it as [X] or [+/−X] interchangeably (*eg* [labial] or [+/−labial]). Chomsky and Halle (1968: 297) claim that since 'phonological features are classificatory devices, they are binary, as are all other classificatory features in the lexicon, for the natural way of indicating whether or not an item belongs to a particular category is by means of binary features'. Of course, the postulation of binariness at the classificatory (or contrastive) level does not mean that, **phonetically**, features have to be binary. For instance, nasality is not distinctive for vowels in English, but a vowel may exhibit a small amount of nasality either inherently or under the influence of a neighbouring nasal consonant. In this case, the features are functioning as scales. Technically, the attribute is the same but the value, instead of ranging over a set with two members $\{+,-\}$ (or $\{1, 0\}$), ranges over numerical parameters (see *eg* Ladefoged 1982: 268–9). For instance, one might want to say that while, phonologically, nasality is zero for all English sounds ([−nasal]) except for nasal consonants which are 100 per cent nasal ([+nasal]), phonetically, vowels are 20 per cent nasal before a nasal consonant.

The issue of the mapping between phonology and phonetics is

an extremely controversial one. Some researchers see phonetics as a non-linguistic subject dealing directly with properties of the speech signal. The position taken here is that phonetic properties which are not mechanically determined and can come under linguistic control are part of a linguistic description. Thus, the use of various types of /l/ in English does not result from necessary mechanical adjustments of the tongue-position and is part of the system of English which has to be learned by speakers. At the very least, properties which can be contrastive across languages should be included within a phonetic transcription. But S. R. Anderson (1985: 262–6) argues very persuasively that all physical features which can constitute an aspect of the difference between one language and another should be part of a phonetic transcription and belong to linguistic phonetics. Arguably, however, many of the fine-grained aspects of a transcription should be accommodated within a linguistic phonetic module which operates from the output of the phonological component, rather than within the phonological module itself (cf 5.2.7). However that may be, the phenomena dealt with in this book are so tightly integrated to the linguistic system as a whole that their inclusion in the phonological component is hardly debatable.

2.3 The phonetic features and their articulatory correlates

For expository reasons, the set of features given below will be cast within *SPE*-like headings. These headings have no theoretical import. The definitions are in the main borrowed or paraphrased from *SPE* or Halle and Clements (1983), unless otherwise indicated. The reader should be aware that many features are discussed again at various points of this book and some features will be argued to be unnecessary. Some features which prove problematical and are not discussed later are considered in more detail here.

2.3.1 Major class features

1. Syllabic/non-syllabic: [+/−syll]. Syllabic sounds are those which constitute peaks of syllables, non-syllabic sounds are those which are in the margins of syllables. Examples: *cat*, [kæt], where the [æ] is [+syll] and [k] and [t] are [−syll]; *cattle* [kætl̩] with [æ] and [l̩] as [+syll], Serbo-Croat *krv* [kr̩v] 'blood' with syllabic [r̩].
2. Consonantal/non-consonantal: [+/−cons]. Consonantal sounds are produced with a constriction in the vocal tract at

least equal to that found in the fricative consonants; non-consonantal sounds are produced without such a constriction. Obstruents (plosives, fricatives, affricates), nasals, and liquids are [+cons]. The [−cons] class includes the vowels and the glides (a category made up of the semi-vowels and the glottal sounds [ʔ] and [h]).

3. Sonorant/obstruent: [+/−son]. Sonorant sounds are produced with a vocal tract configuration sufficiently open for the intra-oral air pressure to be approximately equal to the ambient air pressure. By contrast, obstruents are produced with a constriction sufficient to generate intra-oral pressure much greater than that of the surrounding air. (Vowels, liquids, glides, and nasals are [+son]. Stops, fricatives and affricates are [−son].)

Also included in SPE is a vocalic–non-vocalic [+/−voc] feature (already part of Jakobson, Fant and Halle, 1952) which allowed an opposition between (voiced) vowels and liquids, both labelled [+voc], and all other sounds labelled [−voc]. In SPE it is indicated that this feature should be dropped in favour of [+/−syll]. Since then, [+/−voc] has made many comebacks (eg Grace 1975), and it is not uncommon for simplifications of the feature-system to be accompanied by a reintroduction of this feature (eg Spencer 1984).

2.3.2 Cavity features
2.3.2.1. Primary strictures

1. Coronal/non-coronal: [+/−cor]. Coronal sounds are produced with the blade of the tongue raised from the neutral position. The neutral position comes from SPE where it is assumed that there is a speech-ready position defined as follows: (i) the glottis is narrowed so that the vocal folds will vibrate spontaneously in response to normal airflow; (ii) the velum is raised; (iii) the tongue, which normally lies on the floor of the mouth, is raised to a mid-front position (approximately between Jones's cardinal vowels 2 and 3)[1] but with lowered tongue-blade as in quiet breathing. (Dentals, alveolars, palato-alveolars and palatals are [+cor]. Labials, velars, uvulars and pharyngeals are [−cor].)

2. Anterior/posterior: [+/−ant]. Anterior sounds are produced with a primary constriction located at or in front of the alveolar ridge; posterior sounds are produced with a constriction behind the alveolar ridge. (Labials, dentals and

alveolars are [+ant]. Palato-alveolars, palatals, velars, uvulars and pharyngeals are [−ant].)

2.3.2.2 Tongue-body features

1. High/non-high: [+/−high]. High sounds are produced by raising the body of the tongue towards the roof of the mouth or, in *SPE* terminology, above its neutral position (that is, approximately the position of [e] in RP which is between cardinal vowels 2 and 3); non-high segments are produced without such a raising.
2. Low/non-low: [+/−low]. Low sounds are produced by lowering the body of the tongue to a level below the uvula or, in *SPE* terminology, to a level below the neutral position; non-low sounds are produced without such a lowering.
3. Back/non-back: [+/−back]. Back sounds are produced by retracting the body of the tongue towards the rear wall of the pharynx or, in *SPE* terminology, from its neutral position; non-back sounds are produced without such a retraction.

The three features above are used for both vowels and consonants. The main point to observe in connection with vowels is that high, low and back together allow for a maximum of three levels of height and a simple front–back opposition from a **phonological** standpoint. One of the (system-internal) reasons why the high–low (or close–open) dimension is limited to three values despite the theoretical possibility of four value-combinations for two binary features is that the grouping [+high, +low] is ruled out: the body of the tongue cannot be simultaneously raised towards the roof of the mouth and lowered to a level below the uvula. It is useful to realise that [+high] implies [−low] and [+low] implies [−high], since the redundant values are not normally mentioned in rules or in referring to segments.

Combined with [+/−round], the above three features give rise to matrices of the type given in [2]. Although the IPA symbols [y, ø, œ] are used in this book for the front rounded vowels, generativists often use [ü, ö, œ] instead. The symbols given in [2] correspond only partially to the IPA system which derives from Jones's cardinal vowel scheme based on four vowel heights (primary cardinal vowels: i, e, ɛ, a, ɑ, ɔ, o, u). Thus when only one a-type vowel is used contrastively within a language, it is typically classified as [+back, −round, +low] in generative writings (recall the Midi French system in Chapter 1) but still

[2]

	−back		+back	
	+round	−round	+round	−round
+high −low	y	i	u	ɨ
−high −low	ø	e	o	ʌ
−high +low	œ	æ/ɛ	ɔ	a

symbolized as /a/ which clashes with the IPA value attached to this symbol. Note too that [ɨ] has been used instead of IPA [ɯ]. In Chapter 4, a description of the vowel system of RP will be offered within the format of [2].

The *SPE* way of structuring the vowel space has given rise to an enormous literature both from a phonetic and a phonological point of view (since it has often been argued that various languages may require four and perhaps five degrees of vowel height at the contrastive level). This issue will be considered again in 2.5.2, 3.2 and in Chapter 8 from a variety of angles.

As far as non-vowels are concerned, [high], [back], and [low] fulfil two functions:

1. They characterize primary articulations directly in so far as these involve displacements of the body of the tongue. For instance, the palatals [c, ɟ, ʎ, ç, j] and velars [k, g, x, ɣ, w] all involve close approximation or contact with the roof of the mouth and will be classified as [+high]. But the palatals do not involve a retraction of the tongue from the neutral position and will therefore be [−back]. The velars, on the other hand, involve a retraction of the body of the tongue away from its neutral front position and will be [+back]. As for the pharyngeals [ħ, ʕ], they involve both a retraction and a lowering of the body of the tongue towards the pharynx and will be [+back, +low]. Segments for which displacements of the body of the tongue are not crucial, say labials such as [p, b, v, f], will have a neutral tongue position [−high, −low, −back].

2. They also characterize secondary articulations: palatalized segments involve the superimposition of a [j] articulation on a primary gesture and will be categorized as [+high, −back]; velarized segments involve the superimposition of an [ɨ] articulation and will be [+high, +back] and

pharyngealized segments involve the superimposition of a back [a] (IPA [ɑ]) articulation and will be [+low, +back].

Some examples of classification for typical places of articulation are provided in [3].

[3]

Example:	Labials f	Dentals s	Palatals ç	Velars x	Uvulars χ	Pharyngeals ħ
Coronal	−	+	+	−	−	−
Anterior	+	+	−	−	−	−
High	−	−	+	+	−	−
Low	−	−	−	−	−	+
Back	−	−	−	+	+	+

Let us now turn to the glides, a class assumed to include the semi-vowels and the 'glottal' sounds [h, ʔ] – a grouping whose validity will be re-examined in 3.5.2. The semi-vowels are symbolized in this book by IPA symbols [j, w, ɥ] but alternative symbols often used by generativists are [y, w, ẅ] respectively. In terms of the features presented above, the glides would be classified as in [4] which departs from *SPE*: 307 in that [j] is classified there as [−cor] but as [+cor] here in line with recent work.

[4]

	j, ɥ	w	h, ʔ
Coronal	+	−	−
Anterior	+	−	−
High	+	+	−
Low	−	−	+
Back	−	+	−

4. Advanced/Unadvanced Tongue Root: [+/−ATR]. A positive value for [ATR] corresponds to the drawing of the tongue root forward, thus enlarging the pharyngeal cavity and often raising the body of the tongue as well; [−ATR] sounds do not involve this gesture.

This feature, added to the universal inventory by Halle and Stevens (1969) on the basis of work discussed below, accounts among other things, for vowel harmony processes well represented in Niger–Congo languages of West Africa and Nilo-Saharan languages of East Africa (*cf* Lindau 1978; Kaye 1982, in press: Ch. 4). Thus, the ten phonetic vowels of the Akyem dialect of Akan are subdivided into two sets of five each distinguished by an advancement vs. retraction of the tongue root in [5]. The vowels within a morpheme must all belong to one set only and the vowel harmony rules also apply across morpheme boundaries. The personal pronouns in Akan, for example, harmonize with the vowels in the stem. The verb for 'to leave' is [fĩ] with a [+ATR] vowel and the verb for 'to vomit' is [fĩ] with a [−ATR] vowel. The prefixed pronouns show [ATR]-based alternations in the quality of the vowel: [mì fĩ] 'I leave', [òfĩ] 'he leaves' vs. [mʊ fĩ́] 'I vomit' and [ɔ̀fĩ́] 'he vomits' (cf Lindau 1978: 550–1 and 7.1.5).

[5]

+ATR		−ATR	
i	u	ɪ	ʊ
e	o	ɛ	ɔ
ɜ		a	

Such alternations were treated in terms of features such as [+/−tense] or [+/−covered] by Chomsky and Halle among others. Radiographic data has, however, shown conclusively that the relevant physiological parameter is the movement of the root of the tongue (cf Ladefoged, 1968: 33–9; Stewart 1967; Lindau 1975, 1978 for detailed discussion and further references). As the displacement of the root of the tongue in [+ATR] sounds is accompanied by a lowering of the larynx and sometimes with movements of the back pharyngeal wall, it has been argued by Lindau that the physiologically relevant parameter is the expansion of the pharyngeal size. A better name for this feature would, in her view, be [expanded]. (But see Hall and Hall 1980, for reservations on [expanded].)

One possible problem is that under either proposal, as they stand, a wider pharyngeal cavity is turned into the marked value [+ATR], which the opposite set lacks. Now, this is definitely what is required phonologically for many vowel harmony systems, including Akan (Stewart 1967) and Kpokolo (see 8.4). But, there are also cases where, phonologically, retraction of the tongue-root seems to be the relevant parameter (eg Yoruba, see Archangeli and Pulleyblank (to appear); and Nez Perce, see Hall and Hall 1980). Moreover, phonetically, [+ATR] and [−ATR] vowels are equally 'marked': while [+ATR] vowels can be produced by advancing the tongue root beyond a kind of 'normal' position and lowering the larynx, [−ATR] vowels often involve retraction of the tongue from this 'normal' position and raising of the larynx (Lindau 1978: 551; Ladefoged 1982: 206, as well as Hall and Hall 1980). Therefore, it appears that we have two gestures in opposite directions from a 'neutral' position of the root of the tongue: either advancement or retraction. On the basis of phonology and phonetics, we should arguably allow for two features [+/−Advanced Tongue Root] (ATR) vs. [+/−Retracted Tongue Root] (RTR) and, in a familiar way, rule out the combination [+ATR, +RTR] as an impossible articulatory manœuvre.

One area where [+/−RTR] seems relevant is the treatment of the pharyngeals. While it was suggested above that pharyngealized consonants could be distinguished from other types of normal or secondary articulation by the feature combination [+low, +back], it is more accurate to consider that the relevant parameter is in fact a retraction of the root of the tongue and a general constriction of the pharynx. In other words, pharyngeals are [+RTR]. Note that, in Jakobsonian terms, the retraction of the tongue is marked: according to Maddieson (1984), only Arabic, Tuareg and Shila are reported to have pharyngeal plosives and only subsets of the stops in these languages allow a contrast between plain and pharyngealized consonants. Selecting a positive property [RTR] rather than the absence of [ATR] is arguably a better way of bringing out the markedness of pharyngeals.

2.3.3 Lip-attitude

1. Rounded/unrounded: [+/−round]. Rounded segments are produced with a protrusion of the lips. Unrounded segments have a spread or neutral lip position. The feature [+round] is applied not only to rounded vowels (u, o, y, ø, etc.) but also to labialized consonants (p^w, t^w, k^w, etc.) by contrast with unrounded vowels and consonants.

It has been suggested, on the basis of the Swedish vowel system, that feature systems should allow two degrees or types of contrastive rounding (see Malmberg 1971: 153–4, 164–7; Fant 1971: 231 ff; Lass 1984). The mid-high front vowel of Swedish *hus*, transcribed here as /ɨ/, 'house', is said by Lass to differ from /e/ and /ø/ solely in terms of lip gesture. Whereas /e/ is unrounded and /ø/ has protruded lip-rounding, /ɨ/ involves vertical lip-compression. In terms of Catford (1977), /ø/ would be endo-labio-endolabial: both the lower lip and the upper lip are pushed forward so that their inner parts are juxtaposed producing a rounder, pouting effect. On the other hand, /ɨ/ would be exolabio-exolabial, that is, a sound produced by juxtaposition of the more external parts of the lower lip and upper lip. Lass puts forward a feature called [+/−inrounding], a translation of the Swedish term *inrundning*, where /ɨ/ is [+inrounding] and the other round vowels are [−inrounding]. The front vowels of Swedish are given the following matrix representation by Lass 1984: 88 (who, it will be noted, uses a feature [+/−mid]) [6].

[6]

	i	y	e	ø	ɨ	ɛ	a
High	+	+	+	+	+	−	−
Mid	−	−	+	+	+	+	−
Round	−	−	+	+	+	−	−
Inrounded	−	−	−	−	+	−	−

On the other hand, it is suggested in *SPE*: 315 that /ɨ/ could be distinguished from /y/ in Swedish by means of a feature [+/−covered] which is correlated with a constricted pharynx and a noticeable elevation of the larynx, and Chomsky and Halle cite work by Fant as lending some plausibility to this idea. However, according to Fant (1971: 231), there is no evidence to back this suggestion. There is no doubt, from the phonetic literature on Swedish, that /ɨ/ is distinguished from /y/ in terms of types of lip-rounding. As supplementary evidence, let us point out that the high long vowels of Swedish are pronounced as diphthongs towards a homorganic glide or fricative and, whereas /y:/ is made with a closing element which is palatal [ɥ], /ɨ:/ moves towards a bilabial fricative [β] (*cf* Malmberg 1971: 166). An extra feature such as [+/−inrounding] or [+/−compressed] (Lindau 1978) is therefore required.[2]

2. Labial/non-labial: [+/−lab]. 'As the term implies, labial sounds are formed with a constriction at the lips, while non-labial sounds are formed without such a constriction. (Labial consonants, rounded vowels vs. all other sounds.)' (Halle and Clements 1983: 6.)

This feature is not part of the *SPE* inventory. Yet, there is plenty of evidence that the following groups of sounds form a natural class: labiodentals [p, b, f, v, β, ɸ, m], doubly articulated labial-velars such as [kp, gb], labialized consonants (*eg* [pʷ, bʷ], round vowels and semi-vowels (*eg* [u, o, y, ø, w]). One example of the relevance of [+/−labial] has already been given from English phonotactics in 1.3.2.1. Another example is provided by Finnish (*cf* Vennemann and Ladefoged: 1971) where /ɣ/ (derived from /k/ by weakening) is changed into [v] between high round vowels (*ie* u __u and y __y):

[7] ɣ → v / $\begin{bmatrix} +\text{high} \\ +\text{round} \end{bmatrix}$ ____ $\begin{bmatrix} +\text{high} \\ +\text{round} \end{bmatrix}$

Without a feature [+/−labial], this change does not receive a natural interpretation since /ɣ/ is a velar unrounded continuant which becomes an anterior unrounded continuant in the context of high round vowels. On the other hand, positing the feature [labial] allows us to express this change along the following lines:

[8] $\begin{bmatrix} +\text{high} \\ +\text{back} \\ +\text{cont} \\ +\text{voice} \end{bmatrix}$ → [+labial] / $\begin{bmatrix} +\text{high} \\ +\text{labial} \end{bmatrix}$ ____ $\begin{bmatrix} +\text{high} \\ +\text{labial} \end{bmatrix}$

which shows that the process at work here is a straightforward case of assimilation.

2.3.4 Length of stricture

Distributed/non-distributed [+/−distr]. Distributed sounds are produced with a constriction that extends for a considerable distance along the mid-sagittal axis of the oral tract; non-distributed sounds are produced with a constriction that extends only for a short distance in this direction. (One example is that of sounds produced with the blade of the tongue – laminals – which are [+distributed] vs. sounds produced with the tip of the tongue – apicals – which are [−distributed]).

The reader will have noticed that, while there is no single parameter corresponding directly to the traditional notion of place of articulation, the features presented so far allow us to characterize major locations along the vocal tract. Nevertheless, languages do exhibit consonantal systems that fall outside our provisional feature-set. In *SPE*, it is argued that there are a quite a number of languages with obstruent systems as in [9]:

[9] p t̪ t ṭ k₁

where [t̪] is dental, [t] is alveolar, [ṭ] is retroflex and [k₁] is palato-alveolar plosive. While these differences could be handled by multiplying subzones along the roof of the mouth, Chomsky and Halle (1968) claim that, in each case, there are also characteristic differences in the length of the zone of contact. Thus [t̪] might

be apical and [t] laminal or vice versa. This claim was based on
instrumental work by Ladefoged (1968) on West African
languages where differences in the denti-alveolar region were
shown to be systematically correlated with differences in the
nature of the constriction. Chomsky and Halle summarize the
relevant data in [10].

[10]

	Teeth and teeth-ridge	Front of teeth-ridge	Back of teeth-ridge
Twi		Apical	Laminal
Ewe	Laminal		Apical
Temne	Apical	Laminal (affricated)	
Isoko	Laminal (affricated)	Apical	

The feature [+/−distributed] is not solely applied to the
laminal–apical distinction. The distinction can also be applied to
such distinctions as that of bilabials ([+distr]) vs. labiodentals
([−distr]) and 'soft' ([−distr]) vs. 'hard' ([+distr]) dentals in
Polish. Finally, the retroflex consonants examined by Chomsky
and Halle (1968) are tentatively labelled [−distr]. Under one
interpretation, therefore, the obstruent system given above could
be characterized in [11] where all the consonants can be seen to
be pairwise distinct (see §3.3).

[11]

	p	ṭ	t	ṭ	k₁
Anterior	+	+	+	−	−
Coronal	−	+	+	+	+
Distributed	+	−	+	−	+

Notice that the laminal–apical distinction, subsumed under
[+/−distributed], instead of being treated as an 'intensifier' of
small differences in place of articulation, has become a primary
distinguishing feature. On the other hand, differences in place of
articulation such as dental vs. alveolar, traditionally seen as basic,
are now relegated to low-level phonetic adjustments. Chomsky
and Halle (1968: 312) tell us: 'This is by no means an empty
claim. It would be controverted if, for example, a given language
were shown to have dental and alveolar consonants which both
had apical articulation.' Ladefoged has mentioned the Dravidian

languages as falsifying the *SPE* claim (*cf* Ladefoged 1971: 38–41, 1982: 145). Thus, he describes Malayalam as a language illustrating the necessity for six places of articulation:

[12] Malayalam places of articulation (the subscript indicates dentality and the dot marks retroflexion)

Bilabial	Dental	Alveolar	Retroflex	Palatal	Velar
kʌmmi	pʌn̠n̠i	kʌnni	kʌṇṇi	kʌɲɲi	kʌŋŋi

Despite this *prima facie* counter-example, the *SPE* scheme is still adhered to in a great deal of work. A mixed scheme where traditional labels like 'apical' and 'dental' play a role beside 'distributed' is advocated in Spencer (1984).

2.3.5 Secondary apertures

1. Lateral/central [+/−lat]. 'Lateral sounds, the most familiar of which is [l], are produced in such a way as to prevent the airstream from flowing outward through the centre of the mouth, while allowing it to pass over one or both sides of the tongue; central sounds do not involve such a constriction' (Halle and Clements 1983: 7). Lateral sonorants, fricatives and affricates are [+lat]; all other sounds are [−lat].

Lateral is one of the least controversial features of phonological theory. It is, however, argued in Spencer's 'Eliminating the feature [lateral]' (1984) that its relative phonetic transparency does not constitute a strong argument for its inclusion in a restrictive set of DFs.

2 Nasal/oral: [+/−nasal]. 'Nasal sounds are produced by lowering the velum and allowing the air to pass outward through the nose; oral sounds are produced with the velum raised to prevent the passage of air through the nose' (Halle and Clements 1983: 7). Nasal stops, nasalized consonants, vowels and glides are [+nas]; all other sounds are [−nas].

The above definition of [+/−nasal], as well as that of *SPE*, simplifies the phonetics considerably but is sufficient from a phonological standpoint (see Laver 1979 and van Reenen 1982 for thorough discussions of nasality).

2.3.6 Manner of articulation features

1. Continuant/stop: [+/−cont]. Sounds produced with a primary constriction which allows the air to flow through the mid-sagittal region of the vocal tract are [+cont]; sounds

produced with a sustained occlusion are [−cont]. (Vowels, glides, r-sounds, fricatives are [+cont]; nasal stops, oral stops and laterals are [−cont].)

The distinction between stops and non-stops is well grounded in the phonology of languages. The inclusion of r-sounds in the above list, borrowed from Halle and Clements (1983), requires some comment. Chomsky and Halle (1968), who adopt a slightly different definition, warn the reader that some care is needed in applying this feature to the liquids. For instance, while General American or RP [ɹ] is clearly [+cont], how should one classify trilled [r], taps and flaps? Trilled [r], they argue, is [+cont] because the repeated occlusions are a side-effect of the narrowing required for the Bernoulli effect to take place. They do not come up with a final conclusion on taps and flaps but would seem to be in favour of a [−cont] assignment.

The difference between taps and flaps is controversial (see Catford 1977: 128–35 for a possible account) but, if one thing is agreed on, it is that taps and flaps are not, properly speaking, vibrants but very brief stops. Catford offers the figures of 1–3 centiseconds for the duration of the closure in taps as opposed to 5–6 centiseconds for stops. In fact, whereas a stop can be prolonged without losing its identity, taps/flaps simply cannot be prolonged and therefore cannot be [+cont]. Note, on the other hand, that it is not because a sound is prolongable that it is necessarily [+cont]: the nasals and laterals are both prolongable but involve a sustained occlusion and are classified as [−cont] according to the above definition. It is worth pointing out that Chomsky and Halle (1968) did not see the assignment of laterals as + or −cont as an easy matter, but rather suggested that it depended on whether or not the laterals patterned with the stops within a language. The most debatable classification in the above definition by Halle and Clements (1983) is that of the glides (semi-vowels and [h, ʔ]). [h] and [ʔ] are best treated as [+cont] and [−cont] respectively (see 3.5.2). As for the semi-vowels, they are primarily distinguished from high vowels by their momentariness. If it were agreed that [+cont] segments have to be prolongable, as assumed above, then the semi-vowels cannot be [+cont]. On the other hand, they do not involve a sustained closure. A better definition would be: sounds which do not involve a total blockage within the oral cavity and are prolongable are [+cont], other sounds are [−cont].

2. Delayed/instantaneous release: [+/−delrel].
There are basically two ways in which a closure in the vocal

tract may be released, either instantaneously as in the plosives or with a delay as in the affricates. During the delayed release, turbulence is generated in the vocal tract so that the release phase of affricates is acoustically quite similar to the cognate fricative. The instantaneous release is normally accompanied by much less or no turbulence (*SPE* p 318).

This feature which is restricted to sounds produced with a closure, is not part of the Halle and Clements (1983) set. Within *SPE* it accounts for the contrast between plosives and affricates. [p, b, t, d, k, g] are [−delrel]; [č] and [ǰ] are [+delrel].

3. Tense/lax: [+/−tense]. Tense sounds are produced with a greater (vs. smaller) amount of deformation of the vocal tract away from its neutral, rest position. Their tongue-body configuration involves a greater degree of constriction than that found in their lax partners and this is often accompanied by greater length. An example of [+tense] vs. [−tense] opposition is provided by the vowels of modern German, for instance: *ihre* 'her' vs. *irre* 'err', 1st sing.; *Huhne* 'chicken' vs. *Hunne* 'Hun'; *Düne* 'dune' vs. *dünne* 'thin'; *wen* 'whom' vs. *wenn* 'if'; *wohne* 'reside', 1st sing.; vs. *Wonne* 'joy'; *Haken* 'hook' vs. *hacken* 'hack'.

[±Tense] has proved to be one of the most controversial features in the history of phonology. Whereas specialists have often been able to accept its validity for consonants, in the case of vowels it has been felt that the evidence for muscular tension/laxness was lacking and that [+/−tense] merely conflated other distinctions which were independently needed such as [+/−long] or [+/−centralized] (see Lass 1976, 1984 and Catford 1977 for a criticism of this feature and the defence in Wood 1982: 157–82). In 3.2, a possible argument for the relevance of [+/−tense] is cited from standard French.

A further consideration is that no language is known to use distinctively both [+/−tense] and [+/−ATR] (Advanced Tongue Root). It may well be that these features are variant implementations of a single classificatory dimension. But, these two features are not totally interchangeable. In the French data of 3.2, /a/ (IPA [a]) patterns with /ɛ, ɔ, œ/ as [−tense] by contrast with /ɑ, o, e, ø/ which are [+tense]. In ATR systems, a backish /a/ (IPA [ɑ]) tends to pattern with /ɛ/ and /ɔ/ as [−ATR], and its [+ATR] partner is often a centralized vowel such as [ɜ] grouped with [e] and [o] (see [5] above and 7.1.5).

2.3.7 Source features
2.3.7.1 Voicing and types of phonation
In *SPE* a standard feature [+/− voice] is offered. This can be briefly defined as follows:

1. Voiced/voiceless: [+/−voiced]. Sounds produced with vibrations of the vocal cords are voiced; voiceless sounds are produced with a glottal opening so wide that it will prevent vocal vibration if air flows through it. (For many languages, vowels, liquids, nasals, voiced obstruents vs. voiceless obstruents.)

This feature is perfectly adequate to characterize oppositions based on glottal states in many familiar languages. On the other hand, it does not fit very well a number of languages which have contrasts involving much more complex glottal configurations: *eg* breathy voice or creaky voice (laryngealization). Halle and Stevens (1971) have put forward a different system of four binary features which are claimed to be able to characterize not only glottal configurations but also tonal phenomena and differences in voice onset time. These features are presented in a single block for obvious reasons. We examine further down the way they can be combined to characterize various sound types.

2. Spread/non-spread glottis: [+/−spread]. Spread sounds are produced by a displacement of the arytenoid cartilages creating a wide glottal opening; non-spread are produced without this gesture. (Aspirated consonants, breathy voiced or murmured consonants, voiceless vowels and glides are [+spread]; all other sounds are [−spread].)
3. Constricted/non-constricted: [+/−constr]. Constricted sounds are produced by adduction of the arytenoid cartilages causing the vocal cords to be pressed together and preventing normal vocal cord vibration; non-constricted (non-glottalized) sounds are produced without such a gesture. (Ejectives, implosives, glottalized or laryngealized consonants, vowels and glides are [+constr]; all other sounds are [−constr].)
4. Stiff vocal cords/non-stiff vocal cords: [+/−stiff]. Sounds produced with tense vocal cords are [+stiff], otherwise they are [−stiff]. (Voiceless unaspirated or aspirated obstruents, voiceless ejectives, glottalized vowels are [+stiff]; all other sounds are [−stiff].)
5. Slack vocal cords/non-slack vocal cords: [+/−slack]. Sounds made with slack, non-tense vocal cords are [+slack], otherwise they are [−slack]. (Obstruents which are breathy,

glottalized or laryngealized, 'normal' voiced obstruents, creaky voice vowels are [+slack]; all other sounds are [−slack].)

Given the definitions, the feature combinations [+stiff, +slack], [+spread, +constr] are ruled out as physiologically impossible. As a result the four features yield nine distinct phonetic categories which are exemplified in [13] and [14]. For convenience, all the examples in [13] have been drawn from plosives as representatives of the class of obstruents. The symbols [p_k] and [b_1] are borrowed from Halle and Stevens (1971). The first one stands for the weakly aspirated Korean stop which stands in opposition to a strongly aspirated stop [p^h] and an

[13]

	+stiff −slack	−stiff −slack	−stiff +slack
+spread −constr	Voiceless aspirated plosive p^h	Voiceless partially aspirated plosive p_k	Voiced (breathy) aspirated plosive b^h
−spread −constr	Voiceless unaspirated plosive p	Lax voiceless plosive b_1	Voiced unaspirated plosive b
−spread +constr	Ejectives p̓ (=IPA [p'])	Implosives ɓ	(Pre)glottalized or laryngealized obstruents ʔb, b̰

[14]

	+stiff −slack	−stiff −slack	−stiff +slack
+spread −constr	h, W, Y (voiceless)	Voiceless vowels	ɦ (voiced) breathy vowels
−spread −constr		'Normal' vowels/glides	
−spread +constr	ʔ, ʔw, ʔy (voiceless), glottalized vowels		Creaky voice vowels, ʔ̰ (voiced)

unaspirated stop [p]. The second one represents sounds such as the lenis voiceless stop of Danish or the initial *b* of many varieties of English. Note that traditional voiced–voiceless contrasts are now expressed as [+stiff, −slack] (voiceless) vs. [−stiff, +slack] (voiced).

The features discussed above also apply to vowels and glides. We exemplify the various combinations in figure [14] where the terminology and the symbols are borrowed from Halle and Stevens (1971) (note that [y] is IPA [j]).

In [14], Y, W stand for the voiceless glides established by Sapir for Southern Paiute and [²w, ²y] are the glottalized glides of Nootka. Barred 2 is a voiced glottal stop which 'appears to be attested in Jingpho' (Halle and Stevens 1971: 209). The glottalized vowels are given with reference to Vietnamese, Nez Perce and Acoma. Halle and Stevens also include the Danish stød in this category arguing that it is produced with a constricted glottis ([+stiff]).

Finally, the feature [+stiff] is also argued to be the articulatory correlate of **high pitch** and [+slack] of **low pitch**, neutral pitch being the result of [−stiff, −slack]. Since voiceless stops ([+stiff]) tend to raise the pitch of adjacent vowels whereas voiced stops ([+slack]) tend to cause a downward shift in pitch, the use of the same features for these two domains allows a unitary explanation of the facts. The connection between a constricted glottis and pitch also turns out to be relevant for the Danish stød since the latter has often been claimed to be genetically related to the first tone of Scandinavian languages such as Swedish (see Staun 1987, for a discussion of stød and further references).

Halle and Stevens's approach has been heavily criticized by a number of phoneticians (*cf* Fromkin 1972: 38–47; Ladefoged 1972; Catford 1977: 107–9). One standard objection is that the theoretical model posited by Halle and Stevens does not match observations of glottal activity. Thus, it is objected that the supposed states of stiffness of the vocal cords are unsupported or irrelevant. For instance, Ladefoged (1972) presents as unlikely the hypothesis that in creaky voice sounds the vocal cords are [+slack, −stiff]. And Catford objects to a distinction being made between implosive [ɓ] and 'normal' [b] in terms of vocal cord tension when the crucial difference between them is one of airstream mechanisms (glottalic suction vs. pulmonic pressure).

One of the problems here is that the technical literature on the subject does contain conflicting statements. Lieberman (1977: 90–1) describes vocal 'fry' (a term often used in the USA for creaky phonation) as 'appear(ing) to involve very slack tension and a large vibrating mass'. On the other hand Laver (1979: 122–6) provides a very thorough physiological and acoustic description of 'creak', where the quotes from physiologists do not give rise to a fully coherent picture. While Monsen and Engebretson (1977) do speak of 'slack vocal folds', other researchers stress that what is important is that the vocal cords should form an 'unusually thick and compact (but not necessarily tense)' structure which may well involve the false vocal cords. But, these researchers are physiologists usually dealing with 'creaky phonation' as a type of speech defect. On the other hand, linguistic phoneticians such as Catford and Ladefoged, who are interested in creaky voice as a potentially contrastive type of phonation, stress that only a small portion of the vocal folds, near the thyroid, is vibrating (see the photographs of the glottis in Ladefoged, 1971: 6, 1982: 128). The only component on which there is universal agreement is the fact that very low mean rates of flow through the glottis are required for creaky voice and this is precisely the factor that receives no translation in the Halle–Stevens model. The classification by Halle and Stevens was perhaps premature in that it attempted to bring under a fairly simple model a set of sounds whose description is still uncertain. A good example is Halle and Stevens's postulation of a 'voiced glottal stop' in Jingpho. Given that voiced segments require sustained periodic vibrations of the vocal folds, it is difficult to understand how a sound could simultaneously be a glottal stop – which requires total closure of the vocal folds – and voiced.

While the spread-constricted parameter seems less debatable than stiffness–slackness, in view of the uncertainties echoed above, I will feel free to continue to operate with traditional features such as [+/−voiced] and [+/−aspirated] (but cf 7.3.2).

2.3.7.2 Stridency
Strident/non-strident [+/−strident]. Strident sounds are produced with a constriction forcing the airstream to strike two surfaces producing a high-intensity noise. Generally, the strident sounds are distinguished from their non-strident counterparts by faster airflow, a rougher surface and an angle of incidence closer to 90 degrees. This feature is restricted to fricatives and affricates. (In English, the sibilants [s, z, š, ž, č, ǰ] and [f, v] are [+strident]. All other sounds are [−strident].)

2.3.8 Airstream mechanisms
Features relating to airstream mechanisms (pulmonic, glottalic, velaric) will be only briefly mentioned here. In SPE global

features such as 'glottal pressure', 'glottal suction' and 'velar suction' are postulated to account respectively for 'ejectives', 'implosives' and 'clicks'. It seems preferable, following Lass (1984: 93–4), to separate the parameter which refers to the initiator of the airstream mechanisms from the initiation itself (pressure vs. suction). Initiation can, for instance, be specified by two features [+/−glottalic] and [+/−velaric]. A negative value for both these features specifies pulmonic sounds as a default value. One feature (*eg* [+/−pressure]) is sufficient for initiation. Ladefoged and Traill (1984) should, however, be consulted for a detailed criticism of the description of clicks adopted in all standard feature systems (including Ladefoged 1971, 1982).[3]

2.3.9 Prosodic and other features

Section 2.3 has offered a fairly detailed overview of a well-known set of features. Many other features and feature-systems have been discussed in the literature. A review of even a small portion of the relevant works would take us too far afield and some counter-proposals to the 'standard' set will, in any case, be discussed in the chapters that follow. Two other features which will be used in the rest of this book and which figure prominently in the *SPE* tradition will be introduced here:

1. [+/−long]: this feature applies to long vs. short segments and is often in competition with [+/−tense].
2. [+/−stress]: this feature, which is a property of [+syll] segments, is either binary or n-ary according to the language. Thus, the *SPE* treatment of stress in English uses a system where [1stress] marks a main stress, [0stress] marks an unstressed segment and non-primary stresses are indicated by multiples of [1stress]: [2stress] = secondary, [3stress] = tertiary, and so on.

Finally, tones can also be analysed in terms of binary features typically assigned to vowels: parameters such as [+/−high], [+/−low], [+/−rise]. [+/−convex], etc. have been advocated in the classical generative literature (see Wang 1967; Woo 1969). And we have also seen in 2.3.7.1 that [+/−stiff] and [+/−slack] had been put forward as tentative tonal features. While tones will not be extensively discussed in this book, the question of tonal features will be re-examined in our developments on Autosegmental phonology (see 7.1 and note 1 of Chapter 7 for further references). In later chapters, we shall also see that a richer conception of suprasegmental structure renders a number of features introduced above redundant.

2.4 Universalism revisited

The postulation of a universal set of DFs is by no means accepted
by all linguists. A familiar criticism of the 'weak' approach to
universalism made, for instance, by Leech (1981: 232) in the area
of semantic universals, is that it is so 'weak as to be vacuous'.
This position has not uncommonly been echoed in criticisms of
the generative tradition where it is objected that lists of DFs have
predictably grown in generative phonology and that, in view of
the possible requirements of hitherto unanalysed languages, the
assumption of certainty cannot be made. This type of objection
can be traced to Martinet (1955), who, criticizing the 'binarist
theory' of Jakobson, Fant and Halle (1952), said:

> But who could boast of having examined exhaustively all the
> existing and attested languages? And what about all the
> languages which have disappeared without leaving traces and
> those which will appear on the earth tomorrow? Even if these
> authors were to base the binarist theory on an exhaustive and,
> above all objective examination of a respectable sample of
> languages, we would be entitled to reserve our judgement and to
> refuse to draw the general from the particular – even if the
> latter is fairly vast [my translation – JD].

While one has to admit that the interpretation of universals
adopted for DF inventories is, *ex definitio*, not as strong as one
which requires that every language have a particular category, it
is by no means vacuous. It would be vacuous if it were not open
to empirical debate and if no finite list had been proposed as has
usually happened in semantic theories which posit the existence
of a universal set of sense-components but do not provide a
closed list of these. The fact that the list changes or has grown
is not, in itself, a particularly strong objection but merely exemplifies the **tentative** nature of hypotheses in this domain as in
others. But, in any case, we should not get carried away by the
terms 'strong' and 'weak' here. What is important is not to decide
a priori on the relative merits of 'strong' vs. 'weak' universals but
to see which interpretation can lead to the best theory of a
particular domain. It is a fact that languages vary in their
phonetic and phonological inventories very much as individuals
differ from one another (as **phenotypes** in the vocabulary of
biology). But this does not mean that the variation we observe
cannot be the result of different combinations of fixed, universal
parameters in the same way as a biologist might argue that the
phenotypes are the result of varying combinations of universal
underlying properties (**genotypes**). What the quote from Martinet
further assumes is that it makes no sense to embark on a univer-

salist enterprise unless **all** the facts have been charted and **all** the (past, present and future) languages have been surveyed. Since this is impossible, a universalist approach is by definition ruled out. However, if one were to generalize the strictures that Martinet wishes to impose on all linguistic research then there is nothing that could be said about language. Martinet, for instance, assumes that one of the definitional properties of human language is its double articulation – that is, the assumption that all utterances can be split up into minimal signs which have a form and a meaning (morphemes or monemes), and that these minimal signs can in turn be analysed as made up of contrastive units, the phonemes. But how do we know this? Have we examined ALL languages to state this with certainty? Can we be sure that languages that will arise will be structured in the same manner? Linguistics then could only be a catalogue of what exists and not a set of hypotheses on the nature of language that can be confronted with 'facts'.

In so far as distinctive features are concerned, there is indeed no direct evidence that our brain is wired up in terms of feature-detectors corresponding to each of the parameters posited by DF theorists. Species for which feature-detectors have been localized in the brain such as the bullfrog (*cf* Capranica 1965; Lieberman 1984: 132–4) have extremely simple communication systems. Each signal carries a meaning, in the broadest sense of the word, whereas DFs (in their classical interpretation) separate phonemes which in turn separate words. In addition, studies of human beings are always limited by the indirect techniques that can be used. There is a fair amount of evidence, however, that the processing of speech and the processing of other sounds involve different neural mechanisms (*cf* Jakobson and Waugh 1979: 29–35; Darwin 1987: 73–5), even if the question as to whether the very young infants' perception of speech reflects innate abilities which are uniquely human is still controversial (*cp* Eimas *et al.* 1971 and Kuhl and Miller 1978). In so far as the notion of a specialized phonetic module characterizing human beings makes sense (*cf* Liberman and Mattingly 1985), then DF theory is a step based on linguistic evidence towards the specification of this module. Even if the hypotheses entertained by DF theory were to be shown as misguided by future research on speech processing, it is important to realize that universalism can still be defended on methodological grounds. By formulating strong hypotheses about language-structure, we are more likely to unearth facts which may be significant. By suggesting, for instance, that a single distinctive feature, [+/−flat], could account phonologically for pharyngealization, velarization, labialization and retroflexion, Jakobson, Fant and Halle (1952) forced researchers to examine the interaction between these phonetic dimensions in a new light. The rejection of this hypothetical feature in later research is not to be seen as a negative comment on the original proposal but as a positive step in our understanding of language.

2.5 The acoustic/auditory basis of distinctive features

In 2.3 we have given only articulatory correlates for the distinctive features and postponed the problem of choice – if a choice is indeed required – between acoustic (or more properly auditory) and articulatory correlates. The pre-eminence of the auditory dimension in the treatment of DFs is usually traced back to Jakobson, Fant and Halle's *Preliminaries (to Speech Analysis)* (1952: 3) where, to determine DFs, the emphasis was placed on the receptive side of the communication circuit:

> Any minimal distinction carried by the message confronts the listener with a two-choice situation. Within a given language each of these oppositions has a specific property which differentiates it from all the others. The listener is obliged to choose either between two polar qualities of the same category, such as grave vs. acute, compact vs. diffuse, or between the presence and absence of a certain quality, such as voiced vs. unvoiced, nasalized vs. non-nasalized, sharpened vs. non-sharpened (plain). The choice between the two opposites may be termed distinctive features.

Recently, Halle (1983: 94) has claimed that, given that articulatory correlates were also mentioned in *Preliminaries*, the intention of the authors was in fact to remain neutral between production and perception. This is simply not the way that the book was universally interpreted by later commentators and Jakobson's writings do not appear to support this reconstruction. The most detailed exposition of Jakobson's point of view on the basis of DFs is to be found in Jakobson and Waugh (1979). What these authors stress repeatedly is that we speak to be heard and that articulation is no more than a means to an end. Chistovich is quoted approvingly when he says: 'In order to describe and model the process of speech production, it is necessary to turn to such a notion as the aim of the motor act, and the solely evident aim is the production of a definite acoustic effect accessible and "understandable" to the listener' (cited in Jakobson and Waugh 1979: 27). The evidence that Jakobson and Waugh give to bolster this point of view is that there is an imbalance between production and perception: invariance for them is to be found at the acoustic and not at the articulatory level. Let us turn to some exemplification of this claim.

2.5.1 The feature [grave]

The feature [+/−grave] is defined in Jakobson, Fant and Halle 1952: 29 as involving acoustically 'the predominance of one side of the significant part of the spectrum over the other. When the lower side of the spectrum predominates, the phoneme is labelled grave; when the upper side predominates, we term the phoneme acute.' This feature cross-classifies consonants and vowels. The following examples are given in the same work:

Grave vs. acute vowels: Turkish /kɨs/ 'malevolent' – /kis/ 'tumor'; /kus/ 'vomit!' vs. /kys/ 'reduce!'; /an/ 'moment' – /en/ 'width', /on/ 'ten' – /øn/ 'front'.

Grave vs. acute consonants: English fill – sill, pill – till, bill – dill, mill – nill.

It must be pointed out that, as always, the labelling of a phoneme as + or − grave is a relational question: it depends on the structure of the system that we are trying to characterize. But, generally, we can say that labial and velar consonants as well as back rounded vowels are [+grave] whereas dental, alveolar, palatal consonants and front unrounded vowels are [−grave]. Jakobson and Waugh (1979) support the cross-classification of vowels and consonants with the following examples which involve the change of grave into acute consonants in the environment of acute vowels: 'the Eastern Czech shift of labials into dentals in examples such as [ti:vo] from [pi:vo] 'beer'; [četice] from [čepice] 'cap, headgear', [ni:ň] from [mi:ň] 'less' . . . and the widespread appearance of palatal substitutes for velars before front vowels' (Jakobson and Waugh 1979: 98). The Eastern Czech shift belongs to a class of examples where the high front vowel is linked to the palatals and dentals and its translation into the DF framework explored in 2.3 is not self-evident. This does not mean that an articulatory explanation could not be made available (see Pagliuca and Mowrey 1980 for a counter-proposal to the feature [grave] and more exemplification). On the other hand, in terms of our DF set, the fronting of velars into palatals is formulable as:

$$[15] \begin{bmatrix} C \\ +back \end{bmatrix} \rightarrow [-back] \;/\; \underline{\hspace{1em}} \begin{bmatrix} V \\ -back \end{bmatrix}$$

which is as simple as

[16] $\begin{bmatrix} C \\ +\text{grave} \end{bmatrix} \rightarrow [-\text{grave}] \;/\; \underline{} \begin{bmatrix} V \\ -\text{grave} \end{bmatrix}$

and therefore does not provide compelling evidence for an acoustically based account.

What is more striking within the present context is the well-known grouping of labial and velar consonants in a variety of processes: *eg* the change of [x] to [f] in words like *enough* in the history of English, the Dutch shift of [ft] to [xt] (*after* > *achter*) or the [p] to [k] change in the Eastern Toba–Batak Indonesian dialect (see Jakobson and Waugh 1979: 22). Such substitutions are difficult to explain by recourse to the articulatorily based features presented above. For what affinity is there between the lip-gesture which defines labials and the raising of the back of the tongue towards the velum which defines velars? As [+/−coronal] is currently defined, labials and velars can be grouped together as [−coronal] vs. dentals and palatals which are [+coronal]. But, in *SPE*, palatals were [−coronal] and it is indeed possible to make a palatal consonant without raising the tongue blade towards the teeth or the hard palate as required by the definition of [+coronal]. In addition, since [−coronal] sounds are defined **negatively** – *ie* as involving the absence of a raising of the tongue blade – the interplay between labials and velars remains unexplained.

A further example of the grouping of the velars and labials is given by Hyman (1973, 1975). In Feʔfeʔ-Bamileke the phoneme /a/ is realized as a back [ɑ] before [p] and [k], but as front before [t]:

[17] [vɑp] 'to whip'
     [čɑk] 'to seek'
     [fat] 'to eat'

The use of a low back vowel before [p, k] does not receive a perspicuous translation with articulatorily based features:

[18] $\quad$ V $\qquad\qquad$ C
     $[+\text{low}] \rightarrow [\alpha\text{back}] \;/\; \underline{} [\alpha\text{coronal}]$

On the other hand, low back [ɑ] is characterized by a large oral cavity in the same way as labials and velars and, acoustically, this produces a concentration of energy in the lower frequencies of the sound spectrum (gravity). The determination of the extrinsic allophones of the low vowel /a/ is straightforward in acoustic terms:

[19] $\quad$ V $\qquad\qquad$ C
     $[+\text{low}] \;\rightarrow\; [\alpha\text{grave}] \;/\; \underline{} [\alpha\text{grave}]$

2.5.2 The vowel space

A second area which is taken by Jakobson and Waugh, along
with other specialists, as providing strong evidence for the
primacy of the auditory–acoustic dimension is the specification
of vowels. We have seen above that the features [high], [low] and
[back] were defined in terms of tongue height and tongue retraction. If we leave aside the question of binarity, this position
follows a long tradition in phonetics which has been aptly
described by Wood (1982) as the 'tongue arch' model. Jakobson
and Waugh argue that such descriptions suffer from a kind of
'tongue fetishism' which is perhaps supported by the closeness
between the words for 'anatomic tongue' (langue, jazyk) and
'tongue = language' (langue, jazyk). They point out, in
particular, that there is a long documented history of subjects
who lost the greatest part of their tongue but were able to
produce well-differentiated vowels through adjustments in supralaryngeal configurations. But, in fact, we do not need to go into
the case-history of such unfortunate individuals. While there is
evidence that the traditional notion of tongue height does correspond to the articulatory manoeuvres of some speakers (see
Lindau 1978), there is also available data casting strong doubt on
the traditional theory (but see Fischer-Jørgensen 1985).
According to Ladefoged (1967), the only published radiographic
study of a set of cardinal vowels is that of S. Jones (1929). The
results are given below and are quite at variance with the idea
that the tongue is moving down the front axis and up the back
axis in a series of approximately equidistant steps (see [20]).

[20] Measurements in millimetres of the distances between the highest
points of the tongue in the only published X-ray photographs of a
complete set of authentic cardinal vowels (Ladefoged 1967: 71).

[20]   ——— i ———   ——— u ———
              0.75
     ——— e ———
              1.75
     ——— ɛ ———   5.25
              1.75
     ——— a ———
                     ——— o, ɔ same tongue
                              height
                     1.25
                     ——— ɑ ———

More recently, in a detailed experimental study of vowel
articulation, Wood (1982) has claimed that tongue height is
hardly a physiologically relevant parameter of vowel production.
Some of the evidence for this counter-claim is a collection from

the literature of thirty-eight sets of X-ray tracings of vowel articulations in fifteen languages. The results, given in [21], are, once again, strongly at odds with traditional assumptions about tongue movements.

Comparison of tongue heights of [o, ɔ, ɑ, a]-like vowels from a large number of sets of published X-ray tracings (Wood 1982: 12).

[21]

	[ɔ] higher than [ɑ, a]	[ɔ] same as [ɑ, a]	[ɔ] lower than [ɑ, a]	[o] same as [ɑ, a]	[o] lower than [ɑ, a]
Czech	1			1	
English (Am.)	1	1	1		1
English (S. Br.)	1	1			
French		3	1		
German	2		1		1
Icelandic	1				
Italian			1		1
Japanese					1
Korean	1			1	
Polish			1		
Portuguese		1			
Russian			1	2	1
Spanish		2		1	1
Swedish	1			1	
	8	8	6	6	6

By contrast with the variability observed in the articulatory implementation of the vowel dimensions, it is claimed that the relevant parameters are auditory–acoustic. Thus, in terms of the formant frequencies which are displayed in spectrograms, vowel 'height' is not a true physiological dimension but the inverse correlate of the first formant frequency F_1; F_1 is highest for low vowels (IPA [a], [ɑ]) and lowest for high vowels ([i], [u]). And the 'front'–'back' dimension is best thought of as a reflex of the distance between the first two formants: F1 and F2 are far apart in the front vowels and close together in the back vowels. Furthermore, the distance between F1 and F2 decreases in the front vowel series, which corresponds nicely to traditional diagrams showing the front vowels in a slanting line. In that sense, as maintained in Ladefoged (1967, 1982), formant charts such as the one in [22] give a much more accurate picture of reality than the pseudo-articulatory descriptions in common accounts of the structure of vowels.

A formant chart, using the Mel scale, plotting the vowels of standard French. The first formant, F1, is plotted on the ordinate (the vertical axis) and the difference between the frequencies of the first and second formants on the abscissa (the horizontal axis). The formant values are borrowed from Delattre, 1965 p 49.

[22]

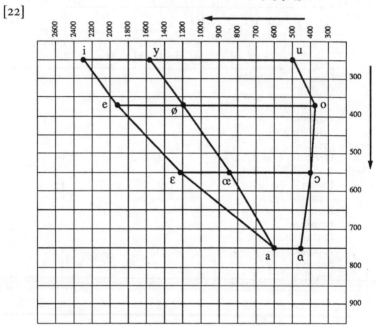

2.5.3 Retroflexion

The third example to be considered here in favour of an acoustic basis of DFs is that of retroflexion. We have seen in 2.3.4 that retroflex consonants, in the *SPE* mould, could be characterized in terms of a feature such as [+/−distr(ibuted)]. In a sense, recourse to [+/−distr] follows phonetic tradition which tends to describe the production of retroflexes as a gesture involving the tip of the tongue: a retroflex is often said to involve contact or approximation between the tip or the underside of the tongue tip and some portion of the post-alveolar zone. But, as carefully argued in Delattre (1967), if we consider in detail one example of retroflexion – the American English /r/ – the articulatory facts turn out to be much more complex than this.

On the basis of X-rays and cineradiography, it can be shown that two very dissimilar articulations can be used to produce this /r/. In the retroflexed version (in the precise use of the term 'retroflex'), the tongue tip rises towards the post-alveolar area to produce a constriction, while the dorsum forms a low arch and the root comes close to the pharyngeal wall. In the other version, called 'bunched /r/' by Delattre, the tongue tip does not rise. Instead, the constriction is produced by raising the dorsum of the tongue towards the hard palate or the prevelum while the root of the tongue approximates the pharyngeal wall creating, however, a constriction which is narrower than for the retroflexed variety. Overall, in the bunched version, the tongue takes the odd shape of a ball with the lowered tip of the tongue tucked away underneath it. Some speakers use one of these articulations predominantly but, argues Delattre, some speakers can shift from one gesture to the other within one single phonetic [r]. Yet, in all cases, the acoustic structure remains identical. Acoustically, the 'retroflex' and the 'bunched' varieties are characterized by identical formant patterns and transitions. In the simplified account of Ladefoged (1982), this is described as 'a marked lowering of the third formant'. As Delattre (1967: 22) argues, this is a striking 'case of different articulatory patterns which can produce similar acoustic patterns or, to express it differently, of differences in articulation which do not result in significant differences in the spectrograms'. He notes further that auditory perception matches the spectrographic evidence since listeners cannot detect by ear whether the /r/ is bunched or retroflex.

2.6 Invariance and distinctive features

The examples we have just considered would appear to deal a death-blow to the claim that the basis of features could be articulatory. But the idea that the basis of distinctive features must be 'acoustic', on the grounds that the only purpose of articulation is as a means to an end, is itself quite controversial. It has often been pointed out that there are cases where the acoustic signal does not contain any one invariant feature, whereas the articulation involves a single, unitary manoeuvre. For example, experimental phoneticians have repeatedly pointed out that the formant transitions which correspond to what is subjectively perceived as, say, a [d], vary according to the nature of the vowel that follows. There is no single acoustic feature that could be isolated as corresponding uniquely to [d]. By contrast, [d] is always articulated by contact between the tip or blade of the tongue and the denti-alveolar region. The argument then goes as follows: as listeners, we hear the same [d] in [di], [du], [da] because we decode the acoustic patterns in terms of the articulatory gestures that we use in speech (*cf* Liberman *et al.* 1967; Lieberman 1975: 76–8; 1977: 120–2; 1984: 146–8). This is known as the **motor theory of speech perception** and has been argued for in a variety of contexts. Recently, for instance, Ladefoged (1982: 104) has pointed out that:

> It is difficult to define stress from a listener's point of view. A stressed syllable is often, but not always, louder than an unstressed syllable. It is usually, but not always, on a higher pitch. The most reliable thing for a listener to detect is that a stressed syllable frequently has a longer vowel. But, as stress can be correlated with something a speaker does, the speaker will find that it is easier to tap on a stressed syllable. This is because it is always easier to produce one increase in muscular activity – a tap – exactly in time with an existing increase in activity. When as listeners we perceive the stresses that other people are making, we are probably putting together all the cues available in a particular utterance in order to deduce the motor activity (the articulations) we would use to produce those same stresses.

The issue of invariance is an extremely complex one. In recent work, Blumstein and Stevens (1981) contend that, if the acoustic property is appropriately chosen, then place of articulation has a unique trace in the acoustic record independently of speakers, vowel contexts or voicing. According to them, the relevant acoustic property is obtained from the spectrum sampled over a short period of about 20 milliseconds at the release of the consonant. It is at this point in time that the articulators are close to being in the target position appropriate for the stop consonants. The property can be defined in terms of a unique, gross spectrum shape for each of the places of articulation (labial, alveolar and velar). Conversely, retroflexion which was presented above as a good prima facie case for acoustic invariance is argued by Lindau (1978), on the basis of X-ray spectrograms, to involve an invariant articulatory manoeuvre: viz. a small retraction of the root of the tongue, 4–6 centimetres above the larynx.

But claims in favour of the motor theory of speech perception do not ultimately rest on across-the-board articulatory invariance at a surface level. Advocates of this theory know very well that the same acoustic effect can be achieved by different articulatory manoeuvres. Thus lowering the larynx by 1 centimetre can induce the same formant shift as would have resulted from a 1 centi-

metre protrusion of the lips (Lieberman, 1977: 44). A defence
of the motor theory of speech perception can only be mounted
at a relatively abstract level. Whereas earlier versions of the
theory linked the gestures used by hearers to decode speech to
key articulators, recent expositions do not see these **gestures** 'as
peripheral movements, but as the more remote structures that
control these movements . . . (which) correspond to the
speaker's intentions' (Liberman and Mattingly 1985: 23). Critics
of the motor theory of speech perception often dub this move
'the retreat up the vocal tract'. On the other hand, auditory
theories of perception have to face the fact that there usually is
not a single cue corresponding to a phonetic category (*eg* some
eighteen potential cues to the voicing distinction are mentioned
in the literature) and that the correspondence between acoustic
records and auditory percepts is extremely indirect (see the
excellent section on this topic in Lieberman 1977: 36–9). In fact,
as pointed out by Liberman and Mattingly (1985: 5), even if the
invariant cues presented by Stevens and Blumstein for place
identification are removed, listeners are nevertheless able to
separate stops at different locations.

From the point of view of phonology, the best position to
adopt is that advocated by Delattre (1967) and Halle (1983).
Distinctive features are neutral between production and perception. They must not be confused with their actual phonetic
implementation. They are abstract, classificatory dimensions
which provide a link between the articulatory and the acoustic
dimensions of speech. In some cases, the tie between a distinctive
feature and its typical implementation is more direct on the
articulatory side and in other cases on the acoustic side. A good
illustration of the situation is provided by [23], borrowed from
Halle (1983: 95).

[23]

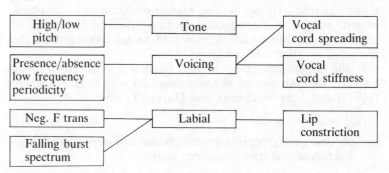

In perception, detectors sensitive to the properties on the left would be activated and the information passed on to the centres corresponding to the distinctive feature boxes. This would be used along with other information by the central nervous system to decode the signal. In production, instructions would be sent from the feature boxes to the control mechanisms on the right-hand side which would activate the relevant muscles to set up appropriate configurations for speech to occur. Note that the properties on the left and the right are themselves high-level control mechanisms and not surface properties of the encoding–decoding system.

It should not be thought, however, that every feature needs to be on-line in speech perception. It can be shown that the time required to decode speech on the assumption that the hearer proceeds on a feature-matrix by feature-matrix basis is astronomical. By contrast, speech decoding is fast and seemingly effortless. But the actual interpretation of speech is known to involve pragmatic and other factors and not to rely on the linguistic modules alone. In perception, therefore, features must be understood as playing a fail-safe role. It is possible that the full set of features, as pointed out by Jakobson and Halle (1956), will only be used in situations where background information is weak (eg introductions at a party).

The above is no doubt speculative. Phoneticians who have worked on the phonology–phonetics interface (such as Ladefoged, 1977, 1980, etc.) argue that the correspondence between phonology and phonetics is typically indirect with many-to-many mappings. But this is not a reason for the phonologist to adopt a purely abstract position (cf 2.2). Many of the **recurrent** features identified in phonological systems throughout the world have been shown to have reasonable (if complex) phonetic translations. And the postulation of less traditional properties is leading to fruitful research in experimental phonetics (see eg Ohala and Kawasaki 1984). By not burning his/her phonetic boat, the phonologist adopts a responsible position towards the data of phonology without which there would be no constraint on the choice of notation and primitives.

If the arguments given in this chapter are accepted, they motivate the NATURAL RECURRENCE assumption of J. M. Anderson (1980a) and J. M. Anderson and Durand (1986):

[24] NATURAL RECURRENCE NR

(a) phonological groupings (paradigmatic and syntagmatic) are
     not random; certain groupings recur;

(b) phonological groupings and the relationship between them have a phonetic basis; they are natural.

In turn, NR imposes a strong requirement on the character of phonological representations expressed in [25]:

[25] NATURAL APPROPRIATENESS NA

A phonological notation is such as to optimize the expression of phonological groupings and relationships which are natural and recurrent.

Notes

1. On cardinal vowels, see Jones (1964: 31–9); Ladefoged (1982: Ch. 9).
2. The distinction between two types of lip opening can be traced to Sweet's *Handbook of Phonetics* (1877).
3. See, however, Sagey (1986: Ch. 3) for a detailed study of airstream mechanisms with standard features within the framework sketched in 7.3.2.

Chapter 3

Binarism, full and partial specification, markedness and gestures

3.1 Binarism

In this chapter, a number of related issues concerning distinctive features (DFs) and the representation of segments are explored. First of all, the pros and cons of binary features and multivalued features are re-examined. Thereafter, we shall see whether segments should be represented in terms of partial feature matrices (archisegments) or fully specified matrices and whether markedness considerations should be incorporated into the model. These discussions will pave the way for a presentation of recent work in Chapter 5 – Underspecification Theory – where it is argued that strict binarism should be abandoned at the lexical level in favour of one-valued features. In the closing section of this chapter (3.5), we consider the advantages of giving more internal structure to segments in the form of 'gestures'.

3.1.1 Binarism, privativeness and equipollence

The adoption of binarism in generative phonology can be traced back to the work of Roman Jakobson. For Jakobson, it is clear that binarism is something that pervades the whole of the human psyche. Thus, Jakobson and Waugh (1979: 20) cite Peirce approvingly when he says: 'The natural classification takes place by dichotomies' or 'existence lies in opposition merely'. In Jakobson's work, binarism was not purely a question of metaphysical speculation but was also to be related to the structure of the brain (cells working on an on–off basis) and to the functioning of communication. The hearer has to go through a series of yes–no questions to apprehend the message.

We saw, however, in 2.6, that the role played by features in perception is controversial and that, as a hypothesis, it applies to high-level cognitive processes rather than as a strategy for interpreting raw acoustic input. In any case, binarism cannot be defended as such on the basis of performance data. The reason is that, while the input to the rules of the phonological component is coded in terms of binary features, the output is usually assumed to be an allophonic representation corresponding roughly to the 'narrow transcription' of British phoneticians (see 2.2). Now, at the phonetic level, many features patently do not function in a binary manner but as scales.[1] For instance, vowels in English are phonologically [−nasal] but phonetically a vowel such as [æ] is slightly nasalized (*cf* Ladefoged, 1982: 267) and some degree of nasalization occurs when a vowel precedes a nasal consonant within the same syllable (*eg plant*). If a model of performance was closely based on the phonological component as it stands, then it is the output of the latter which would be relevant and, as nasality shows, representations at that level are often graded rather than binary.

Not surprisingly, most of the recent work in generative phonology does not attempt to defend binarism in psycholinguistic terms but in terms of expressive power. In *SPE*, there is very little discussion of binarism as such. In fact, the only **direct** justification given by Chomsky and Halle (1968: 297) is that binary features are 'the natural way of indicating whether or not an item belongs to a category'. But close examination of the correlates of DFs suggests that binarism is not simply a question of presence vs. absence of a given property. A voiceless segment is not characterized by the simple absence of voice. If [+voice] corresponds to a particular glottal configuration – say, vibrations of the vocal cords – so does [−voice] which refers to a wide open glottis. And well-known cases of assimilation to [+voice] (*eg* Fr [diznœf] *dix-neuf* 'nineteen' vs. historical [disnœf]) are paralleled by equally well-known cases of assimilation to [−voice] (*eg with* [wɪð] vs. *with thanks* [wɪθ θæŋks]). It does not make sense to think of assimilation to [−voice] in terms of absence of a property. Rather, the assimilation is to a specific configuration, briefly definable as an open glottis. A similar point could be made for practically all features.

On the other hand, if we took a rather less concrete view of phonetics, the 'presence' vs. 'absence' idea might be defended for a feature like [nasal]. Nasal segments involve the addition of an extra resonator (the nasal cavity) which their oral counterparts lack (*cf* Jakobson 1968: 71–3). To complicate matters further, we have to consider the case where a minus value denotes both a positive phonetic property and the absence of that property. Take [strident], for instance, as defined in Chapter 2. In so far as it applies to fricatives and affricates, [+strid] and [−strid] can be argued to refer to two different types of vocal tract configuration. But sonorants in fully specified matrices are also [−strid]. In this latter case, [−strid] seems to denote the absence of stridency. One solution is to leave [strident] unspecified for sonorants. Notationally, this is often represented by entering a zero in the relevant box of feature-matrix. But, as we shall see in 3.3–4, standard generative accounts have assumed that the negative value [−strid] characterizes sonorants at the underlying level. If we use the attribute-value terminology introduced in Chapter 2, it is therefore arguable that the + and − values of given attributes do not have a unique interpretation (cf Wilson 1966 for an interesting early discussion of this topic).

In the above paragraph, it has been suggested that DFs could potentially be looked at in two different ways: either as indicating the absence vs. presence of a property or as attributes which have two 'polar', but mutually incompatible, values. Is there any phonological sense in making such a distinction? Trubetzkoy (1969) thought so and drew a well-known distinction between **privative** and **equipollent** oppositions. A privative opposition exists between two phonemes when one of them possesses some positive property (or mark) that the other one lacks. The phoneme which is positively specified is said to be 'marked' and the non-specified one is 'unmarked'. An equipollent opposition, on the other hand, is a relation in which each of the contrasting phonemes possesses a positive property. How can the distinction be established in practice? Two types of evidence can be mentioned at this stage: first of all, cross-linguistic regularities may give us some information concerning 'markedness'; secondly, patterns of neutralization in a given language might give us a clue. The second type of evidence was paramount in Trubetzkoy's work and, while his classification of phonological systems was seminal, the implication of typological regularities for markedness derives mainly from Jakobson's work (see, in particular, Jakobson 1968) although it is not translated in the resolutely binary notation the latter adopts. Let us now illustrate the discussion with a couple of examples.

If we take nasality in vowel systems, the following universal seems well supported:

[1] In a given language, the number of nasal vowel phonemes is never greater than the number of non-nasal vowel phonemes (cf Trubetzkoy 1969: 120; Ferguson 1963; Ruhlen 1978).

Universals such as [1] are often referred to as Greenbergian universals in recognition of the pioneering work of Joseph Green-berg in the investigation of cross-linguistic regularities. Conservative standard French, with its four phonemic nasal vowels /ɛ̃, œ̃, ɑ̃, õ/ and twelve oral vowels, provides a typical illustration of [1]. In statistical terms, the nasal vowels seem more 'marked' than their oral counterparts.

Let us now check, in the footsteps of Trubetzkoy, whether there is any evidence of neutralization in French confirming the cross-linguistic generalization stated in [1]. By neutralization is meant a situation where the opposition between two phonemes is suspended.[2] A standard example of neutralization is that of [+/−voice] after /s/ in initial clusters in English. As (2) shows:

[2a] pit, bit, spit
[2b] till, dill, still
[2c] cot, got, Scot

the opposition between /p/−/b/, /t/−/d/, /k/−/g/ is neutralized in English after /s/ since only [p], [t], [k] are attested. Trubetzkoy used these positions of neutralization as evidence for markedness: it is the unmarked property which occurs in a neutralization environment. In English, since [p], [t], [k] occur in the context [#s ___ V], Trubetzkoy would conclude that the voiceless plosives lack [voice] which is the marked property. Now, to go back to French vowels, there is a neutralization of the oral–nasal opposition before a tautosyllabic nasal consonant within morphemes (that is, a nasal within the same syllable). Only oral vowels are allowed in this environment:

[3] /samdi/ *samedi* 'Saturday', /ɔmlɛt/ *omelette* 'omelette', /ram/ *rame* 'oar', /pɛn/ *peine* 'sorrow'.[3]

The conclusion has to be that the oral vowels are 'unmarked' in relation to the nasal vowels. The opposition between the oral and the nasal vowels in French is of the privative type.

By contrast with the previous two examples of neutralization, let us consider the opposition between the plosives of French /p/−/b/, /t/−/d/ and /k/−/g/. In terms of cross-linguistic evidence, the voiceless series appears to be unmarked. According to Maddieson (1984: 27), who bases his observations on the UCLA Phonological Segment Inventory Database (UPSID): 'A language with only one stop series almost invariably has plain voiceless plosives (49 out of 50) and the one exception, the Australian language Bandjalang (369) [its UPSID reference number – JD], may be incorrectly reported as having voiced plosives'. But, if we turn to the structure of French, the voice–voiceless opposition is not neutralized after /s/ word-initially where one observes a minimal pair such as [4]:[4]

[4] sbire 'henchman' vs. spire 'spiral'

and in other positions within the word (initially, intervocalically, finally) the voiced–voiceless correlation is extremely stable. The only vacillations in voicing result from assimilation and this works in both directions: compare *subtropical* [syptrɔpikal] and *anecdote* [anɛgdɔt] with historical /bt/ going to /pt/ and /kd/ going to /gd/ (*cf* Walter 1976: 410ff). The voice–voiceless opposition in French can therefore be analysed as a plausible case of equipollent opposition. One way of representing this formally would consist in positing a unary (or singulary) feature NASAL for the privative opposition between oral and nasal vowels in French, whereas the voice–voiceless opposition within plosives would be represented with the help of standard binary features. Example [5] gives a sample representation of /p, b, a, ã/ in terms of these assumptions:

$$
[5]
\begin{bmatrix}
/p/ \\
-\text{syll} \\
-\text{cont} \\
-\text{low} \\
-\text{high} \\
-\text{back} \\
+\text{labial} \\
-\text{voice}
\end{bmatrix}
\begin{bmatrix}
/b/ \\
-\text{syll} \\
-\text{cont} \\
-\text{low} \\
-\text{high} \\
-\text{back} \\
+\text{labial} \\
+\text{voice}
\end{bmatrix}
\begin{bmatrix}
/a/ \\
+\text{syll} \\
+\text{cont} \\
+\text{low} \\
-\text{high} \\
+\text{back} \\
-\text{labial} \\
+\text{voice}
\end{bmatrix}
\begin{bmatrix}
/ã/ \\
+\text{syll} \\
+\text{cont} \\
+\text{low} \\
-\text{high} \\
+\text{back} \\
-\text{labial} \\
+\text{voice} \\
\text{NASAL}
\end{bmatrix}
$$

An alternative formalization, linked to recent work considered in Chapter 5 (*cf* Goldsmith 1985, 1987), allows one-valued features beside standard two-valued features in underlying representations. As a result, [5] would become [6], where [nasal] is a one-valued feature:

[6]

	/p/	/b/	/a/	/ã/
Syll	−	−	+	+
Cont	−	−	+	+
Low	−	−	+	+
High	−	−	−	−
Back	−	−	+	+
Labial	+	+	−	−
Voice	−	+	+	+
Nasal				+

(Since [6] characterizes very recent developments, the discussion here will be based on [5] alone.)

Trubetzkoy himself did not pursue the formalization of this problem and, in standard generative phonology, his insights were not integrated as such. Part of the explanation rests with the status of a notation such as [5]. A representation along the lines of [5] is mixed and would inevitably complicate the statement of rules. Moreover, unary features have been considered inadequate in generative phonology by the following reasoning: it is true, it is argued, that we can differentiate /ã/ from /a/ by assigning a mark NASAL to the former that the latter lacks. But there may well be a rule within the phonological component of French which affects only non-nasal vowels. In that case, how can we specify this set? Sommerstein (1977: 110) says, 'Only by referring, in one way, or another, to the absence of a feature – which is, again, to introduce binarity by the back door' (cf 3.1.2).[5] In addition, it was felt that Trubetzkoyan procedures for deciding whether oppositions were privative or equipollent often led to uncertainties (cf 3.4). Finally, a number of technical problems with zero specifications were pointed out by Stanley (1967) which led *SPE* into fully specified entries as an interim solution before advocating a markedness theory of a binary kind quite different in structure from Trubetzkoy's ideas (cf 3.5).

All in all, therefore, the possible defect of two interpretations of binary distinctive features (presence vs. absence of a property or dichotomous splits based on two 'polar' properties) was discarded in the interest of formal unity. After all, whatever intuitive difference the linguist might have felt between these two interpretations, they could be argued to be conflatable logically: in both cases, the negative value refers to the complement of a set. Whether or not the complement was characterized by a positive property was presumably not felt to be a serious problem when compared with all the advantages of a uniform notation.

3.1.2 The expressive power of binary features

The penultimate paragraph of the previous section included a classical objection to unary features in their privative interpretation. It is worth noting that some non-generative theories which operate with features (*eg* Martinet's functionalist school) do not use an attribute-value formalism. Instead they have recourse to 'atomic' labels such as 'voice', 'voiceless', 'nasal', 'non-nasal', etc. Note that such features get round objections to unary features (since 'non-nasal' allows reference to segments lacking nasality) but that they too conflate privative and equipollent oppositions.

However, atomic labels of this type are less adequate than the binary notation presented so far.

First of all, this symbolization does not reflect the fact that a segment cannot be simultaneously 'voiced' and 'voiceless'. Some external convention would have to be imposed to exclude such combinations. Even if this was done, it can be shown that a variety of generalizations concerning phonological systems would remain unexpressed under this hypothesis. Consider, for instance, nasal–plosive sequences within English morphemes. The range of possibilities is exemplified in [7] with respect to the voiceless stops:

[7a] /−mp/,   */−np/,   */−ŋp/
[7b] */−mt/,   /−nt/,   */−ŋt/
[7c] */−mk/,   */−nk/,   /−ŋk/

That is, while [hɪnt] *hint*, [entrɪ] *entry*, [ræmp] *ramp*, [bʌmpɪ] *bumpy*, [sænk] *sank*, [bʌŋkə] *bunker* are all attested, there are no morphemes such as *[æmt], *[enkɪ], etc. (But such sequences may be allowed at the phonetic level: *cf* [egzemt] as a variable realization of /egzempt/.) The generalization is that the nasal consonant and the plosive agree in 'point of articulation'. Let us, as a first approximation, formulate this in terms of distinctive features along the lines of [8]:

[8]

$$
[+\text{nasal}] \rightarrow
\left\{
\begin{array}{l}
\begin{bmatrix} +\text{lab} \\ -\text{cor} \\ +\text{ant} \end{bmatrix} / \underline{}
\begin{bmatrix} -\text{son} \\ -\text{cont} \\ +\text{lab} \\ -\text{cor} \\ +\text{ant} \end{bmatrix} \quad [8a] \ /mp/ \\[4ex]
\begin{bmatrix} -\text{lab} \\ +\text{cor} \\ +\text{ant} \end{bmatrix} / \underline{}
\begin{bmatrix} -\text{son} \\ -\text{cont} \\ -\text{lab} \\ +\text{cor} \\ +\text{ant} \end{bmatrix} \quad [8b] \ /nt/ \\[4ex]
\begin{bmatrix} -\text{lab} \\ -\text{cor} \\ -\text{ant} \end{bmatrix} / \underline{}
\begin{bmatrix} -\text{son} \\ -\text{cont} \\ -\text{lab} \\ -\text{cor} \\ -\text{ant} \end{bmatrix} \quad [8c] \ /ŋk/
\end{array}
\right\}
$$

Once the rule is expanded as in [8], it is quite clear that we are missing a generalization. If we left the rule as it stands, it would not be any different from a rather implausible process which, say, made a nasal stop [+lab] in front of a [−lab] plosive but also [+cor] in front of [+cor] and [−ant] in front of [+ant]. The formal solution has, however, been anticipated in 1.3.2.2. It involves the use of Greek letter variables (α, β, γ, δ, etc.) which range over the values of the feature coefficients ($+$ and $-$). As a result, [8] can be abbreviated as [9]:

[9] Nasal Place Assimilation

$$[+\text{nasal}] \rightarrow \begin{bmatrix} \alpha\text{lab} \\ \beta\text{cor} \\ \gamma\text{ant} \end{bmatrix} / \underline{} \begin{bmatrix} -\text{son} \\ -\text{cont} \\ \alpha\text{lab} \\ \beta\text{cor} \\ \gamma\text{ant} \end{bmatrix}$$

where, as is familiar from elementary algebra, once a value is selected for a variable all occurrences of that variable must be replaced by this value. An implausible rule with random matchings of the values for labiality, coronality and anteriority could not be so abbreviated. It should be clear now that if atomic names had been chosen for each phonetic dimension (e.g. labial–non-labial, voice–non-voice), the overall pattern would not be reducible to the simple statement given in [9]. In that sense, the variable convention made possible by the $+/-$ values supports the binary notation and can be claimed to be a first step towards a fulfilment of the NA principle put forward at the end of 2.6 (but see 3.5 on gestures).

Further support for the binary notation and the associated use of variables can be drawn from the linking of values affecting different features. Chomsky and Halle (1968: 352) cite an example given by Trubetzkoy (1969) from the dialect of German spoken in Vienna. In this dialect, the front vowels are non-round before /r/ and round before /l/: thus standard German *vier* 'four' and *für* 'for' are both pronounced [fir]; *Heer* 'army' and *hör* 'listen!' are pronounced [he:r]; on the other hand, *viele* 'many' and *fühle* 'feel' are pronounced [fy:l], and *hehlen* 'hide' and *Hölen* 'caves' are pronounced [hø:lən]. These data are naturally formalized as follows:

$$[10] \begin{bmatrix} +\text{syll} \\ -\text{cons} \\ -\text{back} \end{bmatrix} \rightarrow [\alpha\text{round}] / \underline{} \begin{bmatrix} -\text{syll} \\ +\text{cons} \\ \alpha\text{lateral} \end{bmatrix}$$

Chomsky and Halle (1968) argue that if we operated with unary features and assumed, as Trubetzkoy did, that assimilation can only occur between identical features, then the only solution open to us would be to invoke some property that differentiated /r/ and /l/ and was linked to rounding. For instance, we might treat /l/ as labialized – that is, as having the value ROUND). But, since there is no direct evidence in this dialect in favour of this beside the observations above, the formalization in [10] must stand.

The advantage of the variable notation for handling feature agreements can also be supplemented by feature disagreements. Dissimilations can be treated by permitting specifications of the form $[-\alpha$ feature X], where the convention, once again, holds that $- - = +$, and $- + = -$. And, over and above dissimilations, Chomsky and Halle (1968: 356) argue that value switches are well attested in what are called 'polarity rules'. One example they quote is provided by the West Semitic languages (Arabic, Hebrew and Aramaic). In the conjugation systems of these languages, the verbal stem vowel undergoes ablaut. The perfect, which is formed by suffixation alone, exhibits one vowel whereas the imperfect, formed by suffixation and prefixation, exhibits a different vowel. The example they give from biblical Hebrew is the following:

[11] | PERFECT | IMPERFECT | | |
|---|---|---|---|
| a | o | *lamad-yilmod* | (learn) |
| o | a | *qaton-yiqtan* | (be small) |
| e | a | *zaqen-yizqan* | (age) |

The pattern is clear /o/ and /e/ in the perfect correspond to /a/ in the imperfect, and /a/ in the perfect corresponds to /o/ in the imperfect. This is easily formalizable by a polarity rule such as [12]:

$$[12] \begin{bmatrix} +syll \\ \alpha low \end{bmatrix} \rightarrow \begin{bmatrix} +back \\ -\alpha low \\ \alpha round \end{bmatrix} / \underline{\qquad} C + Imperfect$$

Once this rule is expanded by replacing the variable by $+$ or $-$ (applying the convention that $- + = -$ and $- - = +$), we obtain two rules which describe the alternations in [11]. See [13a] and [13b]:

$$[13a] \begin{bmatrix} a \\ +syll \\ +low \end{bmatrix} \rightarrow \begin{bmatrix} o \\ +back \\ -low \\ +round \end{bmatrix} / \underline{\qquad} C + Imperfect$$

$$[13b] \begin{bmatrix} e, o \\ +syll \\ -low \end{bmatrix} \rightarrow \begin{bmatrix} a \\ +back \\ +low \\ -round \end{bmatrix} / \underline{\qquad} C + Imperfect$$

The inclusion. of /i, u/ in [13b], which is entailed by the specification $[-low]$ in [13b], is innocuous in that these two segments do not participate in the process. The conclusion to be drawn is that the linking of variables across features, which is made possible by the binary notation, once again provides a more elegant formalization of well-attested processes.

3.2 Multivalued scalar features

The preceding paragraphs have discussed some of the advantages claimed for the binary notation over unary features but have not mentioned an alternative – that is, the possibility that features be **scalar**. It has already been pointed out that many-valued features are allowed at levels of derivation near the phonetic output but not underlyingly. This decision goes against much traditional and more modern work in phonology which assumes that, beside binary oppositions which play an important role in the organization of phonological systems, we should also recognize gradual oppositions (Trubetzkoy 1969). Thus a vowel system such as the standard French one (recall [22] of Ch. 2) has often been argued to be organized in terms of two binary oppositions round–non-round, back–non-back and a gradual opposition on the height axis:

[14] Standard French phonemic system (schwa excluded)

	−back		+back	
	−round	+round	−round	+round
high	i	y		u
mid-high	e	ø		o
mid-low	ɛ	œ		ɔ
low	a		ɑ	

But labels such as 'high', 'mid-high', 'mid-low' and 'low', which are often used in descriptive works, are unsatisfactory since they denote atomic values and do not show formally that, on the height dimension, we are dealing with degrees of the same property. They trade upon our intuitive understanding of what is involved. To show this, consider a language where there is a process of palatalization (k → č and g → ǰ) which occurs in the environment of the non-low vowels /i, e/. How would we capture this natural and recurrent class with the above notation? Unless some new convention was invoked, the only solution would be to characterize the /i, e/ grouping as in [15]:

[15] [+syll, −back, −round, $\left\{ \begin{array}{l} \text{high} \\ \text{mid-high} \end{array} \right\}$]

The curly brackets are necessary because notions such as non-lowness, midness, etc. are not accessible, as such but only implicit in the naming. If scalar features are to be adopted, the

[16]

	−back		+back	
	−round	+round	−round	+round
4 high	i	y		u
3 high	e	ø		o
2 high	ɛ	œ		ɔ
1 high	a		ɑ	

solution consists in allowing feature-values to range over natural
numbers. The French vowel system would be classified as in [16]
where [high] is just the name of the height scale. Within this
notation (*cf* Contreras 1969; Ladefoged 1971, 1982; Lindau 1975,
1978; Sommerstein 1977) natural classes can be captured by
permitting variables to range over numbers. Thus the class /i, e/
can be characterized as in [17]:

[17] [+syll, −back, −round, j high] where $j \geqslant 3$.

The question now is whether scalar features should be
permitted beside binary features. In the 'standard' generative
tradition, even vowel height, as we saw in Chapter 2, would be
treated in a binary manner by combinations of [+/−high] and
[+/−low]. If vowel height is envisaged in terms of acoustics (*cf*
2.5.2), the notion of a mid-point (the 'neutral' position), from
which one can depart in the up and down direction does not
make much sense since, clearly, one is dealing with a continuum.
Indeed, Jakobson and Halle (1968) acknowledge the peculiar
structure of the high–low parameter in acoustic terms. The single
acoustic dimension they use, compact/diffuse, is allowed to be
split into two features ([+/−compact], [+/−diffuse]). And,
unlike *SPE*, where the mid-point is the base line, mid-vowels are
described as [−compact, −diffuse], thus conceding that they
are in between two 'polar' qualities. Jakobson and Halle
(1968: 444) even claim that psychological experiments show that
/e/ is a mixture of /æ/ and /i/ which 'confirms the peculiar structure of this vocalic feature'. Recent work within the 'standard'
tradition does not display the same reservations about the peculiarity of vowel height. It is therefore instructive to see whether
vowel systems of languages like French, as well as processes
affecting vowel systems, can be handled in a satisfactory way
without scalar features.

The most problematic area for a binary treatment of the standard feature system in [13] is the /a/–ɑ/ opposition. In varieties of French which have only one low vowel /a/, the classification in [18] can be offered (recall [33] in Ch. 1).

[18]

	−back		+back	
	−round	+round	−round	+round
+high −low	i	y		u
−high −low	e	ø		o
−high +low	ɛ	œ	a	ɔ

The system in [18] is the one covered by Dell (1973), for instance, who does not deal with the /a/–/ɑ/ problem. In the pioneering work of Schane (1968), the stance adopted *vis-à-vis* the a–ɑ opposition, exemplified by a minimal pair such as *patte* – *pâte* ('leg' – 'paste'), is highly ambivalent. As noted in Durand and Lyche (1978: 260), on the one hand, Schane observes that it does not exist in all accents of French, that there is 'considerable fluctuation as to which pairs of this type are distinguished' and that it could perhaps be treated by a feature to be drawn from 'a set of affective, i.e. stylistic features, features which Trubetzkoy referred to as *expressive*'. On the other hand, it is clear that, in his system, the back /ɑ/ (sometimes realized as long [a:]) can be accounted for by deriving it from the underlying sequence /as/ on the basis of alternations like those in [19]:

[19] pâte – pastel ('paste' – 'pastel')
   bâton – bastonnade ('cudgel' – 'drubbing')

But neither solution is satisfactory. It is one thing to restrict one's attention to an accent which does not have this contrast as Dell (1973) does. But to point out that various dialects or styles do not use a certain opposition in a consistent way does not prove that in each dialect (or idiolect) the opposition, if it happens to be used, has a fictitious or paralinguistic existence. As for alternations such as those in [19] they are so idiosyncratic within the phonology of French that to derive every /ɑ/ from /as/ on that basis would elevate the very marginal to the general.

Another solution, which can ultimately be traced to Jakobson, Fant and Halle (1952: 36–7), appeals to the feature [+/−tense]. This is, among others, the position of Morin (1983) and Plénat (1987). The inventory in [14] can then be structured as in [20].

[20]

			−back		+back	
			−round	+round	−round	+round
+high		+tense −tense	i	y		u
−high	−low	+tense −tense	e ε	ø œ		o ɔ
	+low	+tense −tense			ɑ a	

Two phonological arguments are put forward by Plénat (1987: 870ff) in favour of this classification. The first one is indirect. The existence of alternations such as the following:

[21] ε–a clair – clarté ('clear' – 'clearness')
    œ–ɔ fleur – floral ('flower' – 'floral')

dealt with by Dell and Selkirk (1978) on the basis of the system in [14], supports the classification of /a/ as [+back]. The rule given by Dell and Selkirk retracts /ε/ to /a/ and /œ/ to /ɔ/ as in [22], where the morphological conditioning has been omitted:

[22] Learned backing (*cf* Dell and Selkirk 1978; Durand and Lyche 1978)
$$\begin{bmatrix} +\text{syll} \\ +\text{low} \end{bmatrix} \rightarrow [+\text{back}] / \_\_ \ C_o + C_o \ V$$

A rule of backing can be maintained by structuring the vowel system as in [20]. The rule (not formalized by Plénat) would be:

[23] $\begin{bmatrix} +\text{syll} \\ \alpha\text{round} \\ -\text{high} \\ -\text{tense} \end{bmatrix} \rightarrow \begin{bmatrix} -\alpha\text{low} \\ +\text{back} \end{bmatrix} / \_\_ \ C_o + C_o \ V$

On the other hand, if we classify the standard French system as in [16], where /ɑ/ is front and /a/ back, no generalization can be expressed.

The second argument proposed by Plénat comes from phonotactics. He points out that in some people's speech, /a/ and /ɔ/ become /ɑ/ and /o/ before the suffix -*tion* (*eg admiratif*

[admiratif] vs. *admiration* [admirɑsjõ]). As he classifies the nasal vowels as tense, we are dealing with an assimilation of tension in the non-high back vowels. Likewise, in some accents /œ/, /ɔ/ and /a/ are never used before the final sequence /-z#/ and we get /ø/, /o/ and /ɑ/: *gueuse* [gø:z], *Berlioz* [bɛrljo:z], *gaz* [gɑ:z], *base* [bɑ:z]. The converse generalization is that a non-high vowel preceding a word-final /r/ can only be lax. That is, we do not observe ∗[−e:r#], ∗[−ø:r#] or ∗[−ɑ:r#]. 'It is difficult', argues Plénat (1987: 871), 'to see how these generalizations could be formulated without referring to the feature [+/−tense].'

Plénat's overall argument is compelling. It shows that even sophisticated phonetic realism in the form of acoustic charts should not be allowed to dictate phonological analyses. But we should also note that the use of [+/−lax], or [+/−ATR], does not seem supported for all vowel systems similar to the standard French one. A variety of authors have argued that Danish requires more than three levels of vowel height (see Martinet 1937; Basbøll 1968, 1984; Basbøll and Wagner 1985; Rischel 1968). The contrastive system of advanced standard Copenhagen is, for example, given by Basbøll (1968) as:

[24] i   y   u
      e   ø   o
      ɛ   œ   ɔ
      æ   ɑ

and none of the specialists quoted above has found any evidence favouring a feature [+/−tense] over the traditional scalar analysis (see too Fischer-Jørgensen 1985). Just as crucially, there are cases showing that we miss generalizations if we do not treat vowel height as a single dimension.

In Fe2fe2-Bamileke, for instance, there is a synchronic process of lowering of the back rounded vowels which has the following effect (Hyman 1972, 1975: 123):

[25] (a) u → o (b) o → ɔ.

The simplest standard formulation appears to be [26]:

$$[26]\begin{bmatrix} +\text{syll} \\ \alpha\text{high} \\ -\text{low} \\ +\text{round} \end{bmatrix} \rightarrow \begin{bmatrix} -\text{high} \\ -\alpha\text{low} \end{bmatrix}$$

[26] requires paired variables and disjunctive ordering of the two subparts [27] and [28] that it abbreviates (*ie* do not subject the output of [27] to [28]):

$$[27] \begin{bmatrix} +\text{syll} \\ +\text{high} \\ -\text{low} \\ +\text{round} \end{bmatrix} \rightarrow \begin{bmatrix} -\text{high} \\ -\text{low} \end{bmatrix} \quad (u \rightarrow o)$$

$$[28] \begin{bmatrix} +\text{syll} \\ -\text{high} \\ -\text{low} \\ +\text{round} \end{bmatrix} \rightarrow \begin{bmatrix} -\text{high} \\ +\text{low} \end{bmatrix} \quad (o \rightarrow \jmath)$$

But in terms of feature-counting [26] is costlier than a statement of a process which would have the following effect (a) ɨ → i (b) ʌ → e. The latter within many systems would be simply statable as [29]:

$$[29] \begin{bmatrix} +\text{syll} \\ -\text{low} \\ +\text{back} \end{bmatrix} \rightarrow [-\text{back}]$$

Why a lowering (or conversely a raising) process along the height dimension should be more costly than [29], which is probably quite marked as an unconditioned process, is not at all clear. This is where recourse to a scalar feature can help. Assuming three levels of height for Feʔfeʔ-Bamileke, all we need to write is:

$$[30] \begin{bmatrix} +\text{syll} \\ n\ \text{high} \\ +\text{round} \end{bmatrix} \rightarrow [n-1\ \text{high}], \text{ where } n > 2.$$

Processes of raising or lowering along the height dimension are well attested. The English Vowel Shift provides a more complex example of the same type (*cf* Ch. 4) in either its synchronic or diachronic interpretation. Another well-known case is Kiparsky's (1968b) example of diphthongization in Eastern dialects of Finnish. The process in question affects all the mid and low long vowels. If these are analysed as sequences of identical vowels (geminates), we can describe the process as affecting the first element (mora) of each geminate. The mutations are given in [31]:

[31] ee → ie
    oo → uo
    øø → yø
    aa → oa
    ææ → eæ

If the overall system is structured as in [32], the process is easy to formalize as shown in [33] below.

[32]

	−back		+back
	−round	+round	
3 high	i	y	u
2 high	e	ø	o
1 high	æ		a

[33] $V_i \rightarrow$ [n + 1 high]/ ___ V_i, where n < 3.

(The subscript i indicates that the two vowels are identical.) Since rounding is not contrastive in the back vowels, it has been left out. A late redundancy rule would make non-low back vowels [+round] and the low back vowel [−round]. As a result, no rounding adjustment is required and the rule can be left in its general form (see 5.1 for ways to formalize this).

It is, however, pointed out in Creider's (1986) critique of non-binary features that an equally good formalization is possible with binary features, viz. (34):

$$[34] \begin{bmatrix} V_i \\ -high \\ \alpha low \end{bmatrix} \rightarrow \begin{bmatrix} -\alpha high \\ -low \end{bmatrix} / \text{_____} V_i$$

and that no real gain in simplicity can be claimed for [33] over [34]. He argues that, although [33] uses one feature only as opposed to two features in [34], the value of n has to be fixed. But he fails to point out that it is also customary in approaches which advocate feature counting not to assign a cost to certain symbols or conventions and, in assessing [34], Creider does not count the α variable in $-\alpha high$ as an extra symbol (see 3.5). But a more important question is whether [34] is an appropriate formalization. The problem with paired variables is that recurring pairings like [34] are not distinguishable from the accidental or the absurd. Consider a rule such as [35] below in a vowel system of the following type /i, e, a, o, u, ĩ, ẽ, ã, õ, ũ/ (Maithili):

$$[35] \begin{bmatrix} V \\ \alpha nasal \\ -high \end{bmatrix} \rightarrow [-\alpha low]$$

It would convert /ã, õ, ẽ/ to /õ, ũ, ĩ/ respectively, and /a, o, e/ to /a, ɔ, ε/ respectively. In anybody's book, this is a 'crazy' rule. Yet, [35] comes out as formally simpler than [34]. This problem has already been mentioned in connection with Fe?f?e-Bamileke and is ignored in critiques of multivalued features from a binary point of view.

Many other features have been mentioned as plausible candidates for a non-binary treatment. For instance, instead of the binary features for glottal activity mentioned in 2.3.7.1 ([+/−stiff], [+/− slack], etc.), which we saw were problematic, Ladefoged (1971, 1982) puts forward a scalar parameter of vocal opening coupled with an aspiration feature. And 'place of articulation' is also treated as a continuum in Williamson (1977) who takes on board Ladefoged's critique of the reliance of [+/−distributed] in handling various place of articulation contrasts (cf 2.3.4).[6] Moreover, there is evidence, as was argued in connection with vowels, that binary features do not always provide the best formalization. But, it must be pointed out that, apart from specific counter-arguments that can be formulated against scalar treatments (see Creider 1986),[7] the adoption of multivalued features presents two problems.

First of all, what range of values is permitted? Ladefoged, in his work, assigns a figure which corresponds to the highest attested number of known phonemic contrasts. Thus, 'place of articulation' has an upper value of 7, 'vowel height' of 4 and 'nasality' of 2. No predictive power is assigned to the value system: discovery of a language with nine places of articulation and four degrees of nasality would in no way affect the network of features. The multivalued theory is therefore much less restrictive than the binary one. Secondly, the scalar notation encounters problems of its own in the specification of natural classes. Recall the process of lowering of Fe2fe2-Bamileke. The formulation, reduced to its essentials, says: [n high] → [n − 1], where n > 2. The question is how n > 2 compares with n > 1, n > 3 or = 2 in terms of natural classes. For instance, the specification [−back, −round, n high], with respect to [32], remains formally the same whether n ranges over 1, 2 or 3. But, if $n \geqslant 3$, we are dealing with a unique segment /i/; if $n \geqslant 2$, we are dealing with /i, e/ and if $n \geqslant 1$, it is the whole set of front unrounded vowels which is involved /i, e, æ/. In so far as it is accepted that the notation should become simpler (ie require less symbols) as the generality of the class increases, the scalar notation appears to be unsatisfactory. For these reasons, we will continue to operate with binary features for the most part of the book (but see Ch. 8 on the Dependency Phonology alternative).

3.3 Contrastivity, archiphonemes and redundancy rules

Until now, we have skirted round the issue of how fully specified underlying representations should be. At various points, we have adopted representations (*eg* Finnish vowels in [32] in terms of the minimal set of features capable of differentiating the phonemes of the language. There are, in fact, good grounds for not wanting the distinctive units of the language to be specified positively or negatively for each DF used in the language. Consider, once again, sequences of nasal + plosive within morphemes in English. In 3.1.2, we saw that the nasal had always the same place of articulation as the following stop. But, then, there is no contrast between /m/, /n/ and /ŋ/ in this context. This is another example of neutralization *à la* Trubetzkoy and it makes sense to say that the segment which occurs before the plosive is simply a nasal consonant, conventionally represented by a capital letter: /N/. So, whereas the underlying representation of *mat* is /mæt/, that of *ramp* is /ræNp/. In terms of DFs, the English nasals, /N/, /m/, /n/, and /ŋ/ might be classified as in [36], assuming for exemplification that the features mentioned are all the features in the language:

	/N/	/m/	/n/	/ŋ/
[36] Syllabic	−	−	−	−
Nasal	+	+	+	+
Sonorant				
Labial		+	−	−
Voice				
Coronal		−	+	−
Strident				

On the basis of [36], the Redundancy Rules (RRs) of the language combine with the phonological rules to produce a derived phonetic representation. The RRs are either language-specific or universal and they either state redundancies concerning feature co-occurrences within a single segment (Segment Structure Rules) or within sequences (Sequence Structure Rules which include our Phonotactic Rules, called Morpheme Structure Rules in standard generative work). Two examples of Segment Structure Rules are given in [37] and [38]:

[37] [+son] → [−strid] (universal RR)

[38] [+nas] → $\begin{bmatrix} +\text{voice} \\ +\text{son} \end{bmatrix}$ (language-specific RR)

A common-or-garden example of the Phonotactic Rules[8] is the one that states that, in English, if a morpheme begins with three consonants the first one must be /s/, the second one a voiceless stop and the third one a liquid or a glide:

[39] If: + [−syllabic]   [−syllabic]   [−syllabic]
     Then: $\begin{bmatrix} +\text{strid} \\ +\text{ant} \\ +\text{cor} \\ -\text{voice} \end{bmatrix}$ $\begin{bmatrix} -\text{delrel} \\ -\text{voice} \end{bmatrix}$ $\begin{bmatrix} +\text{son} \\ -\text{cons} \\ -\text{nas} \end{bmatrix}$

Nasal Place Assimilation (rule 8 above) is a Sequence Structure Rule, and could be formulated in the format of [39], which would turn /ræNp/ into [ræmp].

In the late 1960s, this mixing of phonological rules and RRs was objected to. One of the main reasons lay in the possibility of an improper use of blanks (zero specifications) which could lead to a ternary use of binary features. Part of the demonstration runs as follows (*cf* Stanley 1967; *SPE*: 381–9). Let R stand for any rule of the form A → B/ X __ Y which abbreviates XAY → XBY, where XAY is the Structural Description (SD) and XBY is the Structural Change (SC). A plausible convention on rule application is the following:

[40] A rule R applies to a matrix M only if M is a submatrix of the SD of R.

Consider two segments such that all features (the attribute-value pairs) of one form a subset of the features of the other, as in the examples of [41] below:

[41] [−syll] $\begin{bmatrix} -\text{syll} \\ +\text{nasal} \end{bmatrix}$

Let us suppose now that rules are applied in accordance with [40]. Given the rules in [42]:

[42a] [−syll]   → [−lab]
[42b] [+nasal] → [+lab]
[42c] [−lab]   → [+nasal]

We obtain the derivations in [43]:

[43] Input: [−syll] $\begin{bmatrix} -\text{syll} \\ +\text{nasal} \end{bmatrix}$

     Rule [42a] $\begin{bmatrix} -\text{syll} \\ -\text{lab} \end{bmatrix}$ $\begin{bmatrix} -\text{syll} \\ +\text{nasal} \\ -\text{lab} \end{bmatrix}$

     Rule [42b] $\begin{bmatrix} -\text{syll} \\ +\text{nasal} \\ +\text{lab} \end{bmatrix}$

     Rule [42c] $\begin{bmatrix} -\text{syll} \\ +\text{nasal} \\ -\text{lab} \end{bmatrix}$

Thus, two matrices which were non-distinct (in an intuitive sense which is made more precise below) have been converted into two distinct matrices.

Of course, the demonstration depends on convention [40] and on the presence of pairs of matrices such as the hypothetical ones in [41] at the same point of the phonological chain. The problem can be circumvented to the extent that we require underlying representations to be pairwise distinct. The notion of distinctness appealed to here is a technical one and can be defined semi-formally as follows:

[44] Definition of 'distinctness'
Two matrices, M and N, are distinct if there is some feature F for which M is specified as +F or −F, and N has the opposite specification. Two morphemes, A and B, are distinct if A contains a matrix which is distinct from a matrix in B or if A differs from B in the number of units they contain.

The formal definition of *SPE* (*p* 336) is given in [45]:

[45] Two units U_1 and U_2 are distinct if and only if there is at least one feature F such that U_1 is specified [αF] and U_2 is specified [βF] where α is plus and β is minus; or α and β are integers and $\alpha \neq \beta$; or α is an integer and β is minus. Two strings X and Y are distinct if they are of different lengths, that is, if they differ in the number of units that they contain, or if the *i*th unit of X is distinct from the *i*th unit of Y for some *i*. (We assume 'distinct' to be symmetrical.)

Here /N/ is not distinct from /m/, /n/ and /ŋ/, but this is harmless since the presence of /N/ in a neutralization context excludes the more fully specified nasals. What is, indeed, forbidden by the condition that morphemes be pairwise distinct is that one item, in the same language, could be represented as /ræNp/ and another one as /ræmp/. The difficulty, however, is that within a derivation the presence of non-distinct matrices could arise in the same environment. Note, for instance, that in English we have alternations such as the following:

[46] bomb–bombard, iamb–iambic, dithyramb–dithyrambic

where the first word of each pair ends in /m/ and a /b/ appears in the longer derivative. Say that we relate all these words by postulating that the base ends in a /b/ underlyingly which is deleted during derivations. If so, the representation of *bomb* should be /bɔNb/ since the fact that the nasal is a bilabial is predictable by Nasal Place Assimilation [29] But we can see that potentially, if /b/-deletion operated before rule [29], we could end up with words in /N/ not being pairwise distinct from words ending in /m/ or /n/ underlyingly (e.g. *rim*, *sin*, etc.). Of course, there is no reason to think that derivations would be so constructed that this possibility would arise and, indeed, they were not within approaches which mixed redundancy rules and **bona fide** phonological rules.

While adopting the principle of pairwise distinctness of lexical entries might appear to impose a suitably strong condition on phonological representations, Stanley (1967) and Chomsky and Halle (1968: 384–5) object that it gives rise to problems of a different sort. They consider the following observations on lexical items in English:

[47a] The segment preceding a final string made up of a liquid
       followed by one or more consonants is always a vowel.
[47b] The segment following an initial liquid is always a vowel.

These two observations can be embodied in the two RRs in [48], where [+seg] stands for a segment (a feature column) and where the feature [+/−vocalic] is used (*cf* 2.3.9):

$$
\begin{array}{ll}
[48a] \ [+\text{seg}] \rightarrow & \begin{bmatrix} +\text{voc} \\ -\text{cons} \end{bmatrix} \Big/ \underline{} \begin{bmatrix} +\text{voc} \\ +\text{cons} \end{bmatrix} \begin{bmatrix} -\text{voc} \\ +\text{cons} \end{bmatrix} {}^+_1 \\[12pt]
[48b] \ [+\text{seg}] \rightarrow & [+\text{voc}] \Big/ + \begin{bmatrix} -\text{voc} \\ +\text{cons} \end{bmatrix} \underline{}
\end{array}
$$

Given these two rules, it is unnecessary to specify the initial segment of a morpheme such as *ilk* or the second segment of a morpheme such as *rip* as [+voc, −cons]. Therefore the features [vocalic] and [consonantal] can be specified as in [49] for these two morphemes:

[49a] *rip*	voc	+	−
	cons	+	+
[49b] *ilk*	voc	+	−
	cons	+	+

These two matrices are not distinct in the technical sense, thus violating our condition on lexical representations. To make them distinct we would have to specify [consonantal] as + or − in one of them. But which one is arbitrary and, furthermore, the chosen specification would be redundant since it is independently predictable by [48]. It would seem, therefore, that adopting the principle of **pairwise distinctness** leads to unmotivated analyses.

Whether these examples would be as telling once the full contrastive specification of morphemes was given is questionable. Be that as it may, the conclusion that Chomsky and Halle drew from a battery of arguments, including the above, was that, if partial specifications were allowed, it could only be at the lexical or dictionary level. Before lexical items entered the phonological component, the (unordered) set of morpheme structure rules would apply and replace all zeros by positive or negative specifications. The phonological rules proper would operate on fully specified representations. Indeed, in a logical move, it was even argued by Stanley (1967: §5.5) that, to avoid arbitrary decisions (*eg* when segment redundancies clashed with sequence redundancies), lexical representations too should be fully specified. Redundancy Conditions (not RRs) no longer filled in blanks but some evaluation measure could still apply to the lexicon. The most highly valued lexicon is not the one with most zeros, but the one in which the least number of redundancy conditions characterize the greatest number of lexical entries.

The decision to place RRs outside the phonological component did not go unchallenged. Brown (1970, 1972), for instance, gives detailed evidence from the Bantu language, Lugisu, for allowing the output of phonological rules to be recycled through RRs (see too Hooper 1975). Some preliminary examples have already been given suggesting that full specification leads to non-optimal solution and this thesis will be defended at length throughout the book. Indeed, we shall see that much current work starts from streamlined representations which are not even **pairwise distinct**; *SPE*, however, led people in a different direction. Whatever inadequacies could be noticed in the full-specification approach were, so to speak, judged irrelevant, as a radically different conception of lexical organization was advocated in Chapter 9 of *SPE*. This was the introduction of Markedness Theory within the model. It is to a brief consideration of this issue that we now turn.

3.4 Markedness Theory

At several places above, it has been pointed out that, given the feature-set at our disposal and standard abbreviatory conventions, some groupings which are 'unnatural' are easier to state than more 'natural' groupings (*cf* 3.2). Consider, as a further example, the existence of a language where all sonorants (including vowels) are voiceless. This, by all accounts, would be an exceptional language. Yet, marking sonorants underlyingly as [−voice] is as simple as marking them as [+voice[and writing a redundancy rule such as [+son] → [−voice] is as simple as writing [+son] → [+voice]. Chomsky and Halle (1968: 400) point out that this kind of problem is extremely serious since, if we

were to systematically interchange features or to replace [αF] by
[−αF] (where α = +, and F is a feature) throughout the whole
of *SPE*, there is nothing in their account of linguistic theory to
indicate that the result would be the description of a system
which violates principles governing human languages.

The problem lies in the fact that features have 'intrinsic'
content unexpressed by the formal structure. Chomsky and
Halle's solution involves the reintroduction of markedness. It was
pointed out in 3.1.1 that markedness for Trubetzkoy was essentially a language-particular fact. Trubetzkoy repeatedly emphasized
that **unmarked** and **marked** members of an opposition exist only
in the case of neutralizable oppositions. Only in such cases does
the distinction between unmarked and marked members of an
opposition have an objective phonological existence. But, then,
neutralization is relative and there are indeterminate cases. Thus,
in German, the voice–voiceless opposition is contrastive intervocalically for obstruents: *cf reissen* [raisǝn] 'to tear' vs. *reisen*
[raizǝn] 'to travel'. But the obstruents are neutralized in final
position and only a voiceless realization is attested in this context:
words like *Reis* [rais] 'rice' are never in opposition to *[raiz]. The
conclusion would appear to be that /s/ is unmarked and /z/
marked. However, in initial position, /s/ and /z/ also neutralize
but in this case as [z]. This time /s/ seems to be the marked
member. Appeal to other criteria (*eg* frequency counts) will
become necessary if we insist on talking in terms of
marked–unmarked.

This type of indeterminacy does not occur in the generative
interpretation of markedness. Markedness theory is seen by
Chomsky and Halle and their followers as universal and innate.
In a more recent vocabulary, it is the part of core grammar which
provides a formal theory of the substantive universals of sound-
structure and which sets absolute and parametrized constraints
on possible phonological systems (Kean 1981: 360). Marked
segments or feature-values will be established by a consideration
of cross-linguistic universals, distributional frequency, text
frequency, language change, language acquisition, language loss,
etc. An example has already been considered, that of nasality in
vowel systems (3.1.1). We saw that, in terms of Greenbergian
universals and, arguably, in terms of phonetics, nasality is a
marked value. In languages like French which have nasal vowels
their text frequency is, overall, lower than that of the oral vowels
(see *eg* Valdman 1976: 65). Moreover, while spontaneous nasalization is rare (barring cases of analogy or borrowing, nasal
vowels almost always arise through the influence of adjacent

nasal consonants), context-free denasalization is well attested, supporting the idea that marked segments are reverting to their normal unmarked state (*cf* Ruhlen 1978: §5). Finally, in languages like French, nasal vowels (as phonemic entities) are acquired later than their oral counterparts. The representation of markedness in generative phonology, with respect to this example, is as follows.

Let us assume that an unmarked feature-value is represented by *u* and a marked one by *m*. The presence of *u* in a lexical entry is cost-free whereas *m*, + and − each cost one point. Thus, as a first attempt, we might represent oral vowels as [+syll, −cons, *u* nasal] and nasal vowels as [+syll, −cons, *m* nasal]. The features *u* and *m* are converted to + and − by marking conventions such as:

[50]   [*u* nasal] → [−nasal] / $\left[\begin{array}{c} \underline{\hspace{2em}} \\ +\text{syll} \\ -\text{cons} \end{array}\right]$

Rule [50] says: convert a *u* specification of nasality into a minus one if the segment is a vowel. By convention, any rule such as [50[stands for a 'complement' rule of the form of [51], which converts *m* to +, and vice versa:

[51]   [*m* nasal] → [+nasal] / $\left[\begin{array}{c} \underline{\hspace{2em}} \\ +\text{syll} \\ -\text{cons} \end{array}\right]$

This interpretive convention can be formalized as [52] where 52a and 52b entail each other:

[52]   Complement convention (Kean 1981: 572)[9]
[52a] [u F_i → [αF_i] / in context F
[52a] [m F_i] → [−α F_i] / in context F

Ultimately, all segments can be represented in terms of the coefficients *u* and *m* for all features (although Chomsky and Halle keep + and − in a few cases where no decision can be reached). Chomsky and Halle (1968: 409), for instance, give the following partial classification for standard vowels:

[53]

	a	i	u	æ	ɔ	e	o	y	ɨ	œ	ø	ʌ
Low	*u*	*u*	*u*	*m*	*m*	*u*	*u*	*u*	*u*	*m*	*u*	*u*
High	*u*	*u*	*u*	*u*	*u*	*m*	*m*	*u*	*u*	*u*	*m*	*m*
Back	*u*	−	+	*m*	*u*	−	+	−	+	*m*	−	+
Round	*u*	*u*	*u*	*u*	*m*	*u*	*u*	*m*	*m*	*m*	*m*	*m*
Complexity	0	1	1	2	2	2	2	2	2	3	3	3

Given [53], /a/ comes out as the maximally unmarked vowel, and a system such as /a, i, u/, if we add up the cost of all the components, would be more highly valued than /i, ø, œ/ and be more expected to occur in the phonology of languages. As Kean (1981: 560) puts it, 'A theory of markedness will assign 'probabilities' to the occurrence and variation of substantive elements within and across grammars.'

All the *u*'s and *m*'s will be replaced by +'s and −'s as the lexical entries are converted to underlying phonological representations. The conversion is effected by universal markedness conventions such as [50] above or [54] below:

[54]

$$[u \text{ round}] \rightarrow \begin{cases} [\alpha \text{ round}]/ & \begin{bmatrix} \alpha \text{ back} \\ -\text{low} \end{bmatrix} & [54a] \\[2ex] [-\text{round}]/ & \begin{bmatrix} \overline{} \\ +\text{low} \end{bmatrix} & [54b] \end{cases}$$

What [54] says is that for non-low vowels rounding and backness agree (/i, e, o, u/ represent the norm), whereas for low vowels (/a/ is the intended segment here) non-round is the normal value. Rules of the form of [54] are supplemented by rules which state incompatibilities between features. An instance of the latter is [55] for vowels:

$$[55] \quad \begin{bmatrix} +\text{syll} \\ -\text{cons} \end{bmatrix} \rightarrow \begin{bmatrix} -\text{lat} \\ -\text{ant} \\ -\text{strid} \\ +\text{cont} \\ \ldots \end{bmatrix}$$

The set of markedness conventions is extrinsically ordered in *SPE* but need not be (*cf eg* Kean 1980, 1981 where the ordering is intrinsic).

While the above calculus takes place outside the phonological component, it is further suggested by Chomsky and Halle that markedness conventions could also be 'linked' to phonological rules. Consider a synchronic or diachronic change such that all nasal + stop sequences become nasal + nasal sequences (*eg* onto → onno). This must minimally be formulated as in [56]:

$$[56] \quad [-\text{nasal}] \rightarrow \begin{bmatrix} +\text{nasal} \\ +\text{voice} \end{bmatrix} \; / \; [+\text{nasal}] \underline{}$$

The problem with [56] is the presence of [+voice] given that nasals are typically voiced and that the set of markedness conventions would include [57]:

[57] $[u$ voice$] \rightarrow [+$voice$] / \left[\dfrac{}{+\text{nasal}} \right]$

Suppose that we allowed any feature in the output of a rule which is dependent on the value of another feature for its markedness specification to be automatically assigned its unmarked value. In that case, [56] could be reformulated as [58]:

[58] $[-$nasal$] \rightarrow [+$nasal$] / [+$nasal$]$ ____

and the [−voice] specification of some inputs (say, /p, t, k/) would be 'corrected' by the 'linking rule' [57]. On the other hand, if the assimilation of a stop to a nasal was accompanied by a rather unexpected devoicing (both /ondo/ and /onto/ → onno), the value [−voice] (or equivalently [m voice]) would have to be explicitly mentioned in the rule, as eg in [59]:

[59] $[-$nasal$] \rightarrow \left[\begin{array}{c} +\text{nasal} \\ -\text{voice} \end{array} \right] / [+$nasal$]$ ____

Under the metric of simplicity [59] is more costly than [58].

A full discussion of Markedness Theory would not be in order here. A number of 'philosophical' objections have been raised by Lass (1975, 1980, 1984), in particular, against the erection of statistical frequencies into what he calls a 'pseudo-mathematical' evaluation in terms of cost, value and quantified complexity. But, even if a tightened definition of this area is possible (*cf* Kean, 1980, 1981 for such an attempt), the problem with Markedness Theory is that the whole apparatus it offers is external to the notation. In so far as the notion of complexity of segments makes sense – and it has been suggested above that it is plausible to see nasality as a marked feature – the notation does not reflect it. All markedness theory does is offer a conversion from feature-values of one kind (u, m) into feature-values of another kind (+, −) in the lexicon-to-phonology interface. Indeed, in one type of treatment (Vennemann 1972a; Goyvaerts 1978), it is suggested that even lexical specifications should be in terms of + and −, and that the markedness conventions should be conceived as an interpretive device characterizing the naturalness of segments – a move similar to the one considered at the end of the previous section where RRs were turned into Redundancy Conventions linked to fully specified matrices.

Another problematic area is the pre-eminence given to the complexity of segments in the absence of a discussion of processes. Thus, an unconditioned change of /u/ to /y/ is, perhaps correctly (but see Lass 1975), predicted as complex. But a change such as [60] – a subpart of i-umlaut considered again in Chapter 8:

[60] u → y / ___C_o i

which involves a fronting of /u/ under the influence of the front vowel /i/, is widely attested. Yet the use of linking conventions forces us to state this as [61]

$$[61] \begin{bmatrix} +\text{back} \\ +\text{high} \end{bmatrix} \begin{bmatrix} -\text{back} \\ +\text{round} \end{bmatrix} / \underline{\quad} C_o \begin{bmatrix} -\text{back} \\ +\text{high} \end{bmatrix}$$

given condition [54] which renders front rounded vowels costly (*ie* u → i is, counterfactually, predicted as more natural here). Two solutions have been advocated for this kind of problem: either we devise a set of rule and string markedness conventions (*eg* Schachter 1969) and/or we further complicate the availability of features in markedness conventions. Kloeke (1981), who follows Kean (1980), suggests for instance that [labial] is not available for linking and, if [+labial] is what distinguishes [y] from /i/([−labial]), the [+labial] characterization of the input /u/ need not figure explicitly in the statement of the rule. It will consequently be carried at no cost from the source to the target. Such extra conventions are quite arbitrary and not untypical of work within Markedness Theory.[10] They remind us of the situation in pre-Keplerian astronomy where, to maintain the assumption that planetary orbits were circular, astronomers had recourse to *ad hoc* accretions in the form of epicycles on the circles and eventually epicycles on epicycles. What is needed is, as much as possible, a direct mirroring of complexity and naturalness within the notation and not some external price-keeping device assigning a cost to statements (see 3.5 for a first example and Chs 7–8).[11]

With a few exceptions, work in Markedness Theory seems to have stopped, although it is often referred to as a useful component of Universal Grammar (see *eg* Kiparsky 1985: 135, n. 3). One of the tenets of Markedness Theory is that, at all levels of derivation, phonological representations are fully specified (see Kean 1981: 575). But this book offers many examples showing that full specification prevents the expression of a number of generalizations concerning phonological derivations. What is interesting is that in one recent strand of research explored in Chapter 5 (Underspecification Theory), universal RRs which are essentially the markedness conventions of the *SPE* tradition play a role reminiscent of the 'linking' device of *SPE*. The markedness conventions introduced in this section are therefore a useful backdrop to these further developments.

3.5 Gestures

Within the 'standard' framework adopted so far, phonological representations are two-dimensional matrices which correspond to the consecutive segments of speech. The rows represent particular features and + or − specifications determine the status of each segment with respect to each DF. In other words, a segment is an unordered, unstructured set of simultaneous attribute-value pairs. Technically, $/p/ = \{\langle voice, -\rangle, \langle labial, +\rangle, \ldots, \langle cont, -\rangle\}$. On the other hand, from the perspective of articulatory phonetics, it is customary to point out that speech results from the simultaneous conjunction of independent components which are usually larger than single features. Thus, Ladefoged (1971) distinguishes four major components: the airstream process, the phonation process, the articulatory process and the oro-nasal process. Catford (1977) offers three main components: initiation (airstream mechanisms), articulation and phonation. Only the first two are absolutely basic since, for instance, an ejective does not involve phonation as such. (For him, the closure of the glottal cords that an ejective requires has an initiatory function.) Articulation, for Catford, includes two subcomponents: stricture-type and location. Stricture-type corresponds, roughly, to 'manner of articulation' and location includes three major areas: nasal, oral and pharyngeo-laryngeal.

One of the intuitions behind these divisions is the observation that while major components are largely independent of one another, there are tighter restrictions between the elements of a given component. Thus, within the category of pulmonic egressive sounds, vocal cord activity is relatively free with respect to supraglottal articulation. On the other hand, the features corresponding to supraglottal articulation are not equally independent of one another. For instance, lateral release is not available for sounds which are non-high, stridency applies only to affricates and fricatives, nasality is not contrastive for pharyngeals, and so on. In so far as these restrictions should be incorporated into our feature theory in the form of general redundancy statements (*eg* [−high] → [−lat], [+son] → [−strid]), a partitioning of the set of features into subsets would provide better motivation for such statements. But, beside this, there is a great deal of evidence that

dividing segments into groups of features is relevant for the statement of regularities in sound-systems. This is the issue to which
we now turn.

3.5.1 Nasal assimilation

In 3.1.2, it was argued that the assimilation process whereby a
nasal consonant inherits the place of articulation of a following
plosive within morphemes could be adequately formalized as in
[62] (= [9]):

[62] Nasal Place Assimilation

$$[+\text{nasal}] \rightarrow \begin{bmatrix} \alpha\text{lab} \\ \beta\text{cor} \\ \gamma\text{ant} \end{bmatrix} / \underline{\hspace{2em}} \begin{bmatrix} -\text{son} \\ -\text{cont} \\ \alpha\text{lab} \\ \beta\text{cor} \\ \gamma\text{ant} \end{bmatrix}$$

But, of course, at that stage the argument was advanced in favour
of binary features and Greek variables against atomic labels (and
implicitly against indivisible phonemes). What is striking about
[62], though, is that the assimilation process is by no means simple
to state and requires explicit mention of **all** the relevant features.
Yet, this is a natural and widely attested process. It could be
objected that talking in terms of the nasal assimilating to the stop
assumes a directionality which is not there. Why is it not the stop
which assimilates to the nasal?

One argument in favour of nasals assimilating to stops, rather
than the other way round, is that the same phenomenon takes
place across morpheme- and word-boundaries and supports a
regressive (right-to-left) interpretation, although there is more
variability in these contexts. Consider, for instance, the negative
prefix *in-*. According to Jones's *English Pronouncing Dictionary*
(1977), it is pronounced [ɪn] before a vowel (*inaccessible*) and an
alveolar stop (*indecent*) but [ɪm] before a bilabial stop (*impure*)
and either [ɪn] or [ɪŋ] before a velar stop (*incoherent*). The [ɪn]
realization before a vowel favours the postulation of /in/ as the
underlying form with assimilation to the place of articulation of
a following stop. Across word-boundaries, the preposition *in* can
be realized either as [ɪn] or as [ɪm] and [ɪŋ] before a bilabial stop
and a velar stop respectively (*eg in class* [ɪnklaːs] or [ɪŋklaːs]).
Given that the word *in* is pronounced [ɪn] in isolation, /ɪn/ is the
most plausible underlying form. There is therefore a direction:
the assimilation is regressive.

The same phenomenon of homorganic assimilation by nasals
is widely attested in a variety of languages and its naturalness

should be captured within the notation. What we would like to write is something along the following lines (*cf* Hyman 1975: 91):

[63]
$$[+\text{nasal}] \rightarrow [\alpha\ \text{place}] \ / \ \underline{\qquad} \begin{bmatrix} -\text{son} \\ -\text{cont} \\ \alpha\ \text{place} \end{bmatrix}$$

But such a formulation is purely expository and has no theoretical status within the standard framework.

Following a tradition which can be traced to Lass and Anderson (1975) and Lass (1976), let us now posit within the representation of segments submatrices called *gestures* which can be invoked as units. The precise organization of segments in terms of gestures is very much a matter of debate (see 7.3.2 for other proposals). Here, we shall follow Ewen (1986) and Anderson and Ewen (1987) who suggest, within the framework of Dependency Phonology, an assignment to segments of the internal structure given in [64] below. Although their proposal is cast in terms of a feature system quite different from the *SPE* features, the content of these gestures and subgestures can be glossed as in [65]. Thus, /n/ and /p/ for instance might be

[64]

```
                              Segment
                 _____/        _____
        Categorial gesture                 Articulatory gesture
         /          \                        /           \
Phonatory        Initiatory          Locational        Oro-nasal
subgesture       subgesture          subgesture        subgesture
```

[65]

Categorial gesture	Phonatory subgesture	Consonantality Sonorance Voice Continuancy
	Initiatory subgesture	Glottal stricture Glottalicness Velar suction
Articulatory gesture	Locational subgesture	Place Height Rounding Backness
	Oro-nasal gesture	Nasality

partially represented as in [66]:

[66]

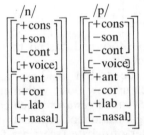

Still keeping quite close to the standard notation, all we need to do to invoke gestures within rules is allow a variable to cover a whole (sub)matrix. By convention, any combinations of feature values within a (sub)matrix will agree with those of any other corresponding (sub)matrix mentioned in the formulation of the rule. In the present context, Nasal Place Assimilation can be reformulated as in [67]:

$$[67] \quad [+\text{nasal}] \rightarrow [\alpha \text{ LOCATION}] / \_\_\_\_ \begin{bmatrix} \begin{bmatrix} -\text{son} \\ -\text{cont} \end{bmatrix} \\ \alpha \text{ LOCATION} \end{bmatrix}$$

[67] formalizes the intuition that homorganicity is not about pairwise agreement between individual features, but about identity of articulation of segments as wholes. Let us now pursue some of the consequences of the gesture hypothesis in connection with the laryngeal glides ([h] and [ʔ]).

3.5.2 The laryngeal glides and dearticulation

In our presentation of DFs in Chapter 2, based on Chomsky and Halle (1968) and Halle and Clements (1983), [ʔ] and [h] and the semi-vowels were grouped together within the category of 'glides' – that is, segments which are characterized as [−cons, +son]. Furthermore, we saw that the 'laryngeal glides' were assigned tongue-body features (−cor, −ant, −high, +low, −back) like any other consonants. This grouping has a long history in generative phonology since it ultimately goes back to Jakobson, Fant and Halle (1952). It presents a serious challenge to traditional phonetic classification where [ʔ] is described as a 'glottal stop' and [h] as a 'glottal fricative'.

From the point of view of phonetics, the traditional classification makes sense if what is meant by a glottal stop is a unit which corresponds in **production** to a complete closure of the glottis with no extra constriction of the larynx and which corresponds, in the **acoustic** (spectrographic) record, to a short period of silence with abrupt rise 'time and cut-off in relation to a following and preceding vowel. An [h] is plausibly classified as a 'glottal fricative' if it is a unit which involves in production an open glottis typical of voiceless sounds but with turbulent airflow, and which corresponds in the **acoustic** record to broad spectrum noise from about 400 to 6500 hertz. But, in practice, what phonologists transcribe as [h] and [ʔ] may well be a voiced breathy onset ([ɦ] as in *ahead*) and a glottal constriction respectively. These latter realizations are much better candidates for the status of sonorants. Since, once again, phonetics does not give us an unambiguous answer, let us turn to examples of the phonological behaviour of [ʔ] and [h] and see whether the 'glide' classification is motivated.

In many accents of English, the voiceless plosives /p, t, k/ can be optionally realized as glottal stops. Thus, in Cockney, one can observe the following pronunciations: [fɪlɪʔ] *Philip*, [ɑ lɪʔɪʔ] *I lit it*, [ə búʔ] *a book* (Wells 1982: 323). Now, these realizations are subject to a great deal of sociolinguistic and phonological variation. In particular, /t/ is much more commonly realized as [ʔ] than either /p/ or /k/. But while other sounds are mentioned in the literature as taking part in this reduction to [ʔ] (*eg* [f] and [d] for Cockney), their participation in the process appears to be much more sporadic and phrase-bound. The question is how to formalize the reduction of /p, t, k/ to a glottal stop. If we assume the standard classification given in Chapter 2, the /t/ → [ʔ] change, to take only one example, will entail extensive feature-values switches. Leaving voicing aside, we have at least:

[68] /t/ → [ʔ]

$$\begin{bmatrix} +\text{cons} \\ -\text{son} \\ -\text{cont} \\ +\text{ant} \\ +\text{cor} \\ -\text{low} \end{bmatrix} \begin{bmatrix} -\text{cons} \\ +\text{son} \\ +\text{cont} \\ -\text{ant} \\ -\text{cor} \\ +\text{low} \end{bmatrix}$$

The same pattern emerges if we consider [k] → [ʔ] and [p] → [ʔ] and it is clear that any statement of the reduction of voiceless plosives to [ʔ] will prove cumbersome, to say the least. Suppose, however, that we stay close to tradition and define [ʔ] as a plosive which is voiceless on account of the period of silence which corresponds to it in the spectrographic record and the absence of voice bar (*ie* [ʔ] = [−son, −cont, −voice]). All the major class changes charted above will not be required. Let us assume, in addition, that phonologically [ʔ] is to be characterized as an incomplete stop – a stop whose articulatory gesture is lacking. Of course, we know that the supraglottal articulators are in some position or other, but we are saying that this is irrelevant to the phonological classification of [ʔ]. The description of /p, t, k/ → [ʔ] becomes quite simple. It involves the deletion of the whole articulatory gesture of the source segments. It is an example of weakening which can be referred to as 'dearticulation'.

An analysis in terms of weakening is well supported by cross-linguistic evidence. As mentioned in Lass (1976), the historical account of many languages often involves a depletion of the voiceless plosive inventory through a reduction to [ʔ]. Ultimately, we can expect the [ʔ] itself to disappear and it is interesting to note that, according to Wells (1982: 325), one can find in Cockney the occasional zero realization in intervocalic position – [beə] for *better* and [lɪo] foɪ *little* – where zero is in sociolinguistic variation with a voiceless stop, a tap and a glottal stop. In terms of gestures, the weakening path can be represented as in [69].

[69]

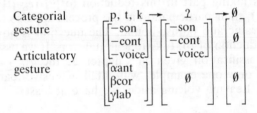

Now, the same demonstration can be given for [h], both synchronically and diachronically. While English has only marginal weakenings such as *thanks* pronounced as [hæŋks], many languages illustrate alternations between the voiceless fricatives and [h]. For instance, some varieties of modern Spanish have alternations between [s], [h] and zero in final position (see 4.4.1). And, historically, well-known changes such as Latin *filia* > Spanish *hija* [ixa] 'daughter', bear testimony to the sequence f > h > ∅, the intermediary [h] being reflected in the spelling. In fact, the [h] mid-way station from full specification to zero, is still present in the Gascon variety of Occitan where we have phonetic [h] corresponding to Latin [f] and Spanish zero (*eg hilha*

[hilja] for Lat. *filia*). By representing [h] as a voiceless fricative which lacks an articulatory gesture, the above phenomena can be explained quite naturally.

3.5.3 Glides and nasalization in Malay

The above section argues against the grouping of [h, ʔ] with the semi-vowels within a category of glides. But, we have considered only some examples and mainly restricted our attention to synchronic and diachronic weakening processes. In the following paragraphs, a further case which has been mentioned in the literature as providing strong evidence for the *SPE* category of glides will be examined. The data are borrowed from Malay and the reader is referred to Durand (1987) for a detailed study of the same phenomena.

In standard Malay, there is a process of progressive (left-to-right) nasalization, whereby one or more vowels to the right of a nasal consonant are nasalized. The spreading of nasalization operates both morpheme-internally and across morpheme boundaries. Onn (1980: 45) gives the following examples (where = is a prefix boundary and + a suffix boundary):

[70] /minum/	[mĩnũm]	'to drink'
/makan/	[mãkan]	'to eat'
/naik/	[nãĩk]	'to ascend'
/baŋun/	[baŋũn]	'to rise'
/məŋ=aŋin+i/	[məŋãŋinĩ]	'to cause to ventilate'

The twist in the story of Malay nasalization is this: the feature of nasalization spreads rightwards to any number of vowels provided that the only non-syllabics between them are [ʔ, h, j, w]. Onn (1980: 45) gives the following examples:

[71] /mewah/	[mẽwãh]	'to be luxurious'
/majan/	[mãjãn]	'stalk (palm)'
/maap/	[mãʔãp]	'pardon'
/məŋ=ajak/	[məŋãjãʔ]	'to sift (act)'

For Onn, who adopts a standard analysis of glides, the explanation for the fact that [j, w, h, ʔ] do not block nasalization is that they collectively form the class of [−syll, −cons, +son] segments. If we assume that the rule which spreads nasalization is **iterative** (that is, keeps reapplying to its own output), the formulation of [72] can be adopted:

[72] Vowel nasalization

$$[+\text{syll}] \rightarrow [+\text{nasal}] / [+\text{nasal}] \begin{bmatrix} -\text{syll} \\ -\text{cons} \end{bmatrix}_0 \underline{\hspace{2cm}}$$

The spreading and blocking of nasalization is interesting in that it is attested in other languages, not all belonging to the same language group (*cf eg* Robins 1957 on Sundanese, Bendor-Samuel 1960, on Terena, Halle and Vergnaud 1982a, on Capanuha).

There are, however, three independent arguments within Malay phonology showing that /h, ʔ/ pattern with the obstruents and not with the semi-vowels. To quote only one of them, there is a complex adjustment which affects a prefix ending in a nasal consonant when it is adjoined to a stem with an initial **voiceless** obstruent: viz. the nasal consonant assimilates the point of articulation of the following obstruent and the obstruent is deleted. Some examples borrowed from Onn (1980: 14) are listed in [73]:

[73a]	/pəŋ=tulis/	[pənūles]	'writer'
	/məŋ=pukul/	[məmūkol]	'to beat (active)'
	/məŋ=kawal/	[məŋāwāl]	'to guard (active)'
[73b]	/pəŋ=boroŋ/	[pəmboroŋ]	'wholesaler'
	/məŋ=baja/	[məmbaja]	'to pay (active)'
	/məŋ=daki/	[məndaki]	'to climb (active)'

Onn does not raise the question of what happens if a stem begins with *h* or ʔ. Yet, one of his sources, Hassan, is quite explicit on this point: /p, t, f, k, s, ʔ, h/ undergo deletion in this context. Thus *menghakis* 'to erode (active)', which is made up of the prefix /məŋ/ and the stem /hakis/ is pronounced [məŋakes]. Such examples show that /h/ behaves like a voiceless obstruent here and not like [j,w].

How can we therefore reconcile the above facts with the spreading of nasalization? The fact that [j, w] let nasalization through is not surprising since they are non-syllabic vowels ([−cons, −syll]). In fact, on instrumental and auditory grounds, they appear to be nasalized. The real question is the following: since [+cons] segments are 'opaque' to the spread of nasalization, why do [h] and [ʔ] behave as 'transparent' segments if they are obstruents ([+cons, −son]) as claimed here? But note that there is one characteristic which sets them apart from the other consonants of Malay: they lack an articulatory gesture at the phonological level. If we think in terms of the gestural organization offered above, it is as if nasalization skipped the glottal segments on account of their empty articulatory components. If we assume a 'geometrical' interpretation of gestures, such that each gesture is the labelling of a node and nodes are linked to other nodes in the same segment by lines of association (*cf* Ch. 7), an interpretation can be offered which brings out this intuition [74].

[74] Malay Nasalisation (iterative)
[74a] SD (Structural description)   [74b] SC (Structural Change)

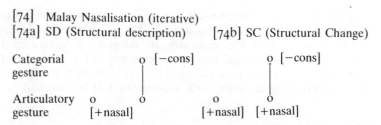

Rule [74] says that, if on the articulatory 'tier', there is an articulatory gesture bearing the label [+nasal] next to an articulatory gesture which is linked ('associated') to a categorial gesture bearing the label [−cons], then the feature [+nasal] is to be copied on to the second articulatory gesture. What is crucial here is that adjacency is expressed only at the level ('tier') of articulation. Nothing is said about articulation except for the segment which is going to inherit nasalization. The configuration in [75] below corresponding to /mahal/ would therefore be an input to the rule [74]. The feature [+nasal] would be copied from left to right yielding first of all [māhal], at which point the feature [+nasal] will be adjacent on the articulatory tier to a segment (the second /a/ of /mahal/) whose categorial gesture is [−cons] and will spread to it. Here /h/ will be invisible since it lacks an articulatory gesture.[12]

[75]

m	a	h	a	l
$\begin{bmatrix}-\text{syll}\\+\text{cons}\end{bmatrix}$	$\begin{bmatrix}+\text{syll}\\-\text{cons}\end{bmatrix}$	$\begin{bmatrix}-\text{syll}\\+\text{cons}\\+\text{cont}\end{bmatrix}$	$\begin{bmatrix}+\text{syll}\\-\text{cons}\end{bmatrix}$	$\begin{bmatrix}-\text{syll}\\+\text{cons}\end{bmatrix}$
o	o	o	o	o
o	o		o	o
[+nas]	[+low]		[+low]	[+lat]

If our argumentation is correct, and some extra evidence is offered in the following chapters, then we are abandoning two tenets of the standard *SPE* framework: (i) the assumption that the set of features has no internal organization; (ii) the assumption that segments should be fully specified. In the case of nasal–plosive sequences within morphemes, representations such as /bæNk/ for *bank* seem licit and well motivated. In terms of gestures and subgestures, /N/ can probably be distinguished from all other segments by classifying it as [+cons], categorically, and [+nasal] in the oro-nasal subgesture. Since the locational subgesture of /N/ is empty (*cf* [65]), there is no need to think of the reformulation of Nasal Place Assimilation offered in [67] as changing any place of articulation features within morphemes.

Rather, the nasal inherits all the features characterizing the following stop. We have also argued that nasalization in Malay could be accounted for, elegantly, by adopting a 'geometrical' interpretation of internal segmental structure. The 'geometrical' structure of segments is reconsidered in Chapter 7 where a radical departure from the *SPE* framework will be outlined.

Notes

1. Representations as scales are only a first approximation: see 5.2.7.
2. The phonemes cannot be taken at random but must be the members of a 'bilateral' opposition in Trubetzkoy's terms: that is, pairs or sets of phonemes which are alike in all features but one. For instance, in English /p/–/b/ are in bilateral opposition since they are the only two sounds characterizable as 'oral labial stops' ([−nas, +lab, −cont]) and differ in voicing. The pair /p/–/m/ is not bilateral. All the features shared by /p/ and /m/ ([+lab, −cont]) also characterize /b/. The reader is referred to Trubetzkoy (1969) as primary source and to the excellent accounts of Praguian phonology in Hyman (1975: 26–9), Sommerstein (1977: 45–53) and Lass (1984: Ch. 3).
3. This is not true at the phonetic level where one can observe [sɔ̃mtɥø] from /sɔmptɥø/ *somptueux* 'sumptuous' and does not apply to some recent borrowings (*eg Honda* [ɔ̃nda] – for the Japanese car make): see Tranel (1981: 76–7). I leave aside the issue of whether French nasal vowels should ultimately be derived from VN sequences for expository reasons.
4. The absence of words beginning with #sd or #sg seems to be due to an accidental gap. Note that the #sf – #sv contrast (*sphère* [sfɛr] – *svelte* [svɛlt]) is also stable although attested for very few pairs of words.
5. Whether this is entirely correct is a question which will preoccupy us elsewhere in this book (*cf* especially Ch. 8).
6. *Cf* too Lass for tentative suggestions in the same direction. On vowel height, lowering in the Scanian dialect of Swedish is often mentioned as evidence for scalar approaches: Lindau (1975, 1978), Lass (1984). See, however, the critique of Lindau in Yip (1980) and Schane's objections to the latter (1984a: 143).
7. I must, however, record some reservations about Creider's general point that we should not be surprised if vowel height too is binary in view of 'the impressive tendencies of humans to operate with binary distinctions elsewhere (in phonology, morphology and semantics)' (Creider 1986: 2). But, I know of no convincing demonstration that the relationship between lexemes in scales such as {excellent, good, fair, poor, bad, atrocious} is best described in terms of binary features (*cf* Lyons 1977: 289). It is too easy to put the burden of the proof, as he does, on advocates of scalar features on the simple grounds that binary features are more restrictive.

8. Phonotactic Rules also include negative conditions (see 1.3.2.1) and positive conditions stating what the overall shape of morphemes must be like. In a language where every monosyllable is of the type consonant + optional liquid + vowel, there will be a positive condition: + [−syll] ([+son, −nas]) [+syll] + (where + marks the beginning and end of morphemes).

9. Kean also includes the complements of contexts in her formulation. This extension will not be considered here.

10. Already in *SPE* the cost of certain segments had to be 'corrected' by recourse to conventions such as 'No vowel segment can be marked for the feature "round" unless some other vowel segment in the system is marked for the feature "high".' And, it was argued that 'linking' could only work if one abandoned the standard (Markovian) theory of rule application. (Put informally, this latter requires that all the information available for the application of a rule must be contained in the input string.) By contrast, linking conventions applied to chains of features with a kind of memory device built into the application (*SPE pp* 425 ff).

11. For further details and references to the early work within Markedness Theory, the presentation of Hyman (1975) is highly recommended, and see Kaye (in press Ch. 3) for a recent presentation. *Cf* Ewen (1980: §2.4.1) and J. M. Anderson and Ewen (1987: §1.3.2) for incisive discussions of this issue.

12. Hayward and Mickey (1987) in '"Guttural": arguments for a new distinctive feature' give solid cross-linguistic evidence suggesting an affinity between [h, ʔ] and 'guttural' sounds which motivates a new distinctive feature [+/−guttural]. This is not incompatible with the claims made here. It shows that phonetics underdetermines phonological analysis – a point I take for granted.

Chapter 4

The derivational issue: aspects of the abstractness–concreteness debate

4.1 Preliminaries

In Chapter 1, it was mentioned that standard generative phonology rejected classical phonemic representations and licensed underlying representations which can be quite remote from allophonic representations. The practice in this area is not monolithic and there are competing schools of thought. Nevertheless, there is an unbroken tradition of MIT-based work going back to the early 1960s and embodied in the monumental *Sound Pattern of English* (Chomsky and Halle 1968) which endorses representations far removed from the surface in order to capture **linguistically significant generalizations**. Researchers in this tradition do accept some kind of **naturalness** principle: other things being equal, underlying representations should be identical to surface representations. But other things are not equal and the body of regularities and subregularities characterizing natural languages requires abstract representations connected to the surface by an intricate set of rules and principles. The area considered in 4.2 is a small but crucial portion of English segmental phonology – namely, the English Vowel Shift (well known as a diachronic process but argued below to be part of a synchronic account of English) and its implications for other rules of the phonology. The main signposts guiding the presentation here are Chomsky and Halle (1968), Halle (1977), and Halle and Mohanan (1985).[1] Since Halle and Mohanan's article is cast within the framework of Lexical Phonology and integrates concepts of metrical structure to be introduced later in Ch. 6, the presentation will attempt to concentrate on the core of arguments lying behind the analyses considered here which have remained relatively stable since *SPE*. Some of the representational issues will be raised again in the following chapters. In 4.3, a number of objections to *SPE*-type analyses of modern English are presented and, in 4.4, an alternative framework – Natural Generative Phonology (NGP) – is outlined and discussed. Section 4.5 offers a brief reconsideration of the Vowel Shift in the light of our discussion of NGP.

4.2 Aspects of the segmental phonology of English

The vowel systems of various accents of English are well known to differ in terms of inventory and realizations. In this chapter, we shall start from an inventory of segments for two major accents – RP and GA (General American) – which corresponds to a classical phonemic inventory. The choice of symbols and feature-analysis has, however, been dictated by the need to fit in with the analyses offered in the generative literature and, particularly, Halle and Mohanan (1985). The argumentation will aim at showing that, to account for rule-governed alternations in English, the underlying inventory of English vowels needs to differ quite substantially from traditional phonemic inventories.

Let us assume that, at some level of representation, our inventory of vowels and diphthongs includes the sounds classified in [1]. The notation and some of the assumptions will be explained immediately after.

[1] Surface vowels

	−back	+back	
		−round	+round
+high −low	i *bit* ij *beat*		u *book* uw *boot*
−high −low	e *bet* ej *bait*	ʌ *but*	o: *baud* (RP) ow *boat*
−high +low	æ *bat*	a *bomb* (GA) a: *balm* aj *bite* aw *bout*	ɔ *bomb* (RP) ɔ: *baud* (GA) ɔj *boy*

Here [1] is organized in terms of binary features which, as explained in Chapters 2 and 3, allow only for three levels of vowel height and a binary front–back opposition. It includes the segments which are traditionally referred to as the short vowels,

the long vowels and the rising diphthongs. Note that the diphthongs are transcribed with a glide as second element as is
customary in American transcriptions (although IPA /j/ is used
instead of /y/: eg /bejt/ corresponds to *SPE* /beyt/). Long vowels
are marked by a length mark but the vowels in *beat, bait, boot*
are treated as vowel + glide sequences. At the phonetic level,
the vowels grouped in pairs in [I] (*eg beat–bit*) are known to be
distinguished by a mixture of length and tension (or centralization). The question of tension will be mentioned at several points
of the presentation below. We shall, in fact, assume that underlyingly a long–short contrast is sufficient.[2] A few other vowels are
not included in [I]: *ie*, in terms of RP, [ə] *ago*, [ə:] *bird*, and the
centring diphthongs [iə] *beard*, [eə] *laird*, [uə] *gourd*. We turn
briefly to a possible treatment of these segments in RP.

Schwa is well known to alternate with full vowels within the
phonology of English. Derivational series such as *photograph*
[fówtəgræf], *photographic* [fòwtəgrǽfik], *photography* [fətɔ́grəfi],
show that full vowels under stress correspond to schwas in
unstressed position. If the most abstract level of representation
were a phonemic transcription, the various occurrences of *photograph* in the above words would not be connected. Under this
hypothesis, the learner of English simply has to memorize the
above forms or, at best, to hypothesize relational statements such
that when -*y* is added to a base like *photograph* the initial [ow]
is not stressed and turned into a schwa, and the schwa of the
second syllable is stressed and turned into [ɔ], etc. But all this
word-bound machinery misses obvious generalizations. The
above   pattern   is   far   from   isolated   (*cf   telegraph–
telegraphy–telegraphic, lithograph–lithography–lithographic*, etc.).
And to account for alternations such as *telegraph–telegraphy*,
[téləgræf]–[təlégrəfi], we would now have to state that, when -*y* is
added, the /e/ in the first syllable is turned into schwa and the schwa in
the second syllable is turned into an /e/. A much more attractive
description is available if we posit underlying forms which are
composites of the surface variants. For instance, *photograph*
would be /fowtɔgræf/ and *telegraph* /telegræf/ which are subject
to stress rules. Under various conditions, unstressed vowels
would be reduced to schwa. The advantage of this approach is
that it is not limited to the above alternations but applies at large
within the phonology of English (*cf* the underlined vowels in
explain–explanation, provoke–provocation) and is further illustrated in 4.2.1. Moreover, the treatment of schwa as the
reduction vowel of English is well motivated synchronically and
diachronically.

Reduction of full vowels to schwa, in a variety of contexts, is widely agreed to have long been an active process in English. For instance, the pronunciation of *November* is given, using our transcription, as [nowvémbə] in Jones's (1977) *English Pronouncing Dictionary* (*EPD*). This reflects the traditional pronunciation, but speakers are known to alternate between [nowvémbə] and [nəvémbə] and the latter is probably the more usual realization for some speakers of English. Words such as *yellow, window, piano*, which end in unstressed [ow] in RP, show reduction of [ow] to [ə] in popular speech. In turn, schwa tends to drop in some unstressed medial syllables in frequently used nouns such as *fact(o)ry, slav(e)ry, nurs(e)ry*. This is reminiscent of our discussion of incomplete segments in 3.5.2. Although the discussion there dealt with consonants only, so that [h] and [ʔ] were treated as consonants with empty articulatory gestures, there is no reason not to extend this treatment to vowels. Phonologically, schwa is a segment specified categorially as a vowel [+syll, −cons] but with **zero articulation**. The disappearance of schwa in unstressed contexts is yet another example of weakening, supporting our phonological hypothesis. Phonetically, schwa needs to have some articulation but we can assume that this is given by universal or language-specific default rules.

The examples given above involve schwa as a **reduction** vowel. But, in some unstressed contexts, schwa may be in opposition with other vowels without any evidence of its alternating with a full vowel. Wells (1982: 167) gives pairs such as *rabbit–abbot*, [ræbit]–[æbət], and *Lenin–Lennon* [lenin]–[lenən]. Since the [ə] in *abbot* and *Lennon* never alternates with a full vowel, the analysis of schwa as an unspecified vowel can also be adopted at the underlying level and, for convenience, we can transcribe these two words as /æbVt/ and /lenVn/ (where V stands for an unspecified vowel).

We can now turn to the representation of /ə:/ (sometimes transcribed /ɜ(:)/) in items such as *bird, nurse, word*, etc. In GA, all these words have a long rhotacized central vowel but this can be interpreted as /Vr/. The realization of /Vr/ as [ə:] is a late allophonic adjustment (see *eg* Wells 1982: 199–203 on what he calls 'the NURSE merger'). In RP, positing an underlying /r/ in a word like *purr* is acceptable since it surfaces across morpheme- and word-boundaries as a 'linking r' (*cf stirring, stir it*). But, in words like *bird* and *nurse*, there is no evidence, apart from the spelling, for postulating an /r/. Since a short, unspecified vowel, /V/, is already within the system, we can treat the vowel in *bird* as its long partner: /V:/. And the word *stir* would underlyingly be represented as /stV:r/. This is why Jones's transcription [ə:] was preferred above over the more modern [ɜ(:)]. As for the diphthongs [iə], [eə], [uə], once an unspecified vowel is accepted in the system, there is no strong reason not to use it for representing these segments: /iV/, /eV/, /uV/. In other words, we can adopt a representation which is identical to the traditional one to all intents and purposes. The reader should note that hereafter the symbol V is used ambiguously: sometimes it is a cover symbol for the class of vowels and, at other times, it denotes the unspecified vowel (schwa). The contexts make clear which is which.

4.2.1 The Vowel Shift

For many analysts, the inventory of [1], supplemented by /ə, ə:, iə, eə, uə/, constitutes the underlying system of English but, within the *SPE* tradition, there are good reasons not to accept this assumption. The starting-point of the *SPE* treatment is the observation that the alternations in [2] are well grounded in the phonology of English and found in a large number of contexts:

[2]

	A	B	C
aj–i	divine–divinity	crucify–crucifixion	satire–satiric
ij–e	serene–serenity	intervene–intervention	metre–metric
ej–æ	sane–sanity	abstain–abstention	volcano–volcanic
aw–ʌ	profound–profundity	_____	_____
ow–ɔ	verbose–verbosity	_____	cone–conic
uw–ʌ	_____	assume–assumption	_____

In the context -*ity*, further illustration of the above alternations is provided by pairs such as *sterile–sterility* [aj–i], *volatile–volatility* [aj–i], *severe–severity* [ij–e], *obscene–obscenity* [ij–e], *opaque–opacity* [ej–æ], *chaste–chastity* [ej–æ], *bellicose–bellicosity* [ow–ɔ], and so on. And each alternation is found in other contexts than the above. To take only one example, in addition to *divine–divinity* (adj–n), [aj]–[i] is also found in *define–definitive* (v–adj), *child–children* (n sing–n pl), and *slide–slid* (v pres vs. past).

Since all these alternations involve 'mutations' triggered by the presence of a suffix, an obvious way to account for them would be to postulate a set of rules taking the left-hand-side vowel as input and producing the right-hand-side variant as output. Limiting our attention to the front vowel alternations, rules such as the ones in [3] would be required.

[3] aj → i
   ij → e
   ej → æ

If we tried to express [3] in terms of features, the rule would be quite complex and would not reveal any underlying generalization. However, alongside the alternations in [2], there exist in English alternations which appear to go in the opposite direction:

[4]

A	B	C	A	B	C
ə –	æ	– ej	marginal –	marginality –	marginalia
ə –		– ij	manager		managerial
ə –	ɔ	– ow	harmony –	harmonic –	harmonious
ʌ –		(j)uw	Lilliput		Lilliputian

Some explanations about the forms in [4] are in order. All the schwas listed in [4A] are the reduced, dearticulated, realization of a full vowel. The vowels underlined in the [4B] forms (when they occur), and not those in [4C], provide the underlying segments. Thus *marginal* is underlyingly /ma:ginæl/ in RP (/marginæl/ in GA) and *harmony* is /ha:mɔni/ (GA /harmɔni/) as is shown by the following considerations.

Before segmental rules apply, the underlying form is subjected to rules of stress. The account of stress has undergone some major revisions since the publication of *SPE* (see Ch. 6). What has remained, however, is the assumption that word-stress is, by and large, predictable by a battery of rules provided it is formulated with reference to the morphological structure of words and in terms of underlying forms of the type exemplified for *photograph* above and not surface realizations.[3] The account of stress is intimately bound with the segmental analysis outlined below. Let us assume, very much as a first approximation, that the main stress rule that applies to nouns and adjectives, runs along the lines of [5] below, secondary stresses being assigned by separate statements:

[5]   Stress in nouns and adjectives (informal statement)
[5a] stress the vowel of monosyllables (*cát, táll*)
[5b] in plurisyllables:

     (i) if the last vowel is long/diphthongized stress it:
        machíne, supréme
    (ii) if the last vowel is short ignore it and stress the

vowel in the penultimate syllable if one of the
following conditions is fulfilled:
α) it is long/diphthongized (*aróma, desírous*)
β) it is followed by a strong CC cluster (*agénda, dialéctal*)
γ) the item is bisyllabic (*pérson, vúlgar*)
(iii) if neither (i) nor (ii) applies, then stress the
antepenultimate (*vénison, pérsonal, benévolent*)

Given [5], the second and third vowel of *marginal* and
harmony cannot be long underlyingly as otherwise they would
attract stress. Note that the main stresses in *màrginálity* and
hàrmónic do not prove that the accented vowel is underlyingly
long. Rather, they fall under different generalizations from [5]:
the suffixes *-ity* and *-ic* attract stress on the syllable preceding
them: *cf cómplex–compléxity, móral–morálity, méthod–methódic,
ángel–angélic*.[4] Therefore, the diphthongs that occur in [4c] must
be attributed to some other factor than underlying length. The
considerations given so far favour the assumption that a word like
marginal has the underlying representation /ma:ginæl/. It would,
first of all, undergo the stress rules – /má:ginæl/ – and then the
segmental rules would apply. Some late rules would reduce the
unstressed /æ/ to [ə]. In the case of *manager*, the evidence
concerning the underlying quality of the final vowel is quite
indirect. Essentially, given that line 1 of [4c] shows underlying
/æ/, line 2 fits the pattern if there is an underlying /e/ in
manager. The underlying /e/ does not, however, surface in any
form containing *manager*.

Now, if the above arguments concerning underlying vowels in
the examples of [4] are valid, and, if we attempt to relate the
vowels in [4A, B] to those of [4C], it looks as if we need to
postulate rules such as: *e → ij, æ → ej, ɔ → ow*. But these rules
are the mirror-images of the rules in [3], which is puzzling. It
does look as if there are underlying generalizations that we are
missing. So far, we have argued that to capture certain generalizations we needed to posit underlying forms which were
amalgams of portions of the surface allomorphs. Suppose, now,
that we allowed for the possibility that the underlying vowel
system includes segments which are not in one-to-one correspondence with those of [1] and which 'mediate' between the
surface variants. Let us assume that (leaving aside /ə, ə:, iə, eə,
uə/) the abstract vowel system of English contains only an
opposition between **long** and **short** vowels and that diphthongs
are created by rule within derivations. More specifically, limiting
ourselves to front vowels, let us suppose that the vowel which

mediates, in either direction, between [i] and [aj] is [i:], between [ij] and [e] is [e:] and between [ej] and [æ] is [æ:]. In line with this hypothesis, the phonological transcription of some representative examples is given in [6]:

[6]
[6a] *divine*   /divi:n/   [6b] *divinity*   /divi:n+iti/
     serene   /sere:n/   *serenity*   /sere:n+iti/
     sane   /sæ:n/   *sanity*   /sæ:n+iti/

The easiest task is to account for the forms in [6b]. The phonology of English includes a rule of shortening which applies in three contexts:

[7] Shortening

$$V \rightarrow [-\text{long}] / \underline{\hspace{1cm}} C_o \begin{cases} \begin{matrix} V\ C\ V \\ [-\text{str}] \\ C\ C \\ + ic \\ \ldots \end{matrix} \end{cases}$$

[7a] Trisyllabic Shortening
[7b] Cluster Shortening
[7c] -ic- Shortening

Subrule [7a], Trisyllabic Shortening, applies to any long vowel which is followed by two syllables, provided that the immediately adjacent syllable to the right is unstressed. This is the rule which takes care of /divi:n+iti/, etc. Subrule [7b] shortens a long vowel followed by two or more consonants and will take care of the B forms in [2] – *eg crucifixion*. Subrule [7c] applies before *-ic* and other suffixes and caters for the C forms in [2] – *eg satiric*. There are some well-known exceptions to [6a]: *obesity, hibernate, isolate.* Thus the second vowel in *obesity*, [owbísiti], should be short, *[owbésiti], but it is not. Such forms have to be marked in the lexicon as exceptions to the Shortening rule: [−rule 7].

Let us now turn to the base forms in [6a]. How can we derive [divajn] from /divi:n/, [sərijn] from /sere:n/ and [sejn] from /sæ:n/? The answer for Chomsky and Halle lies in the postulation of a rule of Vowel Shift, coupled with a process of glide-insertion (diphthongization), as an active component of the majority of dialects of English. The effect of the Vowel Shift is presented diagrammatically in [8]. The main steps in the deri-

[8] Vowel shift mutations

vation of *divine* would therefore be: /divi:n/ → divị:n (stress) → divæ:n (Vowel Shift) → divæ:jn (diphthongization). Such mutations are known to have occurred in the early sixteenth century in Southern British dialects. Yet, for most scholars, the Great Vowel Shift has been regarded as the crucial watershed separating Middle English from modern English. Wells (1982: Ch. 3), for example, speaks of a 'great divide' between the pre-1750 period in which the effects of the Vowel Shift were still affecting the segmental system and the modern period that followed. Therefore, the many *SPE*-based analyses defended in the literature offer a challenging claim in asserting that, far from being dead, these changes are still an integral part of modern English phonology.

The formalization of the Vowel Shift is given in [9]:

[9] Vowel Shift

$$
\begin{bmatrix} +\text{syll} \\ +\text{long} \end{bmatrix} \rightarrow
\begin{cases}
[-\alpha\text{high}] \ / \ \begin{bmatrix} \overline{\alpha\text{high}} \\ -\text{low} \end{bmatrix} & \text{[9a]} \\[2em]
[-\beta\text{low}] \ / \ \begin{bmatrix} \overline{\beta\text{low}} \\ -\text{high} \end{bmatrix} & \text{[9b]}
\end{cases}
$$

(Note that instead of giving two inputs to the rule of Vowel Shift, the features [high] and [low] have been shifted to the environment of the rule.) The Vowel Shift rule (VS hereafter) is restricted to long vowels. It includes two subparts often described as 'exchange rules' (or switching rules). Here [9a] interchanges the high and the mid vowels, while [9b] converts the new mid vowels (that is, the original high vowels) into low vowels, whereas the low vowels become mid. Diagrammatically, the two steps are given below in [10]:

[10]	i:	e:	æ:	ɔ:	o:	u:
STEP 1	e:	i:	___	___	u:	o
STEP 2	æ:	___	e:	o:	___	ɔ:

Following the VS rule, there is a process of glide-insertion formulated in [11], which epenthesizes /j/ after a long front vowel and /w/ after a long back vowel:

[11] Diphthongization

$$
\emptyset \rightarrow
\begin{bmatrix} -\text{syll} \\ +\text{high} \\ \alpha\text{back} \\ -\text{cons} \end{bmatrix} \ / \
\begin{bmatrix} +\text{syll} \\ +\text{long} \\ \alpha\text{back} \end{bmatrix} \_\_\_\_\_
$$

The conjunction of [10] and [11], and other rules, produces outputs such as [diva:jn], with a long first element for each diphthong. Although Halle (1977) offers such a transcription for the diphthongs, we will assume here, in line with *SPE* and Halle and Mohanan (1985), that the first element of a diphthong represents one unit of length (divine = [divajn]). This is achieved by the length adjustment rule in [11], which also tenses the first element of the diphthong:[5]

[12] Length adjustment rule (length adj.)

$$[+\text{syll}] \rightarrow \begin{bmatrix} -\text{long} \\ +\text{tense} \end{bmatrix} \Big/ \underline{\hspace{1.5cm}} \begin{bmatrix} -\text{syll} \\ -\text{cons} \end{bmatrix}$$

We need to return now to the forms in [4] which underpinned the search for deeper segmental representations. We have given some justification for taking the underlying form of the stem *marginal*, which occurs in *marginalia*, as /ma:ginæl/. The long vowel which appears before −*ia* is the result of a quite general rule which lengthens a low vowel followed by one consonant and a suffix made up of /i/ + an unstressed vowel (*ie* -*ia*, -*ian*, -*ious*, etc.):

[13] *CiV* lengthening

$$V \rightarrow [+\text{long}] \quad \Big/ \begin{bmatrix} \underline{\hspace{1cm}} \\ -\text{high} \end{bmatrix} C \text{ i} \begin{bmatrix} V \\ -\text{stress} \end{bmatrix}$$

This rule is responsible for the long vowels in *Caucasian, custodial, felonious, remedial*, etc.[6] and will lengthen the /æ/ in *marginalia* (/mà:ginǽliæ/ → /mæ̀:ginǽ:liæ/), the /e/ in *managerial* (/mæ̀nægér+iæl/ → /mæ̀nægé:riæl/) and so on. At that point, we can see that the conditions for VS are fulfilled since we have long vowels and the mutations /æ:/ → [e:] and /e:/ → [i:] will start us off on the route to the correct allophonic forms. Some sample derivations are given in [14] below to help the reader, who should note that the rules are **extrinsically** ordered (although only some of the motivation for given orders is provided here):

[14a]

	divine	*serene*	*sane*
Underlying form	/divi:n/	/sVre:n/	/sæ:n/
Stress assignment	diví:n	sVré:n	sǽ:n
CiV lengthening	————	————	————
Shortening	————	————	————
Vowel Shift	divǽ:n	sVrí:n	sé:n
Diphthongization	divæ:jn	sVrí:jn	sé:jn
Length adj.	divǽjn	sVríjn	séjn
Other rules	[divájn]	[səríjn]	[séjn]

[14b]

	sanity	*managerial*
UF	/sǽ:n + iti/	/mænVger + iæl/
Stress assignment	sǽ:n + iti	mænVgér + iæl
CiV lengthening	_____	mænVgé:r + iæl
Shortening	sǽn + iti	_____
Vowel Shift	_____	mænVgí:r + iæl
Diphthongization	_____	mænVgí:jr + iæl
Length adj.	_____	mænVgí:jr + iæl
Other rules	[sǽniti]	[mǽnəʤíjriəl]

'Other rules' is a blanket term for additional processes which apply within derivations: *eg* dearticulation, spelling out of the unspecified vowel as [ə] and various quality adjustments. Thus in [14a] the diphthong [æj] is further adjusted to [aj] giving the same starting-point to [aj] and [aw] as in a common variety of GA and RP. But it would remain as [æj] for other equally well-attested varieties. A statement should also be added so that every short vowel which has not been attributed the feature-value [+tense], will be specified as [−tense] by default. In other words, the output of our rules would correspond to narrow transcriptions such as [dɪvájn]–[dɪvínɪtɪ], for example. The reader is asked to do the necessary readjustments when the symbols of [ɪ] appear at the output of derivations.

The rules posited so far account for all the words which alternate given in [2] and [4] but they also apply to words that do not alternate. If we represented a word like *seed* as /si:d/ at the phonological level, it would be turned into [sæjd] by the battery of rules explored above. Instead of making the large set of words behaving in this manner exceptions to VS, we shall take advantage of the **free ride principle**. By representing *seed* as /se:d/, which is incidentally very close to the spelling, it will automatically fall prey to VS and be turned into the correct surface form [sijd].

Finally, we need to start taking a look at the back vowels. An example of application of the VS to back vowels is that of *harmonious*. This word is /ha:mɔn+iɔs/ underlyingly, and it goes through the following stages: /hà:mɔ́niɔs/ (stress) → /hà:mɔ́:niɔs/ (CiV lengthening) → /hà:mó:niɔs/ (VS) → /hà:mó:wniɔs/ (diphthongization) → [hà:mówniəs] (other rules). Parallel to the case of *seed* above is a word like *food*: its representation is /fo:d/ and it is turned into /fuwd/ by our battery of rules. In *SPE*, a word like *house* was represented as /hu:s/ underlyingly, which resembles some dialectal forms in Scottish English. The VS and diphthongization rules turned this into [hɔ:ws], an output which had to be corrected to [haws]. The VS rule was limited to front unrounded vowels and back rounded vowels. Halle (1977) and Halle and Mohanan (1985) do not restrict the VS rule in this manner. A word like *house* would now be represented as a high back unrounded vowel [ɨ] (IPA [ɯ]) which is automatically converted to [aw] by the processes discussed so far. What remains to be discussed is how the long vowels in *balm* and *baud* (see [1]) can be exempted from VS. We examine these questions at more leisure in 4.2.3.

4.2.2 Three arguments for the Vowel Shift

If VS was motivated only by the above alternations, it might be objected that the abstractness it entails is a rather high price to pay. But, as argued by Halle (1977), there are three areas where generalizations can be captured by accepting the above hypotheses. First of all, English exhibits a phenomenon of 'velar softening' whereby /k/ → /s/ and /g/ → /ǰ/ in the environments detailed in [10].

[15a] Halle (1977: 614)

	k	–	s	g	–	ǰ
	critic	–	criticism	analogue	–	analogy
	cynic	–	cynicism	rigour	–	rigid
	electric	–	electricity	ideologue	–	ideology
[15b]	critical	–	criticize	analogous	–	analogize
	reduction	–	reducent	tautologous	–	tautologize
	medicate	–	medicine	intellect[gt]	–	intelligentsia

The examples in (15a] suggest that we are dealing with a natural rule of 'palatalization' before the palatal vowel /i/. However, the examples in [15b], taken at surface value, force us to abandon such a rule. Velar softening seemingly takes place in disparate contexts since it also occurs before [e] (*intelligentsia*), schwa (as a reduced form of /e/ in *reducent*), and before [aj]. On the other hand, Velar Softening is blocked before [ej] in *medicate* and the schwa in *medical* (derived from /æ/). No generalization is possible. But, if we assume that Velar Softening applies **before** VS (and, obviously, schwa-reduction), the contexts turn out to be much more transparent. If we posit underlying forms along the lines of [16]:

[16] criticize /kritik + i:z/ analogize /ænælɔg + i:z/
reducent /redʌk + ent/ tautologize /tɔ:tɔlɔg + i:z/
medicate /medik + æ:t/ intelligentsia /intelig + entsiæ/

it can be seen, on the basis of [15a] and [16], that Velar Softening takes place in the context of a non-low front vowel (/i, i:, e/).

A motivated rule can be maintained, stated semi-formally in [17]:

[17] Velar Softening

$$\begin{bmatrix} k \\ g \end{bmatrix} \rightarrow \begin{bmatrix} s \\ \check{j} \end{bmatrix} / \underline{\hspace{1cm}} \begin{bmatrix} V \\ -\text{low} \\ -\text{back} \end{bmatrix}$$

The existence of Velar Softening explains why *manager* was given as /mænæger/ above: the underlying /g/ can take a free ride on rule [17]) and surface as [ǰ] as required. But note that only morphemes marked as [+latinate] will undergo this rule: we do not want *kill* /kil/ to be turned into [sil]!

The second argument in favour of a synchronic VS rule comes from the special class of words in [18] made up of bound morphemes (prefix+stem).

[18a]	consign–resign	[18b]	incite–recite
	consist–resist		incipient–recipient
	consult–result		concede–recede
	consent–resent		concession–procession

We see that, in [18a], if the first morpheme ends with a vowel, an underlying /s/ is voiced. Rule [19] provides an informal characterization of this process (where = is the boundary between such bound morphemes):

[19] s-voicing rule
$$s \rightarrow z / V = \underline{\hspace{1cm}}$$

However, the forms in [18b] seem to provide systematic exceptions to [19]. The exception is only resolved if we consider that all the bound stems in [18b] have underlying /k/'s which undergo Velar Softening **after** [19] has applied. Some partial derivations of relevant forms are given in [20] to help the reader.

[20]

	Consist	Resist	Concede	Recede
	kVn=sist	ri=sist	kVn=ke:d	ri=ke:d
Stress	í	í	é:	é:
s-voicing		z		
Velar Softening			s	s
Vowel Shift			í:	í:
Diphthongization			í:j	í:j
Other rules	[kənsíst]	[rizíst]	[kənsíjd]	[risíjd]

The third set of data supporting a rule of Velar Softening is provided by the vowel alternations in the 'strong' (alias 'irregular') verbs in English. Only a few examples are considered here (see Halle and Mohanan, 1985: 104–14, for extensive discussion). Consider the present–past patterns exhibited in [21].

[21a] lie–lay [aj]–[ej]; choose–chose [uw]–[ow];
  eat–ate [ijt]–[ejt], swim–swam [i]–[æ];
[21b] find–found, bind–bound [aj]–[aw]
  break–broke [ej]–[ow]

No coherent picture seems to emerge and typical treatments split all these alternations into separate boxes corresponding to the surface alternations. For instance, in Quirk *et al.* (1985) *swim–swam* belongs to class 7A which groups together *begin, drink, ring, shrink, sing, sink, spring* and *stink*. But, if we reconstruct the pre-VS form for each of the alternants of [21], a very different picture calls our attention:

[22a] /li:/–/læ:/, /čo:z/–/čɔ:z/
  /e:t/–æ:t/, /swim/–/swæm/
[22b] /fi:Nd/– /fi:Nd/, /bi:Nd/–/bɨ:Nd/
  /bræ:k/–/brɔ:k/

Let us take the present form as the unmarked stem form. All the past tenses in [22a] can be obtained by making the stem vowel [+low], and the forms in [22b] by making the stem vowel [+back]. In the [22b] set, the simplicity of the backing rule supports the earlier suggestion that surface [aw] derives from the high back unrounded vowel /ɨ/. Let us assume that in the lexicon each 'strong' verb is marked with an arbitrary diacritic which will be used to trigger the correct allomorph in the past context. Say, for instance, that the lexical representation of *lie* is as in [23]:

[23] Partial lexical entry of *lie*
[23a] Phonological and morphological information
  /li:/, [+D]/ past
[23b] Syntactic and semantic information

If the surface representation of a sentence contains the verb *find* with the tense marker [+past], then the information in [23], will be used by rules of allomorphy such as the ones in [24] to derive the underlying forms in [22a].

[24] Past tense allomorphy
[24a] V → [+low] / [_____ , +past, +D] 'drink'
[24b] V → [+back] / [_____, +past, +F] 'find'

Features like [+D] and [+F] are arbitrary symbols whose function is merely to trigger the correct allomorphy rules. The allomorphy rules are 'readjustment rules' mediating between syntax, the lexicon and the phonological component. The standard phonological rules will apply after [24] and crank out the correct surface variant.

If this is accepted a great deal of apparently arbitrary verbal and nominal morphology (*eg* alternations such as *foot–feet, mouse–mice* beside the strong verbs), can be seen to fall within the scope of the VS.

4.2.3 A further look at the back vowels

We have seen that the back unrounded vowels included /i:/, from which [aw] could be derived via VS and diphthongization. In addition, two back rounded vowels have been mentioned: /ɔ:/ whose reflex is [ow] (*aroma, harmonious*) and /o:/ whose reflex is [uw] (*food*). Several questions still need to be answered: (i) If we represent *balm* as /ba:m/ and *baud* as /bɔ:d/, how come they do not undergo VS? (ii) How can we account for alternations such as [aw]–[ʌ] (*profound–profundity*), on the one hand, and [(y)uw]–[ʌ] (*assume–assumption*–see [2]/[4] on the other? (iii) How can we represent /ɔj/ underlyingly?

The representation of *balm* as [ba:m] and *baud* as [bo:d] given in [1] is, in fact, different from the one adopted by Halle and Mohanan who transcribe these sounds as [aₜ] and [oₜ] – that is, tense short [a] and [o]. Since they do not postulate a tense–lax opposition underlyingly, but only a long–short opposition, these segments are represented as /a/ and /o/ underlyingly and become tense by a late rule (*a/o*-tensing) shared by GA and RP. The reason that /a/ and /o/ fail to be affected by VS is simply that they are short. In GA, /o/ is also lowered so that *baud* is represented as [bɔₜd] by Halle and Mohanan (vs. [bɔ:d] in [1]). We shall, however, see that this treatment is quite problematic for RP.

The alternation *profound–profundity* can be related to earlier discussions of [aw]. If the underlying form of this diphthong is /i:/, /profi:nd/ will be turned into [profawnd] as expected. In the case of *profundity*, /prVfi:nd+iti/ – [prəfʌnditi], the underlying /i/ falls prey to Trisyllabic Shortening (rule [7a] and becomes /i/. A rule of i-lowering is postulated whereby /i/ → [ʌ]. The alternation *assume–assumption* exhibits a short [ʌ] in the derived noun. If we posit that *assume* is underlyingly /æsʌ:m/, neglecting the internal morphological structure for expository reasons, we can derive both forms as follows. In the case of *assumption*, Cluster Shortening (rule [7b]) applies and long /ʌ:/ becomes /ʌ/, which is the desired result. On the other hand, for *assume*, the long /ʌ:/ undergoes VS and diphthongization: [iw]. If, like Halle and Mohanan, we posit a rule of *j-preposing* ([iw] → [jiw]) and a rule of *i-rounding* ([jiw] → [juw]) the surface form will be derived. By the principle of **free ride**, which simplifies the underlying inventory, a word like *cube* will also be represented as /kʌ:b/ and turned into [kjuwb] by exactly the same set of rules.

We can finally turn to the status of [ɔj] (*boy*) underlyingly. Two solutions are available to us. We can treat [ɔj] as underlying /y:/ (*boy* = /by:/) – that is, a long rounded front vowel – or as underlying /u:/ (*boy* = /bu:/) since this vowel is still free. The first solution leads to the correct surface quality if, in addition to VS (by: → bœ:) and diphthongization (bœ: → bœj), we posit an œ → ɔ retraction rule (bœj → bɔj). Its drawback is that it leads to a marked underlying system with an isolated front rounded vowel ([y]). The second solution also requires some extra machinery since by VS and diphthongization we get sequences such as /bu:/ → [bɔ:] → [bɔ:w]. A glide switching rule (w → j) is required so that [bɔw] → [bɔj]. An /u:/ source is, however, preferred by Halle and Mohanan. It makes the system more symmetrical since otherwise /u:/ would be missing and it receives support from alternations such as *join–juncture, destroy–destruction*, etc.

The underlying system of English, following Halle and Mohanan, is as given in [25].

[25] Short vowels

	−back		+back	
			−round	+round
+high −low	/i/	bit	/ɨ/ venue[7]	/u/ book
−high −low	/e/	bet	/ʌ/ but	/o/ baud
−high +low	/æ/	bat	/a/ balm	/ɔ/ bomb

[26] Long vowels

	−back		+back	
			−round	+round
+high −low	/i:/	bite	/ɨ:/ profound	/u:/ boy
−high −low	/e:/	seed	/ʌ:/ cube	/o:/ boot
−high +low	/æ:/	bait		/ɔ:/ boat

4.2.4 The linking 'r' and panlectalism

To complete our picture of the segmental phonology of English, one further phenomenon characterizing the conservative variety of RP as described by Jones and Gimson will be examined: the so-called 'linking r'. Mohanan (1985, 1986) mentions alternations such as the ones in [27]. (All the examples are Mohanan's but his transcription has been modified to fit in with [1].)

[27]   Linking /r/ (Mohanan 1986: 36)
[27a] soar [so:] vs. soaring [so:riŋ]
[27b] bear [beə], bearness [beənes] vs. bearest [beərəst]
[27c] star [sta:], starless [sta:les] vs. starry [sta:ri]
          The star [sta:r] is dirty
[27d] saw [so:], sawing [so:iŋ]
[27e] idea [ajdiə], ideology [ajdiɔləǰi]
          (cf nonsense form *bearology* [beərɔləǰi])
[27f]   spa [spa:]; The spa [spa:] is dirty

The standard way of handling the alternations in [27] in generative phonology is to separate the words of RP into two classes. The words in [27a–c] have an underlying /r/: *star* /star/. This /r/ is deleted before a pause or when the next word or morpheme begins with a consonant. The rule can be formulated as follows:

[28]   /r/-deletion
$$r \rightarrow \emptyset / \underline{\hspace{1cm}} \left\{ \begin{array}{l} \#_0 \ C \\ \# \ \# \end{array} \right\}$$

On the other hand, the words in [27d–f] end in a vowel underlyingly. Once again, we notice that the underlying forms postulated for RP are close to historically older forms and to the spelling, and that, in morpheme-final position at least, the difference between a rhotic accent such as GA and a non-rhotic accent such as RP is only superficial. One of the claims of *SPE* was that it seemed likely 'that the underlying lexical (or phonological) representations must be common to all English dialects, with rare exceptions, and that much of the basic framework of rules must be common as well' (*p* x). In other words, what is often referred to as a 'panlectal' account was claimed to be feasible. The validation of that claim was left to future research and it is interesting to see that Halle (1977) and Halle and Mohanan (1985) do attempt to demonstrate that major dialects of English conform to the guess that *SPE* was hazarding. By and large, according to these accounts, the modern dialects of English share the same underlying forms and the same set of core processes such as VS, diphthongization and Velar Softening. The differences in surface realizations between two dialects, say A and B, are usually attributable to additional rules in A and not in B (*eg* r-deletion), to different orderings of rules (*cf* Ch. 1) and to slightly different rule formulations or allophonic processes (*eg* [ow], the surface reflex of /ɔ:/, is further realized as [əʊ] in RP, as [ʌʊ] in Cockney, etc.).

In the next section, however, we examine the phenomenon of 'intrusive r' where the correct synchronic account is as an inversion of /r/-deletion before moving on to a critical assessment of the above assumptions.

4.2.5 The intrusive 'r'

The account of linking /r/ as absence of r-deletion is quite explicitly restricted by Mohanan to the conservative non-rhotic variety of RP described by Jones and Gimson (or to the New England accent of American English covered in Kenyon and Knott 1944). It is not meant to include the phenomenon of 'intrusive r' – that is, the pronunciation of a non-historical 'r' in sequences such as *idea*[r] *of it*. The intrusive [r] is used both across word boundaries (as above) and across morpheme boundaries (*draw*[r]*ing*). While it is often frowned upon by purists, the use of intrusive [r] is described by Hughes and Trudgill (1979: 32) as 'so automatic that speakers are usually unaware that they do it. Generally, too, we can say that the tendency is now so widespread that if a speaker with a southeastern-type English accent fails to use intrusive [r], especially after /ə/ or /ɪə/, he is very probably a foreigner.' They point out, however, that many RP speakers are careful not to use an intrusive [r] within words.

Now, for speakers using an intrusive [r], is there any reason to postulate a distinction between a linking [r] in *soar up* [sɔ:rʌp] and an intrusive [r] in *draw up* [drɔ:rʌp]? Hughes and Trudgill do not take this course and postulate a rule of [r]-insertion which can be informally stated as follows:

[29] [r]-insertion

$$\emptyset \rightarrow r \; / \; [ə, ə:, ɪə, eə, oə, a:, ɔ:] \; \#_o \; V$$

Rule [29] accounts for [r]'s in *idea*[r] *of it*, *better*[r] *and better*, *Sir*[r] *Andrew*, *milieu*[r] *is*, *India*[r] *and*, *here*[r] *is*, *bear*[r] *it*, *bore*[r] *it*, *Shah*[r] *of Persia*, *far*[r] *away*, and so on (*cf* too Wells 1982: 222–7).

But what evidence do we have that all these [r]'s could still not be underlying? After all, how can we know that native speakers do not analyse any word-final /ə/ and /a:/ as /ər/ and /a:r/

underlyingly: *eg* /iːdiər/ *idea*, /betər/ *better*, /šaːr/ *Shah*, /faːr/ *far*, etc. One type of evidence mentioned by Wells is a tendency by some Southern English speakers to intrude an [r] in foreign names and expressions. Some examples he quotes are *déjà*[r] *ici, ich bin ja*[r] *auch fertig* and choirmasters are reported as having to admonish against *gloria*[r] *in excelsis* and, more demotically, *viva*[r] *España*. But, of course, one might still object that these foreign endings are reanalysed according to the native template which requires word-final /r/ after /aː/ underlyingly.

Fortunately, there is another type of evidence which appears incontrovertible. An intrusive [r] is attested after schwas which are reduced variants of full vowels such as *tomato*[r] *and cucumber, the window*[r] *isn't clean, I don't know* [dʌnər] *if he is* (Wells 1982: 226–7). Since the full form (*eg* [now] *know*) does not permit intrusive [r], the [r] must be inserted only after [ow] has been weakened to [ə]. Trudgill (1974: 162) gives data of this type for another non-rhotic dialect of English (Norwich): he reports *out to*[r] *eat* and *quarter to*[r] *eight* with a schwa in both occurrences of *to*. The evidence therefore favours for these phenomena a rule of insertion which is the opposite of the historical rule. This is usually referred to as **rule inversion**. Many reanalyses of *SPE*-style treatments in terms of rule inversion have been put forward by linguists who favour concreteness in phonology (see 4.4).

4.3 Objections to the Vowel Shift and Velar Softening

The above sections have presented as objectively as possible an analysis of the vowel system of English which attributes a central role to rules such as VS and Velar Softening. We must now turn to possible lines of objection to such a treatment. The first problem is how to square this account with the facts of language acquisition. Wells (1982: 188) puts the problem like this:

> It implies that a child who hears everyday words such as *knee, piece, bean* (which have no derivationally related words with other vowels) somehow realizes that he must store them lexically with the phonological representations /neː/, /peːs/, /beːn/ since otherwise the VS rule, needed for pairs of related words which a child mostly does not learn till puberty, would not allow them to have the correct phonetic output.

But, of course, this cannot quite be what Halle and his associates would claim. They are well aware that many of the alternations underpinning their analysis are learned late. Furthermore, the knowledge of given alternations is going to vary from individual to individual. However, we must assume that, for all mature speakers of English, there are enough of these alternations to justify the radical abstracting away from the surface proposed earlier. The learner will initially set up /niː/ as the underlying form of *knee*. But, at some point, **reanalysis** will take place on the basis of exposure to a large set of alternations such as those in [2] and [4] above. One source for reanalysis has been claimed to be the learning of the strong verb patterns (Kiparsky and Menn 1977).

Much seems to depend, in critiques of VS, on what faculties linguists are ready to attribute to the mind. On the one hand, some scholars would reject such an account as unnecessary and implausible: humans prefer to memorize as much as possible and keep to surface patterns and they find 'concrete' solutions (*cf* 4.4) better than 'abstract' ones. The human mind is a special kind of computer which prefers to maximize storage and use fairly simple operations rather than store a small number of primitives organized in terms of a complex body of rules (Jaeger 1986 and the references therein). On the other hand, Halle and Clements (1983: 2) suggest that various facets of language behaviour favour a more abstract approach. If asked to rank pseudo-words like *sprash, sknap, strup, sdrut* on a scale ranging from those that could easily be adopted in English to those which could not, we would certainly rank *sprash* and *strup* high and *sknap* and *sdrut* low. Halle and Clements (1983: 2) suggest that our knowledge of phonotactic patterns cannot depend on our having been made to memorize the list of all admissible onsets of English words. The answer to the puzzle of where this knowledge stems from is that: 'our memory is so constructed that when we memorize words, we automatically also abstract away their structural regularities. We suppose, to be specific, that human storage space for memorizing words is at a premium so that every word must be memorized in a maximally economical form in which redundant (predictable) properties are eliminated.'

Because of our lack of understanding of how the mind actually organizes linguistic data, I will try and steer away in what follows from any aprioristic position on the question. It may well be that language is stored in a mixed manner or that different subjects adopt different strategies when confronted with similar bodies of data. Even if this is the case, descriptions *à la SPE* can be argued to provide an abstract characterization of the declarative knowledge that speakers of English have of portions of their own language. I see nothing reprehensible in a process of idealization which asks, at least as an initial step: if a speaker knew all this data and connected all these forms, what would the system look like? At the same time, the account has to be potentially vulnerable, to be compatible with psycholinguistic evidence, if this is available, and to require a minimum of *ad hoc* machinery to work. Let us, therefore, look at a number of areas where the postulation of VS can be, or has been, criticized.

One of the major areas where the abstract analysis presented above seems to be unsatisfactory is with respect to the back vowels. Let us start with the vowels in *balm* and *baud* in RP. The transcription adopted initially for these words was /baːm/ and /boːd/, to keep close to Halle and Mohanan's (1985) analysis. But, later on, it was mentioned that these authors represent these sounds as short /a/ and /o/ underlyingly and tense them by a late rule. In their account, the surface representation of these words is [baₜm] and [boₜd]. Let us leave aside the question of the quality of these vowels which in some accounts of RP are transcribed [bɑːm] and [bɔːd] (Gimson 1980; Wells 1982) since the adoption of a binary framework makes comparisons quite difficult. The major problem is the length of these vowels.

Halle and Mohanan (1985: 75) do mention in a footnote that Jones's *EPD* (1977) represents the vowel in *balm* as long and they could have added that words like *baud* (*eg laud, law, staunch*) also have a long vowel in Jones's *EPD* (as, in fact, reflected in Halle's (1977) transcriptions). The selection of tension over length as a characteristic of these two vowels at a near-realizational level is odd if we limit the discussion as Halle and Mohanan do to conservative RP. If we take the pair [æ]–[aː] (*Pam–palm*) in this (probably moribund) variety of English, the quantity difference is always there whereas a tension difference might be absent. Thus Jones in *Outline of English Phonetics* (1964: 72, fn. 15) stresses that [æ] is normally tense. Of course, there is nothing that would prevent Halle and Mohanan from adding a rule that made tense [o] and [a] in RP long or from reformulating the rule of *a/o*-tensing as a rule of lengthening. But the question remains: why should these two vowels be classified as short underlyingly? The answer seems to lie in a desire to make VS look more general than it really is. Since VS applies only to long vowels, by making /oː/ and /aː/ short, they are automatically skipped and the rule can be maintained in its generality. But what tells us that these two vowels are not short underlyingly? One good reason for questioning this assumption is provided by the phonotactics of English: like all long vowels and diphthongs, /aː/ and /oː/ are acceptable in final position within monosyllables: *cf law* [lo:], *raw* [ro:], *shah* [ša:], *bra* [bra:]. By contrast, the short vowels are not allowed in the same environment: *[lɔ], *[rɔ], *[šæ], *[bræ]. It does look as if, at least for RP[8], VS should be restricted, as in *SPE*, to vowels which agree in backness and rounding. This way /a:/ words will not have to be treated as exceptional but /o:/ words (*baud*), which agree in backness and rounding, will have to be marked as [−VS].

The diphthong [ɔj] has also proved problematic ever since *SPE*. In *SPE*, this vowel was analysed as underlying /œ:/, a much-criticized analysis. The new analysis by Halle and Mohanan, who derive [ɔj] from /u:/, is not much more compelling since, once VS and diphthongization have taken place (/u:/ → [ɔw]), an *ad hoc* glide-switch is needed [ɔw] → [ɔj].[9] But what about alternations such as *adjoin–adjunction, destroy–destruction, join–junction–juncture* quoted by Halle and Mohanan as supporting a /u:/ source for [ɔj]?

The first thing to note is that while a short vowel in the second syllable of *eg destruction* can be motivated as the result of Cluster Shortening [7b], the vowel we expect from underlying /u:/ (assuming the stem is /de=stru:+k/) should be [u] not [ʌ]. A special rule will be needed to unround and lower this [u] to [ʌ]. Even if we assume that the lowering could take a free ride on ɨ-lowering (used to derive [prəfʌnditi] < prəfɨnditi < prVfɨ:nditi – see 4.2.3), it is not the case that ɨ-lowering is independently motivated. The underlying form will also require an underlying /k/ which does not surface when *adjoin* is used in isolation. If we further look at nominalizations in *-ion* (*-ation, -ion, -tion, -ution, -ition*), as documented in Aronoff (1976: 99–110), it is clear that any analysis must make room for a great deal of arbitrary stem allomorphy. For instance, stems in *X-olve* appear as *X-olution* (*solve–solution, resolve–resolution, revolve–revolution*) where [v] alternates with [u], whereas we get [v] alternating with [p] in *receive–reception, conceive–conception*, etc. It is at least plausible that the relation between [ɔj] and [ʌk] in these words might be determined by a phonologically arbitrary rule of allomorphy (Aronoff 1976: 110) without increasing the depth of phonological representations.

If we now turn to the alternation [aw]–[ʌ] mentioned in 4.2.3, the situation is hardly better. Halle (1977) tells us that the only examples of related words known to him are:

[30] profound–profundity; pronounce–pronunciation; similarly
      announce, denounce, etc.); South–Southern;
      abound–abundant, flower–flourish, tower–turret

We have pointed out that the phonological derivation of the longer forms required an *ad hoc* rule of i-lowering. But, even if we disregarded this, it is clear that the forms in [30] are, as Halle would probably admit, a hodge-podge. Doublets such as *tower–turret* are generally unconvincing. Forms such as *South–Southern* are related but the [aw]–[ʌ] alternation does not derive from general phonological processes. That is, there are no independent **phonological** rules predicting [ʌ] from /u:/ in the context __ Cə(C)C#. As for the derived word *pronunciation*, very many speakers pronounce it as [prənàwnsiéišən] and the spelling *pronounciation* is so common that some teachers of linguistics at university level make a point of drawing students' attention to it. This 'error' is revealing: it is expected if many of the phenomena covered above are largely morphologized and speakers prefer a transparent derivative to fairly arbitrary stem-allomorphy. On the other hand, if the whole underlying system of English is structured so as to make VS pivotal, why should speakers break quite general rules in order to produce such an aberrant form?

The arguments presented above suggest that the treatment of the back vowels entailed by the postulation of VS as a core process of modern English leaves something to be desired as it stands. The reservations expressed above concerning the analysis of English offered in the wake of *SPE* are echoed in a series of recent psycholinguistic experiments aimed at probing the reality of VS (*cf* Jaeger 1986; McCawley 1986; Wang and Derwing 1986). These experiments, which complete some well-known earlier studies (*eg* Ohala 1974; Steinberg and Krohn 1975), involve production tests, preference tests, recall tests and concept formation tests and thus tap a wide range of verbal abilities. Some of the findings which have emerged from this research can be summarized as follows:

1. Subjects exhibit a preference for non-VS alternations over VS alternations. For example *obtain+atory*, if elicited, will be typically pronounced [əbtéinətri] rather than *obtanatory* [əbt@nətri] predicted on the basis of *exclaim–exclamatory*, *inflame–inflammatory* and the morphemic make-up of *obtain*. This does not fit in with the claim that VS is a general phonological rule which requires all underlying representations to be restructured to reflect its effect.

2. There is a great deal of inter-subject and inter-pattern variation which once again argues against VS as being learned as a single, broad generalization by speakers.

3. The back vowel alternations [ɔj]–[ʌ], [aw]–[ʌ] are generally rejected whereas [(j)uw]–[ʌ] and [ow]–[ɔ] are accepted. On the other hand, alternations such as [uw]–[ɔ] (*fool–folly*), [ɔj]–[ɔ] (*joy–jolly*), [ɔj]–[ow] (*voice–vocal*) and even [aw]–[ɔ] (*astound–astonish*), which are attested for very few pairs of words and not included in the most recent versions of VS, fare somewhat better than [ɔj]–[ʌ] and [aw]–[ʌ].
4. For a number of subjects, there is a dramatic improvement in performance if the tests are linked with the presentation of written material. (Note that the experiments did not rest on spelling.)

All the authors quoted above share the belief that the relations that speakers establish between VS pairs are to a large extent **orthographical** and appear to be based on the 'long-short' spelling rule commonly taught in schools. The rejection of pairs modelled on *profound–profundity* or *join–juncture* with radical spelling changes as opposed to the acceptance of *produce–production* (with ⟨u⟩ in the spelling in each case) fits in well with this hypothesis. Just as crucially, the preference for poorly attested alternations such as [aw]–[ɔ] or [ɔj]–[ɔ] could correspond to an implicit reference to spellings ⟨ou⟩–⟨o⟩ and ⟨oy⟩–⟨o⟩ with first letter identity (see the careful argumentation in Wang and Derwing 1986: 110–13).

Whether the explanation of the knowledge speakers exhibit of some vowel alternation pairs is ultimately to be attributed to orthography is an issue which I leave open.[10] The above-mentioned experiments do **not**, however, prove that speakers fail to establish relations between words involving various allomorphic changes. Indeed, McCawley's study shows precisely the opposite. For a majority group, VS alternations such as [ij]–[e] (*serene–serenity*) present no real obstacle to the perception of two words as morphologically related. What they suggest, however, is that an account involving VS as a pivot of modern English phonology, while compatible with a subset of possible alternations, is clearly at odds with other posited relations.

The authors of the various experiments reported above recommend a wholesale abandonment of VS and, in some cases, of the phonological paradigm developed in the wake of *SPE*. Many critics of VS (*eg* Jaeger 1986) seem committed to a 'concrete' view of phonology as advocated in Natural Generative Phonology (NGP), for instance. Since NGP was constructed very much in reaction to *SPE*, whose analyses were felt to reach a 'comble de l'absurdité', it will be useful to take a close look at this model before returning briefly to the VS issue in 4.5.

4.4 Natural Generative Phonology

In the 1970s, a strong reaction took place against *SPE*-type analyses on the part of a number of linguists grouped under a variety of banners. One famous example is that of NGP, a movement spearheaded by Hooper and Vennemann which spawned a great deaL of descriptive and theoretical work during the 1970s and early 1980s. The most complete exposition of NGP is Hooper's 1976 book, *An Introduction to Natural Generative Phonology* (*INGP* hereafter). A detailed application of basic principles of NGP to a well-studied language is Tranel's *Concreteness in Generative Phonology: Evidence from French* (1981).

Natural generative phonology starts from the assumption that abstractness should be banned from the grammar. Rules involving unpronounceable elements are not acceptable since 'the hypothesis may not be tested' (*INGP p* 13). Underlying forms must bear a much more direct relationship to surface phonetic representations. There are, however, several positions which have been advocated conforming with this need for more concrete representations (sometimes called the STRONG NATURAL- NESS CONDITION):

1. One solution is to legislate that the underlying representation of a morpheme must be one of the surface allomorphs. This, for instance, would allow /s/ or /z/ or /iz/ as possible underliers of the plural allomorphs. It would also force the analyst to choose between /divajn/ or /divin/ as underlying forms of the morpheme *divine*, but would rule out /divi:n/ which is not a possible realization of this morpheme. By definition, 'fictitious' segments such as Halle and Mohanan's high back unrounded /ɨ:/ (*profound*) that speakers of English cannot pronounce would be excluded.

2. A more radical alternative solution advocated by Vennemann (1974) dispenses with underlying forms altogether. The lexicon for Vennemann is made up of complete words, not morphemes, in their surface phonetic forms (although most examples he gives are in phonemic representations). Phonological rules function as redundancy statements. To quote Vennemann (1974: 359) on the plural suffix in English:

   What is the 'underlying representation', /s/, /z/ or /iz/? What are the rules? In the system I am discussing, the situation is this: Since plural nouns are words, and words are in the lexicon, and are there fully specified, plural nouns are there fully specified. Thus, /s/, /z/, and /iz/ all occur in the lexicon, e.g.

in *cops* /kʰɑps/, *cobs* /kɑbz/, and *arches* /arčiz/. The rule is: The plural suffix is /s/ if the singular ends in a voiceless non-sibilant, the plural suffix is /z/ if the singular ends in a voiced non-sibilant; the plural suffix is /iz/ after a sibilant. Formulated in this way (the traditional formulation to be sure), the rule is always 'true on the surface' and involves no ordering problems.

3. A third position advocated by Hooper (1975, 1976) is less concrete than Vennemann. She argues that the conditions on abstractness should be placed on rules rather than representations. More specifically, she thinks that 'all rules should express transparent surface generalizations, generalizations that are true for all surface forms and that, furthermore, express the relation between surface forms in the most direct manner possible' (*INGP p* 13) This principle is called the TRUE GENERALIZATION CONDITION (TGC) and a consequence of it is that 'No phonological features appear in the lexical representations of a morpheme except those that occur in some surface representation of that morpheme' (*p* 20). She does, however, assume that underlying forms are never directly accessible, and archisegmental representations are acceptable since they do not violate the TGC. An archisegmental representation stands in a subset relation to the surface realizations and does not contain features not present on the surface.

Whichever of these positions is adopted, it is quite clear that other assumptions have to be made about the organization of the phonological component if some version of the strong naturalness condition is to be imposed. All versions of NGP share the following two features:

1. Many rules that are presented as **phonological** (e.g. the VS in English) in the *SPE* paradigm are, on the contrary, argued to be **morpho(phono)logical** in NGP and, in some cases, not to be rules at all. The phonological component should be split into blocks of different rule-types and divisions along traditional lines such as that between morphophonemic and allophonic rules make a comeback.
2. The only order which is allowed is **intrinsic** ordering (all rules apply in random sequential order – that is, a rule can apply whenever its structural description is met) unless the ordering can be predicted on universal grounds. This is called the NO ORDERING CONDITION (NOC). Vennemann (1974: 372) puts this in rather provocative terms: 'Writing

grammars with ordered rules is a systematic way of lying about the language.'

The work within NGP has led to some interesting reanalyses of data which had been used to support abstract analyses. One example borrowed from a dialect of Spanish is presented in 4.4.1–2. The organization of the NGP model is summarized in 4.4.3 and a discussion of NGP and concreteness is offered in 4.4.4 and 4.4.5.

4.4.1 Rule morphologization in Andalusian Spanish

Many dialects of Spanish have a five-vowel inventory /i, e, a, o, u/ at the phonemic level and share the tendency for vowels to have two realizations: an open variant in closed syllables and a close variant in open syllables. The open–close realizations are interpreted in terms of tension by Hooper (1974, 1976), who bases herself on Saporta (1965). Some illustrations involving /e/ are given in [31]:

[31] /lej/   [lɛj]   *ley*   'law'
     /le/   [le]   *le*   'him/you'
     /lerdo/   [lɛrdo]   *lerdo*   'slow'
     /piedra/   [pjedra]   *piedra*   'stone'
     /ekuestre/ [ekwɛstre] *ecuestre*   'equestrian'

The rule laxing vowels in closed syllables would have to be stated as [32] in the standard framework:

[32] Vowel laxing (non-syllabic version)

$$[+\text{syll}] \rightarrow [-\text{tense}] \, / \, \underline{\quad} \, [-\text{syll}] \left\{ \begin{array}{c} \# \\ [-\text{syll}] \end{array} \right\}$$

where $[-\text{syll}][-\text{syll}] \neq$ obstruent + liquid/glide

The reason for the disjunction on the right is that *SPE* does not recognize the syllable as a unit of analysis. A closed syllable, in Spanish, has to be defined as involving either one non-syllabic before a word-boundary (*eg ley* in [31]) or two non-syllabics (*eg lerdo*) provided they are not an obstruent followed by a liquid or a glide. But what do a word-boundary and a consonant have in common to be grouped between braces? And why should a liquid + obstruent (*eg* /rd/) have a different effect from an obstruent + liquid (*eg* /dr/) in an intervocalic position? Not recognizing syllable boundaries forces a complex statement on us. Moreover, this type of rule is **recurrent**: we have already seen a similar disjunction at work in the case of /r/-deletion in English (4.2.4) and mid-vowel lowering in Midi French (Ch. 1). If we take the NA principle stated at the end of 2.10 seriously, our notation should optimize the expression of recurrent groupings.

The solution advocated soon after the publication of *SPE* by Hooper (1972) and Vennemann (1972b), among others,[11] involved the recourse to syllable boundaries ($) which were assigned by universal rules. If we divide the words of [31] into syllable stretches as in [33]:

[33] /lej/   [lɛj]
     /le/   [le]
     /lerdo$/   [lɛrdo]
     /piedra$/   [piedra]
     /$e$kuestre/ [ekwɛstre]

the statement of vowel laxing can become much simpler:

[34] Vowel laxing (syllabic version)
     $[+syll] \rightarrow [-tense] / \_\_ [-syll] \$$

But what about tense vowels in open syllables? Assuming the underlying vowel-phonemes are not marked for [+/−tense], all we need to do to derive surface forms is add rule [35] to our battery of processes:

[35] $[+syll] \rightarrow [+tense] / \_\_ \$$

It can be seen that the structural description of [35] is more general than that of [34] and rules standing in this kind of general are often conflated as a single Elsewhere rule:

[36] $[+syll] \rightarrow \begin{Bmatrix} [-tense] / \_\_ [syll] \$ \\ [+tense] \text{ elsewhere} \end{Bmatrix}$

[36] is no more than a convenient way of stating two rules plus an ordering. If you rewrite [35] as [37] below (which is a simpler formulation since the $ boundary has been left out) and let the more general case [37] apply **after** the more specific one [34]:

[37] Vowel tensing
     $[+syll] \rightarrow [+tense]$

you get the effect of [36]. The simpler formulation of [37], compared with [35], might be claimed to be offset by the fact that [34] and [37] must apply in this order whereas rules [34] and [35] do not need to be ordered. However, the ordering between [34] and [37] need not be stated **extrinsically**. Rather, NGP assumes the validity of a universal principle of Proper Inclusion Precedence (Koutsoudas, Sanders and Noll 1974), or Elsewhere Condition (Kiparsky 1973a) such that, if the SD of a rule A properly includes the SD of a rule B, then A applies first. 'Properly includes' means roughly that A contains all the information contained in B and more. Proper Inclusion Precedence is widely

accepted in generative phonology and will play an important role
in Underspecification Theory (Ch. 5) under the name 'Elsewhere
Condition'.

The application of vowel laxing [36] in Spanish dialects is
particularly striking in noun, adjective and verb morphology. The
classical statement of noun and adjective plural formation is that
/s/ is added to a vowel-final stem and /es/ to a consonant-final
stem. The second person singular of several verb tenses is also
marked by /s/. One can therefore observe alternations like those
in [38], where the verbal forms are in the present indicative:

[38] [klase]–[klasɛs] *clase–clases* 'class-sg'–'class-pl'
     [tɔnto]–[tɔntɔs] *tonto–tontos* 'stupid-sg'–'stupid-pl'
     [kor:e]–[kor:ɛs] *corre–corres* 'run-3sg'–'run-2sg'

Now, various dialects of Spanish, particularly those spoken in
southern Spain and in many parts of America, weaken the
pronunciation of syllable-final /s/ to the point where it is either
reduced to [h] or lost entirely. This has profound repercussions
on the surface morphology of these dialects. In those situations
where [s] is the marker of morphological categories in standard
Spanish (*cf* [38]), these dialects can end up relying on vowel
quality alone as a morphological differentiator. Thus, *clases,
tontos* and *corros* have been claimed to be respectively pronounceable as [klasɛ], [tɔntɔ] and [kor:ɛ] in accents which allow
final /s/ deletion (Uruguay). Saporta (1965) provides an *SPE*-
style account (called 'the standard analysis' from now on) of such
dialectal pronunciations. He assumes underlying forms with
plural /s/ and then posits a rule of syllable-final S-deletion which
is **extrinsically** ordered after vowel laxing:

[39] S-deletion
     s → ∅ / __ $

The plural noun *clases*, for instance, will go through the
following stages: /klase+s/ → [klasɛs] (vowel lowering) →
[klasɛ] (S-deletion). Note that S-deletion if applied first would
bleed vowel lowering (*ie* deprive it of input).[12] Saporta's analysis
has to be rejected in NGP since **extrinsinc** ordering is banned by
the NOC and the presence of a lax vowel in the absence of its
phonetic conditioning contravenes the TGC. Instead vowel laxing
would have to be formulated in morphological terms – *eg* as in
[40] which does not cover verbal morphology:

[40] [+syll] → [−tense] / $\left[\dfrac{}{+\text{plural}} \right]$ #

Either analysis accounts for the facts but Hooper (1974, 1976) in order to settle the matter prefers to turn her attention to the Andalusian dialects of Spain which exhibit similar phenomena and are well documented.

For ease of reference, it should be pointed out that S-deletion from the angle of the 'standard analysis' should really be split up into two rules: a rule of weakening of /s/ to [h] and a rule of [h] deletion formulated below.[13]

[41] S-aspiration

$$s \rightarrow h / \underline{\quad} \$$$

[42] H-deletion

$$h \rightarrow \emptyset$$

In Western Andalusia, Hooper (1976: 34) claims that the rule of vowel laxing is live but that, when the /s/ is dropped, a close (tense) vowel appears. According to her, deletion of a final /s/ 'causes restructuring of any lexical items that contain /s/, including the plural morpheme and the second person singular morpheme for most tenses'. She further observes that while the potential for a situation which would be describable by extrinsic ordering exists in this dialect, this potential is not realized and the path chosen is that of phonetic transparency.

Hooper then turns her attention to the Eastern Granada dialect of Andalusian (called Granadino) which, as is shown below, exhibits extensive vowel laxing in plural forms. In this dialect, the tense-lax difference is not related to syllable structure but governed entirely by morphological categories. Basing herself on Alonso, Vicente and Canellada (1950) she provides the examples in [43] below:[14]

[43] Orthography	Singular	Plural	Gloss
pedazo	[peðaθo]	[pɛðäθɔ]	piece
alto	[alto]	[ältɔʰ]	tall
cabeza	[kaβeθa]	[käβɛθä]	head
selva	[selva]	[sɛlvä]	forest
lobo	[loβo]	[lɔβɔʰ]	wolf
tonto	[tonto]	[tɔntɔ]	stupid
piso	[piso]	[pɪsɔʰ]	floor
fin	[fin]	[fɪnɛʰ]	end
grupo	[grupo]	[grʊpɔʰ]	group

At first sight, it might look as if these examples could be accounted for as in the standard analysis: plural is marked by an /s/ underlyingly, this /s/ triggers vowel laxing and then there is a right-to-left spreading of the [−tense] value. Note that in this dialect, /s/ is categorically weakened to [h], and then [h] is

variably deleted. But words such as [selva] 'forest-sg' suggest that
vowel laxing does not operate systematically in closed syllables
as otherwise [sɛlva] would be attested. Moreover, there are
examples which are odd, as Hooper points out, if we make this
assumption. In Castilian Spanish, the word for 'Tuesday' has the
same form, *martes*, in the singular and the plural (*el martes*
'Tuesdays' and *los martes* 'On Tuesdays'). But in the Granada
dialect the singular of *martes* is [marte] and the plural [märtɛ].
If a final [s] triggers laxing, it is odd that an etymological or
underlying [s] should have been dropped without surface trace
in the singular. The restructuring is less odd if we interpret laxing
as morphologically conditioned.

The morphological conditioning is also attested in the verbal
morphology: for instance, *corro* 'I run' is [kor:o] whereas *corres*
'you-sg run' is [kɔr:ɛ]. Once again, Hooper points out, we find
that underlying or etymological /s/'s have been wiped out
without causing surface laxing since Castilian *es* /es/, third
singular present of *ser* 'to be', is pronounced [e] in the Granada
dialect. Finally, Hooper stresses that according to Alonso,
Vicente and Canellada (1950) the phonetic difference between
tense and lax vowels is much more striking in the Granada dialect
than in Castilian. This makes sense if the distinction has taken
on a semantic significance as marker of separate morphological
categories. Her conclusion is that vowel laxing is a property of
whole phonological words (including, as she shows, verb + clitic
sequences) and is triggered by morphosyntactic features such as
[+plural] in nouns and adjectives and second person singular or
first person plural in verbs. She even remarks that there is no
reason to see laxing as spreading leftwards from the last syllable
since a few words, rather idiosyncratically, appear to have a lax
vowel in the last syllable which does not trigger laxing to the left:
eg Rafael [rafaɛl] or *Tomás* [tomä^h] (see further, 7.1.5).

How does the situation in the Eastern dialect relate to derivations such as the ones put forward by Saporta for Uruguayan?
Hooper's thesis is that rule morphologization did not take place
after but **before** the phonetic motivation for vowel laxing had
been obscured or lost. She assumes an intermediate (unattested)
stage where one had for instance:

[44] Orthography Singular Plural

		Singular	Plural
pedazo	'piece'	[peðaθo]	[peðaθɔ^h]
cabeza	'head'	[kaβeθa]	[kaβeθä^h]
fin	'end'	[fɪn]	[finɛ^h]

The plural forms in [44] could be dealt with by supposing that vowel lowering is triggered by underlying /s/'s (or [ʰ] for that matter). But Hooper asserts that, at such a plausible stage, /s/ would no longer be the plural marker and speakers would adopt a morphological rule like [45]:

[45] Granada plural harmony

$$V \rightarrow [-\text{tense}] \, / \, \left[\underline{\hspace{2cm}} \atop +\text{plural} \right] \quad (h) \quad \#$$

As she puts it, morphologization does not take place **because** the phonetic environment for a rule is lost, rather the phonetic environment is allowed to be lost **because** the rule has been morphologized.

4.4.2 A re-examination of Andalusian Spanish

Hooper's analysis of Andalusian Spanish gives a plausible example of the way speakers of a language can reanalyse surface forms and move to other generalizations than historically based ones. But, as the set of data and argumentation stand, they do not quite deliver the death-blow to the standard analysis that Hooper seems to have in mind. The situation concerning Western dialects is rather difficult to assess since the sources she gives do not offer a proper discussion of the phenomena at hand and many recent studies on Andalusian Spanish contain only the briefest of remarks on the matter (eg Carbonero 1982: 54). Some data given in Vicente (1967) do suggest, however, that her presentation is over-simplified.

The first difficulty with Hooper's account is that she does not discuss the significance of alternations involving [s] at morpheme-boundaries in Spanish. Hooper does mention the existence of pairs such as those in [46], (with neutralization of the /θ/–/s/ opposition of Castilian Spanish) in the varieties under discussion (Alonso, Vicente and Canellada 1950: 215):

[46] | Orthography | | Singular | Plural |
|---|---|---|---|
| voz | 'voice' | [bɔʰ] | [bɔsɛʰ] |
| tos | 'cough' | [tɔʰ] | [tɔsɛ] |

These alternations support underlying forms like [bos] for *voz* and /tos/ for *tos* (which do not break the TGC) with weakening of final /s/ to [h] by S-aspiration and possible disappearance of the [h] by H-deletion. The surfacing of a word-final /s/ is, in general, well attested both inflectionally and derivationally: *inglés* 'English'–*inglesa* 'English-fem'–*inglesismo* 'anglicism', *atrás* 'behind' (adv)–*atrasado* 'behind' (adj), and so on.[15] But Hooper does not seem to relate the [ʰ] which appears in the plural to underlying /s/ seemingly because this would break the TGC since the hypothetical plural morpheme /(e)s/ does not surface as such in Granadino and extrinsic order is required for Uruguayan-like data.

But, here, we have to bear in mind that, if plural /s/ does not surface, it is because it is at the right-hand edge of words and pluralization does not allow further suffixation. Nevertheless, the standard analysis does make a prediction: should a form be lexicalized as a plural and tolerate further affixation, the adding of a vowel-initial suffix would make the /s/ resurface. The structure of Spanish morphology, which is normally theme-based, appears to restrict this possibility to end-stressed nouns. Thus, if we imagine a group of singers calling themselves *los papás* ('the daddies'), which is a good candidate for lexicalization as a plural, the standard analysis would predict the possibility of derivatives such as *papasero* as in *un peinado papasero* (a daddies-like hairstyle). One of my colleagues, who is a Granadino speaker, assures me that this is a potential word and that one would observe the pronunciations: *papás* [päpäʰ] and *papasero* [papasero]. Hooper makes no prediction and has to have two stories concerning final [ʰ]'s. But one fact needs one explanation.

The difference between Granada Andalusian and other dialects is that Granadino has two markers of the plural: final /s/ and vowel harmony (see 7.1.5 for further remarks on the latter). The data suggest the possibility of an eventual loss of underlying plural /s/'s but this has not happened yet. So, when Hooper says of the stage represented in [44] above that speakers would perforce analyse the laxing in a hypothetical intermediary stage, as illustrated in [peðaθɔʰ], as morphologically based, thus discounting the aspiration, this is no more than a *petitio principii*.

Let us now turn to the ordering question. Hooper rejects derivations such as /klase+s/ → [klasɛ+s] (vowel laxing) → [klasɛʰ] (S-aspiration) → [klasɛ] (H-deletion) for Uruguayan as not conforming to the NOC. However, such forms are attested in Vásquez (1953) on which Saporta (1965) is based. She does not provide any real reason for not including these data, and presenting two dialects which function differently does not justify the exclusion. But, let us assume, for the sake of the argument, that the data in Vásquez does not deserve credence. It turns out that there are similar examples in Western Andalusian, if we reconsider pronunciations like [rafaɛl] or [tomäʰ] quoted earlier.

Hooper claims that there are no hints in Alonso, Vicente and Canellada (1950) as to why we have an open vowel in such singular forms and that only seven forms appear in their corpus of 200 words: [tɔʰ] *tos* 'cough', [mjɛʰ] *miel* 'honey', [mjɛʰ] *mies* 'grain', [pjɛ] *pie* 'foot', *color* 'colour' [kɔlɔr] and *portier* 'door-curtain' [pɔrtjɛ(r)]. Her figure is incorrect since the corpus also mentions a lax vowel in the final syllable of such singular forms as *cantor, fiel, coser*, although some of these words have a tense vowel as alternative pronunciation. If we look at these examples from the standard perpective, they all involve a consonant (r, l, s) whose (variable) deletion is well attested in the reference dialect but which is present in inflection and derivation (*eg* [kantɔ]–[kantɔrɛ] *cantor–cantores* 'singer'–'singers'). One explanation for the low vowel in final syllables of singular forms (*cf* Vicente, 1967: 292, 318–19 and Alonso, Vicente and Canellada 1950: 216) on the context of /o/-lowering despite Hooper's claim) is that Eastern Andalusian dialects include a rule of laxing in final closed syllables (except before /n/):

[47] Final syllable laxing
    V → [-tense] / ___C #

Note that [47] has to precede extrinsically the deletion of /r, l/, S-aspiration and H-deletion. Now, this rule, from the data, is either variable within idiolects or across speakers. Be that as it may, it renders unnecessary the postulation of a phonemic contrast for examples like *piel* 'skin' which can be pronounced [pjɛ] and contrasts on the surface with [pje] *pie* 'foot-sg'. Yet, the simple explanation that [47] provides is banned by NGP since it breaks the NOC and the TGC.

A striking illustration of the same phenomenon is provided by some Eastern dialects where phonemic /a/ is fronted to [ɛ] before underlying non-nasal consonants in word-final position. To quote Vicente (1967: 294): 'In this region, the singular–plural opposition is *graná–granÉ; boluntá–boluntÉ*. Moreover, one can observe the changes of this stressed final *-á* brought about by *-l, -r, θ*: ɔʰpitÉ–ɔʰpitale; oliβÉ–oliβárÉ, capÉ–capáse (capaz–capazes)' (my translation with regularized vowel symbols). These alternations are quite easy to explain if we posit the following ordered rules for the dialect in question (most of them have already been covered and are repeated here for convenience):

[48a] Vowel laxing [34]
[48b] Vowel tensing [37]
[48c] ä → ɛ / ___C #
[48d] S-aspiration [41]
[48e] H-deletion [42]
[48f] l, r → Ø / ___#

A sample derivation is given below [49], where capital letters are used to indicate that the vowels are not marked for tension underlyingly:

[49]	*ospital* 'hospital'	*ospitales* 'hospitals'
	\$Os\$pI\$tAl\$	\$Os\$pI\$tA\$lEs
[49a]	ɔspItäl	ɔspItAlɛs
[49b]	ɔspitäl	ɔspitalɛs
[49c]	ɔspitɛl	———
[49d]	ɔʰpitɛl	ɔʰpitalɛʰ
[49e]	———	ɔʰpitalɛ
[49f]	ɔʰpitɛ	
output	[ɔʰpitɛ]	[ɔʰpitalɛ]

Once again, such derivations would have to be banned by NGP, and alternations like those quoted by Vicente would have to reflect a different phonemicization from other Andalusian dialects or different morphophonological rules. But, the *SPE* framework offers an elegant and insightful way of dealing with them. The Andalusian data, if we widen the scope of our investigation, do not support NGP as much as Hooper claims, and, while deserving further investigation, are compatible with an abstract analysis. Before we turn to a general evaluation of NGP's basic principles, let us examine how the phonological component is structured for NGP.

4.4.3 Rule types in NGP
As mentioned before, NGP assumes that the rule system does not form a monolithic block but rather that rules should be divided into different types. The rule blocks adopted in *INGP* by Hooper (1976) are given below going from the lexicon to phonetic forms:

(I) VIA RULES
A via rule is a type of lexical rule of the form

aj ⟨⟶⟩ i

relating for instance *divine* and *divinity*. The forms *divine* and *divinity* are entered in their full form in the lexicon and assumed to be linked by the via rule above. Other rules of the same type would relate *serene–serenity* (ij ⟨⟶⟩ e), *sign–signify* (aj ⟨⟶⟩ ig), etc. These rules are assumed to vary from speaker to speaker. It is quite possible that some speakers of English do not have any of the above.

(II) SPELL-OUT RULES

As in the standard model, these are rules which give an underlying shape to morphosyntactic categories (*eg* in English, *plural* → # z #).

(III) MP RULES

MP rules correspond to traditional morphophonological (or morphophonemic) rules. They change features in environments described in morphosyntactic or lexical terms. They are often inverted rules. For instance, Learned Backing which accounts for alternations like *clair–clarté* [ε]–[a] or *honneur–honorifier* [æ]–[ɔ] in French is an inverted rule in the formulation of 3.2. It retracts /a/ to [ε] and /ɔ/ to [œ], whereas the historical rule, as reflected in Schane's standard analysis (1968), was a rule of fronting. It is an MP rule since it applies to the last vowel of morphemes marked for an arbitrary feature [+L(earned)] in the presence of morphemes which are themselves marked [+L] (see Dell and Selkirk 1978; Durand and Lyche, 1978).

(IV) SANDHI RULES

Rules which make reference to word-boundaries but to no other non-phonetic information (*eg* features such as [+/− Latinate, +/− noun]), are considered as sandhi rules. Both /r/-deletion and [r]-insertion in English are sandhi rules.

(V) P RULES

P rules are phonological rules proper. They are defined as rules which 'describe the way the surface contrastive features will be manifested in a phonetic environment' and which mirror 'processes governed by the physical properties of the vocal tract' (Hooper 1976: 16). P rules cannot refer to morphological or syntactic boundaries. The discussion of phonetic variation in Chapter 7 of *INGP* places P rules within a hierarchy of styles from most formal to most casual (labelled Largo, Andante, Allegretto, Presto). Largo will contain forms corresponding to the most explicit style (roughly, the citation form of a word, *eg* [bɪkɔz] 'because'). Each style is a block or cycle of rules which applies to the output of the higher cycle and the general movement is towards reduction of the phonetic string (*eg* pronunciations like [bɪkəz] → [bɪxəz] → [pxəz] as reported in Brown, 1977: Ch. 4). Hooper (1976: 113) gives an example from Brazilian Portuguese. In Largo, we observe rules of palatalization, which palatalize /t/ and /d/ before /i/ and nasalization, which nasalizes a vowel before a nasal consonant. In Andante, final unstressed vowels become high by a process of vowel raising. This triggers a reapplication of palatalization. In Allegretto, high front vowels are deleted after palatal consonants (vowel deletion). She exemplifies these processes with the variants of *teatrinho* 'little theatre' and *morte* 'death':

[50]	*teatrinho*	*morte*	rules
Largo	[čiatrĩno]	[mɔhte]	patalatization
			nasalization
Andante	[čiatrĩnu]	[mɔhči]	vowel raising
			palatalization
Allegretto	[čatrĩnu]	[mɔhč]	vowel deletion

4.4.4 The NOC, the TGC and underlying forms

In 4.4.2, a number of queries were raised concerning the conclusions that Hooper draws from Andalusian dialects. The difficulty with the NGP model is that it does not just correct what have been seen as 'the *SPE* excesses' but ends up banning much less deep representations and derivations (*eg* the derivation of [pjɛ], *pie*, suggested in 4.4.2 and many of the derivations of Ch. 1). In effect, the strictness of these conditions, as correctly observed by Dresher (1981), is more or less identical to versions of autonomous and taxonomic phonemics which rely heavily on surface contrasts.

Thus, the derivation discussed in 1.2.4 of *writer–rider* in dialects of the [rajɾər]–[raːjɾər] type would have to be banned because it involves rule ordering and also violates the TGC. The pronunciation [rajɾər] (/rajt+ər/) shows that the lengthening rule is not surface-true: if a vowel is lengthened in front of every voiced consonant, why is it not in front of [ɾ]? Although Hooper (1976) does not discuss this problem, Rudes (1976) treats the *writer–rider* problem from the point of view of NGP and ends up postulating in /aj/–/aːj/ contrast underlyingly – a solution which was rejected in 1.2.4 as missing obvious generalizations. It will be recalled that it was pointed out that the two relevant rules (lengthening and flapping) are independently required and that the underlying forms chosen directly reflect the morphological structure. In fact, the listing of all forms in quasi-phonetic representation, advocated by Vennemann, runs into trouble here. Speakers have no difficulty deriving new agentive *-er* or inflectional *-ing* forms from verbs ending in /t/, and, at the point at which a new word is derived, the underlying form will be of the form /Xt+ər/ or /Xt+iŋ/. The assumption that once such words have been made up they must all be memorized in their surface form is gratuitous and does not really enlighten us. Moreover, in this case, for speakers who always flap underlying /t,d/'s, it is clear that an underlying form like /rajt+ər/ does not correspond to any of the surface representations. All the possible constraints on underlying forms summarized at the beginning of 4.4 seem to be inadequate here.

In fact, it is not even clear that Hooper's own treatment is internally consistent since the Brazilian Portuguese example quoted earlier violates the TGC (as noted by Kenstowicz and Kisseberth 1979: 232): the rule of palatalization (t → č / __ i) is not surface-true once the /i/ has been deleted (*cf* [čatrīnu] *teatrinho*).

Where, however, Hooper is correct is in arguing against fully specified representations defended by Vennemann and *SPE*. Let us go back to the Andalusian data and assume that a young Granadino knows the singular form [mono] ('monkey') but has never heard the plural. This child, to be sure, will have no trouble producing [mɔnɔʰ] as a plural form. If the singular has been memorized in its surface phonetic form, to derive the plural, all the [+tense] vowels will have to be made [−tense] by the plural redundancy rule behaving in a dynamic manner and, then, the plural form will be stored in its surface phonetic representation. Such feature-change is unnecessary if underlying forms are partially specified (*ie* if the underlying vowels of *mono* are not specified for [+/−tense]). The plural is created by extending the feature-specification (see *eg* derivation [49] above) and not by changing features. Neither the phonetic representation of the singular nor that of the plural need be memorized as such.

This type of example is far from isolated and slips of the tongue have some bearing on the issue (*cf* 1.2.1). Consider a common type of lapsus: *pik slimp* [pikslimp] for *pink slip* [piŋkslip]. If we assume fully specified underlying forms, the error involves transposing an [m] from the second word to the first one and then letting this [m] be changed into a velar [ŋ]. On the assumption that slips of the tongue can (but need not always) be located at a more abstract level than phonetic form, and that the underlying representation of *pink* is /piNk/ with a nasal archiphoneme, this slip of the tongue is a simple transposition, which feeds the rule of Homorganic Nasal Assimilation (*cf* 3.5.1).

Many variants of concrete phonology seem singularly unaware of this question. They appear to assume that feature-value changes do not induce abstractness. But a rule such as [+tense] → [−tense] is not a simple operation: the notation [−back], as stressed in Chapter 2, stands for an attribute-value pair ⟨back,

$-\rangle$ and changing it to $\langle$back, $+\rangle$ involves two elementary transformations: the value '+' is deleted and the value '−' inserted (see Gazdar *et al* 1985; Bresnan 1982 on the formal definition of features). At this point, of course, one can retreat to the position that, as in current theories of syntax (GB, LFG, GPSG), no mutation should take place. But, phonology is not syntax. Fast speech phenomena (see *eg* the Brazilian Portuguese data of 4.4.3 or the data in Brown 1977) show that the correspondence between surface and underlying structures is very often many-to-many not one-to-one with insertions, deletions and quite radical mutations (but see 7.4).

The above development reinforces our conclusions of Chapter 3. Underlying representations need not be fully specified and many rules should be seen as feature-filling rather than feature changing. However, underlying representations need not correspond to surface representations in a one-to-one manner. Natural Generative Phonology accepts discrepancies between underlying forms and surface forms at the 'phonetic' end but hankers after one-to-one correspondence at the (morpho)phonological level. As we have seen, this does not just dispose of the VS or Velar Softening in the synchronic analysis of English but also of much less abstract representations which seem well motivated.

The derivational issue received a great deal of attention in the 1970s, as reflected in advanced textbooks such as Kenstowicz and Kisseberth (1979) or Sommerstein (1977). There is no doubt that most generative phonologists would prefer, **other things being equal**, to adopt derivations where no extrinsic ordering statements have to be made. To some extent the adoption of a stratal organization and recourse to universal conventions such as the Elsewhere principle will reduce the bulk of extrinsic ordering statements that have to be made but these are still seen as essential in a great deal of current research. By and large, the debates which raged in linguistic journals until comparatively recently (see *eg* Koutsoudas, Sanders and Noll 1974 and Koutsoudas 1980 vs. Noske, Schinkel and Smith 1982) have abated. Many phonologists, feeling that an impasse has been reached, have turned their attention once again to the representational issue or the link-up between phonology and morphology as detailed in the following chapters.

4.4.5 Evaluation of strata in NGP

The rule-blocks adopted in NGP (4.4.3) represent an interesting but not uncontroversial theory of phonological organization. The notion of P rule is somewhat problematic since it is questionable that phonological features and processes should be intended to reflect directly physical properties of the vocal tract as claimed by Hooper. Thus, extrinsic allophones which depend on mechanical adjustments of articulators are, appropriately, not covered in phonological descriptions. Moreover, the splitting of P rules into well-defined compartments (largo, andante, allegretto) is debatable. It may be useful for descriptive purposes or for sociolinguistic research to set up various registers, but there is little evidence of the ultimate validity of such categories (see *eg* Durand 1986b; Encrevé 1983, 1988, for a critique of registers in accounting for French liaison). In so far as extrinsic ordering is dispensed with by recourse to such blocks, one ought to be sceptical of the claim that all the ordering is intrinsic.

Of the other processes, the notion of via rule seems the most problematic. The striking feature of via rules, as they are formulated in the literature, is their vagueness: two segments are mentioned on both sides of the arrow without any attempt at making contexts more precise. The function of the double arrow in these statements is unclear since even a single arrow always expresses the relationship between two levels of representation. If the intention is to suggest that via rules allow speakers to go in either direction more easily than for other rules, then this is quite debatable. Back-formations typically proceed by clipping rather than return to putative underlying forms: *eg self-destruct*, not *self-destroy*, from *self-destruction*, where *stroy-struct* would seem to be a good candidate to via rule status (*cf* Bauer 1983: 230–2 on back-formations).

In one version of NGP, via rules are replaced by disjunctive statements within individual entries (Hudson 1974). For instance, the entry for *divine* would be something like the following:

$$[51] \ \text{div} \begin{bmatrix} i \\ aj \end{bmatrix} n \rightarrow \begin{bmatrix} i/ \ \underline{\quad} \ \text{-ation, - atory, -ity, -ize} \\ \text{elsewhere} \end{bmatrix}$$

But such representations are very much the same as for suppletive alternations such as *go–went*. Hudson defends this on the basis of Anaximander's principle: since no clear-cut distinction exists between minor alternations and 'irregular' forms all alternations should be treated in the same way, all the more so as they are claimed to be subject to historical levelling in the same way. But, the historical stance taken by NGP is debatable and Anaximander's principle ultimately leads to most phonological rules being reduced to disjunctive lists (see Dresher 1981, on both points). For instance, the statement of the 'regular' plural of English becomes no different from that of *foot–feet* or *go–went*. At that point the model loses much of its plausibility. It is true that there is no clear-cut line between various types of alternation. But the reduction of most alternations to lists is no more insightful than the opposite extreme of trying to find one common underlying denominator for all words which are related semantically and historically (*eg father–paternal*).

The merit of NGP has been to force phonologists to think hard about their phonological constructs. It is striking that even non-concrete generative accounts of well-studied languages like French, for instance, have moved away from the remote representations licensed in Schane (1968). The studies of Dell (1979a) and Dell and Selkirk (1978) show conclusively that many alternations covered in early work are too idiosyncratic to deal with, or are morphologically conditioned and represent cases of rule-inversion. As was stressed above, there is still no consensus in the field concerning the derivational issue. The fight for concreteness goes on under other banners – *eg* Natural Morphology (see *eg* Dressler 1985). In so far as such theories adhere to some version of biuniqueness, they would fall under the same criticisms as are formulated here against NGP. But the attempt to set up motivated stratal organization, despite the criticism of NGP above, is a worthwhile one and one (quite different) version of it – Lexical Phonology – will be considered in the next chapter.

4.5 In defence of the Vowel Shift

In 4.3, we presented a number of weaknesses of the so-called 'abstract' analysis of English and considered some possible objections to the VS as a live synchronic rule. On the other hand, the trend of 4.4.4 was to argue *contra* NGP that phonology is inherently 'abstract': neither the underlying representations nor the narrow transcriptions of phonology correspond directly to the physical record of speech. A global rejection of Halle and Mohanan's (1985) account of VS on the grounds that /ɨː/ is **unpronounceable** misses the point to the extent that phonological representations (of all schools) as they stand are, in a sense, **unpronounceable**. It is the task of a phonetic theory to relate the representations of the phonologist to a model of production and perception which will itself be an abstract characterization of the encoding–decoding process.

There is no need to shy away from all criticisms of VS. On the other hand, we should note that behind one line of criticism is the implicit assumption that *SPE*-style analyses are wrong because of the number of exceptions to various rules or the need for lexical marking of items. But, in the main, only low phonetic rules such as aspiration are in fact exceptionless. The regular plural formation (*cf* 1.3.2.2) has exceptions (*mouse–mice, sheep–sheep*). Yet, most linguists would agree that the rule is worth stating and, for instance, sheds light on distinctive feature theory.

Another problem is that the evidence which has been cited in favour of rules such as VS, Velar Softening, etc. is itself part of a larger set of data which bears on the analysis but has, perforce, been omitted from 4.2. For instance, in 1.3.2.1, it was argued that a more insightful statement of the phonotactics of English was possible if the sequence [juw] in *few, cue, beauty*, etc. was considered as a single vocalic unit. This does not prove the correctness of analysing [juw] as /iː/ underlyingly, but it reduces the arbitrariness of the rule of j-insertion mentioned in 4.2.3 and makes the /i/-assumption compatible with interesting claims concerning the sequential structures in English. Indeed, it was argued that the phonotactics of English was best stated at an abstract level and not by reference to the attested strings.

To give a final example, Halle's argument in favour of VS, based on the difference between *consign–resign* vs. *incite–recite*, is often objected to on the grounds that the morphemes making up such words are not 'salient'. It is true that, semantically, *con-, re-, -in- -sist, -cite*, etc. do not have independent meanings. But, as convincingly argued in Aronoff (1976), there are good morphological and phonological grounds for assigning internal structure to these words. First of all, by giving all these Latinate words a prefix-stem structure we account for the fact that the stem behaves uniformly in front of the same suffixes: for instance, corresponding to *resign, consign, assign* with [sajn] ([zajn] by s-voicing) we find *resignation, consignation, assignation* with [sig] ([zig]). Similarly, *deduce, induce, reduce, conduce* give rise to *deduction, induction, reduction, conduction*. Secondly, prefix-stem verbs are stressed on the stem: *consígn, dedúce, resíst*, etc. And nouns derived from these verbs by zero derivation are stressed on the prefix: *áccess, pérmit, próduce*, etc.[16]

Once these boundary divisions are accepted, we note that further sub-regularities can be captured. For instance, Aronoff (1976) points out that, within prefix=stem forms, nominalizations in *-tion* and *-ion* (*subsumption, rebellion*) are root governed. That is, while *-ation* (*cf realization, formation, evocation*) is very productive and not sensitive to the phonological or morphological structures of the base, *-ion* and *-tion* are morphologically governed. They require a Latinate prefix=stem root. But, this does not mean that the selection is phonologically arbitrary. Thus, Aronoff argues that +*tion* is only selected by non-coronals (that is, labials and velars). Consider his set of examples:

[52] duce   deduce   deduction
      scribe   prescribe   prescription
      ceive   conceive   conception
      deem   redeem   redemption
      sorb   absorb   absorption
      stroy   destroy   destruction

As will be obvious to the reader, this small generalization can only be maintained if the morphological affixation (or the RR characterizing the words in [52]) is formulated at an abstract underlying level. That is, we need to assume underlying forms such as /dʌk(e)/, /scri:b/, /ke:v/, /de:m/, /sɔrb/ (GA), /stru:k/. The *-tion* nouns in [52] will be obtained by application of Trisyllabic Shortening and other rules of the phonology, whereas the verbs will undergo VS and other attendant processes.[17]

The problem in assessing the *SPE* analysis, and its more recent extensions, is that we are confronted with a kind of 'package deal'. An intricate set of regularities and sub-regularities can be captured if we assume underlying forms making rules such as Trisyllabic Shortening, VS and Velar Softening pivotal to English phonology. This is at a price since, as was argued earlier, the back vowel set is not totally well behaved and various 'fictitious' segments or *ad hoc* rules have to be posited for the account to work. On the other hand, opponents of VS appear to evacuate the problem completely by locking regularities within lexical entries. And to explain the fact that speakers of English can create new forms such as *morile* → *morility* ([mərajl]–[məriliti]), they usually appeal to perceptual strategies which are unspecified).

In the absence of a detailed alternative to the segmental analysis of English put forward by Halle and his associates, I shall continue to take for granted the basic correctness of the overall hypothesis. In any case, this analysis is assumed in the innovative work in Lexical Phonology presented in Chapter 5, and this framework offers a treatment of a number of facts which were recalcitrant within the *SPE* paradigm. The fate of generative phonology need not rest, however, on VS. The wealth of descriptive and theoretical work spawned by *SPE*, a small part of which is considered here, attests to the fruitfulness of the generative paradigm.

Notes

1. There is a vast literature on the segmental phonology of English within the generative framework. The best compendium on the immediate post-*SPE* scene is Goyvaerts and Pullum (1975). References to more recent work based on Lexical or Metrical Phonology will be given in due course.

2. *SPE* has only a tense–lax position underlyingly and considers tension and length as correlated. On the other hand, Halle (1977) uses both tension and length distinctively, but [+/−tense] is a contrastive feature for long low vowels only. The presentation here follows as much as possible Halle and Mohanan (1985) for whom only length is distinctive and [+/−tense] differences are introduced by rules. As their analysis is non-linear, and requires concepts covered later, a number of expository simplifications have been necessary. However, the main arguments for abstract underlying representations in English can be presented in partial independence of current notation.

3. For an excellent resumé of English stress in the *SPE* mould, see Hogg and McCully (1987: Ch.1).

4. There are a few exceptions to the statement made here about *-ic*: *Árabic, aríthmetic, ársenic, Cátholic, héretic, lúnatic, pólitic, rhétoric.* Guierre (1979, 1984), who uses a quantified, corpus-based approach, gives a percentage of exceptions of 2 per cent in 1000 words.

5. See Halle and Mohanan, 1985: 73 for a more general formulation of tensing.

6. There are lexically marked exceptions to *CiV* Lengthening such as *Italian, gaseous, rebellious*, and systematic exceptions involving *-ion* (*companion, procession, discussion*): see Halle and Mohanan (1985: 78) and Rubach (1984b).

7. The justification for /i/ in *venue* is given in Halle and Mohanan (1985) and will not be discussed here.

8. The argument here on /a:/ and /o:/ is constructed with reference to RP but, as far as I can tell, also applies to varieties of GA as described by Moulton (1977).

9. Halle and Mohanan (1985: 102) claim that it is sufficient to front [w], which would result in [ɥ], 'since the glide is normally rounded and the traditional representation of the diphthong with an unrounded glide reflects the absence in English of a phonetic contrast between rounded and unrounded front glides rather than phonetic reality'. As far as RP is concerned, this contradicts what solid descriptivists such as Jones (1964: 436–8) or Gimson

(1980: 132–4) claim in connection with [ɔj]. Both Jones and Gimson give the second element of the diphthong as [e] or [ë] in narrow transcription, and Jones warns Dutch and German learners against finishing the diphthong with rounded lips as they commonly do. A two-feature mutation [+back, +round] → [−back, −round] does seem required to handle the w → j switch in many accents of English, and the attempt to minimize the arbitrariness of this change is not fully convincing.

10. At least one advocate of VS has explicitly attributed a heuristic role to spelling knowledge in the setting-up of underlying forms (Michaels 1980). There is no reason to deny that, in literate societies, a close link can exist between spelling and pronunciation (*cf* spelling pronunciations such as [foːhed] which is undermining the earlier [fɔrid]). I shall assume, however, that phonological accounts should not depend on knowledge by speakers of the spelling conventions of their own language.

11. The need for integrating the syllable within generative phonology was stressed very early on by authors such as Fudge (1969) and Dependency Phonologists (*cf* J. M. Anderson 1969; J. M. Anderson and Jones 1974; Durand, 1976). But these linguists stressed the need for integrating the syllable as a suprasegmental unit and not in the guise of boundaries: see Chapter 6.

12. The two rules could be applied simultaneously if Koutsoudas, Sanders and Noll's (1974) theory of rule application was accepted. It is assumed in NGP that ordering is **sequential**.

13. For most Latin-American varieties, S-aspiration and H-deletion are variable and syllable-final /s/'s still surface. Moreover, some dialects have extended /s/ deletion to syllable-initial position, although this is statistically infrequent (*cf* Hammond 1980).

14. The symbols are mine. Alonso, Vicente and Canellada (1950) use a variety of diacritics: *eg* é = my [e], è = my [ɛ], etc. The most controversial sound is the *a* used in plural forms. Alonso, Vicente and Canellada describe it as more fronted and having more jaw-opening than the *a* used in plural forms and they transcribe plural *a* as [ä] (hence my [ä]). I shall continue to use tense −lax to refer to the distinction: it is not clear that this is totally adequate nor that [ATR] would fare any better (see the discussions in Vicente 1967: 291 and in Salvador 1977, who proposes a new feature [+/−projected] to handle the singular–plural alternations).

15. It is important to note that the alternations from Granadino are not restricted to the lower strata of local society. As stressed by Alonso, Vicente and Canellada even the most cultivated speakers (*eg* university professors) exhibit the phenomena in question and the vocabulary they cite does not necessarily depart from standard Spanish. For further evidence, see the texts in Carbonero (1982).

16. The rule stressing the stem in prefix-stem Latinate words is given by Guierre (1979, 1984) as 99 per cent correct. The (representative?) counter-example he quotes is *prócess* (n, v). But note that *process*

(v) in the 'procession' sense is end-stressed (*procéss*). Moreover, examples like *prócess* (v) 'treat, develop' might well be apparent exceptions if we assume Kiparsky's Lexical Phonology account of compounding (*cf* 5.2.3). The initial stress in prefix-stem nouns is described by Guierre as 100 per cent correct.

17. See Aronoff (1976: 99ff) for a detailed discussion of *-ion*, *-tion*, *-ation*, *-ition*, *-ution*, including a treatment of counter-examples to the statements made here such as *convene–convention* or *detain–detention*.

Chapter 5

Underspecification Theory and Lexical Phonology

5.1 Underspecification Theory

In this chapter, two recent extensions of the standard theory will be considered: Underspecification Theory (UT) and Lexical Phonology (see 5.2). The first is concerned with the theory of features and the specification of underlying segments. The second one involves a re-examination of the interface between phonology, morphology and syntax. The discussion of UT will be based on Archangeli's major work on the subject 'Underspecification in Yawelmani phonology and morphology' (1984), an unpublished MIT thesis which has already had a great deal of influence on the technical literature. The presentation here will be uncritical but the topic will be taken up again in later chapters of the book (*cf* in particular Ch. 8).

In Chapters 3 and 4, we have presented two views on the specification of underlying segments: a full specification account (see 3.3, 3.4) and a partial specification account exemplified by archisegmental representations which has been argued to be more adequate. In this section we turn to a recent development in this area – the notion of underspecification as developed by Archangeli (1984). It will be recalled that, if full specification is accepted, a value for every feature has to be entered into a phonological matrix. Thus, given an inventory of vowels such as /i e a o u/ and assuming, contrary to facts, that the total set of distinctive features was {high, low, back, round, voice}, the matrix for such a vowel system would be:

[1]

	i	e	a	o	u
High	+	−	−	−	+
Low	−	−	+	−	−
Back	−	−	+	+	+
Round	−	−	−	+	+
Voice	+	+	+	+	+

or its equivalent in markedness terms (*cf* 3.4). By contrast, a partial specification approach would differ in two respects: (a) some predictable features would be left out and it would be assumed that the missing values would be filled in by redundancy rules; (b) there might be the possibility that the contrast between two phonemes was suspended in some context leading to the postulation of archiphonemes. Suppose that language X which has the vowel system above neutralizes the opposition between /i/ and /e/ at the end of words. In addition to the above set, say that we posit archiphoneme /I/ which represents the suspension of the /i/–/e/ contrast and is simply a non-back vowel. Language X might therefore have an inventory such as:

	i	e	a	o	u	I
High	+	−	−	−	+	
Low	−	−	+	−	−	
Back	−	−	+	+	+	−
Round						
Voice						

[2]

All vowels would be redundantly specified as [+voice]: [round] does not need to be specified either since it is predictable by the following statements:

[3a] [αback, −low] → [αround]
[3b] [+back, +low] → [−round]

/I/ is simply specified as [−back] and, assuming that it is realized as /e/ in the context of neutralization, a realization rule would be added to the phonology saying:

[3c] [−back] → [−high, −low] / _____ #

Underspecification theory, like partial specification theory, starts from the assumption that underlying specifications should be as streamlined as possible and that redundancies should be extracted from underlying entries not only for distinctive features but for all other aspects of phonological representations. Archangeli (1984: 50) formulates the following principle:

[4] FEATURE MINIMIZATION PRINCIPLE

A grammar is most highly valued when underlying representations include the minimal number of features necessary to make different the phonemes of the language.

Underspecification Theory is not just an attempt to achieve formal simplicity at the underlying level. At the basis of this approach lies an interest, not solely in neutralizations as in structuralist phonemics, but also in asymmetrical segments (or feature-values) in languages. Take the example of vowel harmony systems. They often contain segments which behave differently from all the other segments of the language in being 'opaque' – that is, they block the spread of a feature-value. (This notion of opacity will be illustrated in 7.1.5.) One possible explanation in terms of UT is the following: vowels which trigger the spread of a feature-value are obviously specified underlyingly for the feature-value which is spreading; vowels which inherit the harmonizing feature-value are unspecified for that feature-value; opaque vowels are exceptionally specified underlyingly for the opposite value of the harmonizing feature-value and so block spread.

Some of the main characteristics of UT are explained below.

1. Only distinctive features are present underlyingly as in partial specification accounts but (leaving aside exceptional cases such as that of opaque segments) **no feature is specified for both values (+ and −) underlyingly**. For instance, the underlying vowel system of Japanese is argued to have the following structure:

[5]

	i	e	a	o	u
High	−		−		
Low		+			
Back			+	+	

2. The missing values are filled in by a mixture of language universal and language specific RRs. The universal RRs are of the following type:

[6] [ ] → [+low] / X __Y

or equivalently

[7] [∅ low] → [+low] / X __Y

and merely extend the feature specification of the input. By contrast, standard phonological rules such as [8]:

[8] [−low] → [+low]/X __Y

are feature-changing.

In the technical parlance of *SPE*, the input and output of a redundancy rule are 'non-distinct' (see 3.3 for a formal definition of 'distinctness'). Here UT assumes that application of a RR for a given feature to a matrix already specified for that feature is blocked. If this principle was not adopted, the application of RRs would have a disastrous effect since, in effect, it would wipe out all underlying distinctions.

3. The choice of underlying values is made on the basis of language particular phenomena and of the universal RRs available to the phonologist.

We now exemplify and develop the basic principles of UT with reference to Archangeli's treatment of Yawelmani before turning to a brief examination of the Midi French vowel system from this point of view.

5.1.1 Yawelmani vowels and underspecification

In the wake of Newman's classic study of the Yokuts language (1944), and the well-known generative reinterpretations offered in Kuroda (1967) and Kisseberth (1969), the vowel system of Yawelmani is assumed by Archangeli to be of the following type underlyingly: /i, a, o, u/ (short vowels) and /i:, a:, o:, u:/ (long vowels). A full matrix interpretation of the short vowels – ignoring predictable features such as nasality, voice, sonorancy, etc. – is given by Archangeli (1984: 74) as:

[9]

	i	a	o	u
High	+	−	−	+
Low	−	+	−	−
Round	−	−	+	+
Back	−	+	+	+

From the point of view of UT, this interpretation suffers from two fundamental inadequacies: it is neither minimal nor expresses the **asymmetric** behaviour of /i/. This vowel is the recurrent epenthetic vowel of Yawelmani and assuming it is fully specified complicates processes such as vowel harmony to which we turn below. Archangeli puts forward the following underlying system where /i/ is empty and where [−high] and [+round] are the only attribute-value pairs used.

[10] Underspecified Yawelmani system

	i	a	o	u
High		−	−	
Round			+	+

It should be noted that the four vowels of Yawelmani are no longer fully distinct from one another but only potentially distinct. Thus /a/ and /u/ are in a subset relation with /o/; and /i/, the zero set, is by definition a subset of all the other vowels of the system. One has to assume, though, that all these vowels are distinguished from consonants by being specified, *eg* as [−consonantal, +syllabic], as otherwise /i/ would only be in a subset relation with all consonants with potential bad consequences. The classification of /i/ in UT is therefore of the same type as the classification of segments such as [h] and [ʔ] discussed in 3.6 which, it will be recalled, were specified as a voiceless fricative and stop at the level of the categorial gesture but unspecified (empty) from the point of view of articulation. And it was pointed out in 4.2 that this treatment could be extended to the neutral schwa vowel of English. This convergence between UT and conclusions reached within other frameworks is therefore interesting.

5.1.1.1 Rounding harmony

Central to the phonology of Yawelmani is a process of vowel harmony which is simple to state: vowels become round to the right of a round vowel of the same value for high. This is summarized in [11]:

[11] $/ \ldots uC_oi \ldots / \rightarrow / \ldots uC_ou \ldots /$
$/ \ldots oC_oa \ldots / \rightarrow / \ldots oC_oo \ldots /$

Examples of rounding harmony (borrowed from Dell 1973) are given in [12], where, phonologically, the stems are assumed to be /xil/, /hud/, /gop/ and /max/, and the suffixes are underlying /nit/, /it/, /ʔas/ and /al/.

[12]	I	II	III	IV
	Future passive	Aorist passive	Precative gerundive	Dubitative
	xilnit	xilit	xilʔas	xilal
	hudnut	hudut	hudʔas	hudal
	gopnit	gopit	gopʔos	gopol
	maxnit	maxit	maxʔas	maxal

The main point made by Archangeli is that the generalization we would want to capture is that the feature-value [+round] spreads from left to right. But, if one assumes fully specified entries, some 'clean up' rules will be required to express roundness spreading in its most general form. If, for instance, we formalize [11] as:

[13] Rounding harmony
$$\begin{bmatrix} \alpha high \\ +syll \end{bmatrix} \rightarrow [+round] / \begin{bmatrix} +round \\ \alpha high \\ +syll \end{bmatrix} C_o \underline{\quad\quad}$$

then /i/ will become [y] and /a/ will become [ɔ], and these inter-mediary values will need to be converted to [u] and [o] respectively (see Kuroda 1967, for a solution along these lines). That is, one needs to assume derivations such as /hud+it/ →

[hudyt] (rounding harmony) → [hudut] ([y]-retraction) which look weakly motivated. Yet roundness spreading is quite general within Yawelmani. On the other hand, if we start from the underspecified system given above and assume that the rule is formulated before the matrices are filled in, no 'clean up' processes will be required.

Before the application of rounding harmony, the vowels are specified as in [14]:

[14]	No harmony				Harmony	
	i	u	a	o	i	a
High		−	−			−
Round		+		+		

Let us assume, with Archangeli, that at this point a RR fills in the value [+high] for vowels not specified as [−high] and leave to the next section the question of how precisely RRs function within the system. The result will be:

[15]	No harmony				Harmony	
	i	u	a	o	i	a
High	+	+	−	−	+	−
Round		+		+		

If rounding harmony [13] applies now to /i/ and /a/, these latter will acquire the feature-value [+round] and merge with /u/ and /o/ respectively as shown below:

[16]	No harmony			Harmony	
	i	u	a	o	i(= u)	a(= o)
High	+	+	−	−	+	−
Round		+		+	+	+

Other RRs apply thereafter to crank out fully specified matrices. Rounding harmony can therefore be maintained in the general form given in [13]. Now, the drawback is that we appear, rather conveniently for us, to have ordered one RR **before** rounding harmony but assumed that other RRs apply **after** rounding harmony. The next section shows that this ordering falls out from the interaction of general principles.

5.1.1.2 Redundancy rules: default and complement rules

The RRs that fill in the missing values fall into two classes: default rules and complement rules. Default rules are, for the most part, universal but can be language-specific. Complement rules are language-specific but result from a universal convention and are, therefore, cost-free. The universal, cost-free, default rules correspond in the main to the markedness conventions examined in 3.4. Thus, since non-low back vowels are typically round, the following cost-free default rule:

[17] [ ] → [+round] / $\left[\begin{array}{c} \text{+back} \\ \text{−low} \end{array} \right]$

will be available unless the opposite value (non-round) has been posited underlyingly for non-low back vowels or a language-specific RR makes these very vowels non-round. Apart from rules such as [17] which express preferred configurations, default rules also include 'logical' statements of the following type:

[18a] [+low] → [−high]
[18b] [+high] → [−low]

The idea of complement rule is original to UT. Whenever a feature-value is selected for underlying representation, a rule inserting its opposite value is created. In the case of Yawelmani, the underlying value for [high] was chosen to be [−high]. There-fore, the complement rule given in [19]:

[19] [ ] → [+high]

was automatically created and, in fact, this is the RR that, as was assumed, applied to [14] to derive [15]. The full set of comp-lement and default rules required to derive the correct surface values for the vowels of Yawelmani are given in [20].

[20] Complement and default rules for Yawelmani vowels

[20a] [ ] → [+high]   (complement)
[20b] [ ] → [−low] / $\left[\begin{array}{c} \text{+round} \\ \text{−high} \end{array} \right]$ (default)

[20c] (i) [ ] → [−low] / $\left[\begin{array}{c} \text{+high} \end{array} \right]$ (default)

     (ii) [ ] → [+low] / $\left[\begin{array}{c} \text{−high} \end{array} \right]$ (default)

[20d] [ ] → $\left[\begin{array}{c} \text{+back} \\ \text{−round} \end{array} \right]$ / $\left[\begin{array}{c} \text{+low} \end{array} \right]$ (default)

[20e] [ ] → [−round]   (complement)
[20f] [ ] → [αback] / $\left[\begin{array}{c} \text{−low} \\ \text{αround} \end{array} \right]$ (default)

The reader is referred back to 3.4 for help with the interpret-ation of the default rules given above except that empty brackets need to be substituted for unmarked values. As mentioned earlier, all the default rules given here for Yawelmani are part of Universal Grammar and therefore cost-free. The complement rules are language-dependent (since each default statement of this form depends on the underlying value chosen) but they are also cost-free in that they result from a universal feature-filling convention.

Let us now turn our attention to the question of rule ordering: how are the RRs in [20] ordered relative to each other and to the other rules of the language? The first general claim made by UT is that RRs apply as late as possible in a derivation. Secondly, complement rules are assumed to be automatically ordered after rules which supply a value for unspecified feature: thus, since rounding harmony supplies the value [+round] to underlying /i/ and /a/, the complement rule inserting [−round], *ie* [20e], will be ordered after rounding harmony. Thirdly, a general principle – the Redundancy Rule Ordering Constraint (see [21] below) – is posited whereby, if a rule X mentions a given feature value (or a variable ranging over the two values of a feature) in its structural description, then the RRs inserting the value(s) in question must have automatically applied before rule X.

[21] Redundancy Rule Ordering Constraint

A RR assigning 'α' to F (where α is either + or −) is automatically ordered prior to the first rule referring to [αF] in its structural description.

In the case of Yawelmani, since rounding harmony, [13], mentions [αhigh] in its structural description, the complement rule [20a] (= [19]) will be ordered before it by principle [21]. Fourthly, much of the ordering is derivable from the Elsewhere Condition (which was already encountered in 4.4.1). The formal version of this condition used by Archangeli is stated as follows:

[22] Elsewhere Condition

Rules A, B in the same component apply disjunctively if and only if
a. The input of A is a proper subset of the input of B.
b. The outputs of A and B are distinct (in the technical sense of definition [44] of 3.3).
In that case, A (the particular rule) is applied first, and if it takes effect, then B (the general rule) is not applied.

The Elsewhere Condition orders [20b] before [20cii] since the SD of [20b] is more specific than that of [20cii] and the output of the two rules is distinct in that [20b] makes a non-high round vowel [−low] whereas [20cii] makes a non-high vowel [+low].

What is interesting about UT proposals is that a great deal of the functioning of the phonological system is derivable from the interaction of universal principles. Strikingly, in the case of Yawelmani, the particular ordering of the phonological rule of roundness harmony after [20a] and before [20b], and the ordering of the RRs among themselves, are predictable on universal grounds. Since Yawelmani does not contain any learned RR but draws all its RRs from the universal inventory which can be equated with traditional markedness principles, the whole treatment will be highly valued on theoretical grounds.

Finally, classical objections by Lightner (1963) and Stanley (1967) to the use of unspecified values beside + and − values, on the grounds that this permitted a 'ternary' use of binary features are dismissed. Stanley and Lightner were correct in pointing out that by assuming unspecified values beside + and − specifications underlyingly, classical phonological derivations could (at least in principle) be produced whereby [+F], [−F] and [ØF] could end up in opposition (see 3.3). Underspecification Theory is protected against this possibility in two ways. Firstly, only one value is given underlyingly for each contrastive feature. Secondly, the Redundancy Rule Ordering Constraint deprives a structure such as that of [23] of any motivation (Archangeli 1984: 88–9):

[23]
	A	B	C
F	+	−	

Suppose, as Archangeli observes, that the following rules were posited, leading to a potential three-way contrast between A, B and C:

[24] Phonological Rule: [24a] [ ] → [−G] / [———, +F][1]
Redundancy Rules: [24b] [ ] → [+F]
[24c] [ ] → [+G]

The rules of [24] could in principle lead to a ternary use of binary features as shown below:

[25a] by application of [24a]:
	A	B	C
F	+	−	
G	−		

[25b] by application of [24b] and [24c]:
	A	B	C
F	+	−	+
G	−	+	+

But the Redundancy Rule Ordering Constraint [21] would auto-matically reorder [24b] before [24a] as in [26]:

[26a] [ ] → [+F]
[26b] [ ] → [−G] / [____ , +F]
[26c] [ ] → [+G]

And the application of [26a] to a putative matrix of the type [23] would merge A and C:

[27]
     A B C
F   + − +
G

thus preventing a ternary use of non-specified values underlyingly.

5.1.2 Brief application of UT to Midi French

In 1.5 we assumed that the underlying vowel system of Midi French was as given in [28] (plus /ə/). And a rule of MVLOW

[28]

		−back		+back	
		−round	+round	−round	+round
+high −low		i	y		u
−high −low		e	ø		o
−high +low				a	

was formulated to account for the complementary distribution of [e, o, ø] and [ɛ, ɔ œ] (*cf* alternations such as [fɛr]–[ferø] *fer–ferreux* ('iron'–'ferrous'), [šo]–[šɔdə] *chaud–chaude* ('hot' masc vs. fem), [avœglə]–[avøgle] *aveugle–aveugler* ('blind' noun vs. verb). The context of the rule discussed in Chapter 1 will not be considered again here since we return to this question in 6.1.9. Rather, it will be recalled that, given standard conventions on rule application, the formulation:

[29] MVLOW: [−high] → [+low]

transforms the [−low] feature-value of the non-high vowels into [+low]. But the choice of [−high, −low] over [−high, +low], as an underlying (default) value, was, in fact, rather arbitrary since there is no evidence as to which value is basic. And a justification in terms of markedness theory in its standard version does not seem to help since the latter provides only an evaluation metric external to the notation (*cf* 3.4).

Suppose, now, that we appeal to the apparatus of UT as defined above. The underlying Midi French vowel system can be analysed as in [30] with only one value for each feature:

[30]	i	y	e	ø	o	u	a	ə
High			−	−	−		−	
Back	−	−	−	−				
Round		+		+	+	+		

Note that schwa has been directly integrated to the scheme by assuming that it is unspecified for all feature- values. By contrast, adherence to full specification would either force us to find an empty niche for /ə/ in [28] or, in view of the rather special nature of this segment, resort to a new feature such as [+/−tense] in addition to the other features of [28].

The formulation of MVLOW can remain as in [29], but the difference is now that this rule does not change any feature value but only extends the feature specification of segments which undergo this rule. The RRs required for Midi French are all universal and spelled out in [31]:

[31] Complement and default rules (MVLOW version)
[31a] [ ] → [−round] (complement)
[31b] [ ] → [+back] (complement)
[31c] [ ] → [+high] (complement)
[31d] [ ] → [+low] / [_____, +back, −round] (default)
[31e] [ ] → [−low] (default)

In this set, default rules [31d] and [31e] correspond to marking convention VI of *SPE* (*p* 405) given below in [32]. Here [31d] will allow /a/ to be specified as [+low]; [31e] specifies as [−low] all non-high vowels whose value for [low] is still open.

$$[32]\ [\text{u low}] \to \left\{ \begin{array}{l} [+\text{low}] / [\underline{\quad}, \text{u back, u round}] \\ [-\text{low}] \end{array} \right\}$$

To take one example, if we consider the underlying vowel of the morpheme *fer*, it will be specified as in [33] for both *fer* and *ferreux*:

[33]	/e/ *fer*	/e/ *ferreux*
High	−	−
Back	−	−
Round		

The vowel in *fer*, which is in a closed syllable, will undergo MVLOW and as a result give rise to [34]:

[34]

	fer	ferreux
High	−	−
Back	−	−
Low	+	
Round		

The application of complement rules [31a] and [31e] will produce the surface values as in [35]:

[35]

	[ɛ] *fer*	[e] *ferreux*
High	−	−
Back	−	−
Low	+	−
Round	−	−

The first advantage of this analysis is, as was pointed out above, that it solves the question of arbitrary selection of an underlying value for the mid vowels. Secondly, MVLOW does not require a feature-value change and, as was the case in Yawelmani, we rely only on filling-in operations of a universal nature apart from MVLOW itself. It should, however, be pointed out that the universal RRs in [31] would predict [ɨ] ([+high, −back, −round]) as a default realization of schwa. But, typically, schwa is either realized as a front rounded vowel or as a central vowel in this accent, and a proper treatment of this vowel would require an examination of alternations such as [møne]–[mɛnə] *mener–mène* ('to lead' – '(s)he leads'). Lack of space prevents us from dealing more fully with this question (see S. R. Anderson 1982; Durand 1986b) but it is clear that language-specific mechanisms would have to be invoked.

This completes our presentation of UT. To summarize, UT advocates an approach which maximizes contrastivity by recourse to one-valued features underlyingly. In other words, all contrasts are formally handled in a privative way (*cf* 3.1.1) initially, although all features end up as two-valued through the operation of largely universal complement and default rules. The advantage of this latter move is that non-contrastive values become available within derivations and can be put to various uses (*eg* block the spread of given features). This chapter and the previous ones have argued that full specification was not always satisfactory and UT provides an interesting solution in that, unlike classical archisegmental solutions, it protects itself against a possible ternary use of zero specifications besides + and −. It should be noted that UT is not applied solely to the underlying specification of segments. In the following chapters, we shall see that phonological representations have been enriched by the addition of quite complex infra-segmental and supra-segmental structures.

Such non-linear analyses are also cast within an underspecification framework. But the essential concepts have been presented above. Indeed, in 'Underspecification and Yawelmani phonology and morphology', Archangeli (1984) herself moves from a presentation of UT in the *SPE* paradigm to a non-linear analysis of the dialects of Yokuts. And her non-linear treatment of rounding harmony will be outlined in Chapter 7. For further study of UT, the reader is especially referred to the essays in van der Hulst and Smith (1988) and volume 5:2 of *Phonology* edited by Archangeli (1988).[2]

5.2 Lexical Phonology

In the *SPE* model, as stressed in Chapter 1, the function of the phonological component was to interpret the output of the syntactic component. From the point of view of morphology, this meant that phonological rules only had access to a surface bracketing of words (their make-up in terms of morphemes) enriched with boundaries (+, #, =, ##, etc.), whatever the complex transformational history that used to be attributed to words. The boundaries were inherited from the **juncture phonemes** of the structuralist tradition, although, unlike the latter, they were explicitly motivated in morphosyntactic terms. The first mechanism adopted in *SPE* for assigning boundaries was as follows:

[36] SPE-I
   The boundary # is automatically inserted at the beginning and end of every string dominated by a major category (N, V, A(dj)) or by a phrasal category (NP, VP, . . ., S)

As a result of [36], *sincerity prevailed* would be analysed as in [37], or its labelled bracketing equivalent [38]:

[37]

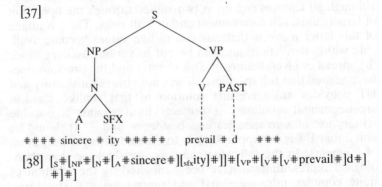

[38] [s#[NP#[N#[A#sincere#][sfxity]#]]#[VP#[V#[V#prevail#]d#]#]#]

The sequence of boundaries was then modified by readjustment rules. For instance, [#[#sincere#][ity]#] was readjusted to [#[#sincere]+ity]#] by a rule informally specified in [39]:

[39] # → + / ___sfx (−*ity* class)

Another convention, given in [40], prevented pile-ups of boundaries:

[40] SPE-II
In the sequence W#ₓ]#ᵧ]Z or W[ᵧ#[ₓ#Z, where Y ≠ S, delete the 'inner' word boundary.

As a result of SPE-II, *sincerity* would have the structure [#[sincere]+ity]#] and the sequence of boundaries in the sentence *Sincerity prevailed* would be reduced to: ##sincer+ity##prevail#ed##.

As work progressed, the *ad hoc* character of the *SPE* theory of boundaries became more and more apparent. The reason, for instance, that -*ity* is preceded by + whereas the past marker (-*ed*) is preceded by # does not follow from any principled assignment but from arbitrary readjustment rules. It was also shown that the boundary theory under-differentiated items which were morphologically different. For instance, *loneliness club* and *re-air condition* have the morphological structure as given in [41], where strong suffixes and prefixes such as -*ness* and *re*- retain the # boundary. But after application of SPE-II, the boundary sequences of [41] are reduced to: #*lonely*#*ness*##*club*# and

[41a]

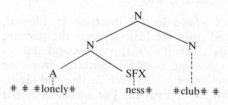

[41b]

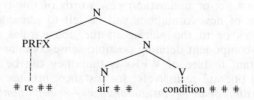

#re#air# #condition#. In other words, the affixation of a suffix before compounding is indistinguishable from the affixation of a prefix after compounding. In so far as our phonological rules rest on boundary assignments, wrong predictions will be made (cf eg 5.2.4). In actual fact, some of these potential weaknesses were often avoided in so far as SPE relied both on bracket information and on boundaries. In other words, it was a mixed theory.

The idea of dispensing with boundaries and allowing direct reference to morphological brackets therefore gained ground, thus favouring a more restrictive theory. At the same time, the transformational approach to word-formation was abandoned in favour of an autonomous morphological component (see eg Aronoff 1976; Dell, 1970, 1979b; Halle 1973 and Scalise 1984 for a thorough review) and convincing arguments were put forward in favour of organizing this latter in terms of ordered levels (cf Siegel 1974). As a result, the need to re-examine the interaction between word-formation rules and phonological rules became more pressing.

5.2.1 The morphological component and level-ordered morphology

We will assume in what follows that, at the core of the morphological component, are word-formation rules (WFRs) along the lines of [42]:

[42a] V → N V   (air-condition, headhunt)
[42b] N → N N   (school board, apple cake)
[42c] V → PRFX V   (re-do, unlock)
[42d] N → A SFX   (happiness, acidity)

These WFRs define trees where lexical insertion is allowed, provided the item extracted from the lexicon bears the relevant label. The lexicon contains a list of stems, prefixes and suffixes as well as words whose meaning is not predictable from the constituent parts. The function of WFRs such as those of [42] is to define the potential words of English. For instance, if our lexicon includes *canny* as A and *-ness* as suffix, [42d] predicts *canniness* as a possible word of English and must underlie our ability to construct or understand new words of this type. The interpretation of new formations will be left to semantic interpretive devices or to the pairing of the above rules with an autonomous component defining possible sense-combinations.

An important feature of WFRs is that they can be chained together and operate recursively: for instance, *institute → institution → institutional → institutionalize → institutionalization*

→ *institutionalizationize* and so on. In fact, some rules such as the nominal compounding rule [42b] are directly recursive as shown by attested compounds such as *UK disco dance marathon record*. No upper limit can be placed on the possible length and complexity of a word, very much as the notion of stating an upper bound on the length of sentences is meaningless.

The recursiveness of WFRs does not mean that any sequence is permitted. Thus, whereas *non-illegal* is possible *il-non-legal* (or *in-non-legal*) is nonsense. And, whereas *bountifulness* is acceptable, *bountifullity* is a joke at best. While the unacceptability of sequences such as *non-in-X or *X-full-ity could be the result of restrictions placed on individual combinations of morphemes, a wide range of sequences can be explained if we divide derivational affixes into two classes as in [43]:

[43] Class 1: -ate, -ion, -ity, -ic, sub-, de-, in-, etc.
      Class 2: -ly, -ful, -some, -ness, re-, un-, non- etc.

and if we also assume that class 1 affixes are always nearer the root than those in class 2.

Class 1 affixes are those which require either a + or = boundary in *SPE*, whereas class 2 require a # boundary. Phonologically, the distinction between class 1 and class 2 affixes is well motivated. Between a class 1 affix and a base, we can observe the following phonological processes: stress shifts (*cf phótográph–phòtográphic*), Trisyllabic Shortening (*cf div*[aj]*ne-div*[i]*nity*), nasal assimilation (*cf illegal* from /in+le:gæl/), etc. By contrast, class 2 affixes do not modify the stress of the base (*cf revénge–revéngeful*), they do not trigger Trisyllabic Shortening (*cf leaderless* [lijdələs] not *[ledələs]) and nasal assimilation is blocked (*cf unladylike* not *ulladylike*).

From a morphological standpoint, there are also important differences between, class 1 and class 2 affixes. For instance, class 1 affixes can attach to stems, whereas Class 2 can only attach to words:

[44]   Class 1   Class 2
       re-mit   re-open
       sub-mit   sub-contract
       de-duce   de-regulate
       dict-ate   peace-ful
       leg-al   kind-ness

And more generally, class 1 morphology is less productive, more exception-ridden and semantically less transparent than class 2. Here, [44] shows that that there are two prefixes *de-*, two prefixes *re-*, etc. The spelling should therefore not be taken at face value in identifying affixes. The class 1 prefixes have already been discussed in 4.5 where we saw that the motivation for assuming the divisions given above are morphophonological not semantic. On the other hand, the class 2 prefixes of 44 are semantically transparent. Thus *re-* in *re-open, re-assess, re-do* can be uniformly glossed as 'do again'.

The integration of the above observations in a level-ordered morphology (as first advocated by Siegel 1974) consists in positing that there is a block of morphological rules (level 1 corresponding to class 1 affixation) which applies first followed by the next block of rules (level 2 corresponding to class 2) and so on. Three examples of derivation are given in [45]:

[45] Dict. ⟦in⟧ ⟦organ⟧ ⟦ic⟧ ⟦un⟧ ⟦organ⟧ ⟦ic⟧ ⟦comfort⟧ ⟦able⟧

> *Level 1*
> +sfx ⟦⟦organ⟧ ⟦ic⟧⟧   ⟦⟦organ⟧ ⟦ic⟧⟧ _____
> +prfx ⟦⟦⟦in⟧⟧⟦⟦organ⟧⟧⟦ic⟧⟧⟧   _____
>
> *Level 2*
> #sfx _____   _____ ⟦⟦⟦comfort⟧⟦able⟧⟧⟧
> #prfx _____   ⟦⟦⟦un⟧⟧⟦⟦organ⟧⟧⟦ic⟧⟧⟧   _____

Note that, in the rest of this chapter, double brackets are used for morphological bracketings to avoid confusion between morphological structures and phonetic representations. This convention is a common one in Lexical Phonology.

As illustrated in [45], level-ordered morphology accounts directly for the sequential constraints mentioned above. A level 2 affix will always be outside level 1 affixation. To derive *in-non-legal*, for instance, we would have to imagine that a form could loop back to level 1 after undergoing level 2 affixation.

The working of WFRs given in [42], as a first approximation, should be re-examined to allow for the complex word-internal layering of morphemes presupposed by [45]. One way of doing this is by adopting a X̄ (X-bar) model where the bar-levels are negative and by assigning categorial labels and subcategorization frames to affixes (see Selkirk 1982b, and Mohanan 1986: 127–44). But it is worth pointing out that not all specialists accept this format in the first place. For instance, Kiparsky (1982a, b), like Aronoff (1976), assumes that affixes are not listed in the lexicon but introduced by the WFRs. He adopts the rule format exemplified in [46] below which accounts for agentive words of the *worker* type:

[46] Insert *er* in env. ⟦$_v$ _____ ⟧$_{N + Agent}$

The structure of the WFRs does have consequences on the

formal mechanics of the morphology–phonology interface but, for our purposes here, and as is customary in much Lexical Phonology work, we shall take the morphological bracketings as given by an independent theory of word formation and avoid controversial aspects of the latter.

Now, if we let phonological rules be interspersed among morphological rules and allowed them to refer only to morphological brackets, we would have a first imprecise model of Lexical Phonology (LP hereafter). The purpose of the following sections will be to articulate such a model.

5.2.2 Lexical rules and cyclicity

The interweaving of morphological and phonological structure alluded to above is not totally new. In *SPE* rules of stress assignment were assumed to be **cyclic**. Starting from a labelled bracketing, a rule is described as cyclic by Chomsky and Halle if, first of all, it applies to the smallest constituent and, then, it keeps reapplying to successively larger constituents. More formally, the cycle is defined as follows:

[47] The cycle (*SPE p* 15):

> we assume as a general principle that the phonological rules first apply to the maximal strings that contain no brackets, and that after all relevant rules have applied, the innermost brackets are erased; the rules then reapply to maximal strings containing no brackets, and again innermost brackets are erased after this application; and so on, until the maximal domain of phonological processes is reached.

One motivation for a cyclic application of rules of stress was the 'protective' function of stress assigned in earlier cycles which prevented the reduction of a vowel to schwa. Consider, for instance, the words in [48]:

[48a] relaxation, emendation, elasticity, connectivity
[48b] illustration, demonstration, devastation, anecdotal

The underlined vowels are reduced to [ə] in [48b] but they retain their original quality in the [48a] forms. Yet, for some of the [48b] words at least, we can recover the underlying quality of the vowel from other derived forms: *cf illustrative* (u = [ʌ] and *demonstrative* (o = [ɔ]). The [48a,b] examples, however, differ in morphological structure. The [48a] forms are derived from underlying forms (*reláx, eménd, elástic, connéctive*) which contain a stressed vowel corresponding to the unreduced underlined vowels of [48a]. On the other hand, the [48b] forms are derived from underlying forms where the underlined vowel is not

stressed: *íllustràte, démonstràte, dévastàte, ánecdòte.* The principle of the cycle, accounts for the distinctions just noted in an
elegant manner. In the case of [48a], stress will be assigned to
the underlined vowel on the first, innermost cycle: [[[reláx][ation]]].
Then, on the next cycle, the main stress is shifted to the suffix
(*-ation*) and the first syllable receives a secondary stress, but the
stress assigned to *-lax-* on the first cycle protects the vowel from
reduction. On the other hand, the underlined vowels in [48b] –
eg [[[compensate][+ion]] – are neither stressed on the first cycle nor
on the second one.

Whereas stress assignment was cyclic, segmental phonological
rules were sensitive to the morphological structure but (with one
exception in *SPE*) non-cyclic. The cyclicity of stress rules is seen
as essentially correct in LP, but the chaining of WFRs provides
a parallel, and arguably better, account of cyclicity than the *SPE*
formulation. All we have to assume is that the stress rules apply
to lexical stems and keep reapplying after every morphological
operation at level 1. However, the major difference between *SPE*
and LP is that, having established that level 1 requires cyclic
application of some phonological rules, it is assumed that this
stratum is cyclic for all rules. That is, all the phonological rules
which are relevant at level 1 are scanned for applicability after
every morphological operation. An example is given in [49],
where TSS is Trisyllabic Shortening (rule [7a] of Ch. 4):

[49] *erectility*
      Level 1   [e:rekt] [i:l] [iti]
      Stress rules   1
      Affixation   [[e:rekt][i:l]]
      Stress rules   1
      TSS   ————————————————
      Affixation   [[e:rekt][i:l]][iti]]
      Stress rules   2 3   1
      TSS   [[e:rekt][il]][iti]]

Once a form has been processed at a given level, all the internal
brackets are erased and the form is then passed on to the next
level. This is a weaker convention than the *SPE* one since
brackets are deleted by [43] after every cycle. (But in some
versions of LP deletion of brackets after every morphological
operation is also assumed.) For instance, assuming that *non-
erectility* is a potential level 2 formation, this would be the result
of combining [non] and [erectility] (where the internal make-up
of *erectility* is no longer available) as [[non][erectility]]. At the
end of level 2, the internal brackets would once again be deleted

and ⟦nonerectility⟧ will be available for further morphological combinations if other levels follow. In order to guarantee these erasures, the following principle is adopted:

[50] Bracket Erasure Convention (BEC)
Erase the internal brackets at the end of each level.

The reader should note that the examples of [45], given as an illustration of level-ordering, should undergo BEC, to fit in with the LP model.

All the rules which apply within the word-formation component are, by definition, lexical. This does not mean, of course, that all rules apply in this manner. Some rules require reference to phrasal information. For instance, /r/ deletion (*cf* 4.2.4) will delete an underlying word-final /r/ if the next word begins with a consonant (*eg bette(r) king*). Such rules can only take place once words have been inserted into syntactic trees. Lexical Phonology posits the existence of a post-lexical module which can rely on syntactic information, and all rules contained within this module are called post-lexical. But post-lexical rules are not restricted to the set of sandhi rules. The rule which aspirates stops in English (*eg* [fətʰɔgrəfi]), traditionally labelled 'allophonic', is also post-lexical. Following Mohanan (1986: 8–10), we can say that any rule which requires morphological information (*eg* categorial labels on brackets or features such as [+/−learned], [+/−Latinate]) is lexical and any rule requiring access to phrasal information is post-lexical. The status of other rules will depend on their position within the rule set. The overall structure of the LP model is given in [51].

[51]

The Lexical Phonology model	
Underlying representations	L
	E
	X
level 1 Morphology ⇄ Phonology	I
	C
level 2 Morphology ⇄ Phonology	O
	N
level n Morphology ⇄ Phonology	
Lexical representation	
Syntax ⟶ Post-lexical phonology	

The BEC also applies in the transition from the lexical to the post-lexical module. At the point at which words reach the post-lexical module, the internal morphological brackets assigned on the last lexical level are deleted. The invisibility of structures assigned within earlier or later (sub-)modules is an important difference between LP and the *SPE* model. In the *SPE* framework, nothing would prevent the analyst from writing a rule such as [52]:

[52] k → č / ___+ i# C ##

This rule palatalizes a /k/ if the next morpheme is /i/ followed by a strong (#-boundary) consonantal suffix provided the latter is phrase-final. A rule of this form makes simultaneous reference to level 1, level 2 and syntactic information. It is impossible within the LP model which is therefore more restrictive than the boundary model. However, Kiparsky (1982a, b) demonstrates that, beside the issue of restrictiveness, LP makes it possible to deal with examples where the boundary theory fails altogether. The arguments involve English compounding processes and are summarized in 5.2.3.

5.2.3 Zero derivation, levels and the Bracket Erasure Convention

The basic observation that Kiparsky (1982a, b)[3] starts from is the presence of two families of noun–verb pairs (related by zero derivation) exemplified in [53]:

[53a] torment$_V$–tórment$_N$
[53b] páttern$_V$–páttern$_N$

In [53a] there is a stress shift between the verb and the noun, whereas in [53b] stress is identical on both. The stress on the verb *páttern* of [53b] is unexpected given the account of stress presupposed by Kiparsky (essentially the development of the *SPE* system to be found in Hayes 1981). A heavy syllable (long vowel, diphthong, vowel + two consonants) should attract the stress as in *appróve, unite, colléct*. The two patterns are well attested:

[54a] *Torment*-words: record, permit, conflict, transfer, rebel, convert, produce, etc.
[54b] *Pattern*-words: canvass. barrack, herald, balance, comfort, doctor, hammer, etc.

What Kiparsky, who posits only two lexical levels, suggests is that the words in [54a] undergo V → N zero derivation (or conversion) at level 1. Thus, tórmènt$_N$ has a nested structure

$[_N[_V \text{torment}_V]_N]$. First of all, the verb, like all lexical categories, undergoes the stress rules and it is stressed on the last syllable. Then, following the morphological conversion, the stress rules are reapplied. The main stress is retracted on to the first syllable in the noun with retention of a tertiary stress on the second syllable for many of these words (which shows itself in a full vowel quality). On the other hand, the words in [54b] are N → V conversions which take place at level 2. It has already been pointed out that the word stress rules are located at level 1 and that level 2 affixation does not affect the stress of the base. We therefore predict that any level 2 zero derivation will be stress-neutral. Granted that this technical solution works, what independent arguments can be given to support it?

First of all, Kiparsky claims that there is a difference in productivity between V → N (level 1) and N → V (level 2): noun-to-verb conversions are much more productive than verb-to-noun ones.

Secondly, the verbs derived at level 2, *pattern, comfort, doctor* cannot undergo level 1 affixation. Compare [55a] and [55b]:

[55a] *pattern+ation, *comfort+al, *doctor+ive
[55b] transform+ation, approv+al, abort+ive

This is exactly what is expected given the strict ordering of level 1 and level 2 operations.

Thirdly, it is predicted that verbs zero derived from nouns (level 2) will be regular in inflection since level 2 is the stratum where 'regular' processes take place: *ring–ringed, wing–winged, ink–inked, link–linked* etc. Kiparsky (1982a: 141) observes that the ablaut rules that account for *ring–rang–rung, sing–sang–sung*, etc. (*cf* 4.2.2 for examples of rules dealing with strong verb allomorphy) can be far more general and that, in fact, 'it becomes a practically exceptionless rule that verbs in *-ing, -ink* are strong'.

Finally, consider the following examples:

[56a] *a publicize, *a demonstrate, *a clarify
[56b] *to singer, *to promptness, *to alcoholism,
      *to sisterhood, *to nationalist
[56c] to pressure, to trial, to engineer, to reference

The examples of [56a, b] seem to indicate that zero derivation is not allowed on suffixed forms. Yet [56c] would appear to show the opposite. But the difference between [56a, b] and [56c] is that the examples of the latter involve suffixation inherited from level 1 since *-ure, -al, -eer, -ence* are level 1 suffixes. Kiparsky, who assumes that zero-suffixation is marked by a null element, argues that if we stipulate that zero suffixes cannot be added to affixed forms by [57]:

[57] *] X] Ø]

all the examples of [56] are readily explained. The offending suffixes of [56a, b] are visible if we assume that [56a] exemplifies V → N conversion at level 1 and [56b] N → V at level 2. So, the hypothetical derivatives will be blocked by [57]. As for the words of [56c], they are formed at level 1 and we saw that at the end of a level all brackets are erased by BEC. Therefore, when nouns such as *pressure* are considered by the morphological rules of level 2, they no longer have a nested structure (⟦⟦press⟧⟦ure⟧⟧) but they behave like monomorphemes (⟦pressure⟧) as far as level 2 operations are concerned.

While this is only part of the evidence that Kiparsky presents, it should suffice to demonstrate the range of observations that can be subsumed under the hypothesis of level ordering and the BEC.

5.2.4 How many levels?
The number of lexical levels is not universally fixed. Halle and Mohanan (1985) and Mohanan (1986) start from the assumption that, other things being equal, rules are going to be post-lexical only. In other words, each and every lexical level has to be argued for. Kiparsky (1982a, b 1985) and Rubach (1984b) have recourse to two levels within the lexical component of English. In a two-level approach, as exemplified in 5.2.3, level 1 corresponds to *SPE* +−affixation (including 'irregular' morphological processes: *sing–sang*) whereas level 2 includes #-derivational processes, compounding and regular inflection. On the other hand, Halle and Mohanan (1985) and Mohanan (1985, 1986) assume the existence of four levels[4] (which they call strata) as summarized in [58]:

[58] The Halle and Mohanan lexical component
    level 1: class 1 +−derivation, irregular inflection
    ↓
    level 2: class 2 #-derivation
    ↓
    level 3: compounding
    ↓
    level 4: regular inflection

The location of regular inflection at level 4 is partially motivated by the fact that the regular inflectional markers are normally outside all other morphemes. Compare [59a] and [59b] in that respect:

[59a] instit-ut-ion-s, work-er-s, house-hunter-s flower-market-s
[59b] *instit-ute-s-ion, *work-s-er, *houses-hunter *flowers-market

Note that, unsurprisingly, irregular plurals formed at level 1 are available for compounding at level 4 (*cf teeth ridge*) as well as inherently plural nouns (*cf alms house, goods train*). But the plural of such compounds is still at the right-hand edge of the whole compound (*teeth ridge-s, alms house-s, goods train-s*).

The justification for Halle and Mohanan's distinction between level 2 and level 3 is phonological. They claim that, in a dialect of English (dialect C in their description), there is a rule (stem final tensing) which tenses the last non-low vowel of a stem in words in isolation, compounds and before inflectional suffixes (*cf* [60a]), but not in other contexts (*cf* [60b]).

[60a] city [sɪti], happy [hæpi]
      city life [sɪtilajf]
      cities [sɪtiz]
[60b] happiness [hapɪnəs]
      various [vɛərɪəs]

By ordering this rule at level 3 in the form of [61]:

[61] Stem final tensing (level 3)

$$\begin{bmatrix} V \\ -low \end{bmatrix} \rightarrow [+tense] \: / \: \underline{\qquad}]$$

they can rely on the fact that, in any suffixed word formed at levels 1 or 2, the short vowel which could potentially be tensed will no longer precede a bracket given the application of BEC. Thus, while at level 2 *happiness* is bracketed [[[hæpɪ][nəs]]], this word reaches level 3 as [[hæpɪnəs]]. Note that a boundary approach would fail to account for these observations since both inflectional and strong derivational suffixes are preceded by # (*eg* ##city#s##. ##happy#ness##).

From a morphological point of view, however, there is evidence that level 2 and level 3 mutually feed each other:

[62a]   [lonely] [ness] [club]
  Affixation   [[lonely][ness]]
  Compounding [[[lonely][ness]][club]]

[62b]   [re] [air] [condition]
  Compounding [[[air][condition]]]
  Affixation   [[re][[air][condition]]]

Whereas such examples are directly accounted for in a two-level model, Halle and Mohanan need to invoke the concept of a loop as in [63]:

[63]
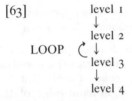

The loop, paraphrasing Mohanan (1986: 51), is a device that allows the output of level 3 to move back to level 2. This does not mean that level 2 and level 3 are unordered with respect to each other. Entry to level 3 from level 1 is only possible through level 2 and entry from level 2 to level 4 is only possible through level 3.

The failure of the *SPE* boundary approach can be further illustrated within the Halle and Mohanan model with reference to compounds and phrasal concatenation. In *SPE*, the boundary sequence ## is assigned both between the elements of a compound such as *mail order* (*mail##order*) and between the (subject) noun and the verb in *The mail offered a bargain* (*mail ## offered*). This can be shown to be inadequate by examining the behaviour of /l/ in English.

In Chapter 1, it was observed that /l/ has two main realizations in RP: a clear or slightly palatalized [l] and a 'dark' or velarized [ɫ] as in [64]:

[64] [l]   [ɫ]
     light   sill
     valley   belt
     please   double

The generalization is that /l/ is dark when it is at the right-hand edge of a syllable (optionally followed by other non-syllabics) and clear elsewhere:

[65] L-velarization
     /l/ → [+back, +high] / ____[−syll]$_0$ \$
[66] L-default (ordered after [65] by the Elsewhere Convention)
     /l/ → [−back]

where it is assumed that /l/ is unspecified for these body-of-tongue values underlyingly. The allophonic rule of L-realization is located by Halle and Mohanan in the post-lexical module.

Now, given that the word *sail* is pronounced [sejɫ], with dark *l* whereas *sailing* is [sejliŋ] with clear *l*, how do we account for this distinction? Halle and Mohanan suggest that there is a rule of L-resyllabification at level 4 which will be informally stated in linear terms as in [67]:

[67] L-resyllabification (level 4)
    [−cons] 1 $ [+syll] → [−cons] $ 1 [+syll]

The syllable-boundaries are inherited from previous levels and L-resyllabification is scanned for application after every morphological operation at level 4. Thus, once ⟦⟦$*sail*$⟧⟦$*ing*$⟧⟧ is formed, the phonetic sequence $sejl$iŋ$ (where two adjacent $$ have automatically been reduced to one) will be converted to sejliŋ$ by L-resyllabification. The operation of L-resyllabification bleeds L-velarization which is ordered after it (since it is post-lexical). As a result, L-default will apply to the /l/ in *sailing* and a front allophone will be produced.

Interestingly, in the majority of accents of English, a contrast between clear and dark *l* can be observed in compounds vs. phrases as in [68]:

[68] [l]   [ł]
    mail order   The mail offered a bargain

This contrast falls out from the assumption that L-resyllabification is a level 4 rule. A compound such as *mail order* will reach level 4 as ⟦mejl$ɔː$dər⟧ after BEC. L-resyllabification will yield ⟦mej$lɔː$dər⟧ and, by the same reasoning as above, a non-velarized /l/ will result. On the other hand, the difference in [68] is inexplicable with reference to boundary information.

5.2.5 Strict cyclicity and abstractness

The sketch of the LP model offered in [51] may have given the impression that every lexical level was cyclic – that is, involved a scanning of phonological rules after each morphological operation. The issue of cyclicity is unfortunately somewhat more complicated than we have assumed so far. To fully understand it, we need to step back and examine some of the motivation which led to the LP model.

After the publication of *SPE*, a great deal of work was devoted to the issue of abstractness. In Chapter 4 we examined and rejected as too strong the NGP constraints on underlying representations and derivations. In a series of influential articles of which NGP can be said to be an offshoot, Kiparsky tried, largely on the basis of historical evidence, to put substantive constraints on abstractness. In two early papers, Kiparsky (1968a, b) argued that the synchronic application of a merger (neutralization) process to all allomorphs of a morpheme – called **absolute neutralization** – should be either excluded (strong interpretation) or specified as highly marked (weak interpretation). This was achieved by the Alternation Condition:

[69] Alternation Condition
Obligatory neutralization rules cannot apply to all occurrences of a morpheme.

What [69] says is that, if the inventory of a language includes the contrasting segments and /X/ and /Y/, the underlying representation of a morpheme may not contain /X/ if the phonetic realization of this segment is always identical with the realization of /Y/. By way of example consider German.

In German, the opposition between voiced and voiceless obstruents is neutralized in word-final position so that *Rat* 'advice' and *Rad* 'wheel' are pronounced identically (3.4). In generative phonology, on the basis of longer forms such as *Räte* [rɛ:tə] 'advice+plur' and *Räder* [rɛ:dər] 'wheel+plur', an underlying contrast would be posited between /t/ and /d/ in word-final position: /rad/ 'advice' vs. /rat/ 'wheel'. The surface neutralization is the result of the application of rule [70]:

[70] Obstruent devoicing
[−son] → [−voice] / _____ #

The question is what to do with words which do not alternate such as *weg* [ve:k] 'away'. While we could posit an underlying form [ve:g] and take a 'free ride' on obstruent devoicing, the Alternation Condition would force us to select /ve:k/ as the underlying form. Kiparsky's argument was based on Lithuanian Yiddish. In that variety of German, rule [70] could be shown to have been operative and then to have ceased to apply with consequent restoration of the underlying voicing contrast (so that *Weg* ('road') had reverted from [vek] to [veg]). But the non-alternating adverb *aweg* [avek] 'away', while etymologically related to *Weg*, had retained the voiceless pronunciation in this dialect in accord with the Alternation Condition.

The Alternation Condition gave rise to a great deal of debate summarized in Kenstowicz and Kisseberth (1979: 211–19) who show that, in its strong reading, it excludes some well-motivated analyses. However, in the course of his investigation of non-alternating vs. alternating forms, Kiparsky (1973b) brought to the attention of linguists a range of cases where rules apply to sequences which arise in the course of derivation but not to sequences originally present in underlying representations. The kind of example Kiparsky considered can be exemplified with respect to Slovak which has received a thorough discussion in Kenstowicz and Rubach (1987).

Restricting ourselves to the etymologically native vocabulary of Slovak, the surface inventory of monophthongs and diphthongs is as follows:

[71]

i	u	i:	u:		
e	o			je	wo
æ	a	a:		jæ	
short vowels	long vowels			diphthongs	

Slovak includes many morphologically conditioned alternations between short and long vowels. Now, in contexts where /i, u, a/ lengthen to /i:, u:, a:/ respectively, we find that /e, o, æ/ lengthen to /je, wo, jæ/. For example, in the genitive plural of feminine and neuter nouns, the final vowel of the root is lengthened giving rise to (phonologically transcribed) alternations such as:

[72]	Nominative singular	Genitive plural	
[72a]	blat-o	bla:t	'mud'
	lon-o	lo:n	'lap'
[72b]	žen-a	žjen	'woman'
	pæt-a	pjæt	'heel'

Conversely, whereas /i:, u:, a:/ shorten to /i, u, a/, the shortening of /je, wo, jæ/ results in /e, o, æ/. On the basis of a wide range of alternations of this type, it is plausible to suggest that the underlying system of Slovak is a symmetric system of six vowels, which occur in short and long forms:

[73]

i	u	i:	u:
e	o	e:	o:
æ	a	æ:	a:
short vowels	long vowels		

It will be assumed that /je, wo, jæ/ derive respectively from /e:, o:, æ:/ by a rule formulated informally as in [74] below (cf Kenstowicz 1972; Kenstowicz and Kisseberth, 1979):

[74] Diphthongization

$$\begin{bmatrix} e: \\ o: \\ æ: \end{bmatrix} \rightarrow \begin{bmatrix} je \\ wo \\ jæ \end{bmatrix}$$

One major problem with this analysis is that it does not apply to etymological loanwords such as:

[75] [legé:nda] 'legend', [afé:ra] 'affair', [metó:da] 'method', [betó:n] 'concrete'

Now, there are hundreds of such lexical items with long mid vowels which should be turned into diphthongs if the standard assumptions are correct. It is, of course, theoretically possible to mark them all as exceptions. But, as Kenstowicz and Rubach observe, there is no evidence that these words behave as exceptions. They are otherwise made up of segments appearing within the phonological inventory of Slovak; they do not show any evidence of being regularized, etc. In addition, they take the same inflections as native items and, even more strikingly, they trigger or undergo some shortening rules operative in the phonology of Slovak at large. For instance, the agentive suffix [-ár] triggers a systematic shortening in long vowels of a preceding syllable in the 'native' vocabulary: cf [pi:s-aṭ,] 'write' vs. [pis-ár] 'writer'. This shortening also applies in examples such as [beto:n]–[beton-ar] 'cement'. But, if the words of [75] have been thoroughly integrated to the phonology of Slovak, why do they fail to diphthongize?

What is even more puzzling is the fact that etymological loanwords can undergo diphthongization in certain contexts. As we have seen, the genitive plural triggers a lengthening in the last root vowel and, even with loanwords, when such a vowel is mid, it appears as the corresponding diphthong:

[76] Nominative singular   Genitive plural
     gitar-a   gita:r   'guitar'
     fabrik-a   fabri:k   'factory'
     omelet-a   omeljet   'omelette'
     bomb-a   bwomb   'bomb'

What Kiparsky (1973b) suggested is that we could deal with this class of cases by modifying the Alternation Condition as in [77]:

[77] Revised Alternation Condition
     Obligatory neutralization rules apply only in derived
     environments.

But the whole problem was put into an entirely new perspective when it was pointed out by Mascaró (1976) that the class of rules which exhibited the 'derived-environment-only' behaviour was identical to the class of cyclic rules and that this behaviour was captured by stipulating that cyclic rules obeyed the Strict Cycle Condition (SCC) (Kiparsky 1982a: 154):

[78] Strict Cycle Condition (SCC)
     (a) Cyclic rules apply only to derived representations.
     (b) Def.: A representation φ is derived with respect to rule R
         in cycle j if φ meets the structural analysis of R by virtue
         of a combination of morphemes introduced in cycle j or
         the application of a rule in cycle j.

The relevance of [78] to the Slovak examples is that, if we assume that diphthongization is a cyclic rule and therefore limited to derived contexts in the sense of [78b], it will not apply to *eg* /afe:r-a/ 'affair' since the vowel length here is part of the underlying representation. On the other hand, if we consider a form like [omeljet] 'omelette-gen.-pl.' (underlying /omelet/), we can see that if the last root vowel is lengthened by the attribution of the morphological features 'gen.-pl.', yielding [omele:t], diphthongization will be able to apply since it will be fed by a rule operating on the same cycle.

Kenstowicz and Rubach (1987) point out that a consequence of treating diphthongization as a cyclic rule is that the diphthongs in roots such as /xvjezd-a/ 'star', /kwor-a/ 'bread crust' and /rjas-a/ 'cassock' must be underlying. On the other hand, in an *SPE*-style analysis, these roots would be derived from /xve:zd/, /ko:r/ and /ræ:s/ by taking a free ride on diphthongization. One advantage of an *SPE* approach is a simplification of the underlying inventory, but a major drawback is that there is no evidence from alternations that these roots have underlying forms that should depart from the surface. By considering diphthongization as a cyclic rule, we favour more concrete representations. Of course, the solution just sketched entails an apparent 'duplication' since we would now be positing both underlying and derived diphthongs. But Kenstowicz and Rubach show convincingly that this duplication can in fact be circumvented if we adopt nonlinear representations of the type advocated in the following chapters.

The best-known example of relevance of the SCC in constraining representations in English is provided by the behaviour of the following words with respect to Trisyllabic Shortening (TSS) (*cf* subcase [7a] of the rule of shortening – 4.2.1):

[79] Oberon, nightingale, Averell, overture, omega

As TSS is formulated in 4.2.1, all these words have to be marked as exceptions. But, very much as in Slovak above, these words do not behave as exceptional in any way. The problem is that TSS is restricted to appear in derived environments only: *cf tri+meter, gran+ular, penal+ty, omin+ous.* But, to formalize this within the *SPE* notation, the environment would have to state a disjunction of pluses as in [80]:

[80] _____ $\langle + \rangle_a$ C$_o$ $\langle + \rangle_b$ V $\langle + \rangle_c$ C$_o$ $\langle + \rangle_d$ V C$_o$
condition: *a* or *b* or *c* or *d*

This complex disjunction is unnecessary if we assume that TSS is cyclic. Because of the SCC, underived forms like those in [79] will be automatically skipped by TSS.

Lexical Phonology specialists seem agreed on treating TSS as a level 1 phonological rule. Since our presentation of the segmental phonology of English in Chapter 4 stayed as close as possible to Halle and Mohanan (1985), we quote in [81] the content of their first stratum with the ordering they adopt. By making our rule set explicit, we have, however, created an apparent problem with respect to the SCC. Since stress is cyclic and feeds the other level 1 rules, why does TSS not apply to the words of [79]? Do they not meet the notion of a derived environment since, by definition, this includes the prior application of a rule in a given cycle? Or, put another way, why is stress allowed to apply to stems as in the first cycle of example [49] (*erectility*)?

[81] *Halle and Mohanan's level 1*

> Stress rules
> CiV lengthening (rule [13] Ch. 4)
> s-voicing (rule [19])
> Shortening (rule [7])

The answer to this problem given by Kiparsky (1982a, b, 1985), and shared *inter alia* by Halle and Mohanan and Rubach, involves a distinction between structure-building and structure-changing operations. Stress assignment, in the case of lexical roots, is structure-building. Kiparsky is referring here to the building of suprasegmental structure covered in Chapter 6, but the theory can be understood without this apparatus. If we assume that lexical entries are unmarked for the feature [n stress] underlyingly, the assignment of a main stress to the lexical stem (*eg erect* in [49]) does not create a representation which is **distinct** (in the technical sense) from the underlying form but merely one which has an extra specification. The position advocated by LP specialists is that only structure-changing operations can feed cyclic rules (see Kiparsky 1985 for a revision of the SCC which makes this proviso explicit).[5]

Having made more precise the notion of cyclicity, let us now see whether it applies uniformly to all lexical levels.

5.2.6 Cyclic and non-cyclic levels
It is, in fact, not the case that all lexical rules which apply in a non-derived environment fall within the class of structure-

building rules. For instance, the VS was argued in Chapter 4 to apply to forms which never alternate and take a free ride on its application (*eg seed* /seːd/ → [sijd]). Whether or not this is thought desirable, VS applies in any case to underived forms such as *divine* (/diviːn/ → [divajn]). If we located the VS at level 1, its application to *divine* would contravene the SCC which is well entrenched at that level. Moreover, the result of its application to stems at level 1 would give rise to forms such as *[divajniti] *divinity*. It should also be noted that, in addition to the VS, Velar Softening applies in non-derived environment (*cf receive* / rV=keːv/ → [rəsijv]). Since *receive* has a morphologically complex structure at level 1 ([[[rV][keːv]]]), the k → s change is triggered wholly by the non-low vowel /eː/ which is present underlyingly and not introduced as a result of a morphological operation.

Booij and Rubach (1987), Kiparsky (1982a, b, 1985) and Rubach (1984a, b) describe rules such as VS and Velar Softening which apply across the board as **post-cyclic**. These rules apply only once after the word has been fully derived from a morphological point of view. Although all the word-internal structure assigned by the word-formation rules which belong to the post-cyclic components are available to the post-cyclic rules, the latter are not subject to strict cyclicity.[6] It is the position of the above specialists that only the last lexical level can escape the SCC. It is, however, worth stressing that, on the assumption that cyclic and post-cyclic rules form separate blocks, the decision to regard a given rule as cyclic or post-cyclic need not be argued for in each case. For instance, Velar Softening and VS were separately shown to be post-cyclic above, but given that Velar Softening precedes VS this latter rule would automatically be assigned non-cyclic status.

The position advocated by Halle and Mohanan is that the cyclicity of levels must be argued piecemeal. Any level can be non-cyclic. Thus, in their lexical model (*cf* [58]), level 2 is non-cyclic whereas levels 1 and 3 are described as cyclic. Level 4, whose cyclicity is not discussed explicitly by these authors, also appears to be non-cyclic since L-resyllabification (in their formulation as well as in the one adopted here) is structure-changing and applies to forms not derived at that level (recall the application at level 4 of L-resyllabification to *mail order*, a level 3 formation). Mohanan (1986), in fact, ends up giving ('arbitrary') preference to the idea that in the absence of counter-evidence it should be assumed that a level is non-cyclic. The exempting of the last level from the SCC by, for example Kiparsky, and the even freer

stance taken by Halle and Mohanan on the cyclicity of levels
have been argued to represent serious weakenings of the lexical
model (*cf* Kaisse and Shaw 1985: 23). It is, however, clear that
requiring of all levels that they should obey the SCC would
destroy most of the phonological rules which are seen as well
motivated by the very authors who subscribe to the LP
framework.

The dust has not yet settled on this whole issue and other
researchers have criticized the LP model altogether in favour of
more classical ideas on the relationship between phonology and
morphology (*cf* Aronoff and Sridhar 1983; Fabb 1988; Halle and
Vergnaud 1987a; Spencer 1988; Sproat 1985). While it may well
be the case that a unification of phonological theories will take
place around some of the concepts articulated in Chapters 6 and
7, the interaction between morphology and phonology is likely
to remain a subject of debate in the years to come.[7]

5.2.7 The post-lexical module

Once a form has undergone all the relevant phonological rules
on the last lexical cycle, all the internal brackets are erased and
a lexical representation is produced, *eg*: [_Adɪvájn] *divine* and
[_Ndɪvɪnɪtɪ] *divinity* for RP. This lexical representation is claimed
to be quite close to classical phonemic representations. This is
not particularly surprising since the phonological rules within the
lexical component correspond, by and large, to the set of *SPE*
rules put forward by Chomsky and Halle, who stopped short of
formulating allophonic rules, and rules involving words in
connected speech. Nevertheless, Mohanan (1986) claims that one
merit of LP is to reconstruct the valid insights of classical
phonemics while avoiding some of the worst methodological
excesses of the post-Bloomfieldians (*cf* 1.2.3).

Words in their final lexical representation are inserted into
syntactic trees and the post-lexical rules apply, if need be, on the
basis of syntactic information (see [51]). As pointed out earlier,
this means that any rule applying over domains larger than the
word is post-lexical. A good example of a post-lexical rule is [r]-
insertion already examined in 4.2.5 (*cf the idea*[r] *of it, the
milieu*[r] *is*) which in the formulation of rule [29] of Ch. 4,
repeated here for convenience, applies across word-boundaries.

[82] [r]-insertion
$$\emptyset \rightarrow r \ / \ [ə, ɔ:, iə, eə, oə, a:, ɔ:] \ \#_o \ V$$

Another example of a rule which is post-lexical is flapping (*cf*
Ch. 1) which was presented in 1.2.4 with reference to words in

isolation (*eg sitting* [sɪɾɪŋ] < /sɪtɪŋ/). But, flapping can also be shown to apply across word-boundaries: *eg si*[ɾ] *in the park*. Therefore, it is post-lexical and any rule which follows it is also post-lexical. Thus, in dialects where lengthening follows flapping, lengthening can automatically be assigned a post-lexical status without having to check its properties.

The post-lexical rules are not restricted to rules which apply within phrases. Since words are present within phrases with their outermost brackets, the latter are available at the post-lexical level. Therefore, classical allophonic rules which may have the word as a domain (*eg* aspiration) apply at this stage too. One criterion for assigning a rule to the post-lexical component is its non-binary nature. Typically, allophonic processes are scalar (*eg* aspiration is a question of more or less not of plus–minus) and this is a sufficient, but not a necessary, condition for treating rules as post-lexical. On the other hand, the lexical module has been claimed to be restricted to the manipulation of binary feature-values. Some other characteristics of post-lexical rules which are mentioned in the literature are their lack of exceptions, the creation of novel forms and their non-cyclicity. These are briefly examined in turn:

1. Lack of exceptions: all segments which fulfil the conditions for aspiration undergo the rule. By contrast, lexical rules are often subject to exceptions (*eg obesity* as an exception to TSS).
2. Creation of novel forms: post-lexical rules create structures which break the lexical templates of the language. Examples of fast speech phenomena have already been given: *eg because* /bɪkəz/ → [bɪxəz] → [pxəz] (4.4.3) with the creation of a cluster [px] which is disallowed within the lexicon.
3. Non-cyclicity: Kiparsky (1982a: 143) claims that 'all and only lexical categories are lexical domains' and that there should be no cyclic application above the word-level. In his account, this yields a neat partition of rule-blocks since post-lexical rules prolong, so to speak, post-cyclic rules in that both do not obey the SCC. This position contrasts sharply with the early work in generative phonology where the cyclic principle received strong support from the syntactic domain (*cf* the *SPE* account of sentence stress in English and Schane's (1968) cyclic treatment of French liaison). But it has been accepted for some time that the candidates for syntactic cyclicity can be treated non-

cyclically (*cf* Liberman and Prince 1977, and Schane 1972). It is, however, unclear why cyclicity should be excluded by definition at the post-lexical level. There is no reason why phonological rules should not work outwards from the constituent parts of sentences to the whole. Indeed, Mohanan (1986) assumes that morphological and syntactic cyclicity share the same structure. It seems preferable to treat cyclicity at the post-lexical level as a matter of empirical (dis)confirmation rather than legislation.

One general problem facing the phonologist at the post-lexical level is the question of conceptual tools. The binary vocabulary and the sharp divisions which characterize lexical rules are not adequate for the specification of many allophonic processes. Mohanan (1986: 157) mentions the possibility of using scalar rules for processes like aspiration in English. The problem is that even scales are only a first approximation. To be properly stated, many allophonic processes require complex equations and weightings. For instance, allophonic vowel length in English is going to be a function of the inherent duration of the vowel, the nature and number of segments that follow, the location of word-boundaries, the stress and intonation pattern, etc. (see *eg* S. R. Anderson 1975; Ladefoged 1977). Mohanan suggests that we should split up the post-lexical module into a **syntactic** module and a **phonetic** module. The latter, where, *eg*, aspiration will be described, will essentially be the province of the experimental phonetician. This move seems by and large correct although it should be noted that the setting up of any division creates boundary problems. It is, in fact, likely that the intermixture of 'phonological' and 'phonetic' rules incisively discussed by S. R. Anderson (1975) will reappear under another guise. For instance, Anderson noted, within the classical paradigm, that in accents which require the lengthening rule to apply before flapping in words such as *rider*, lengthening, which is a clearly phonetic rule, has to apply before flapping, which, as a rule of neutralization, is a good candidate for the status of phonological rule. Be that as it may, the major problem facing phonologists with respect to the post-lexical module is the interaction between syntactic and prosodic information. As the next section shows, we may have been jumping the gun in labelling as 'syntactic' rules which may be more adequately described as 'prosodic'.

5.2.8 Syntax, prosody and the post-lexical module
The previous section discussed criteria for assigning rules to the lexical or the post-lexical module. The general argumentation

which led to the elimination of boundaries in favour of morphological brackets (*ie* constituency information) would apply here as
well and we offer a brief discussion of the inadequacy of boundaries with respect to French liaison further down. But, the **direct**
relevance of syntactic information has been challenged by a
number of authors, and, most eloquently, by Nespor and Vogel
(1982, 1986). These specialists assume, first of all, that as part
of phonological representations, a prosodic hierarchy should be
constructed including units such as the syllable, the foot, the
phonological word, the clitic group, the phonological phrase, the
intonational phrase and the phonological utterance (see Ch. 6 on
part of this hierarchy). In addition, they put forward the thesis
– backed up by the reanalysis of many standard examples – that
post-lexical rules should be formulated only by reference to this
prosodic hierarchy.

Consider, as an example of this claim, the status of r-insertion
in British English given in [82] above. If we abandon boundaries,
the domain of r-insertion would presumably have to be specified
as the sentence since this is the maximal domain of syntactic
analysis. This would account for r-insertion in examples such as:

[83] In America, as you know, doggie-bags are acceptable → . . .
America[r]as you . . .

But r-insertion can equally take place across sentences as in [84]:

[84] I hear. I hear. I hear → I hea[r] I hea[r] I hea[r]

While it might be argued that we could account for [84]
syntactically by allowing an indefinite number of S's (S∗) as
the maximal domain of phonological rules, Nespor and Vogel
(1986: 232ff) argue that this would still lead to an incorrect specification. The reason is that it is not possible to group any two
sentences into a phonological unit. Thus, r-insertion is acceptable
in the following sequence of two declaratives linked by an
implicit 'because' from a logico-semantic point of view:

[85] I have hidden the vodka. Alvin's coming → . . . vodka[r]Alvin
. . .

but not between two declaratives which stand in an implicit
disjunctive ('but') relationship:

[86] I didn't invite Peter. I should have though → . . .∗Pete[r]I
. . .

The domain of r-insertion is what they call the Utterance (U),
a phonological constituent partially based on the syntax since

normally a single S forms a U, but which also requires access to logico-semantic information. Several U's can be restructured into a U only if certain logico-semantic conditions are satisfied. Although mapping rules can be provided from the syntax to the prosodic hierarchy, the latter is the only relevant domain of phonological rules. In that sense, a U is exhaustively defined in terms of Intonational Phrases (I's) and, in turn, I's are exhaustively defined in terms of Phonological Phrases (φ's), and so on and so forth.

Let us examine, as a further example of the relevance of prosodic categories, the process of elision in Midi French which, as we saw in 1.5.1, was responsible for schwa-deletion within words (*cf bêtise* /betə+izə/ → [betizə]) and within phrases (*cf petite amie* /pətitə # ami+ə/ → [pətitami]). In Chapter 1, it was argued that elision should be split into two rules, a surprising result within the *SPE* paradigm given the identity of the processes involved. Within LP, all we need to say is there is one rule which is allowed to span both the lexical and the post-lexical modules. However, what is of direct interest here is the domain of application of phrasal elision. In Chapter 1, this was formulated with a simple reference to word-boundaries as in [87] below (see rule [40] in 1.5.1):

[87] Elision (domain: phrases)
   ə → ∅ / ___ #₁ V

Within Nespor and Vogel's system, it can be observed that, very much like r-insertion above, elision can apply across sentences if they are treated as a single U (*cf* [88]):

[88] Cache la bière. André arrive → . . . [bjɛrãdre] . . . Hide the beer, André is coming.

Moreover, within a sentence, a phrase within which elision takes place need not be said on a single tune: *eg Michèle est venue* can be pronounced [mišɛlevøny] (from /mišɛlə#e#vøny/) with a rise on the NP, *Michèle*, and a fall on *est venue*. In terms of Nespor and Vogel's system, schwa deletion clearly does not apply within an I but within the larger unit, the U. Elision should therefore be reformulated as [89]:

[89] ə → ∅ / _____V   [domain: U]

The above supports the thesis that post-lexical rules are more appropriately discussed with reference to a prosodic hierarchy than to syntactic constituency. But consider now liaison, which was mentioned in Chapter 1 in support of underlying forms which incorporate a latent consonant. Thus the word *petit* was represented as /pətit/ and liaison takes place in the contexts where truncation is disallowed (*eg petit acte* /pətit#aktə/ → [pətitaktə]). Since the conditioning of liaison is the same in Southern French as in standard variety, we can drop the qualification 'Southern' and take advantage for expository purposes of some of the vast literature on the topic of 'French liaison'.

In traditional accounts of liaison, it is assumed that, if the phonological conditions for liaison are fulfilled, three types of grammatical contexts can be distinguished: [90a] obligatory, [90b] optional, [90c] forbidden. Examples of these are given below:

[90a] DET + N	*les amis*	[lezami]	*[leami]
	the friends		
[90b] AUX + ADVP	*est ici*	[etisi] or [eisi]	
	is here		
[90c] NP + VP	*les amis arrivent*	[lezamiarivə]	
	the friends arrive	*[lezamizarivə]	

Where liaison is optional, its frequency will be relative to a variety of 'stylistic' factors. To quote a well-known maxim: 'The more elevated the style the more liaison occurs.' A common way of handling the relative frequency of liaison has consisted in setting up a number of registers or scales of formality: *eg* formal, careful, colloquial.

In major work on this topic, Selkirk (1972, 1974) tried to show how some of the traditional assumptions could be integrated within the generative approach. She took as correct the version of truncation given in Chapter 1 (see rule [49] in 1.5.2). Hence liaison will only occur when at most **one** word boundary separates two units, which is a way of expressing the classical notion that liaison depends on the syntactic cohesion between words. Her argument was that liaison follows directly from the *SPE* universal conventions cited above (SPE-I [36] and SPE-II [40]) coupled with language-specific readjustment rules. Thus, an adjective and a noun should be separated by two word-boundaries but since liaison occurs in *petit acte* [pətitaktə], a convention was proposed which – informally stated – transformed A # # N into A # N. In addition to this, Selkirk contended that the readjustment rules were maximally stated in terms of X-bar syntax. In elevated style, for instance, a boundary between a head and its complement would be optionally deleted to account for liaison (*allait # # en France* → *allait # en France*). On the other hand, liaison was claimed not to occur between heads and modifiers.

A number of difficulties raised by Selkirk's boundary approach
have been discussed in the literature. A major problem, pointed
out by Basbøll (1978: 8), is that it is generally the case that the
more casual or reduced speech becomes the more grammatical
boundaries lose their effect. But in Selkirk's approach exactly the
opposite has to happen. The more elevated the style the more
boundaries have to be deleted (*cf allait en France*). Conversely,
in casual speech the loss of liaison (say, in *très # amusant*) can
only be accounted for by increasing the number of boundaries
surrounding common words like *très* (or *est, ont,* etc.) in order
to fulfil the requirements of truncation. It can be also shown that
a pause in the delivery does not necessarily inhibit liaison: *cf deux
petites . . . z-histoires* 'two little stories' and a variety of other
facts can be adduced against the boundary approach to French
liaison (Morin and Kaye 1982: 299).

An alternative to this approach, first put forward by Rotenberg
(1975, 1978), has consisted in invoking a direct sensitivity to
syntax. The problem is discovering which syntactic configurations
favour liaison. Selkirk's scheme made heavy use of X-bar syntax
– a hypothesis which has received a devastating critique in Morin
and Kaye (1982). Rotenberg, on the other hand, argued that
liaison only occurred between sisters as in [91]. But this requires
too many unmotivated analyses from a syntactic point of view
(*cf* Schane 1978). Thus to account for the liaison in *dans un été*,
the tree needs to be [92a] rather than the well-supported [92b]
(or its X-bar translation).

[91]

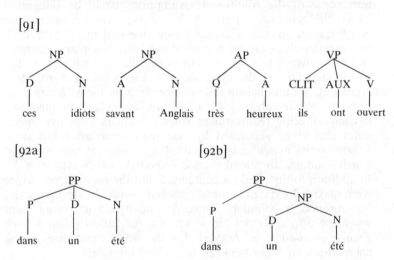

[92a]   [92b]

More recently, Kaisse (1985) has suggested that the relevant condition for liaison was the relation of c-command (*cf* van Riemsdijk and Williams 1986: 141ff). This thesis has been criticized by Morin (1987: 828–30). It seems, in fact, that while the syntactic conditioning of liaison is undeniable, this conditioning does not fully support a strong syntactic hypothesis. Rather, liaison is made on a context-by-context basis, and sometimes a word-by-word basis, a view persuasively defended by Morin and Kaye (1982) and endorsed in Encrevé's (1988) authoritative study of this topic. (See too the discussion in Durand 1986b: 166–8.)

This view of liaison does not seemingly sit very well with Nespor and Vogel's approach. But we have seen that liaison is not blocked by pauses (unlike elision and r-insertion). And Nespor and Vogel point out, citing Morin as their source, that liaison can even apply across speakers as [93] where the hesitation by Speaker 1 leads to a liaison by Speaker 2:

[93] Speaker 1: Je cherchais des [de] . . .
  'I was looking for some'
  Speaker 2 . . . [z]allumettes
  '. . . matches'

On the basis of such examples, liaison could be placed outside the prosodic hierarchy which assumes a normal delivery without pauses and single speakers. One might even go as far as excluding liaison from core phonology altogether. But, surely, this would be an arbitrary move. Liaison is an integral part of the phonological system of French and obligatory liaison is remarkably constant across speakers (see Encrevé 1988). Since, whatever other factors may be involved (see Booij and De Jong, 1987), liaison needs access to syntactic information, it provides reasonable evidence that post-lexical rules cannot be based on prosodic information alone. The debate on the syntactic or prosodic conditioning of post-lexical rules is, in many respects, still in its infancy (see Booij 1985, 1988 and the articles in Zwicky and Kaisse 1987). The point of view adopted in the rest of this book will be that both syntactic and prosodic information should be accessible to phonological rules.[8]

5.2.9 Modularity and Universal Grammar

The specification of the lexical and post-lexical modules is a step towards the **formal** characterization of the grammatical system known as Universal Grammar (UG). This complements the discussion of DFs in Chapter 2, where it was emphasized that work on DFs represents an attempt to fix the **substantive** parameters of phonetic theory. And since many analyses in LP integrate the insights of UT, much of the functioning of phonological systems is derivable from universal principles.

The general organization of phonological operations offered within LP is part and parcel of the modular approach which is central to the Government and Binding paradigm. The theory of rule application provides a striking illustration of the difference between this type of approach and previous efforts. As detailed above, some rules are lexical only and other rules post-lexical only. While this is reminiscent of divisions such as that between MP rules and sandhi-*cum*-phonological rules in NGP, a fundamental difference is that LP also allows a rule to span both the lexical and the post-lexical domain (*cf* elision in Midi French). One possibility which has been raised in LP is that the different properties of rules spanning these two modules might derive from the differences between them (*cf* Kiparsky 1985). If this turns out to be verified, the situation in phonology would parallel that in syntax and logical form. The rule of Wh-movement is available in both these components in English. In syntax, it obeys subjacency, whereas in logical form, it is allowed to violate it. More generally, LP allows the relation between the rule system and the grammatical modules to be envisaged in a new light and some challenging hypotheses can be put forward concerning the phonology of natural languages.

Notes

1. The notation [ ] → [−G] / [____, +F] is equivalent to [ ] → $[-G] / \left[\dfrac{\_\_\_}{+F} \right]$

2. Underspecification has also been explored within LP by Kiparsky (1982a, b, 1985). This is neglected in 5.2 for reasons of space. For a worthwhile exploration of UT with respect to child language acquisition, see Spencer (1985).

3. But see Kiparsky (1983) for a somewhat different position on these formations.

4. See Booij and Rubach (1987) for an attempt to reduce Halle and Mohanan's four levels to three.

5. The fact that stress assignment is structure-building and thus does not obey the SCC is true of English on its first application but not necessarily of other languages. Halle and Mohanan (1985) point out, for instance, that stress asssignment is initially structure-changing in Sanskrit where accents must be specified in underlying representations and thus obeys the SCC.

6. A further complication is that this is, if we follow Booij and Rubach (1987: 30), 'a parameter along which languages vary', since they

argue that in Polish and Dutch inputs to the post-cyclic rules must have no internal morphological structure.

7. The LP model has now been applied to a wide sample of languages. See, for instance, Booij (1984), Durand (1988), Johnson (1987), Plénat (1986) on French; for a thorough examination of one language, see Rubach (1984a); for tones, see Pulleyblank (1986).

8. For a different strand of work on the syntax–phonology interface not explored here, see Pullum and Zwicky (1984), Zwicky and Pullum (1986).

Chapter 6

Metrical structures

6.1 The syllable

In the preceding chapters, although we occasionally made informal reference to concepts such as 'open syllable' or 'closed syllable', the syllable did not play any formal role. Chomsky and Halle, in their attempt to provide formal foundations for phonology, neglected the existing tradition of work on the syllable (*eg* Kuryłowicz 1948; Pike and Pike 1947; Pike 1947, 1967), limiting their attention to strings of segment, their internal structure and operations on segments and features. In 4.4.1, it was pointed out that access to information about syllable boundaries (represented by $) improved matters since more perspicuous formulations of rules became possible. But there is a great deal of evidence that restricting ourselves to the position of segments in relation to syllable boundaries does not go far enough. The syllable needs to be recognized as a **unit**. As simple illustrations of this claim consider the following statements:

[1] Every Mazateco morpheme in its full form consists of bisyllabic sequences (Pike and Pike 1947).
[2] In Polish, stress is penultimate in words of more than one syllable (but monosyllables are stressed).

In each case, the *SPE* translation of these statements has to be made in terms of sequences of segments. For instance, any of the following rules is an appropriate formalization of [2] (where $]_\omega$ is a word-edge):

[3] Polish stress
[3a] $V \rightarrow [+\text{stress}] / \_\_ C_o (V) C_o]_\omega$
[3b] $V \rightarrow [+\text{stress}] / \_\_ C_o (VC_o)]_\omega$
[3c] $V \rightarrow [+\text{stress}] / \_\_ (C_o V) C_o]_\omega$

But these statements are equally arbitrary. Indeed, whether or not the vowel in the last syllable is followed by consonants is irrelevant. If, on the other hand, we recognize that the syllable is a unit, labelled σ from now on, then matters become simpler.[1] The Polish stress rule can simply be stated as [4]:

[4] σ → ó / ——(σ)]$_ω$

and the overall morpheme template of Mazateco is [σ σ].

The Mazateco example may appear over-simple. Nevertheless, it draws attention to the fact that the specification of the phonotactics of a language can be extraordinarily complex without recourse to the syllable. It is no accident that, as in Chapter 2, morpheme-structure conditions in classical generative works were usually restricted to the edges of morphemes, which typically coincide with the beginning and end of syllables. Medial consonantal clusters turn out to be extraordinarily complex if dealt with in isolation from syllable structure. Why, for instance, is a sequence such as [kstr] acceptable medially (*cf extreme* [ekstrijm]) but not the shorter sequence [kps] (*cf* *ikpseme*)? The answer is to be found in the possibility of parsing medial clusters in terms of acceptable syllable-beginnings (onsets) and ends (codas). Thus, to take *extreme*, the sequence [kst] is possible syllable-finally (*cf next* [nekst]) and the sequence [str] is possible syllable-initially (*cf stream* [strijm]). Assuming, as is generally done, that syllable-splits maximize onsets, we can divide up *extreme* in the following way: [$_σ$ek$_σ$][$_σ$strijm$_σ$]. By contrast, there is no way of segmenting hypothetical *ikpseme* into syllables. Neither [kps] nor [kp] is allowed syllable-finally. The first syllable break must therefore be after *ik*: [$_σ$ik$_σ$][psijm]. But, then, neither [kps] nor [ps] is allowed as the onset of a syllable: words spelled with initial *ps* are pronounced with an [s]: *cf psychology* [sajkɔləji]. The only way of dividing *ikpseme* in terms of syllable-stretches is as follows: [$_σ$ik$_σ$] p [$_σ$sijm$_σ$], where a /p/ is stranded between two well-formed syllables.

The exhaustive parsability of medial clusters in terms of possible syllable onsets and codas is a requirement on the well-formedness of morphemes in English and many other languages. And, more generally, it can be said for many languages that morphemes are sequences of possible syllables (*cf eg* Mazateco above). The fact that exceptions are attested (*eg* Italian: *cf* Vincent 1976) does not, of itself, invalidate the centrality of syllable-structure for specifying the phonotactics of languages. The precise relation between syllable-structure and underlying sequences of contrastive segments will be further investigated later. Having affirmed the need for a syllable unit (σ), the ques-

tion that will preoccupy us now is how this unit stands in relation
to its constituents.

The reconstruction of the syllable in 'orthodox' generative
phonology is usually attributed to Kahn (1976), who adopted a
minimalist view. The σ node dominates immediately its constituents (daughters) as symbolized in the representation of *catkin*
in [5].

[5]

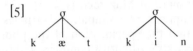

Despite the simplicity of [5], Kahn demonstrated conclusively
that a wide number of generalizations could be captured by reference to syllable-structure rather than segments and boundaries.
Part of the explanatory power of Kahn's examples stemmed from
the formal integration of syllable overlap in his model – an issue
considered in 6.1.8. Another minimalist position is that taken by
Clements and Keyser (1983), who suggest that the relation between σ and segments should be mediated by what they refer to
as the 'CV tier' as in [6].

[6]

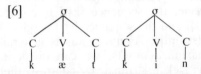

The C and V slots form a set of timing units. They correspond
roughly to the abstract C and V labels which many structuralists
used in stating the shape of the syllable of languages – as, for
example, when Abercrombie (1967) says that the syllable in Cantonese is of type (C)V(C). Although Clements and Keyser argue
at length against giving more internal structure to the syllable,
the persuasiveness of their case lies elsewhere – *ie* in the many-to-
many relationship they allow between the CV tier and the segments. The CV tier is now accepted by most phonologists as an
indispensable component of phonological representations and receives further consideration in 6.1.7 and in Chapter 7. But, there
seems to be a broad consensus that, on the analogy of NP–VP
division of sentences in syntax, there is a major break between
the onset of the syllable (*eg* [tr] in *train*) and the rest of the syllable, which is called the rhyme and is made up of the syllable
peak and all its right-handside satellites (*eg* [ejn] in *train*). It will
be argued here that further sub-units should be recognized; in
particular, that the rhyme should itself be split into a nucleus and

a coda, but this is more controversial. As a starting-point, let us review a number of arguments in favour of the onset–rhyme (O–R) split.

6.1.1 The onset–rhyme split

In this section, three arguments drawn from stress assignment, phonotactics and speech errors will be given in favour of giving a branching O–R structure to the syllable.

The classical statement of stress assignment in Latin is well known (cf Allen 1969, 1970).[2] Stress depends on what is referred to as the 'quantity' (light vs. heavy) of syllables. A syllable is 'heavy' if it contains a long vowel, or a diphthong, or a short vowel followed by a consonant. An open syllable which contains only a short vowel is 'light'. It should be clear that in deciding whether a syllable is heavy or light, the status of the onset of the syllable is strictly irrelevant. Thus *ak* is just as heavy as *brak*, and *gre* is just as light as *ne* or *e*. What matters is the nature of the rhyme. Given this concept, the position of the Latin stress can be stated quite simply: in words of more than two syllables, if the penultimate rhyme is heavy, it is stressed (*relá:tus, reféctus*), but if it is light, the antepenult receives the accent (*exístimo:, ténebrae*). Disyllables are necessarily stressed on the penult (*tégo:, tóga*). The dynamic character of this stress rule can be observed in stress-shifts resulting from the addition of an enclitic (*-que, -ue, -ne, -ce*) to a word: for example, *uírum* but *uirúmque*.

But there remains a problem in the classical formulation: what is common to a long vowel, a diphthong and a short vowel + consonant? The similarity between a short vowel + consonant and a diphthong (a sequence of two vocalic units or of vowel + glide) appears to lie in the fact that in each case two units are involved. But, if we were to represent long vowels as $[+/-long]$, as we have done so far, the heaviness of a rhyme containing a long vowel would be a different matter from that of the other two types of rhyme. One solution to this problem lies in the assumption that long vowels should be treated as 'geminates' – that is, sequences of identical vowels. A heavy syllable in Latin can then be formally defined as a syllable whose rhyme branches as exemplified next page in [7]. This example is important in that the heaviness of rhymes has been shown to condition, again and again, the assignment of stress in a variety of languages. In fact, ever since *SPE*, most generative accounts of English have assumed that principles similar to that of the Latin stress rule were operative in the assignment of English stress (cf [5bii] and [5biii] in 4.2.1).

[7]

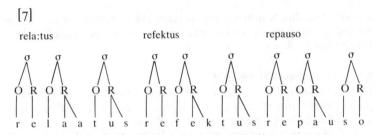

rela:tus   refektus   repauso

Let us now turn our attention to phonotactic arguments in favour of O–R. One very simple but telling argument is offered by Harris (1983: 9–10). Harris observes that any statement concerning syllable-size in Spanish is hopelessly complex if the O–R split is not recognized. Thus, we will need to say, for instance, that

> Spanish syllables have a maximum length of five consonants, if the initial string contains two segments, but a maximum length of four segments if there is one initial consonant, and three segments if there is no initial consonant. One has only to formulate this (non)alternative to see its inadequacy: in fact, rhymes are maximally three segments long independently of onset length.

Moreover, Harris argues that there are strong restrictions between elements of the rhyme in Spanish which are unparalleled by restrictions between the onset and the peak of the syllable. The same argument can be constructed for English and consideration of the data and tables in Fudge (1969, 1987) should convince any reader that the links between the elements of the rhyme are stronger than those between the onset and the peak of a syllable. To exemplify this point briefly, we can see that, given a syllable formula CCVC in English, if the first consonantal slot is filled by /s/ and the V slot is filled by /æ/, the choice of a consonant which can fill the second C slot is going to be more controlled by /s/ than by /æ/. This indicates that a stronger link exists between the first two consonants, as members of the onset, than between either consonant and the vowel (Pike 1967: 386–7). The degree of cohesion within the onset as well as within the rhyme provides strong support for a branching structure.

Fudge (1987), in a short quantitative survey based on Fromkin (1973), also shows that speech errors (spoonerisms, haplologies, blends) shed some light on the matter of syllable division. For instance, spoonerisms such as *cassy put* for *pussy cat* where the substitution involves the onset + peak are attested. But, according to Fudge, the most frequent type of error is on the model *if the fap kits* for *if the cap fits* – that is, the rhyme (peak + coda) is respected and the substitution involves onsets only. Fudge suggests that 'cases supporting that Onset + Rhyme split outnumber those supporting the Onset + Peak + Coda split by about four to one'.

Since further evidence in favour of the rhyme can also be adduced from other areas (*cf eg* J. M. Anderson 1986b; Fudge, 1987, Selkirk 1982a; Vincent 1986), we shall assume that the case for an O–R split is cast-iron. Rules which were formulated in terms of sequences of segments and boundaries can now appeal directly to suprasegmental structure. In Chapter 5, for instance, the rule of L-velarization was provisionally formulated as in [8]:

[8] L-velarization (rule [65] of 5.2.4)
$/l/ \rightarrow$ [+back, +high] / ___[−syll]$_0$ \$

But it can now be reformulated as in [9]:

$$R$$
[9] $/l/ \rightarrow$ [+back, +high] / $\underline{\text{l}}$

which indicates that the relevant context for velarization is that $/l/$ should be part of a rhyme. The presence of optional segments between $/l/$ and the end of the rhyme (*eg belts* [belts]) is strictly irrelevant to the application of [9]. Yet, it was necessary to mention the possibility of these segments in [8], which assumed that information about syllable-structure was restricted to syllable-edges.

6.1.2 The nucleus and the coda

The type of argumentation employed above to motivate an onset–rhyme split can also be used to justify a further division of the rhyme into two parts: a nucleus (N) and a coda (C). The nucleus is the constituent that contains the head of the whole syllable (i.e. the [+syllabic] segment). In a language like English, the nucleus is made up of short vowels (*bit*), long vowels (*palm*), or diphthongs (*like*). And the shortening and lengthening rules which relate short vowels and long vowels/diphthongs in English and other languages have been argued to have the nucleus as domain (see *eg* Kenstowicz and Rubach 1987, on Slovak). Adopting a nucleus is a way of formalizing the traditional intuition that long vowels and diphthongs function as unitary complexes and impose restrictions on the nature of the coda as such. For instance, in English (*cf* J. M. Anderson 1986b), the nucleus /aw/ cannot be followed by non-coronal consonants within the coda as illustrated in [10]:[3]

[10a] down, */−awm/, */−awŋ/
[10b] loud, */−awb/, */−awg/
[10c] tout, */−awp/, */−awk/
[10d] mouth, house, slouch, */−awf/
[10e] mouth (v), rouse, gouge, */−awv/,

A syllable such as *blind* would therefore be represented as in [11].

[11]

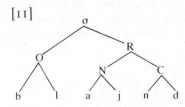

The nucleus is not made of vocalic elements only. Pike (1967: 387), for instance, gives five independent arguments why in Totonaco a post-vocalic glottal stop in CVʔ and CVʔC syllables must be part of the nucleus and not part of a post-nuclear consonantal cluster. And in a language like Slovak, the nucleus can be filled in by long and short liquids (*eg srna* (sr̥na] 'deer' and *kŕmny* [kr̥:mni] 'food' (adj) – see Kenstowicz and Rubach 1987: 473).

One advantage of splitting syllables into an onset vs. a rhyme, and allowing the rhyme to branch into two sub-constituents, lies in the possibility of distinguishing two different modes of integration of semi-vowels within a syllable. Kaye and Lowenstamm (1984) show that in standard French (and their argument carries over to Midi French) a sequence such as [wa] (*watt* [wat], *oie* [wa]) can function in two ways. Either [w] is parallel to the consonants and is within the onset of a syllable or [wa] is a type of rising diphthong – that is, a sequence within the nucleus. Our two representative examples are given in [12]. Kaye and Lowen-

[12]

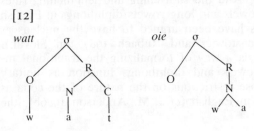

stamm posit that the onset node is universally present within a syllable whether filled or not. The advantage of this assumption is that the onset position is commonly the locus of insertion rules. Many languages require, for instance, the insertion of a glottal stop if a syllable is vowel-initial (*cf eg* Durand 1987 on Malay).

Three arguments can be offered in favour of distinctions along the lines of [12]. First of all, distinguishing rising diphthongs from glide + vowel sequences allows for an elegant account of French liaison and elision. Limiting ourselves to liaison here, it is well known that identical phonetic sequences can behave in two different ways in French, as charted in [13]:

[13a] Onset + nucleus		[13b]	Complex nucleus
les watts	[lewat]		*les oies* [lezwa]
les westerns	[lewestern]		*les oints* [lezwɛ̃]
les week-ends	[lewikend]		*les huîtres* [lezɥitrə]

The words in [13b] behave like vowel-initial words (*les amis* [lezami]) which also have an empty onset. Instead of the linear account of Chapter 1, liaison can therefore be interpreted as a delinking from the coda of the final underlying consonant of liaison words (*eg les* /lez/) which becomes linked (associated) to free onset in [14][4] (where a barred line indicates a delinking – but see 6.1.6). For words like *watt* in [13a] no liaison can occur since the onset is not empty.[5]

[14]

les oies   *les amis*

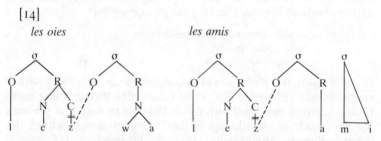

The second argument in favour of distinguishing [13a] from [13b] along the lines of [12] comes from the existence of a conspiracy in French against the sequence Obstruent + Liquid + Glide. Consider the following forms:

[15a] loue	[lu]	louer	[lwe]
tue	[ty]	tuer	[tɥe]
lie	[li]	lier	[lje]
[15b] troue	[tru]	trouer	[tru(w)e]
influe	[ɛ̃fly]	influer	[ɛ̃fly(ɥ)e]
plie	[pli]	plier	[plije]
[15c] *[trwe]	*[ɛ̃flɥe]	*[plje]

We see from [15a] that high vowels in stems are turned into semi-vowels when a vowel-initial suffix is added. But this is blocked when the stem is of the form Obstruent + Liquid + Vowel. We do not either find monomorphemes of the form *[kljɛr], *[plwes], etc. beside *grief* [grijɛf], *brouette* [bru(w)ɛt], etc. In other words, French does not appear to allow onsets of the form Obstruent + Liquid + Glide (OLG). Yet, the sequences of [13b] are allowed after Obstruent + Liquid: *cf croire* [krwar], *pluie* [plɥi], *groin* [grwɛ̃]. This falls out from the assumption that these sequences are part of the nucleus. The constraint barring *OLG applies to onsets and is not broken by a representation such as [16].

[16] *croire*

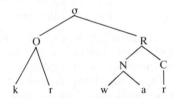

Finally, Kaye and Lowenstamm point out that diphthongs are commonly implicated, synchronically or diachronically, in processes of alternation with simple vowels. In French, alternations such as the ones in [17] can be observed:

[17] ɛ-wa ə-wa verra–voit, devons–doivent
     ø-ɥi peut–puisse
     ə-wɛ̃ fenaison–foin

In each case, the glide–vowel sequence which alternates with a simple vowel belongs to the set of candidates to the 'rising diphthong' status. Connected with this is the observation that whereas the inventory of diphthongs is limited, semi-vowels within the onset collocate freely with any vocalic nucleus (*cf waters, western, whisky, wombat*).

Having established the advantages of the divisions so far postulated, Kaye and Lowenstamm complete the demonstration by showing that in a word like *mouille* [muj], the final [j] does not form a nucleus with the vowel [u], but is part of the coda. It does not constrain the preceding vowel as much as is typical within glides (*ie* all vowels are allowed except [ɔ] and [o], with the exception of foreign borrowing such as *boy*). Unlike the examples of [17], [uj] does not alternate with single vowels. Even more strikingly, when a suffix is added, as in *mouillons*, [j] resyllabifies rightwards like any final consonant [mu$jō]. By contrast, the sequence [aj] of *buy* in English, which is a true diphthong (*ie* a sequence within the nucleus), resists simple resyllabification:*[ba$jiŋ] *buying*. Instead one observes either a hiatus [baj$iŋ] or smoothing ([ba:$iŋ]) (Wells 1982: §3.2.9) as typical realizations in RP for example.

Since as mentioned earlier, additional arguments in favour of the N–C break can be adduced from other languages I shall assume hereafter that branching rhymes are well motivated (but see 6.1.4). We shall see later in this chapter that other advantages accrue from this assumption.[6]

6.1.3 The elimination of [+/−syllabic]

One advantage of introducing the syllable into phonological representation is the possibility of dispensing with the feature [+/−syllabic]. Along with stress and [+/−long] which are reconsidered later, the feature[+/−syllabic] is different from the other features ([+/−cons], [+/−high], etc.) in that it is **syntagmatic**. That is, whether or not a segment is syllabic depends on its position within syllable structure, not on any inherent phonological property of its own. For instance, given the sequence /litl/ in English, the non-syllabicity of the first /l/ and the syllabicity of the second can be determined on the basis of their position within the word. By contrast, /l/ is inherently [+son, +lat, etc.]. If [+/−syll] is eliminated, the contrast between the high vowels /i, u, y/ and the glides /j, w, ɥ/ is not one of feature-value assignment but a question of position within the syllable. Any /i, u, y/ which is in a simple nucleus or is the head of a complex nucleus is automatically syllabic. Any /i, u, y/ assigned to the onset, the coda or a non-head position within the nucleus is non-syllabic. What is needed is not a feature [+/−syll], but a set of principles for defining how all positions with the syllables can be filled in by segments and how heads can be recognized. This issue will be taken up in the following sections.

6.1.4 An argument against the nucleus–coda split

Hogg and McCully (1987: 45–7), who assume that the O–R division is well grounded, provide the following argument against splitting the rhyme into nucleus + coda. They observe that beside *grind, print, pound*, the following syllables are unacceptable:*graimb,*pounk,*faimp. The generalization is that, if there are four elements within a rhyme, then the fourth position must be filled by a consonant which is [+coronal] (Fudge 1969; Selkirk 1982a). By supposing that the structure of the rhymes of *grind* and *graimb* is as in [18],

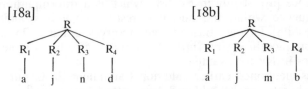

[18a]   [18b]

the constraint is easy to state: *ie* R_4 cannot be filled by [+cor].
On the other hand, Hogg and McCully argue that by positing a
N–C layer, the unacceptability of [18b] can only be clumsily
stated. Given that *clamp, bunk*, etc. are acceptable, they point
out that there are only two options open. Firstly, we can state
that the coda may branch if either (a) the nucleus does not
branch (*bunk*), or (b) the second slot in a two-member coda is
[+coronal] (*grind*). Secondly, we could claim that in examples
such as *clamp*, the /m/ is not part of the coda but of the nucleus
(as does Selkirk 1982a). Neither solution, they conclude, is
satisfactory: the first because it makes the structure of one constituent – *ie* the coda – dependent upon the internal structure of
another constituent – *ie* the nucleus; the second because it allows
nasals, as well as /l/ (and/r/ in rhotic accents), to be systematically ambiguous with respect to their position within the syllable.

Hogg and McCully are correct in rejecting an ambiguous
assignment of sonorants as highly undesirable. But, it is not clear
that the statement of the restriction on R_4 need involve a
complex disjunction. The tree structure representing a syllable
encodes three types of information: a structural hierarchization,
a type assignment (R, C, etc.) and an order relation. Given a
syllable-schema such as [19]; the node R **dominates** (in the formal
sense of the word – see Wall 1973: 144–52) its daughters as well
as any granddaughters: that is, N, C, x, y, z, w. We can therefore
state the restriction on R_4 as in [20], where ⟨ indicates immediate
precedence:

[19]

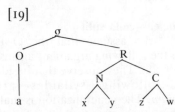

[20] Given segments x ⟨ y ⟨ z ⟨ w, where R dominates x, y, z, w,
     then w must be [+cor]

In view of the fact that Hogg and McCully (1987: 55) adduce themselves some evidence in favour of retaining the N–C split, the elegance of the restriction $N_4 = [+cor]$, does not seem sufficient to tip the balance in favour of unstructured rhymes.

6.1.5 Syllable-templates and the sonority hierarchy

One common way of specifying the possible syllables of a language is by means of a template-schema. A tentative template-schema for English (influenced by Selkirk 1982a, 1984b) is given in [21]. The numbered letters will not be conceived as labels but rather as place-holders for segments and will therefore not be included in syllable representations.

[21]

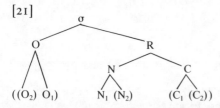

In [21] only the N nucleus position is obligatory and the parentheses indicate optionality. For instance, by omitting the onset positions and maximal expansion within R, we obtain the syllable-template corresponding to words like *old* [owld] as exemplified in [22]. In Chapter 1, it was pointed out that the phonotactics of English must allow for clusters of three consonants initially (*str*). Since [22] allows only for two positions, the status of initial clusters such as *str* will require further discussion. At this stage, we will concentrate on how the various place-holders in [21] become accessible to phonological segments.

[22]

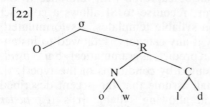

In English, vowels, liquids and nasals – *ie* [+son] segments – can function as head of the nucleus (*cf bottle* [bɔtl̩], *button* [bʌtn̩]). The range of segments which can be syllabic nuclei varies from language to language. Some languages also allow fricatives and even stops have been claimed to be available. Nevertheless, there is a clear ranking of accessibility to the head position. For instance, we expect liquids to be assigned to the syllabic nucleus only when no vowels are available (*eg* Slovak *sŕn* [sr̩:n] 'deer gen. pl.'). The standard distinctive features do not express this relative ranking and there is a long tradition in phonology suggesting that we should have recourse to a **sonority hierarchy**. We will leave aside the question of the phonetic correlates of sonority here and take our evidence from cross-linguistic work on the shape of syllables. One (tentative) example of sonority hierarchy based on Selkirk (1984b) is given below:[7]

[23] Sonority hierarchy

Sonority Index (SI)	Sound
10	a
9	e, o
8	i, u
7	r-sounds
6	laterals
5	nasals
4	voiced fricatives
3	voiceless fricatives
2	voiced stop
1	voiceless stop

Despite the fact that [23] needs to be refined in various respects, it allows us to determine not only the head of the nucleus but it also makes prediction as to the overall shape of syllables. It has often been observed that onsets are typically on an ascending slope in terms of sonority and that codas are on a descending slope (*cf eg flint* with a 3–6–8–5–1 sonority curve). Availability for head status and position within the syllable are not disconnected and this can be captured with reference to the sonority hierarchy. Moreover, recourse to SI allows a compact formulation of conditions on syllable templates. As formulated, [21] overgenerates massively if any category is allowed to instantiate the terminal slots. Thus, it predicts as grammatical *bnit, *psint, etc. It needs to be supplemented by conditions of the type [24], where, for simplicity, we shall assume that the accent described is like American English in allowing syllabic [r]'s (*eg better* [betr]):

[24] Sample conditions on the syllable-template
[24a] SI of $N_1 \geq 5$
[24b] SI of $O_1 > 5$ and < 9 if O_2 is filled
[24c] SI of $O_2 \leq 3$
[24d] SI of $C_1 <$ SI of C_2

Condition [24b], for instance, restricts the O_1 position to values 6, 7 and 8 of [23], that is, lateral, liquids and (non-syllabic) high vowels if O_2 is instantiated (*cf train, clip, queen*). Beside positive conditions as in [24], there will also be negative conditions excluding combinations which might be expected on the basis of the sonority hierarchy, but are nevertheless impossible. For examples of negative phonotactic conditions, the reader is referred to 1.3.2.1 where the syllable should replace the morpheme as the frame of reference (*cf* Fudge 1969; Selkirk 1982a, 1984b; J. M. Anderson, 1986b, for detailed discussions of 'collocational' restrictions within the syllable).

The syllable-template schema, with the set of positive and negative conditions, can be thought of in two ways. It can either function as a generative device, licensing possible syllables, or, by a process of matching, syllable-templates can be paired with underlying strings of segments which fulfil all the requirements on the various terminal positions. However, as it stands, the syllable-template schema will not allow for words such as *backs* [baks] or *act* [akt], since condition [24d] requires that there should be a descending sonority slope within the coda (and [24d] is, in fact, often generalized as a requirement that the sonority slope must rise from the initiation of the syllable to the syllabic and then decline). Examples such as *acts* [akts], *texts* [teksts], or *sixths* [siksθs] apparently pose an even greater problem since the final sequences contain four segments (against two positions licensed by [22] within the coda) with oscillating values of the sonority index.

While it might be argued that the syllable-schema should be modified to accommodate such final sequences as [ks], [kt], [kts], [ksts] and [ksθs], many researchers seem agreed that it is better to appeal to the concept of extrametricality to which we turn.

6.1.6 Extrametricality
If we leave aside the structure of words, we have assumed so far that each and every underlying segment making up morphemes had to occupy a position within the syllable. One fruitful line of enquiry has been been based on the idea that some underlying segments might in fact not be integrated to syllable structure – *ie* be extrametrical. The general idea of extrametricality arose in the context of work on the assignment of stress where it was found that simpler rules of stress-assignment could be formulated if initial or final syllables were ignored (*cf* Hayes 1981, 1982 and the textbook accounts in Halle and Clements 1983: 17–18; Hogg and McCully 1987: §3.6). In assigning Latin stress, for instance,

the last syllable can be considered **extrametrical** (Hayes
1981: 66–74). And in English, simpler stress rules are formulable
if we assume that the last consonant does not count. Consider
verbs such as, those of [25] cited in their underlying forms:

[25] attend /Vten(d)/
     remain /rVmææ(n)/
     astonish /Vstɔni(š)/

If the last consonant is, so to speak, invisible, stress assignment
can be formulated in a simple manner: stress the last syllable if
it is heavy (*atténd, remáin*), otherwise stress the penultimate
(*astónish*).

If we return now to English syllable structure, we note first of
all that there is no reason why the core syllable template should
include derivational and inflectional markers such as *-th* and *-s*.
These are the result of morphological operations which will also
predict their sequencing – as in *widths* (*cf* Ch. 5). At the stage
at which grammatical markers are introduced, they are, in fact,
extrametrical and we shall assume that they are derivatively
attached to the syllable by a rule of 'stray segment adjunction'.
In so far as the grammar contains an independent mechanism for
adjoining stray segments to the syllable, segments such as the
[t] of *act* or the [s] of *axe* [aks] which have the same or a higher
sonority index than the previous consonant can be left unattached
when the syllable-structure of the morpheme is first constructed.
Since all the segments (grammatical or otherwise) that we might
wish to consider extrametrical at the right-hand edge of forms in
English turn out to be [+coronal], the syllable integration of
extrametrical material, which can be located at the end of the
lexical component, need not distinguish between grammatically
stray segments and stray segments breaking conventions
governing sonority values. The worrying sequences considered at
the end of 6.1.5 can therefore be accommodated in a general and
elegant way (but see 6.1.7 on [st]).

' The concept of extrametricality can be insightfully applied to
French. Returning to the sketch of Midi French offered in
Chapter 1, it was pointed out that to account for liaison (*petit
écrou* [pətitekru]), derivation (*petitesse* [pətitɛsə]) and flexion
(*petite* [pətitə]), the underlying form of words like *petit* ([pəti])
should include latent consonants such as the final /t/ in /pətit/.
There is, however, a problem that was noted in our presentation
of liaison in Chapter 1: the underlying liaison consonant does not
trigger MVLOW (a rule reconsidered in 5.1.2 from the point of
view of UT). Consider once again, MVLOW as provisionally

reformulated in [26], in a first attempt to improve the context part by bringing in information about syllable-boundaries (see 6.1.9 for a better formulation):

[26] Mid-Vowel Lowering

$$\begin{bmatrix} V \\ -\text{high} \end{bmatrix} \rightarrow [+\text{low}] / \underline{\hspace{1cm}} C_1 \begin{Bmatrix} \vartheta \\ \$ \end{Bmatrix}$$

That is, a mid vowel is lowered if the next syllable contains a schwa or if it is in a closed syllable. Thus, if the underlying form of *mes* is /mez/ or of *gros* is /groz/, [26] predicts that the mid vowel will be lowered lexically, thus producing *[mɛzami] (*mes amis*) and *[grɔzami] (*gros ami*). But the correct forms for this accent are [mezami] and [grozami].

Now, MVLOW is a lexical rule: it is sensitive to morphological boundaries within words. Thus, it does not occur in prefixes *déstabiliser* [destabilize] or in compounds *autostop* [otostɔp]. An elegant way of accounting for this is to assume that it operates at a level which precedes prefixation and compounding in the LP sense. Durand (1988), based on Johnson (1987), suggests that Midi French MVLOW should be within the productive suffixation strata (level 2), whereas prefixation and compounding are at level 3. On the other hand, liaison is clearly post-lexical (*cf* Ch. 5) and by definition follows MVLOW. If we assume that the liaison consonant is extrametrical, it will be invisible in so far as MVLOW is concerned and a mid vowel preceding the extrametrical consonant will not be lowered (see too Booij and Rubach 1987 on this issue).

The essence of the extrametrical account of French liaison is that the addition of suffixes, which are always vowel-initial in Midi French, as well as liaison, will save the latent consonant which will be attached rightwards to any free onset [27].

[27] *petit écrou*

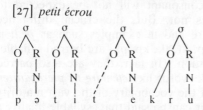

One advantage of treating liaison consonants as extrametrical is that, in any case, we need to differentiate between latent consonants, which are deleted if they are not rescued by a following vowel, and fixed final consonants (*cap* [kap], *sec* [sɛk])

which are never deleted. The classical generative analysis forced one to treat this latter class as marked since they had to be specified as exceptions to the rule of truncation. But this is not a satisfactory move: there is no evidence that fixed final consonants are marked. There are many trends in French expanding this 'exceptional' class: abbreviations (*faculté* [fakylte] → *fac* [fak]), acronyms (*FNAC* [fnak]), etc. By contrast, there has been a long-standing erosion of liaison consonants. The extrametrical account of French liaison correctly treats latent consonants as marked: the underlying representation of *petit* /pətit/, with the unattached final consonant has to be treated as exceptional in some way, perhaps by marking the final /t/ with a diacritic feature which will prevent it from being attached to the coda of the second syllable.

It is sometimes argued that the concept of extrametricality is not inherently superior to analysis of liaison as insertion of a consonant since in both cases some diacritic marking of lexical items is required. It is therefore worth extending the data to see whether there is any further advantage to the extrametrical analysis. In the variety of Midi French described here, unlike in standard French, the following words are pronounced without a final /t/:

[28] contact, infect, intact, correct, direct, tact
  [kɔntak] [ɛ̃fɛk] [ɛ̃tak] [kɔrɛk] [dirɛk] [tak]

But, whenever a flexional or derivational vowel is added as in [29], a /t/ appears (*eg correcte* [kɔrɛktə]):

[29a] flexion: infecte, intacte, correcte, directe
[29b] derivation: contacter, infecter, correctement

These data suggest an underlying /t/, which is also extrametrical, and is deleted if no right-hand-side vowel comes to its rescue. Given that these examples are nouns or predicative adjectives, the underlying consonant will not be expected to surface in liaison and does not. But, the crucial difference between extrametricality here and in examples such as *petit* is that sequences such as [pt, tp, kt, tk, kp, pk] are barred syllable-finally in the accent in question. (In fact, they are also barred syllable-initially if we exclude words like *cténaire* or *ptérosaurien* which are simply not part of the vocabulary of the vast majority of speakers.) Generalizing, it can be said that, syllable-finally, a sequence of two consonants of equal sonority or with a rising sonority slope are forbidden (except for Cs: *thorax, phénix*, etc.). Note that words like *arme* or *boucle* clearly have a schwa so that the syllabification will be [ar$mə] or [bu$klə]. Given these constraints on the syllable-templates of Midi French, the final consonant of *direct* will be **automatically** extrametrical as in [30a], and will be deleted unless, as in [30b], it is saved through the suffixation of a vowel which carries a free onset to which the stray /t/ can be attached.

[30a]

[30b]

In so far as extrametricality here relies on independently established constraints governing syllable-structure, it offers a superior analysis to an insertion account. Given that insertion accounts have not come to grips with the problem of generalizing the consonant which appears in liaison, inflection and derivation (*cf* 1.5.2), appeal to syllable-structure offers a more promising line of investigation of the phenomena at hand.

6.1.7 The CV tier
Beside the enrichment of phonological representations just proposed, most phonologists seem agreed that a tier of abstract timing relations such as the **CV tier** of Clements and Keyser (1983), introduced at the beginning of this chapter, should also be part of suprasegmental structure. Chapter 7 will justify the CV tier (more appropriately called **skeleton**) in more detail. Here, we will outline some advantages of positing an intermediary layer between the segments and suprasegmental structure.

The treatment of some segments such as affricates has always proved problematic. That is, arguments can be found in favour of treating affricates both as single units as reflected in the *SPE* analysis and as sequences of two segments. And, diachronically,

English /č/ and /ǰ/ have developed from single stops (*eg* Middle English *chin* ⟨ CGerm.**kinn*-) and from /tj, dj/ sequences (*eg* *actual*). By assuming that /č/ in *chin* is represented as in [31]:

[31]

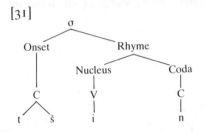

where the first C position is associated with two successive feature-bundles, we can formalize the intuition that /č/ is simultaneously a single entity made up of two articulatory events: a closure phase followed by fricative phase. (If this is correct, a feature like [+/−delayed release] presented in 2.3.6 becomes unnecessary.) Conversely, long vowels, for instance, can be treated as sequences of two V's on the CV tier linked to one feature-matrix as in [32b], where the syllable-structure is left out.

[32a] Bit   [32b] Beat   [32c] Bite

```
C   V   C        C   V   V   C        C   V   V   C
|   |   |        |    \ /    |        |   |   |   |
b   i   t        b     i     t        b   a   i   t
```

Note that a diphthong, such as the one in *bite*, also corresponds to two units of timing, but that each V is associated with a different articulatory complex. The literature, however, also mentions short diphthongs – that is, diphthongs which are grouped phonologically, with short monophthongs (*cf* J. M. Anderson and Ewen 1987: §3.6.4, 7.3.1; Kaye 1981). Once again, we can account for such diphthongs by positing that two feature-bundles hang from a single V position as in [33].

[33]

```
      V
     / \
    a   i
```

We are now in a position to return to the syllable-template for English: *cf* [21]. Following Selkirk, only two members were permitted in the onset and the coda and no allowance was made for final clusters such as /kst/ in *next*. Selkirk suggests that /st/ should be treated as a single unit. One often-quoted argument in favour of this is that, in the inherited Germanic verse, while initial *p-* may alliterate with clusters such as *pr-* and *pl-*, and *h* with *hr-*, *hl-* and *hn-*, *s-* may not alliterate with *sk-*, *st-* nor *sk-* with *sp-*, *st-*, etc. In fact, *sk* can alliterate only with *sk*, *st* only with *st*, and *sp* only with *sp* (*cf* Kuryłowicz 1971: 195). In other words, *sp-*, *st-* and *sk-* behave like single units in such verse. The vague notion of a 'single unit' can be made sense of by appealing to the CV tier. That is, words like *strip* and *next* will be represented as in [34].

[34a]

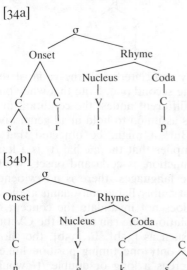

[34b]

One additional advantage of the CV tier is that it allows us to eliminate a feature like [+/−long]. A long segment always corresponds to two slots on the CV tier, whereas a short segment is anchored from a single C or V position. Like [+/−syll], [+/−long] is different from truly paradigmatic features such as [+/−high] or [+/−cons], which indicate a value at one (abstract) point in time, and its elimination leads to a more homogeneous feature-set.

6.1.8 Ambisyllabicity
So far we have assumed that there existed clean breaks between successive syllables. There is, however, evidence that syllables should be allowed to overlap. If we consider, for instance, a word

like *petrol*, it has been observed that the medial [t] has simultaneously syllable-initial and syllable-final characteristics. In
particular, the [r] is voiceless as is typical in syllable-initial [tr]
clusters, but there is also a glottal reinforcement of the [t]
([pe2trəl] or [pe?trəl]). Representations along the lines of [35a]
have been argued for in a variety of frameworks (*cf* J. M.
Anderson and Jones 1974, 1977; J. M. Anderson and Ewen 1987;
Clements and Keyser 1983; Kahn 1976),

[35a]

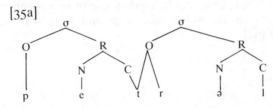

where the [t] is simultaneously associated with the coda of the
first syllable and the onset of the second one. Note that while one
element can be linked to two different nodes, the condition that
association lines cannot cross is assumed to hold in all generative
accounts of ambisyllabicity. But, it might be objected that a
representation such as [35a] implies that the medial /t/ is a long
segment because of its dual function as coda and onset. While
this might be correct for some languages, there is no evidence
in favour of the assumption that ambisyllabic consonants are long
in English. Fortunately, this does not invalidate the concept of
ambisyllabicity since, as one solution, one can invoke the CV tier
and assume a representation such as [35b]. In [35b], the short
bisyllabic /t/ is seen to occupy only one timing position linked
to two different syllables, whereas a long or double /t/ would
have been associated with two slots on the CV tier.

[35b]

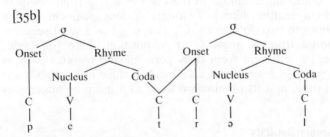

By licensing ambisyllabicity, we can relate the structure of
polysyllabic morphemes to that of monosyllabic morphemes in
English. In the latter, which are usually considered as lexically

stressed, the short (or lax) vowels are not allowed unless a consonant follows. (As pointed out in Hayes 1982, the last consonant of monosyllables in English is never extrametrical.) Compare [36a] and [36b]:

[36a] [bɪp]   [36b]   *[bɪ]
      [læk]   *[læ]
      [nek]   *[ne]

But, in polysyllables, if ambisyllabicity is not allowed, a stressed syllable can be open and yet contain a short vowel (*cf pe$trol, ci$ty, wre$cker* under this assumption). If, on the other hand, we accept (as in [35]) that the medial consonant in such words is ambisyllabic, a single generalization holds: a short vowel cannot be the sole element of a stressed rhyme or, put another way, the rhyme of a stressed syllable must be complex. Assuming ambisyllabicity follows stress assignment in *eg petrol*, it can be argued that the relevant consonant becomes ambisyllabic so that the correlation between stress and syllabic heaviness is maintained. It is also worth noting that ambisyllabicity provides further motivation for a coda slot which, as it were, provides a receptacle for the reassignment of consonants within derivations.[8]

One area of controversy is whether ambisyllabicity, in so far as it is at all accepted, is underlying or derived. While work in Dependency Phonology (*cf* J. M. Anderson, 1986b, J. M. Anderson and Ewen 1987; J. M. Anderson and Jones 1974, 1977) has argued for underlying ambisyllabicity in languages like English, the majority of researchers seem agreed in viewing ambisyllabicity as a derived phenomenon. The issue is complex and heavily bound up with stress in English. The reader is therefore referred to the above-mentioned articles as well as to Selkirk (1982a) for a contrary point of view and further references.

6.1.9 The foot and above

By readmitting syllables to the phonological fold, we are paving the way for a reintroduction of the suprasegmental hierarchy. It has frequently been observed that sequences of syllables, in languages like English, are grouped into rhythmic units called **feet**. In the British tradition represented by Abercrombie (1964a,b), a foot is made up of a stress pulse optionally followed by less salient syllables. Thus, in *This is the house that Jack built*, Abercrombie posits the foot structure of [37] (p. 220), where the stressed syllables are in capitals, and argues in support of these divisions that feet in English tend to be of equal duration – a characteristic often referred to as isochrony (*cf* too Giegerich

1980). The feet exemplified in [37] operate at **utterance level**, but the concept of foot has proved important in the classification of systems of stress at the **lexical level**. In the study of lexical stress assignment from a universalist perspective, feet have been described in terms of a small number of parameters, discussed below, which can be set by individual languages.

[37]

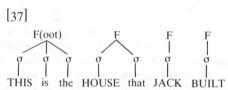

Since feet are assumed to be made up of a stressed syllable optionally preceded or followed by dependants (but not both), one first parameter which will be selected by individual language is whether the foot is **head-initial** (or left-headed) or **head-final** (right-headed). In English, for instance, feet are head-initial but note that feet of one syllable (as in *Jack* or *built* in [37]), often called degenerate feet, are well formed. A second parameter is whether feet are **bounded** or **unbounded**. If a foot is bounded, it will be restricted to an upper limit of syllables. For instance, for Selkirk (1980), feet have an upper limit of three syllables, whereas Hayes (1981) argues that bounded feet should be universally limited to a maximum of two syllables (*ie* be binary). In an unbounded foot, the stressed syllable governs an entire sequence of units on its left or on its right within a given domain (*eg* until the next stressed syllable is reached or until the beginning/end of a word).

An example of bounded foot assignment is provided by Maranungku. In this language, main stress falls on the initial syllable and secondary stress on every second syllable thereafter as in [38]:

[38a] lángkaràtetì 'prawn'
[38b] wélepènemànta 'kind of duck'

The stress assignment rules of this language can be formulated as follows:

[39a] Over the syllables of the word construct left-headed binary trees (left to right).
[39b] Assign stress 1 to the head of every syllable.
[39c] Reassign stress 1 to the first foot of a word (i.e. reduce every [1 stress] by 1).

If we apply [39] to [38a] and [38b] we obtain [40].

[40a]

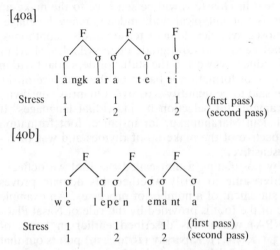

Stress   1   1   1   (first pass)
          1   2   2   (second pass)

[40b]

Stress   1   1   1   (first pass)
          1   2   2   (second pass)

In 40, the concept of foot is used to determine the assignment of stress in the *SPE* mode. But the trend of this whole chapter has been to show that many features could be eliminated by recourse to richer suprasegmental representations. In this case, it is clear that if we had a way of coding heads within feet and reassigning headship within a unit superordinate to syllables, stress as an n-ary feature could be dispensed with entirely. This will indeed be the topic of the following sections.

An example of unbounded foot assignment is provided by Huasteco. In this language, primary stress is assigned to the last long vowel of a word, and, if there is no long vowel, to the first vowel. If we take the case of a word like *hílk'omac* ('leftovers'), where there is no long vowel, we can see that an unbounded foot is formed by default whose first syllable carries the main stress as in [41]. Since we return to stress in Huasteco in 6.2.2.3, we can leave the more complex cases for the moment. It will be noted, however, that in formulating stress-assignment in this language we have appealed to a distinction between long and

[41]

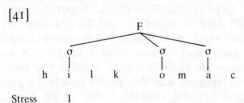

Stress   1

short vowels. In so far as a long vowel will be the head of a foot, we can see that feet in Huasteco will be sensitive to the make-up of rhymes. This is not untypical and, indeed, many languages tend to favour closed syllables, long or tense vowels, diphthongs, full vowels as foot heads and downgrade open syllables, short or lax vowels, and reduced vowels to the status of dependant within a foot. Whenever foot formation is based on the structure of the rhyme, it will be said to be **quantity-sensitive.** Quantity-sensitivity is a further parameter for selection by individual languages. It will be noted that in Maranungku, for instance, foot formation proceeded irrespective of the make-up of rhymes and was therefore **quantity-insensitive.**

In so far as by postulating a unit called the foot we define a domain, it is interesting to verify whether this domain proves essential to the statement of a number of processes. An example of the relevance of the foot is provided by the rule of Nasal Place Assimilation (NPA) which was described earlier in terms of morphemes (*cf* 3.1.2, 3.5.1). Kiparsky (1979: 439) points out that in general 'the foot establishes a domain of **close contact** between adjacent segments in English'. His first example of this is the fact that in words like *ink* or *íncrement*, the nasal is obligatorily assimilated to the following obstruent ([ɪŋk], [ɪŋkrəmənt]), whereas in words like *íncrèase* (n) or *ìncréase* (v) the assimilation is optional ([ɪnkrijs] or [ɪŋkrijs]). His second example involves the Mutual Assimilation (MA) of [k] and [r], which he writes [KR] in words like *crew, increase* ([KR]) vs. *back-rub, cock-roach* ([kr]). If we define the domain of obligatory NPA and MA as the foot an elegant account is possible, as is shown by the following examples (*cf* Nespor and Vogel 1986: 94):

[42a]	ink	[ink]$_F$	→ i[ŋ]k	NPA
[42b]	crew	[crew]$_F$	→ [KR]ew	MA
[42c]	íncrèase (n)	[in]$_F$[crease]$_F$	→ in[KR]ease	MA
[42d]	ìncréase (v)	[in]$_F$[crease]$_F$	→ in[KR]ease	MA
[42e]	increment	[increment]$_F$	→ i[ŋKR]ement	NPA, MA

It should be pointed out that an account of NPA in terms of ambisyllabicity has been advocated by J. M. Anderson and Ewen (1987: §2.3.3) within Dependency Phonology. Kiparsky (1979) rejects any explanation here in terms of syllable-structure, and Nespor and Vogel (1986: 94), who follow his treatment, argue that in an example such as *increment* ambisyllabicity is not acceptable 'because such an analysis would require the entire sequence *nkr* to be tautosyllabic, and this would violate the principles governing English syllable structure'. But if we assume with J. M. Anderson and Ewen that left-headed feet are, perhaps universally, a domain for ambisyllabicity, and that the latter must always yield well-formed codas and onsets, the application of ambisyllabicity to *increment* is as in [43], where the CV tier has been left out for convenience. As is obvious, [43] does not require any ill-formed onset or coda and, on this assumption, a better generalization emerges: obligatory NPA and MA apply to **tautosyllabic** segments.

[43]

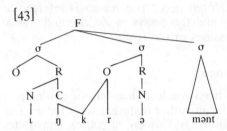

The foot is not of relevance only to English. Thus, if we go back to the Midi French rule of MVLOW, given in [26], we notice that, although this reformulation is simpler than the statement of Chapter 1, the rule still operates in two disparate contexts. Indeed, we might wonder what a syllable-boundary and a schwa have in common. But as emphasized in Chapter 1, the schwa vowel is unstressed (*cf père* [pérə], *autre* [ɔ́trə], *beugle* [bœ́glə]) and can, therefore, be argued to form a foot with its left-hand stressed partner. As a result, rule [26] can be vastly improved by specifying its domain as the foot:

[44] Mid-Vowel Lowering

$$\begin{bmatrix} V \\ -high \end{bmatrix} \rightarrow [+low] \, / \, \underline{\hspace{2cm}} X \,]_F$$

In [44] what conditions the lowering is the presence of any material (X) to the right of the affected vowel. But note that [44] can also be simplified if, once again, we assume that the foot is a domain for ambisyllabicity. If in *père*, the [r] is attached to the rhyme of the first syllable while functioning as onset of the second syllable, [44] can be reformulated as [45], which simply states that the rhyme must branch:

[45] Mid-Vowel Lowering

$$\begin{bmatrix} V \\ -high \end{bmatrix} \rightarrow [+low] \, / \, \underline{\hspace{2cm}}$$

Whether or not ambisyllabicity is adopted, the main point is that the foot is well supported as a domain for various general-

izations (see the survey in Nespor and Vogel 1986 §3.2.2). Many
proposals exist for the grouping of feet into higher phonological
phrases. For instance, it has been argued that above the foot we
need units such as the **prosodic word** (ω) and that prosodic words
are in turn grouped into **phonological phrases** (φ) which are
grouped into **intonational phrases** (I) in order to form **utterances**
(U). The relevance of this prosodic hierarchy has already been
mentioned in Chapter 5 but, for lack of space, these various
suggestions cannot be explored here. The reader is referred to
Nespor and Vogel (1986) and the essays in Zwicky and Kaisse
(1987) for thorough discussions of the issue.

6.2 Stress and prominence

The discussion so far has been conducted within the assumption
that stress was a feature like any other feature, except for the fact
that it could be multivalued (n-ary) which, of course, constitutes
a departure from strict binarism for distinctive features. The *SPE*
account of stress as a feature has been progressively abandoned
in generative phonology in the wake of Liberman and Prince's
seminal article 'On stress and linguistic rhythm' (1977). The full
range of arguments offered by these authors against a featural
representation of stress will not be reviewed here (see Hogg and
McCully 1987: Ch. 3). But, with Liberman and Prince, we will
note that stress is a syntagmatic, not a paradigmatic notion. To
say that the first syllable of *city* is stressed is to say that it is more
salient than the second one. And if, in an *SPE*-style analysis, we
assigned a [3stress] value to the second vowel of *relaxation*
(5.2.2), that feature-value would have no **local** import (unlike
values such as [+low], [−high], [−cons], etc.). It would be only
understandable in terms of the relative ordering produced by the
stress rules – say, for example, a stress contour of the form 2 3
1 0.

In a way, the *SPE* theory of stress assignment recognizes that
stress is syntagmatic since any assignment of primary stress within
a domain weakens all other stresses by one (5.2.2). But this
numerological approach has unfortunate consequences. For
instance, the phrase *sad plight*, which has a 2 1 stress contour in
isolation, ends up with an 8 1 stress contour in the sentence *My
friend can't help being shocked at anyone who fails to consider
his sad plight* (*SPE p.* 23) as a result of reassigning [1stress] to
plight within successively larger domains. The value [8stress] is
plainly absurd. What we need is a formalism whereby relative
degrees of salience between two constituents of a phrase remain

unaffected by the degrees of prominence assigned to that phrase within larger domains. Let us, therefore, consider first an attempt to code prominence values by recourse to metrical trees (6.2.1) before turning to an approach in terms of grids (6.2.2).

6.2.1 Metrical trees

The representation of stress advocated by Liberman and Prince (1977) takes seriously the claim that stress is a syntagmatic notion. In their approach, stress (or prominence) is a binary relation between two constituents: a strong element marked as *s* and a weak one *w*. The trees which make up the suprasegmental hierarchy should be annotated in terms of *s–w* as in [46].

[46] *many*

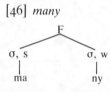

But, in many discussions, only one dimension is considered. Either attention is drawn to the prosodic constituents or to the prominence relation. Thus, for instance, *Many linguists go to Essex* might be represented as in [47] where the prosodic constituents are implicit in the representation. Alternatively, as in [48], the tree (which could just as easily be placed upside-down below the segments) can be supplemented with horizontal lines

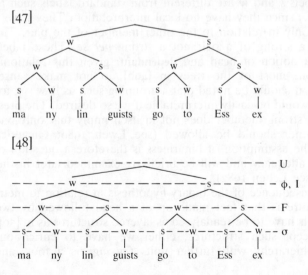

anchoring the *s–w* labels to successive prosodic categories. As is common in the literature, we shall operate with trees of the form [47] unless prosodic categories are relevant to the discussion. Such trees are standardly referred to as **metrical trees** and **metrical phonology** is the branch of phonology dealing with the structures they embody (*cf* Giegerich 1985, 1986a,b and the references therein).

As suggested above, the classical notation of metrical phonology assumes that phonological constituency is binary branching only and that the two sisters of each branch are either [s w] or [w s]. Thus, the tree in [49a] is well formed whereas all the structures in [49b] are ill formed.

[49a]

[49b]

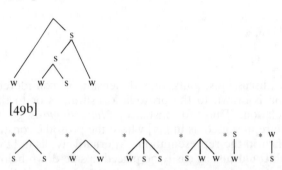

The labels *s* and *w* are different from standard labels such as (σ, F, etc.) since they have no local interpretation. They have a meaning only in relation to the other member of the pair. The strong is a strong of a pair not a strong *per se*. These labels embody a notion of **head** and **dependant**: given this relational assumption, most of the trees in [49b] do not make sense. However, it should be noted that a grouping such as [s w w], for instance, would be easily interpretable if we so desired. The presence of a strong member does not in itself imply that only one weak partner should be allowed (see Ewen 1986; Giegerich 1986a). The assumption of binariness is therefore a question of empirical adequacy and will be briefly re-examined later in this chapter (see Leben 1982).

One consequence of the binary hypothesis in relation to metrical structure is that feet made up of a head followed by two dependants have to be reanalysed as layered structures as in [50]. If we accept such structures, either we have to enrich our prosodic hierarchy with further units (*eg alge* is a foot, and *algebra* a superfoot) or we have to accept that the prosodic hierarchy and the metrical layering do not coincide totally. This second avenue is one which is often adopted, but its consequences are rarely explored in depth.

[50]

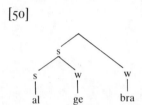

6.2.1.1 *Stress and the Designated Terminal Element*

At the lowest level, the assignment of stress within English words, for instance, would consist in the formation of left-headed feet. Thus, the rules of English foot formation, not analysed here, would produce the trees given in [51]. At the level of the whole word (ω), the prominent element would be derived by some version of rule [52].

[51]

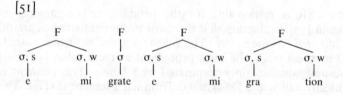

[52] Lexical Category Prominence Rule (LCPR)

For any pair of nodes [N1, N2]ω, where N1 and N2 are feet or dominate feet, N2 is strong if and only if it branches.

Application of the LCPR would produce the trees given in [53].

[53a]   [53b]

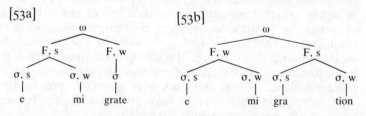

Interestingly, the same basic rule is put forward by Liberman and Prince for handling prominence within compounds:

[54] Compound Stress Rule (CSR)

For any pairs of nodes [N1, N2]_L, where N1 and N2 are lexical categories and L is a lexical category, N2 is strong if and only if it branches.

[55a]

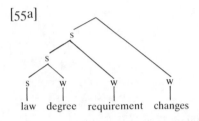

law   degree   requirement   changes

[55b]

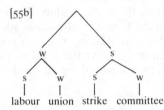

labour   union   strike   committee

The CSR is responsible for the prominence assignments as shown in [55], predicting that the most prominent stresses are on *law* and *strike* respectively. The reason for this assertion is that, in all metrical trees, the most prominent element (alias [1stress]) is the unit which is only dominated by *s* labels. This element is technically called the Designated Terminal Element (DTE). The DTE in [50], for instance, is the first syllable of *algebra* and the reader can verify that in [55a, b] *law* and *strike* are dominated by *s* labels only.

It is important to realize that while *alge* is stronger than *bra* in [50], no direct strength relationship is established between *ge* and *bra*. By contrast, the numerological approach to stress ranked all vowels with respect to this parameter. It is a matter of debate whether metrical trees should tell us more. It would, of course, be possible to impose a convention whereby, in the configuration illustrated in [50], -*ge*- should be stronger than -*bra* on the grounds that it is part of a strong constituent (*alge*-). But in the absence of clear empirical evidence allowing us to rank the relative salience of -*ge*- and -*bra*, it is preferable not to adopt such an interpretation and to leave the relationship between adjacent *w*'s undefined in such configurations.

One of the most interesting applications of the concept of metrical trees has been in connection with patterns of rhythmic

[56a]   [56b]

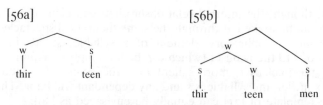

alternations which occur within sentences. Thus, while *thirteen* is end-stressed when pronounced in isolation [56a], in the phrase *thirteen men* there is typically a stress shift as portrayed in [56b]. The stress shift represented by *thirteen men* also accounts for examples such as *hòme-grówn ápples* → *hóme-gròwn ápples, àchromátic léns* → *áchromàtic léns,* etc. The configuration responsible for this shift has been argued to be the presence of a structure such as [57a] within a tree which is changed to [57b] by a rule commonly called Iambic Reversal (or Rhythm Rule).

[57a] Iambic Reversal   [57b]

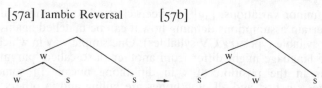

This is illustrated in the shift [58] where the nodes fulfilling the configuration of [57a] are circled.

[58a]   [58b]

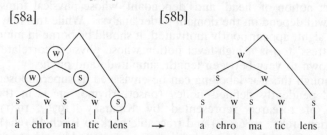

As it stands, rule [57] – which is an optional rule – is obviously too general. To take one example only, it would allow *maròon júmper* to be pronounced *màroon júmper* which would wrongly make the first unstressed syllable of *maróon* strong. Appropriate constraints on the application of [57] are taken care of in the literature on metrical phonology (see *eg* Kiparsky 1979: 425ff).

6.2.1.2 Strength relationships within the syllable
So far, suprasegmental strength relationships have been dealt with in isolation from the internal structure of the syllable.

Clearly, though, the internal relationship between elements of a syllable can be looked at through the same theoretical spectacles. The rhyme, as obligatory element of a syllable, stands in a relation of *s* to the *w* onset (which can be left empty). Within the rhyme, the nucleus is more salient than the coda, and, within complex nuclei, the syllabic is *s* and any dependant will be *w*. The syllable template of [21] can equally be envisaged as [59].

[59]

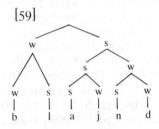

With minor variations, [59] has been claimed to be universal, given certain assumptions defining how it can be matched against simpler syllable types (*eg* CV syllables). One simple way in which a whole language might differ from another (a so-called 'parameter') is in the position of *s* in diphthong nuclei. In some languages *s* is first and all diphthongs are falling and in others *s* is second and all diphthongs are rising. In such representations, of course, *s* and *w* are no longer related to stress but to an abstract notion of 'head' and 'dependant' whose physical translation will depend on the domain under analysis. While this may, at first sight, appear poorly motivated, it should be borne in mind that 'stress' too is a high-level notion whose physical correlates are known to vary between length, amplitude and pitch.

Although the *s–w* labelling can be envisaged as superimposed on independently defined nodes (onset, rhyme, etc.), in the strand of research represented by Kiparsky (1979, 1981), Giegerich (1985, 1986a, b) and traceable back to Rischel (1964), it is argued that the relational structure represented by a metrical template such as [59] is primitive and the labelling derived. That is, terms such as onset, rhyme, etc. would be defined derivatively in terms of metrical structure. The basic idea is that, starting from the top nodes, subtrees of the template define possible syllable structure and that matchings will be constrained by the sonority hierarchy. The reader is referred to Kiparsky (1979: 432–3) for details concerning the association between strings of segments and the syllable-template.

One worry often expressed in connection with the elimination of labels in metrical trees is that this appears to lead to an under-differentiation of contrastive units. Consider, for instance, the following metrical representation of the French word *si* 'if' /si/:

[60]
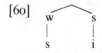

Since in [60] all we have is a binary division onset–rhyme, how can we claim that we are capturing notions such as 'nucleus' or 'syllabic'? This worry is legitimate, but, in so far as the nucleus is defined as the strong element of a rhyme, /i/ in /si/ will be a nucleus by definition, and if, in turn, we define the syllabic as the strong element of the nucleus, /i/ will emerge as a syllabic too. The labelling can therefore be reconstructed from the *s–w* configurations within the syllable. In so far as this approach is accepted, it further reinforces our earlier decision to drop the feature [+/−syllabic]. The syllabic is simply the DTE of the syllable (*eg* /a/ in *blind* – *cf* [59]).

6.2.2 The metrical grid
An important adjunct or alternative to the use of metrical trees for the representation of patterns of prominence is that of **metrical grids** (first introduced by Liberman 1975). We will content ourselves with an informal presentation of the notion of grid here. A metrical grid consists of rows and columns of marks represented by asterisks (or x's) which indicate the relative strength of successive stressable units. Two main rules will be used as a starting-point:

[61a] Assign to each syllable a position (an asterisk) on the metrical grid.

[61b] Starting from the most deeply embedded phrases in a metrical tree, assign an asterisk to each *s* in a *s–w* or *w–s* pair.

The application of [61a] and [61b] to the sentence *many linguists go to Essex*, on the basis of the metrical structure given in [47], would yield:

[62]
						*		L3
	*					*		L2
*		*		*		*		L1
*	*	*	*		*	*	*	L0
many		linguists		go		to	Essex	

In [62], L0 is a base level and L1 to L3 refer to the successive levels entailed by examining patterns of prominence encoded in a metrical tree. The two rules [61a] and [61b] do not, however, suffice as they stand. If we take *thirteen men*, for instance, we can construct the following initial grid based on the sequence of syllables and the stress on the second syllable of *thirteen*:

[63]   *   L1
         * *   *   L0
         thirteen men

But since *men* is stronger than *thirteen*, we could assign a solitary asterisk on L2 above *men*. However, a column with gaps is not allowed by the formalism. Instead the structure must be that of [64], which still does not reflect Iambic Reversal:

[64]   *   L2
             * *   L1
          * *   *   L0
          thirteen men

In other words, if an asterisk is required in a particular slot of a given level to reflect the principle that 'strong is stronger than weak', the slot on each inferior level is automatically filled in with an asterisk. This convention is expressed more technically by Liberman and Prince (1977: 316), who formulate the following principle:

[65] Relative Prominence Projection Rule

In any constituent on which the strong–weak relation is defined, the DTE of its strong subconstituent is metrically stronger than the DTE of its weak subconstituent.

Principles [61a, b] and [65] combined guarantee, in principle, the well-formedness of metrical grids. Let us now examine some potential applications of the notion of grid.

6.2.2.1 Grids, Iambic Reversal and eurhythmy

One of the original arguments in favour of the grid notation was that it provided a perspicuous account of Iambic Reversal. In the example of *thirteen men* above, it will be observed that there is what is known as a **grid clash**: two grid elements are adjacent on two contiguous levels. (Note the asterisks above *-teen* and *men* on L0 and L1 in [64].) The function of Iambic Reversal is to resolve such grid clashes by moving the clashing asterisk to the nearest landing site (*ie* leftwards), thus producing [66]:[9]

[66]   *   L2
             * *   L1
          * *   *   L0
          thirteen men

A further example of Iambic Reversal is provided by *achromatic lens*, already given above in metrical tree notation:

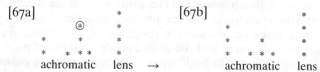

[67a]   *   [67b]   *
              ⊛   *   *   *
       *   *   *   *   *   *   *
       *   * * *   *   *   * * *   *
    achromatic   lens   →   achromatic   lens

In [67a], the circled mark is the one that undergoes Iambic Reversal. Iambic Reversal in grid accounts reduces to a general rule 'Move *' (which is explicitly reminiscent of Move α in such theories of syntax as Chomsky 1981, and, in fact, so formulated in Prince 1983).

The motivation for Iambic Reversal ultimately rests, in the eyes of Prince, Hayes or Selkirk, in the notion of **eurhythmy** or perfect grid. All these authors share the belief that, in a language like English, there is a tendency towards a regular spacing of stress marks (or isochrony: *cf* 6.1.9). Move * is one of the strategies ensuring that grid configurations are eurhythmic. Another strategy is that of 'beat addition' whereby in an example like *Farrah Fawcett-Majors* grid marks are added to provide a more periodic stress structure. The grid predicted from the metrical tree is given in [68a] (*cf* Hayes 1984: 46–8). But what is required is argued to be the more eurhythmic [68b]. An asterisk has therefore been added above *Far(rah)* to produce a better interstress interval and, as a result, the column above the first syllable of *Majors* is strenghtened, since this bears the main group stress. (Recall the principle 'strong is stronger than weak'.)

[68a]   [68b]

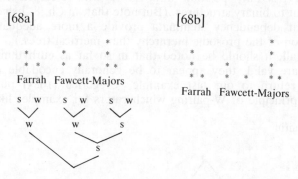

                         *   *
        *   *   *   *   *
        *   *   *   *   *   *   *
     Farrah Fawcett-Majors   *   *   *   *   *
                                       Farrah Fawcett-Majors
       s w   s w   s w
       \/   \/   \/
       w   w   s
        \   \   /
          \   \ /
            \   s
              \   /
                s

6.2.2.2. *Metrical trees or grids?*
In the previous two sections, grids have been presented as parasitic on trees, in a sense, although we have just seen in [68],

the possibility of a divorce between grid and tree representations. In the approach of Liberman and Prince (1977) both trees and grids were used simultaneously. The grids were given a sort of teleological function: grid clashes produce pressure for change and the tree gives permission for reversals to take place. But, given that both the trees and the grids encode patterns of prominence, having recourse to both types of notation simultaneously would not seem to be the most parsimonious approach. Many researchers have therefore attempted to articulate a position which uses only one of these theoretical constructs. Giegerich (1985, 1986a), who develops the insights of Kiparsky (1979), argues that the grid is essentially a visual device, parasitic upon tree configurations, and that the metrical tree formulation of Iambic Reversals, for instance, is basically adequate. On the other hand, Prince (1983) and Selkirk (1984a) articulate a grid-only position which abolishes metrical trees altogether. However, the dual notation has been defended most ardently by Hayes (1983, 1984) on the grounds that trees and grids play sharply different roles – trees encode stress patterns whereas grids reflect patterns of rhythm (*cf* too *inter alia* Hayes and Puppel 1985; Nespor 1988).

A comparison and evaluation of all these approaches would require far more space than is available here (see Hogg and McCully 1987 for a good summary with reference to English). I will therefore declare a preference for the more parsimonious position which favours either trees or grids given the closeness of structure that they display. Moreover, I will support Giegerich's tree-only position although I will reject its full commitment to binary structures. (But note that, in Ch. 8, I shall suggest that dependency stemmata provide a more adequate formalization of the prosodic hierarchy than metrical trees.)

First of all, it should be noted that in so far as eurhythmic principles are valid, they appear to be generally encodable in trees. To return to our last example, Giegerich (1985) puts forward a principle of W-pairing which caters for examples like

[69] W-pairing

condition: nodes 1 and 2 branch [s w]

Farrah Fawcett-Majors [69]. As a result of W-pairing, the metrical tree structure for *Farrah Fawcett-Majors* [70a] would become [70b].

[70a]   [70b]

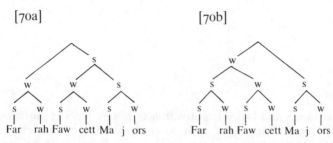

Secondly, as argued by Giegerich, metrical trees provide a uniform notation for suprasegmental patterns of prominence, since both syllables and constituents above the syllable have the same relational structure. By contrast, since all grid-only approaches also require access to information about syllable-structure (*eg* heavy vs. light rhymes), they split up suprasegmental representation into two unrelated formalisms. Yet, and this point will be emphasized again in Chapter 8, it is the head of a syllable which is also the most salient element when that same syllable is stressed within a foot, and that foot is the main stress of a word, and so on.

A third problem is the lack of structure inherent in grids. For instance, while two feet can be reconstructed in *Fawcett-Majors*, what tells us that *-cett* is governed on the left rather than the right? Of course, the general principle that heads are on the left in English can be invoked, but this is not reflected by the notation. Moreover, by decreeing that *eg* level 1 corresponds to a foot, we are not thereby providing the limits of that foot. Yet, the relevance of prosodic categories as domains for rules has received a great deal of attention in recent years (see Nespor and Vogel 1986). More generally, it can be said with Giegerich that the metrical tree model tackles the question of prosodic hierarchy in a more direct way than the grid approach, which, as it were, slips in prosodic constituents through the back door.

This is not to say that the metrical trees displayed so far are fully adequate. Their commitment to binarism leads to a proliferation of structure which has failed to receive strong motivation so far. For instance, the binary subconstituents that are assigned to *algebra* in [71a], do not appear to be required as phonological domains. As we have emphasized that there was little evidence allowing us to rank the last two syllables in terms of prominence, it seems preferable to adopt a non-binary tree such as [71b]:

[71a]   [71b]

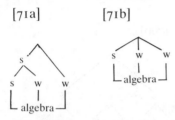

The richness and lack of motivation of binary trees is particularly striking in languages with a single word-stress (whether initial, final, penultimate, post-initial), or in subgeneralizations which have the same effect. Thus, in Huasteco, we saw that in the absence of a long vowel, the first syllable of a word is stressed (*cf* [41]). Since this stress-assignment is unbounded this will lead to left-branching trees such as [72a]. The over-elaborate nature of [72a] has often been used as an argument in favour of grids such as [72b] in so far, of course, as these are not directly linked to binary trees. But [72c] is just as adequate as [72b].

[72a]   [72b]   [72c]

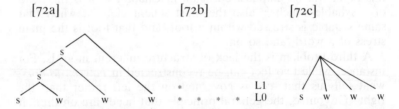

The issue of grids vs. trees is far from settled and the reader must be warned that the position advocated here is by no means universally shared. Moreover, an important variant of the grid approach has recently been put forward by Halle and Vergnaud. This is the topic of the final section of this chapter.

6.2.2.3 Halle and Vergnaud's grid and constituent approach

We conclude this chapter by a brief resumé of a grid approach to stress advocated by Halle and Vergnaud (1987 a, b), who test it against a wide sample of stress systems. This approach is different from Prince's and Selkirk's frameworks, particularly, in that it recognizes constituents, and it is likely to give rise to a great deal of work and debate in the forthcoming literature (see Laks 1988). We shall first of all exemplify this system with the Australian language Maranungku where, it will be recalled, odd-numbered syllables within words are stressed and an extra-heavy stress falls on the initial syllable of the word (*cf* 6.1.9; Hayes 1981 and the sketch in Halle and Clements, 1983).

As in other grid systems, a base line of marks is defined corresponding to every syllable (line 0). Halle and Vergnaud use the term 'line' instead of 'level' for each layer of constituents. More precisely, an asterisk is placed over the stressable units of each syllable (typically vowels). In Maranungku, the vowels but not the consonants are stressable units as reflected in [73]:

```
[73]  *  * * * *      * * *    * *   line 0
      langkarateti  welepenemanta
```

On each line it is possible to define constituents which are bracketed and which each have a head. The head of each constituent on line *n* receives a grid mark on line *n* + 1. For Maranungku, as in 6.1.9, Halle and Vergnaud posit left- headed binary constituents which are constructed from left to right and give rise to [74] (the dots play a formal role in the mechanics of the system but this can be left aside here):

```
[74]  *   .  *  . *       *        .   *      .   *          .  line 1
     (*   *)(* *)(*)    (  *    *) (  *    *) (  *          *) line 0
     langka rate ti   we l e pe n e m a n t a
```

Single syllables at the edge of strings, such as *ti* in *langkarateti*, form degenerate one-syllable feet (unless they are extrametrical and hence invisible). On line 1, a new constituent is formed which encompasses the whole word and which is left-headed. As a result, an asterisk is added on the leftmost asterisk column producing [75]:

```
[75]  *    .   .   .         *     .    .    .       .   line 2
     (*    .   *.  *) (  *    .    *    .    *      .) line 1
     (*    *) (* *) (*) (  *    *) (  *    *) (  *      *) line 0
     langka rate ti we l e pe n e m a n t a
```

The dependants of a head form what is called a domain. The domain is either bounded or unbounded (*cf* 6.1.9). In the case of unbounded constituents, the domain extends to the edge of a string (*cf* [77b] *infra*) or to the nearest head at the same level marked by an asterisk (*cf* [77a] *infra*). In Maranungku, an unbounded constituent has been constructed over line 1 whose head, marked by the solitary asterisk on line 2, is the main stress of the word. On the other hand, since bounded constituents are normally binary, each dependant will be adjacent to the head as exemplified by the feet of line 0 in Maranungku.

Given the notational apparatus just sketched, we can turn to a somewhat more complex illustration involving Huasteco. As mentioned in 6.1.9, stress in Huasteco falls on the last syllable that has a long vowel, but, in words where all the syllables contain reduced vowels, stress is assigned to the first syllable. This type of stress assignment is attested in a variety of other languages (classical Arabic, Chuvash, Hindi) and is illustrated by Halle and Vergnaud with reference to Eastern Cheremis (based on Hayes 1981). But there is some doubt that Eastern Cheremis does exemplify this type of stress, at least as simply as claimed in the literature (see Sebeok and Ingeman 1961). This is why Huasteco (*cf* Larsen and Pike 1949; Laks 1988) has been chosen here.

Consider the following two Huasteco examples in [76], where y is a glide:

[76a] ʔe:la:swá:y   '(they) probably found each other'
[76b] hílk'omac   'leftovers'

The general strategy, when a particular unit (long vowel, branching rhyme, etc.) attracts stress, is to mark it by an arrowhead placed directly below it and to project its prominence on to L1 by assigning it an asterisk at that level. Any construction of bracketed constituents on line 0 will respect this pre-assigned prominence. If we assume that line 0 constituents are left-headed in Huasteco and unbounded, we will produce structures such as those of [77] for our two examples:

[77a]   [77b]

```
   *       *       *                         *      .     .      line 1
( * ) ( * ) ( * )                       ( *    *    * )           line 0
ʔ e: l   a: s ẃ a: y                     h i  lk' o  m a c
  ^       ^       ^
```

In the case of [77b], the left-headed unbounded constituent encompasses the whole word and is reflected on line 1 by the asterisk over *i*. In the case of [77a], every pre-assigned head starts a domain which ends as soon as a new head is encountered. In this particular example, each constituent on line 0 is coterminous with a syllable. To derive the main word-stress all we need to do is construct a right-headed unbounded constituent on line 1, as in [78]:

[78a]   [78b]

```
     .       .       *                     *      .     .       line 2
( *       *       * )                    ( *      .     . )      line 1
( * ) ( * ) ( * )                        ( *    *    * )         line 0
ʔ e: l   a: s w a: y                     h i  lk' o  m a c
  ^       ^       ^
```

In the case of [78a], the rightmost asterisk able to receive a stress is the last vowel. As for [74b], it will be noted that the rightmost asterisk able to receive a stress is, in fact, the solitary initial asterisk of line 1.

There is, unfortunately, one remaining difficulty: if we examine [78a], we can see that we are left with two secondary stresses which are not pre-theoretically motivated. Halle and Vergnaud suggest that a general mechanism of suppression is available, which they describe as a conflation of two lines – lines 1 and 2 in this case. What is meant by the conflation of two lines in this context is that a constituent on the lower line will only be preserved if its head is also the head of a constituent on the higher line. In other words, [78] will surface as [79]:

[79]
```
        .           .           *       line 2
    (   .           .           *   )   line 1
    (  *  )  (   *   )  (   *   )       line 0
       ? e: l      a: s    w a: y
         ^          ^        ^
```

The various steps of grid construction for Huasteco are as follows:

[80a] Stressable elements are vowel.
[80b] Assign line 1 asterisks to long vowels.
[80c] Line 0 constituents are left-headed.
[80d] On line 0 construct unbounded constituents.
[80e] Line 1 constituents are right-headed.
[80f] On line 1 construct unbounded constituents.
[80g] Conflate lines 1 and 2.

The study of lexical stress assignment is a good testing ground for theories of stress structure given the uncertainties that surround prominence assignments within utterances. Halle and Vergnaud present a universal framework for lexical stress such that the stress system of individual languages can be reduced to a number of choices from a small number of dimensions ('parameters'). At the base of the system is the notion of constituent with a head (situated at one edge of the constituent) and dependants forming a domain. A grid representation articulated in levels is projected from the constituents with a view to defining prominence relations between the syllables of each word. The language-specific parameters are: (a) Are constituents left-headed or right-headed? (b) Is the domain bounded or unbounded? (c) Are constituents constructed right to left or left to right? (d) How many levels are there? (e) Are there any extrametrical elements? Note that (a) to (c) can vary from level to level within a single language. A principle of conflation of levels can also be invoked to smooth out prominence assignments not maintained at an upper level. The conflation of levels is not structure-preserving and, therefore, a powerful mechanism to include in any grammar.

While the various approaches sketched here may look like notational variants, there are empirical differences between them. Halle and Vergnaud's grid and constituent approach, unlike grid-only approaches, sees stress as a reflex of the way languages concatenate elements in head-dependant structures. One type of evidence they refer to in favour of their system is the fact that rules of deletion can leave constituent structure intact with reassignment of headship to dependants of the constituent (*cf* Halle and Vergnaud 1987a: 50–1). The testing of their hypotheses will lead to a lively debate in the forthcoming literature. Laks (1988) offers a thorough presentation of the Halle and Vergnaud scheme and a critique from the standpoint of a grid-only approach.

Notes

1. The Polish argument is borrowed from Basbøll (1981) and Lass (1984). It should be noted that there is an exceptional class of Polish words which are stressed on the antepenultimate.
2. This is not to say that the formulation of Latin stress presented here is the best as it stands. See the discussion and references in Vincent (1988).
3. Note that in discussing the syllable in English the 'surface' vowels, rather than the underlying vowels of Chapter 4, are generally being used for convenience. No attention has been paid to dialectal variations (*eg* the fact that forms like *loup* in Scots do not obey [10c]).
4. The status of 'h aspiré' words and many other issues, such as the relation between 'liaison' and 'enchaînement', are neglected here as well as in 6.1.6: see Booij (1984), Clements and Keyser (1983), Durand (1986a, b), Encrevé (1983), Klausenburger (1984) among many others. A comprehensive treatment of liaison using theoretical tools defined in this chapter and the next will be found in Encrevé (1988).
5. It might be thought that the words of [13a] can be disposed of on the grounds that they are foreign. But, in the present context, there is no evidence that using an exception feature such as [+foreign] would have any explanatory value. Taking a word like *input*, we note that it behaves like any other native French word with respect to liaison and elision: *cf les inputs* [lezinput]) and *l'input*. Moreover [13a] contains words like *yole* ('skiff') which while specialized are not foreign in any reasonable sense of the word. In any case, how would

a child learning French know that a word like *water* ('loo'), which belongs to [13a] is foreign? It does not violate any phonotactic constraints on the surface and it belongs to a class [13a] which is larger than that of words like *oie* or *oiseau* [13b] and which is expanding.

6. A very different position on the status of the coda and syllable-structure in general is however taken in Kaye (to appear) and Kaye, Lowenstamm and Vergnaud (1988). A discussion of syllable structure from the point of view of Markedness Theory is outlined in Kaye and Lowenstamm (1981). Hyman (1985) is well worth consulting for an alternative view concerning the status of the syllable in phonological theory.

7. But note that Selkirk (1984b) places [s] out of its 'voiceless fricative' niche ahead of nasals. As this move captures only part of the exceptional behaviour of [s], I have kept here to a class-based index. It should also be noted that Selkirk treats the SI as a scalar feature which is available in phonological rules.

8. Ambisyllabicity is only allowed after a short stressed vowel but not after a complex rhyme (*eg Péter*): *cf* Fallows (1981).

9. To be quite precise, Iambic Reversal never applies in a structure like (a) below, which is a subpart of *maroon sweater* (b) – a type of sequence forbidding 'Move *':

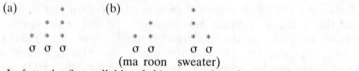

(ma roon   sweater)

In fact, the first syllable of *thirteen* needs to be treated as a foot – that is, as a two-asterisk column, with a consequent reinforcement of adjacent columns.

Chapter 7

Autosegmental and multidimensional phonology

7.1 Preliminary remarks

In this chapter, we turn to the question of phonological representations once again. In Chapter 3, it was argued that various facts pointed to the need for richer infrasegmental structure (*cf* 3.5 on gestures). And in Chapters 5 and 6, we progressively abandoned the unidimensional picture of phonology of *SPE*, in that the string of segments was argued to be linked to suprasegmental structure on the one hand (syllable, foot, etc.), and to morphosyntactic structure on the other. We also saw that, in some theories, an additional structural plane (the grid) was postulated to represent patterns of rhythm and prominence. In such theories, three independent planes (more correctly, half-planes) intersect at the level of segments. We also introduced the notion of a CV tier which was placed between segments and the suprasegmental hierarchy.

In the following sections, we shall move on to the position that the CV tier should be seen as an anchoring device (hence the more appropriate name of **skeleton**) relating the internal content of segments to other types of information. The reader may have noticed, however, that in many respects our approach has remained linear: in particular, the domain of features has been assumed to coincide with that of segment-sized units. But a number of linguistic phenomena suggest that features should not be locked within single segment-sized units but should be allowed to span domains of varying sizes (portions of the syllable, whole syllables, feet, words, etc.). This idea is not new and much work in the Firthian school (or London school: see Palmer 1970; Lass 1984: §10.2) started from this very assumption. In recent years, these insights have been developed and formalized within a framework known as Autosegmental Phonology.[1] As the original and most intuitively convincing examples of autosegmental analysis have come from tonal phenomena, we shall start from examples in this area and then move on to an integration of these ideas into a more complex geometrical model which we shall call 'multidimensional phonology' – a model far removed from many of the assumptions that we started from in the early chapters of this book.

7.2 Tones and the autosegmental framework

Within the *SPE* paradigm, tones were considered to be features on a par with other features. Thus, to describe a language possessing three distinctive level tones (high, mid, low), we could select the features H for a high tone and L for a low tone, and analyse the contrast between three syllables /bá/ (where the acute accent means high), /bà/ (where the grave accent means low) and /ba/ (where the lack of accent denotes a mid tone) as in [1]:

[1]	b	á		b	á		b	a
syll	−	+		−	+		−	+
cons	+	−		+	−		+	−
son	−	+		−	+		−	+
ant	+			+			+	
cor	−	−		−	−		−	−
H		+		−				−
L		−		+				−

In the above matrices, tones are features like any other features: they are considered in [1] not to be applicable to the initial consonant but this in itself does not make them special since we also want to consider other features such as [anterior] as not relevant to vowels. We consider here and below that tones are associated with key elements within syllables: the so-called tone-bearing units. These are typically vowels but other segment-types can also bear tone (*eg* liquids, nasals, etc.).

Let us now turn to examples showing that, if we consider tones as properties of individual segments, some striking generalizations are missed.

7.2.1 A Bakwiri language game

In the Bantu language Bakwiri (*cf* Hombert 1973; Dell and Vergnaud 1984; Vago 1985), there is a language game in which the two syllables of disyllabic words are transposed. Thus, the word for 'dead' is *kʷéli* and would be transposed as *likʷé*. Bakwiri has two contrastive tones – high and low. They can therefore be analysed in terms of the two values of a single feature: *ie* [+H] for a high tone and [−H] for a low tone. For expository purposes, we shall however transcribe this contrast as [+H] and [+L] in the examples below. In the *SPE* notation one way to formalize this syllable switch might be to write a transformational rule as follows:

[2]   [−syll]   [+syll]   [−syll]   [+syll]
     1   2   3   4   ⇒ 3 4 1 2

This formulation would be adequate for the word *kʷélí* where all features (including [+H]) making up the individual segments seem to be transposed. But, if we take a word like *kʷélì* ('falling') where the second vowel bears a low tone, the transposition yields *lìkʷè*. In other words, while the segments making up the two syllables have changed places, the tones have stayed in their original position. Yet, rule 2 would have predicted *lìkʷé*. How can we explain such examples which are representative of the patterns of Bakwiri? What is happening is that the tones are simply not transposed along with the segmental make-up of each syllable. They behave as if they belonged to a separate level or **tier**, as we shall say from now on, in relation to the other features of which the segments are composed.

Suppose that a word like *kʷélì* was represented as in [3], where the phonetic symbols stand for whole matrices of features and where the lines (called **association lines** from now on) connect tones with the relevant tone-bearing units:

[3]   +H +L   tonal tier
      | |
    kʷ e l i   segmental tier

Then, we could maintain our transposition rule [2] by assuming that it applied only to units on the segmental tier but left the tonal tier unaffected. In [3], the tone-features are treated as **autosegments** which are independent from the other features making up a segment – hence the adjective 'autosegmental' used in this chapter.

This simple example illustrates one important piece of evidence in favour of autosegmental approaches to tone – namely, the notion of 'tone stability'. That is, the tonal tier does not necess-arily behave in unison with the segmental tier. We shall see more exemplification of this as we go on. Let us now turn to a different problem: the representation of contour tones.

7.2.2 Contour tones

While some tone languages use only 'level' tones (register tones) such as high, mid, or low, many tone languages use 'contour' tones beside 'level' tones (*eg* fall, fall–rise, etc.). The question is how these should be represented at an abstract, phonological, level. Let us assume we are attempting to represent a falling tone. One interesting suggestion is that we could perhaps treat a falling tone as the sequence [+H][+L]. Although a representation like this gives the starting-point and the finishing-point of a tone, it might well be objected that this does not express the fact that a rising tone is a **movement** from high to low. This is, in a sense, true but not as damaging as one might think at first sight. Consider any representation in terms of segments – say, /pek/. The movement from an [e] position to a [k] position is not sudden but gradual and one inevitably goes through a series of intermediate vowel qualities before reaching the [k] position. But these intrinsic allophones are the result of coarticulation and independently predictable from a theory of phonetic implementation of phonological segments. By the same token, we can assume that an actual falling tone is the inevitable result of moving in time from high-frequency phonation to low-frequency phonation.

Having tried to justify the intuitive plausibility of an analysis of contour tones in terms of more primitive level tones, let us turn to the precise nature of the coding of a contour tone along these lines. One first possibility, then, is to build the sequence [+H][−H] within a standard matrix as in [4] where we work from the hypothetical representation of the vowel /à/ with a falling tone (denoted by a grave accent):

$$[4] \begin{bmatrix} \text{à} \\ +\text{syll} \\ -\text{cons} \\ +\text{low} \\ -\text{round} \\ +\text{H} +\text{L} \end{bmatrix}$$

But, if we do so, we are in fact breaking a fundamental convention on the internal structure of segments within the standard *SPE* mould: that is, within a column of features one and only one feature is formally allowed. The reason is that a segment, as explained in Chapter 2, is an (unordered) set of simultaneous features: {+syll, −cons, +low, −round}. By using [+H][+L] as in [4] we are in effect bringing order as a dimension of classification of features. This is problematic since the whole formalism

is based on a different assumption and would have to be revised
to allow for this theoretical innovation with possibly far-reaching
consequences. If, on the other hand, we adopt representations
such as [5a] or [5b] we create other problems:

[5a] /à/

$$\begin{bmatrix} +\text{syll} \\ -\text{cons} \\ +\text{low} \\ -\text{round} \\ +\text{H} \\ +\text{L} \end{bmatrix}$$

[5b] /à/

$$\begin{bmatrix} +\text{syll} \\ -\text{cons} \\ +\text{low} \\ -\text{round} \\ +\text{H} \end{bmatrix} \begin{bmatrix} +\text{syll} \\ -\text{cons} \\ +\text{low} \\ -\text{round} \\ +\text{L} \end{bmatrix}$$

Both of the above conform to the formalism. However, [5a]
leaves open two phonetic interpretations: does this represent a
movement from +H to +L, a falling tone, or on the contrary a
movement from +L to +H, a rising tone? On the other hand,
[5b] is not the representation of a single segment but that of two
segments. Of course, we might want to claim that contour tones
are only properties of long segments (a tentative claim which was
made in early work in the generative analysis of tone). But this
is simply not true. Cross-linguistically, there is no reliable correlation between contour tones and inherent length.

Let us try another avenue. Why do we not simply postulate
basic tones such as [+RISE] or [+FALL] as part of our theory
of distinctive features? In this case, /à/ would be represented as
in [6a] and a rising tone /á/ as in [6b]:

[6a] /à/

$$\begin{bmatrix} +\text{syll} \\ -\text{cons} \\ +\text{low} \\ +\text{FALL} \end{bmatrix}$$

[6b] /á/

$$\begin{bmatrix} +\text{syll} \\ -\text{cons} \\ +\text{low} \\ +\text{RISE} \end{bmatrix}$$

This does not pose any formal problem as such. But now, let us
examine the formulation of a well-attested type of assimilation
which occurs in tone languages (*eg* Cantonese): a falling tone
becomes a high-level tone when followed by either a high tone
or another falling tone. This regressive assimilation seems
phonetically quite natural. A fall implies a movement from high
to low frequency and when the low-frequency component of the
fall is immediately adjacent to a high frequency (that of the level
tone or the starting-point of another fall) it assimilates to it. But,
if we formulate this in terms of different features for level and
contour tones, we obtain [7]:

[7] $[+\text{FALL}] \rightarrow [+\text{H}] / \underline{\quad} \begin{Bmatrix} +\text{FALL} \\ +\text{H} \end{Bmatrix}$

As it stands, [7] is clearly unsatisfactory. The braces in the environment of the rule collapse elements which are formally unrelated. And the phonetic naturalness of a fall being realized as a high- level tone is not expressed either by [+FALL] → [+H].

Suppose, on the other hand, that we adopt the suggestion put forward in 7.2; that is, that we postulate that tones are represented on a different tier from the rest of the segmental representation and that we use V and C to represent respectively tone-bearing elements and elements not marked for tones. In that case, a hypothetical syllable /ban/ would have the following representations according as to which tone it bore (where the autosegments could just as easily be placed below the segmental tier):

[8]
```
    +H          +L         +L +H     +H +L
    |           |           \ /       \ /
  C V C       C V C        C V C     C V C
high level   low level     rising    falling
```

Now the two inputs to our example of assimilation would be:

[9a]
```
 +H +L   +H +L        [9b]    +H +L   +H
  \ /     \ /                  \ /     |
 C₀ V    C₀ V C₀             C₀ V   C₀ V  C₀
 fall  +  fall               fall  +  high
```

If we assume that the assimilation in [7] refers only to the tonal tier, the formal similarity between the two contexts is striking. Here [9a] is the same as [9b] except for an extra [+L] tone at the extreme right of [9a]. We could therefore write a much more satisfactory rule, either deleting the second [+L] tone in the first fall or assimilating it to the next [+H] value as follows:

[10a] [+L] → ∅   / [+H] __[+H] (deletion)
[10b] [+L] → [+H]   / [+H] __[+H] (assimilation)

Let us, in order to introduce a number of concepts which will be vital later, apply [10b] to the two structures in [9]. The result will be as in [11]:

[11a]
```
 +H    +H    +H    +L       [11b]    +H    +H    +H
   \  /        \  /                    \  /        |
  C₀ V    C₀   V    C₀               C₀ V    C₀  V C₀
 level   +    fall                   level   +  high
```

We can see that the two [+H] tones on the syllable of the ex-fall represent a surfeit of structure since they denote identical phonetic values connected to one position. We could postulate a convention that merged these two [+H] tones to produce [12] below.

[12a]
$$\begin{array}{ccccc} +H & +H & +L & & \\ | & \vee\!\!\!\!\vee & & \\ C_o\ V & C_o\ V & C_o & & \end{array}$$
high + fall

[12b]
$$\begin{array}{ccccc} +H & & +H & & \\ | & & | & \\ C_o\ V & C_o\ V & C_o & \end{array}$$
high + high

Such a convention has fortunately been independently postulated under the name of Obligatory Contour Principle (OCP). The OCP, first put forward in Leben (1973), is formulated as follows:

[13] Obligatory Contour Principle
For any pair of adjacent autosegments a and b, a ≠ b.

The OCP forbids two identical autosegments to follow one another. Crucially, if a sequence of identical autosegments should arise within a derivation, the OCP, functioning as a kind of repair device, merges them. In fact, the OCP (which will be discussed more extensively in 7.3.2) also predicts that the two adjacent [+H] tones of [12a] and [12b] should now merge again, producing [14a] and [14b]:

[14a]
$$\begin{array}{ccccc} +H & +L & & \\ \diagup\ \ \vee\!\!\!\!\vee & & \\ C_o\ V\ C_o\ V & C_o & \end{array}$$
high + fall

[14b]
$$\begin{array}{ccccc} +H & & \\ \diagup\ \ \diagdown & \\ C_o\ V\ C_o\ V & C_o \end{array}$$
high + high

Implicit in the above discussion is some theory of the relation between the tonal tier and the tone-bearing units: a set of rules governing their association. Indeed, given that such a theory is required anyway to account for what happens once tones are, for example, changed or deleted, one might therefore question the validity of the formulation given in [10] which follows the standard *SPE* formalism. A better way of handling this and other examples of tonal change is to operate in terms of deletion, addition or reassignment of association lines. Thus, starting once again from [9] as input, we could have severed the line of association between the affected [+L] tone and its tone-bearer as exemplified in [15] and then let the OCP derive [14].

[15a]
$$\begin{array}{ccccc} +H & +L & +H & +L & \\ \diagdown\!\!\!\!\times & & \diagdown & & \\ C_o\ \ V & C_o & V & C_o \end{array}$$
fall + fall

[15b]
$$\begin{array}{ccccc} +H & +L & +H & \\ \diagdown\!\!\!\!\times & & | & \\ C_o\ \ V & C_o\ \ V & C_o \end{array}$$
fall + high

Although severing a line may appear identical to a feature-deletion rule such as [10a], principles such as the OCP and the conventions dealt with in the following sections have no equivalent in the standard notation and lead to treatments far removed from those possible in the *SPE* tradition.[2]

7.2.3 Principles of association

If we start operating in terms of rules of association governing the relationship between adjacent tiers, one question which should be aired is whether the linking between tones and tone-bearers is given underlyingly or, on the contrary, derivable from general principles. One leading idea of autosegmental phonology is that, in the unmarked case, the autosegments and the segments are not paired underlyingly but associated by **well-formedness principles** given in [16]. In [16] we use tones and vowels to make the discussion more concrete but these conventions are assumed to apply to any autosegmentalized feature and the units it is connected to on the segmental tier.

[16] Principles of association[3]

[16a] **Mapping**: Associate vowels with tones in a one-to-one fashion left to right until we run out of tones or vowels.

[16b] **Dumping**: If after applying [16a] some tones are still free (that is, unassociated) link them to the last vowel to the right.

[16c] **Spreading**: If after applying [16a] some vowels are still free link them to the last tone on the right.

[16d] Association lines are not allowed to cross.

Principle [16a], taking [17a] as input, produces [17b]:

[17a] +H +L   [17b]   +H +L
                                    | |
       b a t a   b   a   t a

Principles [16b] and [16c], taking [18a] and [18b] as inputs, produce [19a] and [19b] respectively. Principle [16d] is a general principle of generative grammar: the representation given in [20a] is no more allowed than the syntactic representation suggested in [20b].

[18a]   [18b]

       [+H] [+L] [+H]   [+H]   [+L]
        | | | | |
    b   a t   a   b a t   a s a

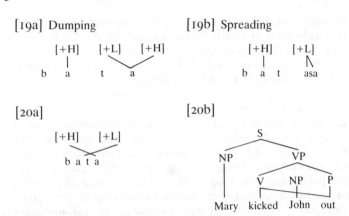

There is some debate in the literature as to whether [16b], dumping, and [16c], spreading, are universal conditions that apply automatically in any language or whether, on the other hand, they are parameters which are fixed by each language individually. The stronger position would treat them as default mechanisms, unless inhibited within individual languages, but Halle and Vergnaud (1982b), among others, argue that they represent marked options which must be specified in the grammar of individual languages.

7.2.4 Exemplification: Margi tones

In the Nigerian language Margi (cf Williams 1976; Dell and Vergnaud 1984, both based on Hoffman 1963), there are three tones phonetically: a high tone, transcribed as v́; a low tone transcribed as v̀ and a rising tone transcribed as v̌. The high tone will be represented as [+H] and, once again for clarity, we will represent the low tone as [+L] (instead of [−H]). The rising tone, following 7.2.2, will be analysed as a sequence [+L][+H] on the tonal tier. Let us now see some evidence for this assumption. First of all, whenever a process of deletion or fusion reduces two consecutive syllables marked as [+H][+L] to one syllable, the resulting syllable displays a rising tone. Examples are given in [21]:

[21a] /tlà + wá/   [tlwǎ]   'to cut in two'
[21b] /ngjɜ̀ + já/   [ngjǎ]   'to fire (pottery)'
[21c] /ngjìr + rí/   [ngjǐr]   'to light'

Assuming the underlying form of [21a] is [22a], after deletion of the /a/ vowel in the first syllable, we obtain [22b]. At that point, principle [16a] links the only vowel to the first [+L] (see

[22c]) and by [16b], **dumping**, the free tone [+H] is also associated with the vowel, thus producing a rising tone (see [22d]).

[22a] [+L]   [+H]   [22b] [+L]   [+H]
      tla   wa   tl   wa
[22c] [+L] [+H]   [22d]   [+L] [+H]
         \ /   \ /
        tlwa   tlwa

On the other hand, Margi – as is common in tone languages – has some suffixes which have no phonological tone. The reason for assuming this is that, in representative examples such as [23a] and [23b]:

[23a] /sá + na/   [sáná]   'to lose'
[23b] /ndàl + na/   [ndàlnà]   'to throw'
[23c] /nǒ + na/   [nǎná]   'to model'

the tone of the suffix is simply inherited from the vowel to the left. This is totally predictable given convention [16c], *ie* **spreading**. Let us assume that the underlying representation of *sá* is {/sa/, [+H]} where the segmental representation and the tone are unsequenced, whereas the representation of *na* is simply {/na/}. After these morphemes have been put together by a morphological rule we obtain [24a]. When we apply the association convention the [+H] tone will first be linked to the first vowel by [16a] and then the free vowel will be linked to the only available tone by spreading, yielding [24b]:

[24a]   +H   [24b]   +H
          | |\
     s a n a   s   a n a

The behaviour of toneless suffixes gives further support to the notion that rising tones are in fact a [+L][+H] sequence on the tonal tier. Notice that in [23c] the rising tone has given place to a [+L] and a [+H] tone split over each of the two syllables. This follows directly from the ideas articulated so far. Thus, if nǒ is underlyingly {/nə/, [+L][+H]}, once suffixation rules put it together with *na*, we obtain [25a] below. But the rules of association state that sequences of free tones and sequences of free tone-bearers will be associated from left to right on a one-to-one basis. Therefore, we predict the distribution of the two tones over the two syllables as given in [25b]:

[25a]   +L   +H   [25b]   +L   +H
                                   | |
      n   ə   n a   n   ə   n a

This example also indicates that the association principles are best applied here after suffixation (a dimension which we expect to vary between languages). If we assumed that, first of all, the tone(s) and the stem were linked and then a suffix was added, we would have to undo the original association and reassociate the [+H] tone to explain [25b] (cf Williams 1976: 467–9 for a tentative discussion of Margi verb phrase morphology).

Further confirmation of our treatment of Margi comes from the tone of some enclitic subject pronouns: it is [+H] when the previous syllable is [+L] and [+L] when the previous syllable is [+H] or rising. Thus, the cliticization of *nda* 'third plural' at the end of the themes *àsá* (present of 'to lose one's way'), *áwì* (present of 'run'), and *ávĕl* (present of 'jump') yields *àsándà*, *áwìndá* and *ávĕlndà* respectively.

If we assume once again that a rising syllable (as in *ávĕl*) corresponds to the sequence [+L][+H], this dissimilation rule will be easily explicable. A simple morphological spell-out rule can be expressed in the way indicated below (where only [+/−high] is used since recourse to two values of this feature is sufficient to handle the tonal patterns of Margi):

SPELL-OUT RULE: $\emptyset \rightarrow [-\alpha\text{high}] \ / \ [\alpha\text{high}]$ ____

7.2.5 Extensions of autosegmental analysis

Tone has been selected above as a particularly striking illustration of the concept of **autosegment**. But, it is by no means the only property whose domain is not tied to the segment. Vowel-harmony phenomena which involve the spreading of a given feature – tongue-body position, tongue-root advancement, lip-rounding, etc. – to a whole domain have also received insightful treatment within the autosegmental framework.

Consider, for instance, the Asante dialect of Akan (cf Stewart 1967; Clements 1976, 1981). This Twi-Fante tone language of Ghana shares with many other African languages a type of harmony in which the vowels fall into two sets of five, each distinguished by advancement vs. retraction of the tongue root ([+/−ATR], as defined in 2.3.2.2). These vowels will be transcribed as : /i, e, ɜ, o, u/ [+ATR] vs. [ɪ ɛ a ɔ ʊ] [−ATR]. As an illustration of the harmony contrast, examine the following sequences of prefix + root + suffix (with tones left out):

[26] e-bu-o   'nest'
      ɛ-bʊ-ɔ   'stone'
      o-fiti-i   'he pierced (it)'
      ɔ-cɪrɛ-ɪ   'he showed (it)'

The selection of a root such as /fiti/ 'pierce' triggers the spreading of a [+ATR] value, whereas that of /cirɛ/ 'show' triggers the spreading of [−ATR]. Therefore, [+/−ATR] is contrastive in roots but not in affixes, although Clements (1981) argues persuasively that the contrast is neutralized in the case of low vowels. (Here /ɜ/ is not an underlying segment but the result of assimilation of /a/ to subclasses of [+ATR] segments.)

Suppose, now, that we applied to this example of vowel harmony the concepts that we have used in connection with tones. Thus, a stem such as *fiti* 'to pierce' which belongs to the [+ATR] class, would be simply specified underlyingly as {/fiti/,[+ATR]}, where [+ATR] is an autosegment:

[27] f I t I
      +ATR

(The capital letters indicate vowels which are unmarked for [ATR].)

An application of the principles of association, discussed in 7.2.3 in connection with tones, to [27] would yield [28c], on the (universal) assumption that the autosegment-bearers (or **P-bearing units** as they are usually called) are vowels for this class of feature.

[28a]   [28b]   [28c]

f I t I ——— mapping → f i t I ——— spreading → f i t i
                              | \⁄
+ATR   +ATR   +ATR

If, as hypothesized above, regular, harmonically alternating affixes do not contain any [ATR] specification underlyingly, and, if the association conventions apply once all affixes have been sequenced, derivations such as those given in [29] will obtain.

[29]

O + f I t I + I → o + f I t I + I → o + f i t i + i
      \⁄   \⁄   \⁄
  [+ATR]   [+ATR]   [+ATR]

One challenging feature of Akan is the fact that [−ATR] /a/ is immune to ATR harmony (does not become [ɜ]) and, when occurring in a root, makes suffixes [−ATR]. The behaviour of /a/ in Akan is typical of what are called **opaque** segments: opaque segments block the spreading of a certain process and may, in addition, determine a domain of their own.[4] To represent the opacity of /a/, we will connect it (or pre-link it) to a [−ATR] value underlyingly as in [30]:

[30] O + b I s a + I 'he asked it'

$$\underset{\text{+ATR −ATR}}{\mid}$$

When this word enters a derivation, [+ATR] will be linked to the segmental domain preceding /a/ by one-to-one mapping followed by spreading. But since, underlyingly, /a/ is pre-linked to [−ATR], the autosegment [+ATR] will not spread to it and cannot either spread to the unspecified suffix /I/ since this would involve a crossing of lines. On the other hand, there is nothing preventing the [−ATR] value of /a/ to spread rightwards to any following suffix. The upshot is [31].

[31]

o + b i s   a + ɩ

[+ATR]   [−ATR]

Another example of autosegmental treatment is that of vowel nasalization in Terena (Bendor-Samuel 1960). In this language, the first person singular (subject of verb or possessive pronoun) is formed by nasalizing all the vowels and semi-vowels in the word up to the first stop or fricative. Consider:

[32]	emo2u	'his word'	ēmõ2u	'my word'
	ayo	'his brother'	ãỹõ	'my brother'
	owoku	'his house'	õw̃õŋgu	'my house'
	piho	'he went'	mbiho	'I went'
	ahya2ašo	'he desires'	ãnža2ašo	'I desired'

The situation depicted here is very close to that in Malay (*cf* 3.5.3), except that the stop or fricative which blocks the spread of nasalization surfaces as a pre-nasalized consonant (which could be transcribed with a raised nasal before the consonant – *eg* [ᵐbiho]). One good argument for treating the nasal+stop articulations as units rather than sequences is that the syllable-template of Terena does not allow consonant clusters: all Terena syllables are of type (C)V.

The blocking of nasalization illustrated above indicates that nasality spreads left to right from a position before the affected morpheme. If we assume that the morphology spells out the above words as nested structures with [+nasal] as an autosegmental marker of 'first person singular' followed by the stem we would have structure of the form [33a] which will become [33b] by mapping and spreading. Since stops and fricatives act as

[33a]   [33b]

[+nas]   [+nas]

[[ayo]] → [[a y o]]

opaque consonants, they will be pre-linked to a [−nas] specification which, in turn, will extend rightwards to following vowels
as in [34b].

[34a]   [34b]

[+nas]   [−nas]   [+nas]   [−nas]

[[o w o k u]] → [[o w o k u]

But [34b], as it stands, does not indicate the pre-nasalization
of the consonant, nor the voice switch of the stop to which we
return briefly later. Pre-nasalized segments involve a lowering of
the velum before the stop or fricative articulation in circum-
stances which require the whole segment to function as one unit.
While a feature such as [pre-nasalized] might appear adequate
(Ladefoged 1971: 35), it is clear that it is unsatisfactory since:
(a) a pre-nasalized segment, like any other [+nasal] segment, can
nasalize a preceding vowel; (b) pre-nasalization can be the result
of a spreading of [+nasal] as in Terena (see S. R. Anderson 1971
and Ewen 1982). One solution in the classical framework would
be to say that a pre-nasalized segment involves the internal
sequence [+nasal][−nasal], but the same objections we formulated against this type of solution for tones would hold here. An
elegant answer to this conundrum is fortunately at hand within
the autosegmental framework. If, by a language-specific association, the feature [+nasal] is associated to a stop or a fricative
as in [35] the move from a nasal to an oral articulation within the
lifetime of the stop will be transparently expressed. The type of
representation made possible within the autosegmental framework for pre-nasalized stops is given in [36a], and the attested
converse situation where a segment is post-nasalized is given in
[36b].

[35] [+nas]   [−nas]

       o w o   k u

[36a] Pre-nasalization   [36b] Post-nasalization
      [+nas] [−nas]   [−nas] [+nas]

            C   C

Note finally that in [32] a pre-nasalized obstruent surfaces as [+voice]. This may be tentatively attributed to the [+nasal] feature which once associated with the consonant triggers by default a [+voice] value.

It is, of course, not the case that harmony processes could not be treated within the *SPE* framework. But it will be noticed that the *SPE* commitment to full specification of segments does not cope very well with cases like the Terena one where a single feature external to the stem is applied to it. Moreover, the elegant treatment of opaque segments and that of pre-nasalization has no equivalent in the standard notation. A typical way of handling harmony processes in the *SPE* framework was to mark the first or last vowel of a given domain for the harmonic feature and then spread this latter iteratively from left to right or right to left. But in many cases, harmonic features are the property of a whole stem (as in Akan) or a whole word without any need for a given vowel to be privileged (see *eg* Kaye, 1971; in press, on Desano) or even, more controversially, a given direction. For instance, in Chapter 4 vowel harmony in Andalusian Spanish was considered. While it was maintained that an underlying /s/ could still mark (residually) the plural, there is no need to assume that the tense–lax opposition observed in singular *vs* plural forms spreads from right to left (as may have happened historically). A simpler solution consists in positing that the morphological choice [+/−plural] triggers the presence of a 'prosodic' feature, [+/−tense], which will spread to all vowels within the specified domain by standard principles of association (see Cerdá-Massó 1984, who advocates a 'Firthian' treatment of the Andalusian vowels). Indeed, Hooper's (1976) formalization which specifies the domain as the phonological word (## . . . ##, which encompasses the verb plus its clitics) just marks every vowel as tense or lax without giving any privilege to the right-to-left dimension.[5]

One obvious consequence of the above remarks is that the notion of segment in its classical sense is beginning to dissolve. Not only tones but other phonetic properties are best thought of as 'prosodies', which are not tied to segments but rather span various **domains** (defined in metrical or morphosyntactic terms). Given that more than one property can be autosegmentalized (*eg* tone and ATR-ness in Akan), the question is how the P-bearing units and the autosegments should be interfaced. Fortunately, an important piece of machinery was introduced in Chapter 6: the CV tier or **skeleton**, as we will call it from now on. We saw there that by introducing a set of timing positions between syllable structure and segmental structure a more adequate treatment of diphthongs, long vowels, affricates, etc. as well as aspects of syllable structure, became possible. But, we left open the question of how the skeleton related to other portions of phonological representations. What we want to suggest now is that all planes (syllable-structure, morphological structure, grid, harmonic features, etc.) intersect in the skeleton core which, for this reason, has often been compared to the spine of a spiral-bound notebook. An illustration of this idea is given in [37] which is a partial representation of the Akan sequence *mifi* 'I leave'.

[37]

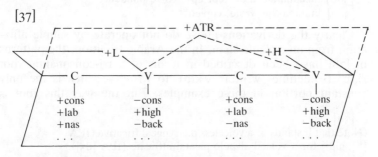

It quickly becomes impossible to represent pictures of intersecting planes on two-dimensional pages and the reader will have to bear this in mind and do the necessary readjustments whenever partial representations are provided. But, the reason for preferring **skeleton** to **CV tier** should be obvious: the latter misleadingly places the timing slots on a par with other autosegmental units. Instead the skeleton should be thought of as what unifies an essentially multidimensional representation.

7.3 The skeleton

In the following three subsections, the notion of skeleton is explored first with special reference to Semitic phonology and then in a broader framework.

7.3.1 Sketch of classical Arabic morphology

At the base of the following description of aspects of classical Arabic phonology is John McCarthy's seminal thesis *Formal problems in Semitic phonology and morphology* (1979) where the inflectional and derivational paradigms of classical Arabic receive extensive discussion.

The most salient characteristic of the morphology of the verb in classical Arabic (and Semitic languages in general) is its **non-concatenative** aspect. Each verb form consists of a root of three or four consonants which defines its lexical identity and these consonants enter a variety of patterns with vowels intercalated between them. As an incomplete example of the morphological family clustering around the concept of writing, consider:

[38a] kataba 'he wrote'
[38b] kattaba 'he caused to write'
[38c] kaataba 'he corresponded'
[38d] takaatabuu 'they kept up a correspondence'
[38e] ktataba 'he wrote, copied'

Clearly the derivations above do not operate by simple affixation from an isolable stem. In the Arabic tradition, the patterns in [38] have been described in terms of a tri-consonantal root /ktb/ (sometimes written √ktb) 'to write' – which is the only constant portion in these examples. But the way this root is

[39]
(Note that ḥ stands or a voiceless pharyngeal fricative (IPA [ħ] and j for a voiced alveolo-palatal affricate (IPA [dʒ]).

	Perfective		Imperfective		Participle	
	Active	*Passive*	*Active*	*Passive*	*Active*	*Passive*
Triliteral roots						
I	katab	kutib	aktub	uktab	kaatib	maktuub
II	kattab	kuttib	ukattib	ukattab	mukattib	mukattab
III	kaatab	kuutib	ukaatib	ukaatab	mukaatib	mukaatab
IV	ʔaktab	ʔuktib	uʔaktib	uʔaktab	muʔaktib	muʔaktab
V	takattab	tukuttib	atakattab	utakattab	mutakattib	mutakattab
VI	takaatab	tukuutib	atakaatab	utakaatab	mutakaatib	mutakaatab
VII	nkatab	nkutib	ankatib	unkatab	munkatib	munkatab
VIII	ktatab	ktubib	aktatib	uktatab	muktatib	muktatab
IX	ktabab		aktabib		muktabib	
X	staktab	stuktib	astaktib	ustaktab	mustaktib	mustaktab
XI	ktaabab		aktaabib		muktaabib	
XII	ktawtab		aktawtib		muktawtib	
XIII	ktawwab		aktawwib		muktawwib	
XIV	ktanbab		aktanbib		muktanbib	
XV	ktanbay		aktanbiy		muktanbiy	
Quadriliteral roots						
QI	daḥraj	duḥrij	udaḥrij	udaḥraj	mudaḥrij	mudaḥraj
QII	tadaḥraj	tuduḥrij	atadaḥraj	utadaḥraj	mutadaḥrij	mutadaḥraj
QIII	dḥanraj	dḥunrij	adḥanrij	udḥranraj	mudḥanrij	mudḥanraj
QIV	dḥarjaj	dḥurjij	adḥarjij	udḥarjaj	mudḥarjij	mudḥarjaj

linked with various vowel sequences or the consonants are organized was typically tackled in a taxonomic way. To gain a more accurate view of the problem, let us consider the derivational patterns recognized in the Arabic tradition. These patterns are usually called **binyanim** (singular **binyan**), a term borrowed from Hebrew grammar. Example [39] on p. 258, borrowed from McCarthy (1979, 1981), lists the fifteen tri-consonantal binyanim and four quadri-consonantal binyanim of the Arabic scholarly tradition, cross-classified in terms of inflectional categories (perfective/imperfective, etc.).

If we compare the active and passive forms of individual binyanim (*eg takattab-tukuttib* in V), it is clear that, while the actual vowels change (a . . . a . . . a, u . . . u . . . i), the sequence of vowel and consonant slots stays stable. With reference to the first column of [39] we observe the following templates (with gaps in the passive):

[40] CVCVC (I)   CVCVVCVC   (VI)
     CVCCVC (II,IV)   CCVCVC   (VII,VIII,IX)
     CVVCVC (III)   CCVCCVC   (X,XII,XIII,XIV,XV)
     CVCVCCVC (V)   CCVVCVC   (XI)

These templates are strangely similar to the notion of skeleton with which we have operated above. Let us assume that, in fact, they are the skeleton but that the difference from previous examples comes from their source: they are not lexically given but supplied by the morphology – a situation also exemplified by Yawelmani (*cf* 7.4.1). The word-forms of [39] could be analysed as the result of associating two types of information to each skeletal template: on the one hand, an inflectional vowel pattern, say /u . . . i/ for *kutib* (I), and, on the other hand, the consonantal root (/ktb/ for 'write'). Following McCarthy, let us array the obviously independent vocalic and consonantal 'melodies' on different planes. The underlying form of *kutib* will therefore be as [41a] – where the phonemic symbols stand, of course, for feature-matrices

[41a]   u   i   [41b]   u   i

    C   V   C   V   C   C   V   C   V   C

    k   t   b   k   t   b

The associations in [41b] are one to one and follow directly from our general conventions.

Leaving aside the vowel melodies for a moment, let us concentrate on the link between the root consonants and the skeleton. A one-to-one mapping is sufficient to account for very many cases; for instance:

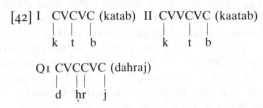

[42] I CVCVC (katab) II CVVCVC (kaatab)

        k t b   k   t   b

Q1 CVCCVC (dahraj)

    d ḥr j

Even apparently wayward forms such as *ktabab* and *dahraj* follow directly from **spreading** by the well-formedness conditions whose interpretation here requires that each slot in the skeleton must be linked with at least one segment in the melody:

[43] IX   CCVCVC (ktabab)   Q4 CCVCCVC (dharjaj)

     kt b   d ḥ r j

If we look, however, at *kattab* (II), whose underlying form is as in [44a], the predicted association in terms of universal conventions is [44b]:

[44a] CVCCVC (kattab)   [44b] CVCCVC (*katbab)

     k t b   k t b

But [44b] would give rise to an incorrect surface form. McCarthy posits here a language-specific rule which severs the first link between a consonant and the first of two C slots as in [45]:

[45] Delinking (Binyanim II, V, XII, XIII)

    CVC

      ⤫╱

   [+cons]

The application of delinking adjusts [44b] to [46a] and, as a result, the association conventions spread the /t/ on to the now vacant C slot in [46b]:

[46a] CVCCVC   [46b]   CVCCVC (kattab)

     k t b   k t   b

Other forms in the first column involve prefixations or infixations. McCarthy assumes that the prefixes and infixes are also on different planes – a particularly attractive solution in the case of infixation which interrupts a morphemic string without threatening its overall identity. A form such as *ktawwab* (XIII) would therefore be the result of, first, fixing *w* on to the skeleton as in [47]:

[47]   w
      |
  CCVCCVC (ktawwab)
  k t   b

and then letting left-to-right, one-to-one association apply (bearing in mind that the C linked to *w* is no longer available). The result is [48a] corrected to [48b] by delinking.

[48a]   w   [48b]   w
       | |
  CCVCCVC   CCVCCVC
  | | |/ | | /
  k t b   k t   b

At this point, two associations are possible in accord with our general conventions. If we link the /w/ to the immediately adjacent free C slot we obtain [49a] below which is our desired result (*ktawwab*). But, if we link the /t/ to the same C slot, we obtain [49b]:

[49a]   w   [49b]   w
       |\ |
  CCVCCVC (ktawwab)   CCVCCVC (ktawtab)
  | | | | | |
  kt   b   kt   b

But, far from being an embarrassing result, [49b] is in fact binyan XII. The indeterminacy in the spreading has, as it were, been used by the language to generate two contrastive forms.

Let us now turn to the vowels. A form such as *kutib* has been used to exemplify a one-to-one association between V slots and vowel melodies. But if we consider a form like *katab* (I), although it may appear as if its full representation might be [50a],

[50a]   a a   [50b]   a   [50c]   a
       | | /\ |
  CVCVC   CVCVC   CVCVC
  | | | | | | | |
  k t b   k t b   k t b

the reader will recall that the OCP predicts that the same vowel melody should be shared by the successive V slots. In other words, [50b] is the correct derived structure from an underlying representation of the form [50c].

On the assumption, then, that successive occurrences of the same vowel correspond to only one vocalic melody underlyingly, how would a form such as *kuutib* (III) be derived? If our starting-point is [51a] below, we predict [50b] *kuitib as output, by one-to-one, left-to-right association and then spreading of /i/ on to the last free V slot:

$$[51a] \quad \text{u i} \qquad [51b] \quad \begin{array}{c} \text{u i} \\ | \hspace{1pt} | \backslash \end{array}$$

$$\text{CVVCVC} \qquad \begin{array}{ccc} \text{CVVCVC} \\ | & | & | \end{array}$$

$$\text{k} \quad \text{t} \quad \text{b} \qquad \text{k} \quad \text{t} \quad \text{b}$$

Let us assume with McCarthy that in such forms a language-specific rule of the form [52]:

$$[52] \quad \begin{array}{c} \text{i} \\ \vdots \\ \text{VC]} \end{array}$$

links the /i/ to the last vowel slot in a stem. Rule [52] will be automatically ordered before the general associations by the Elsewhere principle since it is more specific than these latter (*cf* 5.1.1.2). The application of [52] to [51a], which can be maintained as initial form, yields [53a] from which [53b] is derived by the principles of association:

$$[53a] \begin{array}{c} \text{u} \\ | \end{array} \qquad \text{i} \qquad [53b] \quad \begin{array}{c} \text{u} \\ | \backslash \end{array} \qquad \begin{array}{c} \text{i} \\ | \end{array}$$

$$\text{CVVCVC} \qquad \begin{array}{ccc} \text{CVVCVC} \\ | & | & | \end{array}$$

$$\text{k} \quad \text{t} \quad \text{b} \qquad \text{k} \quad \text{t} \quad \text{b}$$

While much remains to be said, the above should provide a reasonable overview of the interaction of language-specific and universal conventions in the phonology of classical Arabic. We can now turn our attention once again to the OCP.

7.3.2 The Obligatory Contour Principle

When dealing with vowels in 7.3.1, we have invoked principle [13] – the OCP – to bar repeated adjacent occurrences of the same vocalic melody. The OCP would also be invoked in dealing with a form like *samam*, apparently from root /smm/ 'poison'. In so far as *samam* has two adjacent occurrences of /m/, we should in fact assume that this form is derived from a bi-consonantal stem

/sm/ mapped on to skeleton of the form CVCVC by the usual route:

[54]   s   m   (samam)
       | /\
       CVCVC
         \/
          a

The question remains as to why, beyond simplicity, this might be desirable. One first observation is that the one-to-many associations embodied in the OCP allow us to make sense of the intuitively appealing idea that the forms in [39] (*eg kattab*) are all variations on a basic /ktb/ theme. A second observation can be made concerning long segments such as the /u:/ in *kuutib* [53b], treated by the OCP as a single vocalic melody associated with two V slots. Long vowels behave sometimes as if they were a single segment and sometimes as if they were two. This is easy to explain given representations where a long vowel corresponds to two slots on the skeletal core and to one value on the vowel melody. A third observation is that long vowels cannot, for instance, be split by epenthesis of a vocalic element sandwiched between the two V slots. The reason is that this would involve a crossing of lines:

[55] *V V V   (aəa)
        \ /
         X
        a ə

But if we represent long segments simply as geminates, as was done earlier in this book, the reason for their 'integrity' *vis-à-vis* other sequences which are interruptable remains mysterious.

Besides these general observations, there is some very strong evidence within the phonology of classical Arabic – and all the Semitic languages – that the OCP is an explanatory principle (McCarthy 1979, 1981, 1986; Lowenstamm and Prunet 1986). There is a striking asymmetry within the phonology of this language between the possibility of roots of the form $C_1C_2C_2$ such as /smm/ (reducible to /sm/ by the OCP) and the impossibility of tri-consonantal roots of the form $C_1C_1C_2$ such as /ssm/, for instance. Rare exceptions such as the nursery word *dadan* 'plaything' hardly compare with the some 200 words of type $C_1C_2C_2$ (smm, hll, mdd). This follows directly from the OCP: a hypothetical underlying form such as [56a] (see p. 264) would be automatically adjusted to [56b] which is indistinguishable from the structure underlying *samam*.

[56a] s   s   m   [56b]   s   m
   CVCVC   CVCVC
     a   a

If we assume, therefore, that classical Arabic obeys the OCP, the absence of roots with two identical initial consonants falls out from general principles. The alternative requires the postulation of an arbitrary constraint on the shape of morphemes.

The status of the OCP as a universal principle has been the subject of intense controversy. Although we started from the OCP and tones for expository reasons (7.2.2), it is in the area of tones that the most problematic data have been uncovered (*cf eg* Goldsmith 1976, on Etung, Conteh, P. *et al.*, 1983, on Mende). From the non-tonal point of view, the universal status of the OCP has been questioned by Kenstowicz (1982) and Schein (1981) on the basis of Tigrinya. But Lowenstamm and Prunet (1986) offer an elegant demonstration that without the OCP many facets of the phonology of Tigrinya would remain mysterious and argue strongly in favour of the OCP as a defining principle of phonological systems. The issue is considered in depth by McCarthy (1986) who, recognizing the possibility of violations of the OCP, proposes to consider it as a parameter of UG whose unmarked value is 'on'.[6]

7.3.3 The skeleton as a set of pure positions
In this chapter and the previous one, the skeleton has been organized in terms of units labelled C and V in the line of McCarthy's work or Clements and Keyser (1983). We have deliberately refrained from giving them a specific interpretation, relying on a tacit assignment of vowels to V's and consonants to C's. One possible interpretation of V is as subsuming the former feature [+syllabic] and C as [−syllabic] (Clements and Keyser 1983: 10). But, since we have argued in Chapter 6 that the notion of syllabicity could be reconstructed from syllable-structure, this interpretation would merely reintroduce [+/−syllabic] by the back door. The idea therefore arose of treating the skeleton as a set of pure positions (usually represented by X's) which mediate between the various planes (Kaye and Lowenstamm 1985; Levin 1983). One convincing argument used by Kaye and Lowenstamm runs as follows.

In Tiberian Hebrew, in contexts where we observe a gemination of the consonant formally similar to that of *kattab* above (see [57a]) the gutturals fail to geminate. What happens is that the vowel which precedes the guttural is extended over the free slot giving rise to a long vowel by a process of **compensatory lengthening** (see [57b]):

[57a]   i   e   [57b]   i   e

         | | ⌐ |

      CVCCVC (sibber)   CVCCVC (pii?er)

      | |/ | | | |

      s   b   r   p   ? r

But the spreading of /i/ in [57b] is taking place on a C slot which clashes with our former assignment of long vowels to VV sequences. This is avoided if the skeleton is specified in terms of X's as in [58]:

[58]   i   e

       |⸜ |

    X X X X X X

    | | |

    p   ?   r

This type of representation has now become extremely common in phonology and is accepted by most phonologists working within a multidimensional framework. It will be used in the rest of this chapter.

7.4 Further geometrical extensions

Some strong evidence has been provided above in favour of allowing features to belong to different planes linked to a skeleton. But, it has also been argued in the literature that features should be hierarchically ordered and grouped in bundles. The idea of gesture was introduced in 3.5 and will be further explored in 7.4.2 below. For the moment, we will sketch a proposal made by Archangeli (1984, 1985) that more structure should be given to features within a plane.

7.4.1 Yokuts revisited

The data considered by Archangeli are taken from the dialects of Yokuts and have, in part, been dealt with in 5.1, where Archangeli's account of Yawelmani rounding harmony was presented in linear terms. The reader is advised to peruse that section again before turning to the following development.

In her work, Archangeli examines in depth three non-linear solutions to the statement of rounding harmony. All these solutions assume that features for consonants are arrayed on a different plane from vowel features (as shown above for Arabic, for instance).

The first solution, called unitiered harmony by Archangeli, consists in placing all the vowel features in a single bundle (or tier) on a single plane. The form [ʔugunhun], derived from /ʔugun+hn] by vowel epenthesis and rounding harmony, would be obtained from the following intermediate representation:

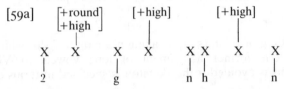

The spreading of [+round] consists in linking the whole matrix which includes [+round] to vowel slots on the right (in two successive steps), while simultaneously delinking the latter from the feature(s) they were associated with. This is exemplified in [59b]:

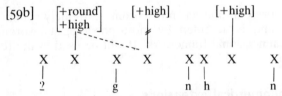

This first solution is not an improvement on a linear statement of harmony since it assumes that all features of the trigger spread on to the victim – hardly a general truth about harmony processes.

A second solution of a familiar kind in autosegmental terms consists in assigning the [+round] feature to a separate plane and in specifying rounding harmony as in [60] below:

[60] Multiplanar harmony

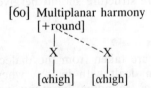

The third solution, favoured by Archangeli under the name of Coplanar Harmony, consists in placing features in separate tiers but within the same plane. She suggests, as part of a universal layering of features, that [high] is anchored closer to the skeleton with [round] and [back] on successive separate tiers (arbitrarily represented here above the skeleton rather than below). A segment such as [y] would therefore be represented as in [61]:

[61] Universal stacking of features

```
Back tier        [−back]
                    |
Round tier       [+round]
                    |
High tier        [+high]
                    |
SKELETON         X
```

Archangeli's formulation of coplanar harmony is as follows:

[62] Coplanar harmony

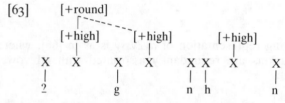

To exemplify with [ʔugunhun] once again, the application of [62]
to an underlying form specified in accord with [61] would yield
[63] below:

[63]

```
        [+round]
        ┌─────────────
    [+high]      [+high]        [+high]
      |            |              |
  X   X        X   X      X X   X       X
  |            |          | |          |
  ʔ            g          n h          n
```

Since the vowels in [63] are not specified for [+/−back], the
actual surface form [ugunhun] would be derived by the operation
of a default rule (see rule [20f] in 5.1) which, other things being
equal, will specify a non-low round vowel as back.

Archangeli's case rests on a close examination of three dialects
of Yokuts: Yawelmani, Wikchamni and Gashowu. She shows
that, while coplanar harmony provides a satisfactory account of
all three dialects, the other two solutions (unitiered harmony and
multiplanar harmony) fail in at least one instance. The
Wikchamni dialect provides a good illustration of the advantage
of coplanar harmony.

Wikchamni has the same vowel system as Yawelmani with the
addition of the front rounded vowel /y/. It too participates in
vowel harmony, as illustrated in [64a, b]:

[64a] dyʔs + ši → dyʔysšy   'sting + aorist'
[64b] hud   + ši → hudšu   'know + aorist'
[64c] tan   + ši → tanši   'go + aorist'
[64d] moxd + ši → mooxidši   'get old + aorist'

As will be recalled from 5.1, /i/, as exemplified by the suffix
-ši, is only specified as a [+high] vowel at the stage at which

Rounding Harmony applies and, if it inherits the value [+round] as in [64b], it will correctly surface as [u]. In [64c] the stem vowel is not round and, by definition, cannot trigger rounding harmony. In [63d], the stem vowel is round but differs from /i/ in terms of vowel height which blocks rounding harmony. The puzzle is why we should observe [y] in *dy2yssy*. If [+round] is the value that spreads to the suffix *-ši* (making the vowel [+high, +round]), then, by default, the expected surface allomorph of this morpheme should be [šu]. How come the [−back] value of the stem vowel spreads as well? Is this a peculiarity of Wikchamni?

The answer that Archangeli gives is that Wikchamni can easily be handled if we adopt coplanar harmony. Let us assume the underlying specification of the vowel system given in [65]:

[65] Wikchamni underspecified vowel system:

	i	y	u	a	o
High				−	−
Round		+	+		+
Back	−				

The underlying representation of *dy2yssy* is as in [66], where the empty brackets are redundantly associated with all vowel slots (free X's):

[66]

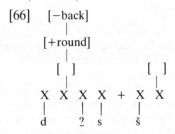

The first stage of the derivation consists in epenthesizing a vowel. This is interpreted, in non-linear terms, as the creation of an extra vowel slot, as in [67], which also receives a set of empty brackets by the RR:

[67]

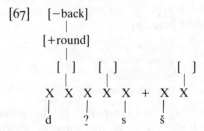

Since rounding harmony (whatever formulation is adopted) makes reference to both values of [high], it will be recalled from 5.1.1.2 that the Redundancy Rule Ordering Constraint [21] forces the introduction of [+high] on segments not specified underlying for [high]. The result is [68]:

[68]   [−back]
         |
       [+round]
         |
    [+high]   [+ high]   [+high]
       | | |
    X X X   X X   +   X X
    | | | | | |
    d   ʔ   s š

Now, coplanar harmony [62] handles the data most elegantly: [+round] is spread from the first [+high] vowel to all following [+high] vowels as in [69] carrying [−back] along for the ride. The upshot is that all the vowels will surface as [y]:

[69]   [−back]
         |
       [+round]
         |
    [+high]   [+high]   [+high]
       | | |
    X X   X X   X   +   X X
    | | | |
    d   ʔ   s   š

By contrast, multiplanar harmony leads to wrong outputs as exemplified in [70], since a [+high, + round] vowel unspecified for [+/−back] is realized by default as [+back].

[70] [+round]
       ┌─────────────────┐
    d X ʔ   X s + š X → *dyʔuššu
       | | |
    ⌈+high⌉ [+high]   [+high]
    ⌊−back⌋

A full demonstration of the advantages of feature-stacking would require much more extensive discussion than is possible here and the reader should consult Archangeli (1984, 1985) for detailed argumentation. Further exemplification of feature-stacking is given in connection with Dependency Phonology in Chapter 8.

7.4.2 A notation for gestures

In 3.5, the idea was defended that sets of features which regularly behave as units with respect to certain types of generalizations (*eg* rules of assimilation) should also be treated as units from the point of view of phonological representation. A particular organization of the internal structure of segments in terms of gestures and subgestures borrowed from Dependency Phonology was introduced and exemplified there with respect to the *SPE* notation. The same hypothesis has been explored in recent work both from a phonetic point of view (see Browman and Goldstein 1986) and from the perspective of multidimensional phonology (see Clements 1985; Sagey 1986). We will limit ourselves to a simplified presentation of some key ideas defended by Clements and Sagey, but keeping close to the proposals of 3.5 in the interest of unity of presentation.

A phonological representation pushing the autosegmental idea to its limits would end up proposing a view of the world where each feature would be assigned to a different plane, all the planes being connected to the common core or 'skeleton' as exemplified earlier in this chapter. The alternative model put forward here is one where the internal structure of segments resembles, in the words of Clements (1985: 229), 'a construction of cut and glued paper'. Example [71] presents an initial example of the kind of structure described here.

[71] A geometrical model of segment – internal structure

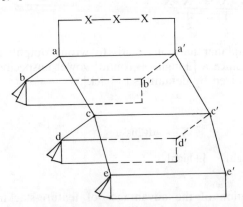

Each fold, obtained by linking the nodes representing the internal structure of two successive segments, is called a 'class tier' (aa', bb', cc', dd', ee'). The lower edges are 'feature tiers' and the upper edge is the skeleton. The fold aa' which is immediately dominated by the X's of the skeleton is a class tier superordinate to all other tiers and labelled 'root tier' for that reason. The justification of the root tier is the following one: we need to be able to characterize processes of **total** assimilation in which a whole segment assimilates all the features of a preceding/following segment. Thus total regressive assimilation can be formalized as in [72] where R1 and R2 on the root tier are the nodes from which all the other features hang:

[72] Total assimilation

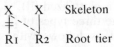

X X Skeleton

R1 R2 Root tier

The feature tiers are justified by cases which affect a single feature (deletion, assimilation). Class tiers correspond to group-ings of features such as were offered and defended in *ch* 3. We argued there for establishing a fundamental opposition between what was called for 'articulatory gesture' which refers to supra-laryngeal articulators and the rest. In Sagey's detailed (1986) study of features and relations in non-linear phonology, a similar picture is offered which can be displayed in a two-dimensional way as in [73]:

[73]

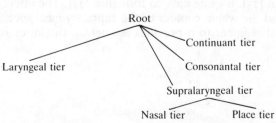

Root

Continuant tier

Laryngeal tier

Consonantal tier

Supralaryngeal tier

Nasal tier   Place tier

From each class tier given above hang a number of features. For our purposes here, we can define each tier as follows (but the reader should note that Sagey's place tier is itself subdivided into further class tiers):

[74] Continuant tier: [+/−cont]
Consonantal tier: [+/−cons]
Laryngeal tier: [+/−voice], [+/− spread],
  [+/−constricted], [+/−stiff], [+/−slack]
Supralaryngeal tier
Nasal tier: [+/−nasal]
Place tier: [+/−round], [+/−anterior],
  [+/−lateral], [+/−high], [+/−back],
  [+/−round] . . .

To illustrate the relevance of this geometrical organization, consider the following set of phonological processes borrowed from Klamath (Clements 1985: 234; Sagey 1986: 46):

[75] nl → ll
    nl̥ → lh
    nl' → l2
    ll̥ → lh
    ll' → l2

(where[l̥] is a voiceless [l] and [l'] is a glottalized [l]).

In terms of feature-specification the three types of [l], [2] and [h] of Klamath can be represented as follows with standard binary features (adapted from Clements 1985):

[76]

	[l]	[l̥]	[l']	[2]	[h]
Voice	+	−	−	−	−
Spread	−	+	−	−	+
Constricted	−	−	+	+	−

The mutations of [75] can be decomposed into two ordered subprocesses: (a) nasals followed by laterals become lateral liquids with the same place of articulation; (b) [l'] → [2] and [l̥] → [h]. The first one, in terms of the kind of organization assumed in [73], is quite easy to formalize [77]. The effect of [77] is to spread the whole content of the supralaryngeal specification of a lateral segment to a previous segment if the latter is nasal.

[77]

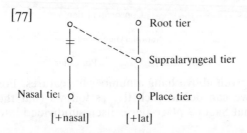

The second set of mutations (l' → 2, l̥ → h) is an example of dearticulation with retention of the glottal configuration. Here [l'] and [l̥] form a natural class – that of [−voiced] laterals. This subprocess can be formulated as in [78]:

The effect of [78] – starting from a structure where two successive laterals have identical articulation and differ only in terms of glottal configuration – is to sever the link between the root node of the second one and all supralaryngeal features. The unaffected first segment survives as [l], but the second segment

[78]

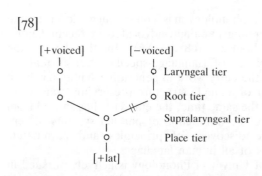

surfaces as [ʔ] if the input was [+constricted] (*ie* [lˀ]) or as [h] if the input was [+spread] (*ie* [l̥]).

Careful argumentation is required to motivate each grouping and subgrouping in this type of approach, and only a flavour of what might count as evidence can be given here. It is as yet uncertain whether the various proposals presented in this chapter can be reconciled. Thus, whether the feature-stacking advocated by Archangeli (*cf* 7.4.1) is compatible with the type of geometry outlined above is still moot (see Sagey 1986: 2.6) and the dissociation of vowel and consonant features required by the morphology of a language like Arabic also needs extensive discussion with respect to geometrical proposals. Nevertheless, there seems to be a fair amount of agreement that any notation must allow features to span domains either larger or smaller than segments in the *SPE* sense while also reflecting the componential (or gestural) make-up of successive timing units.

7.5 Universal Phonology and the 'no rule' approach

In the last three chapters, we have emphasized at various points how aspects of the phonology of individual languages could be derived from the application of universal principles or the selection of one value from a small set of parameters (see, *eg*, the approach to stress in the Halle and Vergnaud system: 6.2.2.3). We have also shown a progressive move away from rule systems in the *SPE* sense in favour of a more 'configurational' approach. Thus, in dealing with classical Arabic morphological patterns, we saw that given representations where various forms of information are arrayed on different planes, and given some local 'wrinkles' (*eg* delinking [45]), the bulk of the phonology was handled by universal principles of association and other general conditions on the functioning of grammatical systems such as the

OCP. In that sense, phonology has come much closer to the Government and Binding paradigm advocated in recent Chomskyan work (*eg* Chomsky 1981, 1986). In the latter, the extrinsically ordered set of (language-specific) transformations which characterized the early work in generative syntax has been abandoned in favour of a single structure-preserving 'transformation' (Move-α). At the same time, the emphasis has shifted from derivational issues to the interaction of parallel systems of representation and the discovery of principles and parameters governing the syntax of all human languages.

The programme of Universal Phonology is actively pursued in various centres throughout the world and has been vigorously defended by Kaye, Lowenstamm and Vergnaud (KLV) in various recent publications (*cf* KLV 1985, 1988, Kaye to appear). In its strongest form, Universal Phonology advocates the abandonment of all rules (in the sense of extrinsically ordered statements) and claims that observed phonological phenomena result from the interaction of general principles governing phonological representations and structures and the parameter values set in particular languages. For instance, vowel-epenthesis in individual languages, far from being an operation which radically distorts underlying structures, might be the simple filling-in (perhaps by a default statement) of potential place-holders in syllable-structure (*eg* an unfilled onset node: *cf* 6.1.1.1).

It is too early to say whether this programme can be successfully completed. Too few in-depth studies of well-known languages, where claims are readily testable, exist within the framework of Universal Phonology (see, however, Encrevé, 1988). Nevertheless, Universal Phonology seems to represent the most interesting option from the point of view of phonology. The range for variation between individual languages is ultimately very vast in the classical *SPE* paradigm given the possibility of long chains of language-specific operations relating underlying and surface forms. Natural Generative Phonology attempted to constrain grammars by various means but only succeeded in consigning to the lexicon the vast bulk of variant forms of morphemes within a fairly poor representational system inherited from *SPE*. If Universal Phonology manages to handle a good portion of the data which has been successfully treated in the classical generative paradigm without *ad hoc* machinery, we might be justified in speaking of progress in the field of phonology.

Notes

1. It is a great pity that American linguists, by and large, failed to perceive the importance of the Firthian insights: compare, in this respect, the fairly negative critique of the London School of Linguistics by Langendoen (1968) with the many extensions of Firthian analyses found in the current literature.

2. While it is argued in the text that contour tones can be handled via level tones, no feature-system for tones is offered here. In 2.3.7.1, it was mentioned that [+/−stiff], [+/−slack] had been offered as possible features for the high–low pitch paremeter. The reader should consult Yip (1980), Clements (1983), as well as thê essays in Fromkin (1978) for insightful discussions of tonal features.

3. The principles of association are sometimes presented in the form of a well-formedness condition requiring that: (i) all tone-bearing units should be linked to at least one tone; (ii) all tones should be associated to at least one tone-bearing unit; (iii) association lines should not cross. Then (i)–(iii) are completed by association conventions specifying the direction of the association (right to left or left to right), its starting-point, as well as the options of dumping and spreading. This variant will not be considered here: see Haraguchi (1977) and Clements and Ford (1979) for authoritative discussions.

4. A fuller discussion of 'opacity' should make room for the converse notion of 'transparency': transparent (or neutral) segments are skipped by harmony processes. For discussions and further references, see van der Hulst and Smith (1986), van der Hulst (1988a: §5).

5. Readers wishing to extend their knowledge of autosegmental phonology are advised to delve into the excellent volumes edited by van der Hulst and Smith (1982, 1985). For introductions to fundamental autosegmental concepts, see Goldsmith (1979), Halle and Vergnaud (1980), and Kaye (in press). For a recent critique of autosegmental work as still too 'discrete' and 'linear' from a Firthian perspective, see Local and Simpson (in press).

6. For further discussion of the OCP, see Yip (1988).

Chapter 8

An outline of Dependency Phonology

8.1 Introduction

The purpose of this chapter is to offer an outline of Dependency
Phonology ((hereafter DP) and present its main theses. Work
within this model goes back to the early 1970s (J. M. Anderson
and Jones 1974), and the first thorough application of DP was
J. M. Anderson and Jones's *Phonological Structure and the
History of English* (1977), followed by Ewen's important 1980
thesis: 'Aspects of phonological structure with particular reference to English and Dutch'. In more recent years, the model has
been tested against a variety of problems, data and languages.
The reader is referred to J. M. Anderson and Ewen (1987) for
a thorough discussion of DP and reasonably detailed syntheses
are available in J. M. Anderson and Durand (1986) and Lass
(1984). Moreover, two recent publications – J. M. Anderson and
Durand (1987), Durand (1986a) – offer a wide range of articles
which complement the reader edited by J. M. Anderson and
Ewen in 1980.[1]

Very much like the developments within metrical and autosegmental phonology considered in Chapters 6 and 7, work within
DP has been animated by the conviction that, in order to satisfy
the NA principle of 2.6, both the internal structure of segments
and their external structure had to be more richly articulated than
assumed in the *SPE* tradition. But the linchpin of this model is
the concept of dependency, or head-modifier relation, claimed
to span the syntactic, morphological and phonological domains.
The notion of constituency, which is central to much modern
work in theoretical linguistics, is claimed not to be primitive, but
to be derivable from the dependency relation coupled with linear

precedence and rules of association. Let us first examine the nature of suprasegmental representations before turning to infrasegmental representations and further implications of this model.

8.2 Suprasegmental representations

Ever since the inception of DP, work within this framework has stressed the need to recognize not only the syllable as a structured unit (*cf* J. M. Anderson and Jones 1974) but also relationships between syllables. As the formalism adopted spans the various components of linguistic description, we shall first illustrate dependency representations with reference to syntax and morphology – which may be more familiar to the reader – and then move on to phonology.

8.2.1 Dependency structures in syntax, morphology and phonology

Dependency representations have been devised in an attempt to formalize the notion of head and subordinate – a subordinate being either an argument or a modifier. These notions are familiar from traditional and recent grammar where, for instance, a verb is said to 'govern' the noun phrases in its frame (in the sense that it imposes restrictions on their nature) so that in *many linguists go to Essex* we would take *go* as the pivot element of the sentence relating *many linguists* and *to Essex*. In turn, prepositions can be argued to govern noun phrases and, at least at surface level, determiners can be taken as dependants of their governing nouns. The kind of representation that has standardly been given in dependency grammar to a sentence such as the above is shown in [1].

[1]

Apart from the labelling, [1] encodes two types of relation: 'government' and 'precedence'. *Go* governs directly *linguists* and *to*, and, in turn, *linguists* governs *many* and *to* governs *Essex*. Government is expressed by placing the node (vertex) corresponding to a head higher than its dependants and connecting them by an arc. A category will be said to be **governed** by, or be the **dependant** of, another category if and only if one arc connects them (*eg many* and *linguists*). On the other hand, a category related to a head by a continuing descending sequence of arcs will be said to be a subordinate (*eg many* as well as *linguists* are subordinates of *go*). As for the relation of precedence – *ie* the fact that *many* immediately precedes *linguists* which immediately precedes *go*, and so on – it is expressed by simple left-to-right ordering on the page.

One major difference between a classical dependency representation such as [1] and a constituency representation (whether or not of the X-bar type) is that in [1] each syntactic category is immediately associated with a terminal. An NP is an N with its dependants, but there is no category NP superordinate to D and N.

While the nodes in [1] are labelled and connected by association with words instantiating the various syntactic categories, an equally adequate representation, favoured from now on, can be devised where the syntactic structure is a projection from the category labels and the words associated with them as in [2].

[2]

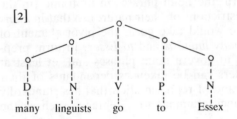

The same type of representation can be adopted in phonology. The syllable also has a head – a vowel in many languages – without which it does not exist as a constituent. That head is flanked by margins and the segments are normally ranked in accordance with the sonority hierarchy (*ie* with an ascending slope from the initiation to the syllabic and then with a descending slope). This is precisely what is expressed by the representation for the syllable *flint* [3], where /l/ and /n/ respectively govern the less sonorous and /f/ and /t/.[2] Note that there is no need for quasi-categorial labels like **strong–weak**, as used in metrical phonology (*cf* 6.2.1.2), since the incorporation of strength relations falls out from our choice of graph representation.

[3]

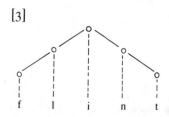

f l i n t

Representations such as [3], used in early work on DP, encounter a problem in that they do not incorporate divisions such as onset vs. rhyme, and nucleus vs. coda, which have been argued to be well motivated in Chapter 6. (That is, there is no vertex in [3] of which one could say, 'this vertex with its dependants comprises the rhyme', the rhyme being the sequence /int/.) The difficulty lies with the assumption made in classical dependency systems that a head is the governor of one and only one construction. But this assumption seems far too strong. Thus, a stressed syllabic within a foot (say /æ/ in *catty*) is successively the head of the syllable that contains it and the head of the foot. And, if that foot is the strong element of a tone group (*eg Dòn't be cátty*), the syllabic will be projected as the head of the whole construction. By the same token, in VP languages, a verb is successively head of the VP and head of the whole sentence (leaving aside the possibility of further protections as defended in X-bar syntax). If we do want to represent the possibility of this type of layering, while retaining the perspicuity of the dependency notation in expressing the notion of head, some assumption(s) of classical dependency systems, as summarized in [4], must be changed.

[4]   Standard dependency graphs
[4a] There is a unique vertex or root.
[4b] All other vertices are subordinate to the root.
[4c] All other vertices terminate only one arc.
[4d] Every vertex is immediately associated with a terminal category.
[4e] No crossing of arcs or association lines is allowed.

Assumption [4d] only allows nodes to be **adjoined** to their heads. If we drop this condition, and also allow nodes to be **subjoined**, we will license representations such as [5], where *go* is successively the head of the VP *go to Essex* and of the whole sentence. This relaxation of [4d] is independently motivated since, if we turn to morphological structure, we clearly need to

[5]

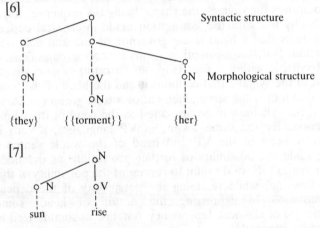

D   N   V   P   N

many   linguists   go   to   Essex

be able to express the possibility of a category node immediately dominating another category node as in denominals [6].[3] Unlike syntactic trees, morphological trees are made up of labelled nodes and involve both subjunction and adjunction as in [7].

[6]

Syntactic structure

Morphological structure

{they}   {{torment}}   {her}

[7]

sun   rise

If we return now to the internal structure of the syllable, we can incorporate the various structural subunits which have been argued to be well motivated in Chapter 6 by invoking both subjunction and adjunction as in [8].

[8] *blind*

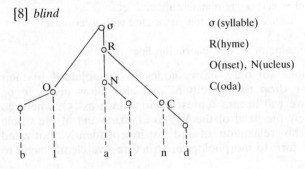

σ (syllable)

R(hyme)

O(nset), N(ucleus)

C(oda)

b   l   a   i   n   d

In [8], both the nucleus /ai/[4] and the coda /nd/ are subunits of the rhyme. The coda (made up of a head, /n/, and a less sonorous dependant, /d/) is adjoined to the node corresponding to the rhyme. The nucleus (also made up of a head, /a/, and a right-hand-side dependant, /i/) is expressed by a node which is subjoined to the rhyme node, itself subjoined to the syllable node. The onset is made up of the left-hand-side dependant (/l/) of the syllable node and all its subordinates (/b/ here). The fact that the node corresponding to /l/ is at the same height as the nucleus node is purely accidental. The labelling used in [8] is, in fact, unnecessary since the constituents of the syllable are uniquely reconstructable from the geometry of the graph. The syllable is the root of the graph or, from another angle, the node which is a third-order protection of the syllabic. A lack of labelling is not peculiar to DP but is a characteristic of much recent work on suprasegmental structure (cf 6.2.1.2).

The relevance of dependency for phonological and morpho-syntactic representations is in accord with what John Anderson (1986a, 1987a, in press) calls the **structural analogy** assumption – an assumption which has its roots in Hjelmslev's 'analogie du principe structurel' (1948). The idea is that we should expect the same structural properties to recur at different levels and that very strong support is required to motivate properties which are unique to a given level. This constraint does not, of course, apply to the basic alphabet, or categories, out of which representations in different components are constructed: the atoms of syntax are not the atoms of phonology. The structural analogy assumption separates DP from much modern work in phonology where the structural constructs of phonology (*eg* the grid or the dependency representations of Dell and Vergnaud 1984) have been developed independently from the representations of morpho-syntax (but see 7.5).

8.2.2. Interconnectedness

In 8.2.1 it was suggested that condition [4d] had to be relaxed. But there is one more condition that is too strong – that of [4c] which requires that each node terminates only one arc. As argued at length in DP (*cf* J. M. Anderson and Jones 1974, 1977; J. M. Anderson and Ewen 1987), and accepted in other frameworks, ambisyllabicity needs to be catered for in many languages (see 6.1.8). Dependency Phonology would propose representations along the lines of [9] (where the labelling is for convenience only) in which the node associated with [p] indicates that this segment functions simultaneously as a coda and an onset. Within the

[9] *tepid*

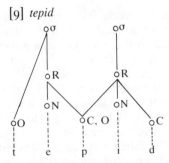

graph linkages which we are licensing, it is easy to integrate, for instance, the concept of **interlude**, which Vincent (1986) defends for medial -NC- clusters (*eg campo*) in standard Italian. Instead of a representation such as [10a], [10b] would be defended in DP.

[10a]   [10b]

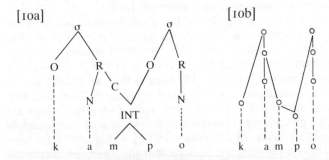

One obvious drawback of [10a], not shared by [10b], is that in so far as INT(erlude) is dominated by both C and O, [mp] is assigned an onset status: mistakenly, given that *[mpo] is not a possible monosyllable. Moreover, [10b] incorporates directly the sonority hierarchy (*eg* the node corresponding to /m/ governs that corresponding to /p/), whereas the INT node of [10a] makes this representation incompatible with a metrical tree.

The degree of interconnectedness (without crossing of arcs) allowed by dependency graphs is particularly useful in the treatment of #sC_1C_2 clusters in English and other languages (*cf* J. M. Anderson and Ewen 1987; Durand 1980; Ewen 1982). Although, different proposals have been put forward in DP, a representation such as that of [11] for *strand* has a number of advantages over other proposals made in the literature. In [11], the onset is correctly treated as a unit (*cf* the node associated with the most sonorous element [r] and all its dependants). But, within this unit, [st] and [tr] are also sub-units – that is, /t/ is an adjoined dependant of both /s/ and /r/. The advantage of assuming this

[11]

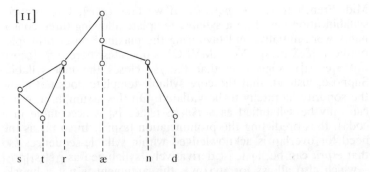

amount of structure is that the restrictions between [s] and C_1, on the one hand, and C_1 and C_2, on the other, generally parallel the restrictions within clusters made up of two consonants only. If, on the other hand, [st] is treated as a single unit, as suggested *inter alia* by Selkirk (1982a) – *eg* by attaching the two segments to a single slot position on the skeleton (*cf* 6.1.7) – , the fact that [#st __] constrains the following slot mostly in the same way as [#t __] becomes coincidental.

This is not to say, however, that the restrictions in the onset can be reduced to pairwise constraints involving adjacent segments as advocated in Clements and Keyser (1983). Thus, /stw/ is not a viable onset despite the availability of /st/ and /tw/ syllable-initially: *stick, tweak*. If we assume with J. M. Anderson (1986b: 71) that the restrictions between contrastive segments hold only between sequences of elements which uniquely share a construction, the various constraints we have just mentioned are all allowed for by the dependency structure assigned to [str] in [11].

The structure assigned to [str] in [11] need not, however, be its initial representation. A number of generalizations can be captured if it is assumed that the core syllable-structure of a language respects the sonority hierarchy. It is therefore arguable that /s/ in #sO and #sOL clusters (where O = Obstruent and L = Liquid) is initially extrasyllabic on the grounds of its higher sonority than that of the following obstruent, and only integrated to the syllable as in [11] within derivations. If this position proves viable, it would mean that the collocational restrictions embodied in [11] are not reflected in underlying syllable structure but, for instance, in the representations at the end of the lexical component. This is not particularly worrying given the amount of underspecification favoured nowadays at the underlying level.

One possible advantage of excluding [s] from initial clusters, pointed out to me by Jonathan Kaye, is provided by MVLOW in

Midi French (*cf* 1.5 *et passim*). If we take *esprit*, for instance, syllabification based on a syllable-template allowing three consonants word-initially, and favouring the maximal onset principle, predicts [\$e\$spri\$]. Yet, MVLOW operates here (*cf* [ɛspri] not *[espri]), suggesting that the /s/ closes the first syllable. Suppose, instead, that the core syllable-template does not allow the sonority hierarchy to be violated. On this assumption, *esprit* can only be syllabified as \$es\$prit\$ (since [s] is acceptable in a coda), thus predicting the pronunciation [ɛspri]. In so far as the need for overlap is acknowledged within syllable-sequences (so that *esprit* can be, at least derivatively, syllabified as [₁ɛ[₂s₁]pri₂] – which also allows for MVLOW), this argument is not a knock-down one but provides an interesting way of looking at these phenomena.

8.2.3 The foot and above
The mode of representation assigned above to syllables is naturally extended to the other units of the prosodic hierarchy. In the foot, assuming a left-strong structure, as in English, the stressed syllabic comes to govern its right-hand-side dependant(s). The formation of groups, etc. involves the projection of foot-heads as governors with non-promoted foot-heads as dependants and so on. The two examples of [12] and [13] illustrate the kinds of representation that would be assigned suprasegmentally in English (see J. M. Anderson 1986b, J. M. Anderson and Ewen 1987: 100–25, Ewen 1986).

[12]

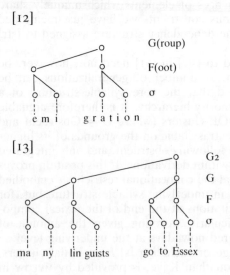

Lack of space prevents the discussion of the mechanisms governing these particular assignments and the nature of the suprasegmental hierarchy. But, it is worth noting that, in [12] and [13], we have representations which combine, in effect, the grid and the metrical tree. The arcs connecting nodes give us the constituency information which is encoded in a metrical tree and is required for the statement of rules which have the syllable, the foot or the group as a domain. The presence of subjunction paths gives us a representation analogous to columns of asterisks (or x's). In so far as it is claimed that both these types of information must be expressed – and Halle and Vergnaud (1987a, b) present an interesting case in favour of this thesis (*cf* 6.2.2.3) – the dependency representation would seem to be a strong contender in this field. To exemplify the analogy with grid phonology, consider the well-known phenomenon of Iambic Reversal attested in English and other languages. If it is accepted that a grid formulation affords a particularly transparent statement of the notion of clash, the same transparency can be achieved with DP representations. Consider [14a].

[14a] Before Iambic Reversal   [14b] After Iambic Reversal

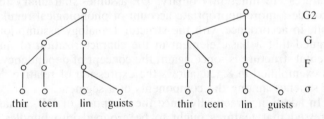

The syllables *-teen* and *-lin* are two successive group heads without an intervening node dominating an immediately lower category, and this configuration can trigger a move-node change whose result is given in [14b]. J. M. Anderson (1986b) and J. M. Anderson and Ewen (1987) argue, however, that Iambic Reversal is better analysed, not as a structural change, but as the reflection of a different mapping between **lexical structure** and **utterance structure** both represented as dependency graphs. The type of association these authors discuss is illustrated in [15] (given next page), which will complete our presentation of DP suprasegmental structures. The reader is referred to these sources for a possible formulation of Iambic Reversal within double representations such as [15].

[15]

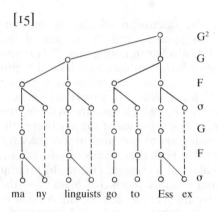

ma   ny   linguists   go   to   Ess   ex

8.3. Infrasegmental representations

Dependency Phonology shares with other modern theories of phonology the assumption that segments are exhaustively decomposable into features (called components) belonging to a universal set. Unlike generative work developed in the wake of Jakobson, Fant and Halle (1952) which takes for granted that features are inherently binary, DP assumes that **unary** features provide a more appropriate account of phonological regularities. But, in accordance with the structural analogy assumption, it is argued that a basic element in the characterization of infrasegmental structure is, once again, the concept of dependency. This, as exemplified in 8.3.1, allows the expression of relative degrees of salience among the components of a segment.

In addition, practically since the inception of DP, it has been stressed that features ought to be grouped into bundles which would capture notions such as 'major class features' or 'cavity features', which were introduced in *SPE* for purely expository convenience. In particular, a major division is established between the **categorial** gesture (which specifies *inter alia* the major class status of each segment) and the **articulatory** gesture (which covers notions such as place of articulation, height, rounding, backness and nasality): *cf* 3.5. In this chapter, we will mainly concentrate on the features characterizing the articulatory gesture of vowels before examining briefly the content of the categorial gesture. The symbols V and C will be used to specify the categorial gestures of vowels and consonants (in the intuitive, pre-theoretical sense) and we shall let them play the role of skeleton in the sense defined in Chapters 7 and 8.

8.3.1 The vowel components

Three components play a crucial role in the definition of the vowel space. These three properties, presented with articulatory/acoustic glosses, are:

[16] i 'palatality' (or 'acuteness' and 'sharpness')
      a 'lowness'   (or 'compactness')
      u 'roundness'   (or 'gravity' and 'flatness')

The above properties (which also function in the characterization of consonants and double articulation) are **resonance components** (*cf* Donegan 1973). With differences, they have been explored within Schane's 'particle phonology' (*cf* Schane 1984a, b) as well as by Kaye, Lowenstamm and Vergnaud (1985) within the theory of 'Charm and Government'.

Vowel systems of the /i, a, u/ type, which are widely attested and constitute the simplest possible vowel systems will be characterized as follows:

[17] {i} /i/   {u} /u/
            {a} /a/

where the symbols between slanted brackets have no systematic import but abbreviate the set-description of the left. Because of the way the resonance components structure vowel systems, they are often referred to as 'tri-directional feature systems', in contrast with classical binary systems, which are then described as 'bi-directional' (*cf* Rennison 1986). Unlike binary or scalar features, unary features are not omnipresent via the attribution of a positive or negative value. Rather, segments can be simply characterized by the absence, as well as the presence, of a given component. In other words, the segment informally called /a/ in [17] is not in any sense [+a, −i, −u] but is simply {a}, with the features **i** and **u** absent. It is important to realize, though, that the issue of binarism and that of tri-directionality are independent. Rennison (1986), for example, uses primitives of the **i**, **a**, **u** type within a binary framework.

Since not all systems are as simple as [17], we obviously need to allow components to be combined and the simple association of two or more components is symbolized by a comma within the set brackets as in [18]:

[18a] {i, a} [18b] {u, a} [18c] {i, u} [18d] {i, u, a}

It should be noted that the ordering of the components does not matter in [18] and that {i, a} is equivalent to {a, i}, and {i, u, a} is equivalent to {u, i, a}, {a, u, i}, etc. On the basis of this convention, if we wanted to describe a system such as /i, e, y, ø, a, o, u/ (which is the sytem of Midi French, *cf* 1.5, except for schwa which can be treated as an unspecified vowel), we would adopt a representation such as [19]:

[19] {i}   /i/   {i, u}   /y/   {u} /u/
      {i, a}/e/   {i, u, a} /ø/   {u, a}/o/
              {a} /a/

In [19], the vowels /y, ø, e, o/ are treated as 'mixed vowels', that is to say, as vowels which have two or more components of equal strength.

One of the contentions of DP, however, is that the simple combination of components does not suffice to handle optimally systems such as the following (*eg* Yoruba or standard Italian):[5]

[20] i   u
        e   o
          ε   ɔ
            a

Rather than classifying /a/ as a back vowel and fitting in the remaining vowels in the quadrangular space of *SPE* vowel features (*cf* 2.3.2.2), DP argues that we should allow for the possibility of one component preponderating over another component. In its terms, this involves treating one component as a governor and another component as a dependant, as in the graphs of [21]:

[21a] /e/ i governor   [21b] /ε/ a governor
           | |
           a dependant   i dependant

Where palatality is dominant, as in [21a], we get the high-mid vowel (/e/), and, where lowness is dominant, as in [21b], we get the low-mid vowel /ε/. As graphs can prove typographically cumbersome, the convention used in DP is to express infraseg-mental government by a semi-colon: /e/ will be represented as {i; a} and /ε/ as {a; i}. As a result the system of [21] can be symbolized as in [22]

[22] {i}   /i/   {u}   /u/
     {i; a}   /e/   {u; a}   /o/
       {a; i} /ε/   {a; u}   /ɔ/
               {a} /a/

Granted that these representations are plausible, let us examine how they fare in the expression of natural classes and rules, and attempt to motivate them in a more general way.

8.3.1.1 Classes and rules

In a system based on unary features which may be absent, certain refinements are necessary to be able to refer – for instance, in rules – to **classes** of segments. While, with reference to the three-vowel system of [17], the simple mention of *eg* {i} in a rule will suffice to pick out the segment /i/, this will not be true of a system like [19]. With reference to the latter, {i} in a rule refers to the set of segments which have the component {i} – that is, all the non-low front vowels: {i} /i/, {i, a} /e/, {i, u} /y/ and {i, a, u} /ø/. In order to refer to /i/ alone, we adopt the following convention: by flanking a component (or group of components) with verticals within curly brackets (*eg* {|i|}) reference is made to the segment characterized by this component (or group of components) alone. Thus, still with reference to [19], {|i|} identifies /i/ and, while {i, a} picks out all the segments which include these two components (/e/ and /ø/), {|i,a|} refers to /e/ only. Further examples based on [19] are given in [23]:

[23] Non-high vowels: {a}   (all vowels except /i/, /u/, /y/)

Round vowels: {u}   (/u, o, y, ø/)

Front rounded vowels: {i, u} (/y,ø/)

Note that the less general the class, the more costly the representation: verticals have to be invoked to refer, in [19], to /i/ alone; and the front rounded vowels, which require two feature values in the standard notation ([−back, -round]), also necessitate more than one component here. In that sense the notation is committed to a simplicity metric of the standard kind, whereby the more general the class the simpler the notation.

Reference to the high vowels in [19] does not appear straightforward since we do not have a component [high] but only **i** and **u**. But, if we invoke the negation operator (symbolized by a tilde: ∼), we can refer to the high vowels by specifying them as vowels which do not contain **a**: ∼{a}. On the other hand, the notation {∼a} refers to the class of segments which contain components other than **a** but which may contain a as well. It might thus be informally glossed as 'these segments which do **not** contain **a** on its own'. In [19], {∼a} refers to {i}, {i, u}, {u}, {i, a}, {i, a, u}, {u, a} – that is, all the non-low vowels. By using the negation operator, we can specify the mid vowels as {a, ∼a}. In reference to [19], {a, ∼a} means something like 'those segments picked out by {∼a} which do in fact contain **a** – that is {i, a}, {i, a, u}, {u, a}.

If we now turn to the system of [22], which involves dependency relations, natural groupings can equally well be defined.

Thus, the front vowels /i, e, ɛ/ are once again {i} – that is, the
class of vowels containing {i}. The mid-high and high vowels /i,
e/ are {i;} (*ie* the class of vowels where **i** preponderates). The
reason is that in a system involving dependency, it is assumed
that {i} is an abbreviation for **i** governing the identity element:
{i; Ø}. Finally, /i/ alone is {|i|}.

Suppose now that, with respect to [22] we wanted to state a
rule lowering /i/ and /u/ to /e/ and /o/ when followed by a low
vowel /ɛ, ɔ, a/ – a type of assimilation which occurred in early
Germanic, for instance. This would be interpreted as the addition
of the component **a** to /i, u/, the only two vowels not containing
a (*ie* ~{a}) in the context of a vowel where **a** preponderates (*ie*
{a;}):

[24]   ~{a} → a / __C₀ {a;}

On the model of [24], in all rules used from now on, the arrow
symbolizes feature-addition not feature-change. For example, a
rule fronting the back vowels /u, o, ɔ/ to [y, ø, æ] in the context
of a right-hand-side /i/ (part of the process often referred to as
I-umlaut: *cf* 8.3.1.3) would be specified as follows:

[25]   {u} → i / __C₀ {|i|}

That is, all vowels containing **u** acquire the component **i** when
the next syllable contains the component **i** and nothing else.

As a last example, consider again the system of [19], which is
that of Midi French, already examined at various points of this
book. If we wanted to formulate the fact that the mid vowels are
lowered to [ɛ, ɔ, æ] in a closed syllable and raised to [e, o, ø]
elsewhere (*cf* 6.1.9), we would write:

[26a] {a, ~a} → {a; ~a} / __C]₀
[26b] {a, ~a} → {~a; a}

where the strength of the relation between the components is
increased from simple co-presence (marked by a comma) to
dependency (marked by a semi-colon).[6] Subrules [26a] and [26b]
are disjunctively ordered by the Elsewhere Condition (or the
principle of proper inclusion precedence). To illustrate: {i,a} /e/
(where the choice of the symbol **e** is arbitrary) will be realized
as {a; i} /ɛ/ by [26a] (*eg mer* [mɛr]), and as {i; a} elsewhere
(*eg mais* [me], *étais* [ete]). And {i, u, a} will be realized as {a;{i,
u}} [œ] (*eg secteur* [sɛktær]), and as {{i, u};a } [ø] elsewhere
(*eg jeu* [žø]).

It is, perhaps, time to comment on one obvious advantage of
the DP notation with respect to the Midi French example. The

standard *SPE* notation forces the analyst to make a choice under-lyingly between a [−high, −low] or a [−high, +low] value for the mid vowel. But we have argued, in 5.2, that there is no strong evidence, in the type of accent described here, favouring one selection over another. By contrast, the unary features allow a neutral selection corresponding to the traditional intuition that, at the contrastive level, we are dealing with **mid** vowels which are allophonically turned into mid-high or mid-low. It is this type of problem which has, in fact, led to a revision of the standard theory in the direction of UT, and an elegant account of Midi French within UT was offered in 5.1.2, where the data were handled solely by recourse to universal redundancy rules. But, a general ('cost-free') solution is equally available within DP: all we need to do is assume that, once a dependency relation is established between two components in a given context, the Else-where rule giving the reverse dependency is available as a default rule (unless overridden by some other statement). The topic of underspecification will be taken up again at various points below (*cf* 8.3.1.5).

8.3.1.2 Fusion, fission and dependency preservation

Much of the motivation for the system of features presented above has come from the difficulty in formulating recurrent examples of 'fusion' and 'fission' in the synchronic and diachronic phonologies of the world's languages. Thus, the diphthongs /ai/ and /au/ are often changed to /e/ and /o/ (with or without length depending on the syllable structure of each language). If we take /ai/ → /e:/ – a change attested in Sanskrit, for example, where length was preserved, the *SPE* transformational formulation is hardly transparent:

$$[27] \quad \begin{matrix} a \\ \begin{bmatrix} +\text{low} \\ +\text{back} \\ -\text{round} \end{bmatrix} \\ 1 \end{matrix} \quad \begin{matrix} i \\ \begin{bmatrix} +\text{high} \\ -\text{back} \\ -\text{round} \end{bmatrix} \\ 2 \end{matrix} \quad \rightarrow \quad \begin{matrix} e \\ \begin{bmatrix} -\text{low} \\ -\text{back} \end{bmatrix} \\ 1 \end{matrix} \quad \begin{matrix} e \\ \begin{bmatrix} -\text{low} \\ -\text{back} \end{bmatrix} \\ 2 \end{matrix}$$

The transfer of features from the left-hand side to the right-hand side is, in fact, arbitrary. In *SPE* notation, an equally natural rule could be [28], which, just like [27], replaces the two input vowels with a long one combining some of the source feature-values:

$$[28] \quad \begin{matrix} a \\ \begin{bmatrix} +\text{low} \\ +\text{back} \\ -\text{round} \end{bmatrix} \\ 1 \end{matrix} \quad \begin{matrix} i \\ \begin{bmatrix} +\text{high} \\ -\text{back} \\ -\text{round} \end{bmatrix} \\ 2 \end{matrix} \quad \rightarrow \quad \begin{matrix} \begin{bmatrix} +\text{high} \\ +\text{back} \end{bmatrix} \\ 1 \end{matrix} \quad \begin{matrix} \begin{bmatrix} +\text{high} \\ +\text{back} \end{bmatrix} \\ 2 \end{matrix}$$

Yet, since [−round] is automatically transferred from source to target in these rules, [28] converts /ai/ into /ɨ:/ ([+back, +high, −round]), IPA [ɯ:]) – not at all a natural or common process. By contrast in DP, if we assume that the input is [29a], the required feature matrix of /e:/ is obtained by simple merger of the two adjacent articulatory gestures, as in [29b]:

[29a] V   V   →   [29b] V.   V
       ⋮   ⋮   ·..·
      {a} {i}   {a, i}

On the other hand, if we consider widespread examples of fission such as Old French /e:/ diphthongizing to /ei/ (in parallel with /o:/ → /ou/), this will be interpreted as in [30]:

[30a] Input   [30b] Splitting   [30c] a-deletion
       V V   →   V   V   →   V   V
       ·.·   ⋮   ⋮   ⋮   ⋮
      {a, i}   {a, i} {a, i}   {a, i} {i}

In [30a], it is assumed, in accord with the OCP (*cf* 7.3.2), that the long /e:/ has one articulatory gesture shared by two V gestures. The change involves the splitting of the two articulatory gesture, as in [30b], followed, in [30c], by deletion of the **a**-component of the second V slot.

While the above is shared by Particle Phonology and DP, DP also asserts the relevance of dependency relations which tend to be preserved through synchronic and diachronic shifts. Thus, the Middle English diphthongs /ai/ and /au/, as exemplified in *day* and *claw*, first developed into long mid-low vowels /ɛ/ and /ɔ:/ (*cf* J. M. Anderson and Ewen 1987: 129). If the input of /au/ → /ɔ:/ is represented as:

[31] V   V
      ⋮   ⋮
      a——u

where **a** governs **u**, as befits a falling diphthong, the change can be described as a subjunction of **u** to **a**, with a reassociation of the whole complex to the two V slots:

[32] /ɔ:/ V   V
           ·.   .·
            ·. ·
             · ·
             a
             |
             u

In terms of the notation adopted earlier, [32] can be alternatively expressed as [33] below:

[33] /ɔ:/ V   V
            ·   ·
            ·   ·
            a; u

If the DP position is correct, a mid-low vowel should be the natural outcome of the fusion of /ai/ and /au/, if they are falling diphthongs. Given, however, that for many systems in which this change has been attested there is no contrast between mid-high /e, o/ and mid-low /ɛ, ɔ/, the predicted phonetic output would not be phonemicized as {a; i} or {a; u} but as {a, i} and {a, u}, as in [31] above, with ultimately variable phonetic realization (as [e] or [ɛ] and [o] or [ɔ]).

8.3.1.3 I-umlaut
One of the diachronic changes which has been claimed as providing strong support for the DP model has been that of Old English I-umlaut – also referred to as i-mutation (*cf* J. M. Anderson and Jones 1977; Colman 1987 as well as Basbøll 1984 on Nordic I-umlaut). Reduced to its essentials, this diachronic change can be depicted as in [34] below, from the point of view of the *SPE* feature-system:

[34] I-umlaut in the standard paradigm

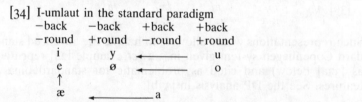

Looked at from the point of view of [34], I-umlaut involves a fronting of back vowels and a raising of /æ/ to /e/. But, this splitting of a natural process into two sub-parts is the result of looking at this phenomenon from the point of view of a quadrangular system. If we look at this change from the perspective of DP as outlined in [35]:

[35] I-umlaut in a DP framework

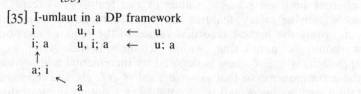

the input segments are attracted towards i by one step. The move towards a component (be it, **i**, **u** or **a**) by one step is assumed to be given by a universal convention. To be more specific, the segments {i}, {i; a}, {a; i}, {a} form a scale from /i/ with maximum preponderance of **i** when it occurs alone, and, obviously, zero preponderance of **a**, to the converse situation for /a/ where **a** is maximally preponderant and **i** absent. We can therefore think of the DP representation as inducing a scale of **i**-ness with values 3, 2, 1, 0 (for /i, e, ɛ, a/ respectively) and a scale of **a**-ness with values 3, 2, 1, 0 for /a, ɛ, e, i/ By universal convention, addition of the **i** component to a subset of the scale involves moving to the next position in the direction of the pole of attraction. In the case of the back vowels in [35], there is no scale between /u/ and /i/ (or /o/ and /e/) of the form: {i}, {i; u}, {u; i}, {u}. Therefore, l-umlaut simply results in the addition of the **i** component to the input segment. When systems do not involve dependency, **i**-attraction or **u**-attraction, or whatever, boils down to simple addition of the relevant component.

One important difference between DP and a scalar approach to vowel representations (*cf* 3.2) is that the second places no upper limit on the number of height distinctions. The DP notation makes the prediction that only five values are possible phonologically, if **mutual dependency** (symbolized by indicating equal preponderance of two components) is allowed, as in [36]:

[36] /i/   /e/   /ɛ/   /æ/   /a/
      i   i; a   a; i   a; i   a

Such representations would allow us to handle the advanced standard Copenhagen system given in 3.2 (*cf* example [24] repeated as [37a] below) and cited as problematic for standard binary features. See the DP analysis in [37b]:

[37a]	i	y	u	[37b]	{i}	{i, u}	{u}
	e	ø	o		{i; a}	{{i, u}; a}	{u; a}
	ɛ	œ	ɔ		{i:a}	{{i, u}:a}	{u:a}
	æ		a		{a; i}	{a}	

The DP system therefore makes a stronger prediction concerning natural languages than an approach setting no inherent limit on possible values of the features – except by accompanying n-ary features by an observational statement concerning the highest recorded value. In the same connection, it should be noted that, within Schane's Particle Phonology approach, where lowness is denoted by incremental additions of the **a** component (so that **ai** = /e/, **aai** = /ɛ/, etc.), a representation such as [**aaaaaaai**] is acceptable as a potential contrastive segment.

8.3.1.4 Markedness

One motivation for the representations adopted in DP, and in much recent work, is an attempt to capture markedness statements directly. Whereas markedness statements in the *SPE* paradigm are essentially external to the notation (*cf* 3.4), the DP combinations of features mirror complexity directly (*cf* too Schane 1984a). Thus, for a system such as /i a u/, the components **i, a** and **u** do not need to be combined. On the other hand, in a system such as /i e a o u/, feature-combinations must be permitted and the mid vowels, often described as mixed, have a more complex internal structure than the three 'quantal' vowels /i/, /a/ and /u/. Finally, dependency has to be invoked when, for instance, vowel height involves more than three positions.

8.3.1.5 Underspecification

As stressed in Chapter 5, a body of recent work going under the banner of UT has been devoted to demonstrating the descriptive advantages of assuming that particular segments may be unspecified with respect to a particular gesture and, more generally, of rendering underlying representations redundancy-free. Given the unary feature hypothesis adopted in DP the possibility of empty gestures is unsurprising. If particular features may be absent or present then, potentially, all relevant features may be absent (*cf* Sanders 1974). And, indeed, the representation of [ʔ] and [h] as a stop and a fricative unspecified for articulation is one which has figured prominently in the DP literature (*cf* Durand 1987 for an illustration in Malay and further references stretching back to Lass and J. M. Anderson 1975). In a series of recent papers, J. M. Anderson and Durand have explored the consequences of the idea of non-specification with reference to a variety of asymmetrical vowel systems. They have attempted to show, on the basis of tentative geometrical principles, that the DP notation makes predictions as to which segment should be unspecified which are partially different from those made in Archangeli's work (*cf* J. M. Anderson and Durand 1988a, b, to appear J. M. Anderson, to appear a, b). Here we shall content ourselves with a brief discussion of the Yawelmani dialect of Yokuts, where the same vowel is selected in DP and in UT (*cf* too Ewen and van der Hulst 1985).

The vowel system of Yawelmani (*cf* 5.1.1, 7.4.1), leaving aside the short–long contrast, is as in [38], in DP notation:

[38] {i} /i/ {u} /u/
  {a, u}/o/
 {a} /a/

The above system is clearly asymmetrical in lacking the vowel /e/. From a componential point of view, /i/ is isolated in that it is the only vowel requiring the component **i**. We also know, independently, that /i/ is the epenthetic (default) vowel of Yawelmani. Let us, therefore, assume that /i/ is unspecified with respect to articulation (indicated below by empty brackets) and that the Yawelmani contrastive system is as in [39]:

[39] { } /i/   {u} /u/
                {a,u} /o/
          {a} /a/

A default rule, linked to the geometrical principles not explored here, spells out the unspecified segment as late as possible within derivations:

[40] Yawelmani default rule: $\textcircled{V} \rightarrow$ i
where a circled V is a vowel with empty articulation.

The central descriptive advantage that flows from these assumptions is the formalization of the process of rounding harmony in Yawelmani. The latter, as stressed in 5.1.1, is simple to state. Vowels become round to the right of a round vowel of the same value for high. For clarity, this is once again summarized in [41]:

[41a] /. . . uC$_o$i . . ./ $\rightarrow$ /uC$_o$u . . ./
[41b] /. . . oC$_o$a . . ./ $\rightarrow$ /oC$_o$o . . ./

Some illustrations of [41] are given in [42] below:

[42a]	xat-mi	'having eaten'
	bok'-mi	'having found'
	xil-mi	'having tangled'
	dub-mu	'having led by the hand'
[42b]	max-al	'might procure'
	hud-al	'might recognize'
	giy'-al	'might touch'
	bok'-ol	'might find'

As we saw in Chapter 5, any direct attempt to represent [41] as a spreading of round in the *SPE* framework requires corrective statements since /i/ will become [y] and /a/ will become [ɔ]. These intermediary values will need to be converted to [u] and [o]. Archangeli's UT account, which treats /i/ as unspecified and /a/ as only specified as [-high], allows a simple spreading of round given the interaction of a complex battery of conventions.

In DP, rounding harmony will be interpreted as a spreading of the **u** component, stated in [43] in autosegmental terms:

[43] Rounding harmony (**u**-spreading)

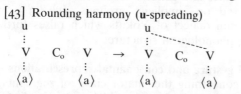

In [43], the requirement that the vowels have the same height is expressed by specifying that they should have the same value for the **a** component (indicated by angled brackets with their standard interpretation). To illustrate with some examples from [42], the underlying form of *dubmu* is:

[44]

$$
\begin{array}{ccccc}
& u & & & u \\
& \vdots & & & \diagup \\
C & V & C & C & V \rightarrow \\
\vdots & & \vdots & \vdots & \\
d & & b & m &
\end{array}
\qquad
\begin{array}{ccccc}
C & V & C & C & V \\
\vdots & & \vdots & \vdots & \\
d & & b & m &
\end{array}
$$

where the consonantal symbols abbreviate the feature-complexes corresponding to each consonant and **u** is an autosegment. The second vowel is unspecified and, by inheriting **u**, becomes /u/. On the other hand, the underlying form of *xilmi* is as in [45a] below, where **both** stem and suffix have a non-specified vowel; [45b] is obtained by a late application of the default rule [40], spelling out the unspecified vowel:

[45a]

$$
\begin{array}{cccc}
C & V & C & C & V \\
\vdots & & \vdots & \vdots & \\
x & & l & m &
\end{array}
$$

[45b]

$$
\begin{array}{ccccc}
C & V & C & C & V \quad \text{(by rule [40])} \\
\vdots & \vdots & \vdots & \vdots & \vdots \\
x & i & l & m & i
\end{array}
$$

In the case of *bok'ol*, the underlying form is as in [46a], from which [46b] is obtained by **u**-spreading:

[46a]

$$
\begin{array}{ccccc}
& u & & & \\
& \vdots & & & \\
C & V & C & V & C \\
\vdots & \vdots & \vdots & \vdots & \vdots \\
b & a & k' & a & l
\end{array}
$$

[46b]

$$
\begin{array}{ccccc}
& u & & & \\
& \vdots \diagdown & & & \\
C & V & C & V & C \\
\vdots & \vdots & \vdots & \vdots & \vdots \\
b & a & k' & a & l
\end{array}
$$

A slot linked to **a** and **u** is equivalent to {a, u} – *ie* the DP interpretation of /o/.

In so far as the DP approach does not require the panoply of complement, default rules and general conventions used in UT, it should be preferred on simplicity grounds. In 8.3.3, we consider the Wikchamni dialect of Yokuts which raises further questions concerning phonological structure.

8.3.2. The categorial gesture and consonantal representations

In DP, information concerning the 'major class' of segments is made available in the **categorial** gesture which is itself split into two subgestures: a phonatory subgesture which is comprised of those sonority-based components which determine the basic 'syntax' of segments and an initiatory subgesture which is concerned with airstream mechanisms. For simplicity, we will leave aside initiation and use the term 'categorial' to refer solely to the phonatory subgesture (*cf* J. M. Anderson and Ewen 1987; Davenport and Staun 1986).

The categorial gesture contains information which, in standard generative feature-sets, would be dealt with by notions such as consonantality, voice, continuancy, sonorance. Two components are used in the categorial gesture: **V** and **C**. On the one hand, **V** can be defined in Jakobsonian terms as corresponding to a maximally periodic structure and vowels with their well-marked formant structure will be defined as |V|. On the other hand, **C** is a component of 'periodic energy reduction' and voiceless plosives with their obstruction of the airway and their lack of periodic source at the glottis are classified as |C|. These two components are clearly related to the Jakobsonian features [vocalic] and [consonantal], but, unlike the latter, they are not binary. The presence of, say, **C**, in a segment does not imply that the segment is in simple binary opposition to an otherwise identical segment which does not contain **C**. Like the vowel components examined earlier, **C** and **V** can either occur alone or in various dependency combinations. Here [47] sets out, in the form of graphs, part of the universal inventory of categorial types:[7]

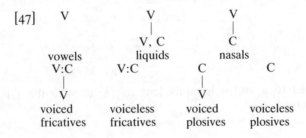

[47] V	V	V
|	|	|
	V, C	C
vowels	liquids	nasals
V:C	V:C	C C
|	|	|
V	V	V
voiced fricatives	voiceless fricatives	voiced plosives	voiceless plosives

As before, natural classes can be defined over these feature-complexes. Thus, the obstruents are segments which contain a governing C, the sonorants are segments which contain a V which is ungoverned, the plosives contain an ungoverned C and so on. Markedness is also mirrored by the notation since vowels and voiceless plosives come out as simplest, in accord with standard observations about developmental or cross-linguistic data, with other segment types falling in between them. Clearly, too, the above classification defines a hierarchy of sonority from |V| to |C| without recourse to an n-ary feature of the type defended by Selkirk (1984b). The governing relations within a syllable mentioned in 2.1 would, therefore, be directly read off the information in the categorial gesture. A universal hierarchy on which language-specific constraints will be based is provided in [47]. Thus, French allows only |V| segments as syllable-heads, lexically, whereas rhotic accents of English widens this to all sonorants (symbolized as {|V|;}. In all languages, the nucleus, rhyme and syllable can, therefore, be defined as first-order, second-order and third-order projections of the head; and the class of possible heads, depending on the language, will be {|V|} or some dilution of the V component.

Two additional arguments have been put forward in favour of the above representation of the categorial gesture. First of all, [47] is intended to allow a natural expression for processes of strengthening and weakening which are arbitrary from the point of view of standard feature-sets and have led to the postulation of strength scales external to the notation (eg Hooper, 1976: Ch. 10). Secondly, it has been argued by J. M. Anderson and Ewen (1987) and Ewen (1986) that the categorial gesture functions like the skeleton (as exemplified informally for the Yawelmani data above) and renders the latter superfluous. But the arguments in 7.3.3 in favour of a skeleton made of pure positions (X's), as against Clements and Keyser's CV labelling, would also seem to apply to DP. One solution, adopted in some recent DP work, consists in appealing to underspecification, thus leaving many of the categorial positions unspecified. Whether this is enough to cope with the wide range of examples involving a skeleton made of pure positions still remains to be demonstrated.

A full inventory of components characterizing the articulatory gesture of consonants in DP lies beyond the scope of this presentation. It is important to underline that the component u (roundness/gravity) cross-classifies consonants and vowels. The labials and velars contain u but, in addition, the velar is specified as l (linguality). A wide array of phenomena in favour of a lingual feature (applied to any segment whose articulation involves the tongue) is surveyed in Lass (1976: Ch. 7 and Lass 1984: 11.5). Thus the series /p, b, t, d, k, g/ would be characterized as follows:[8]

[48] /p/   /b/   /t/   /d/   /k/   /g/
     {C}   {C;V}   {C}   {C;V}   {C}   {C;V}
      ⋮   ⋮   ⋮   ⋮   ⋮   ⋮
      u   u   l   l   l,u   l,u

8.3.3 Geometrical extensions

Many current developments articulate a position where features, gestures and subgestures are organized in a geometrical space (*cf* 7.4.2). While the issue of geometry has not been pursued as such in DP, it is certainly possible to think of the gestures and subgestures as part of a geometrical structure not unlike that advocated in recent work in multidimensional phonology. This whole issue would take us far beyond the confines of this chapter. But, we will outline a possible geometrical reorganization of the resonance components on the basis of rounding harmony in the Wikchamni dialect of Yokuts (influenced by Archangeli 1984, 1985) before taking a brief look at Turkish vowel harmony.

It will be recalled from 7.4.1 that Wikchamni has the same vowel system as Yawelmani with the addition of the front rounded vowel /y/ and that it too participates in vowel harmony, as illustrated in [49a, b]:

[49a] dyʔs + ši → dyʔysšy 'sting + aortist'
[49b] hud   + ši → hudšu   'know + aortist'
[49c] tan   + ši → tanši   'go + aorist'
[49d] moxd + ši → mooxidši 'get old + aorist'

The problem posed by Wikchamni is the following: if the vowel /i/ is also unspecified in this dialect, why do we not observe *dyʔysšu, after spreading of the **u** component in [49a]? Archangeli achieves a pan-dialectal treatment of rounding harmony by suggesting that, universally, [high], [round] and [back] should be ordered in terms of anchorage to the skeleton. As a result, a simple rule of spreading of [+round] can be maintained for all dialects of Yokuts.

In DP, the vowel system of Wikchamni would be represented as in [50]:

[50] /i/ { } /y/ {i, u}   /u/ {u}
                            /o/ {a,u}
          /a/ {a}

Let us assume that, universally the DP features are stacked as follows (where the vertical lines no longer indicate dependency but geometrical anchorage):[9]

[51]

o i	i-line
o u	u-line
o a	a-line
V	

This type of representation is adumbrated in Kaye, Lowenstamm and Vergnaud (1985) with respect to the closely related A, I, U elements of Charm and Government (but the U- and I-lines are not ordered) and it has received an elegant illustration in Kenstowicz and Rubach (1987: 476ff).

Following [51], the vowels of Wikchamni can be specified as in [52]:

[52]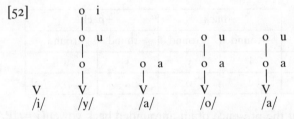

where, by universal convention, any labelled node on a given tier presupposes the presence of nodes in lower tiers. As in Archangeli's account, the surface form of *dy?ysšy* can be easily derived by assuming an underlying form as follows:

[53]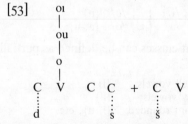

[53] becomes [54] by epenthesis of a slot between /?/ (represented by a **C** without articulatory content) and /s/, and spreading of the **u**-component – and of the **i** carried on its back – to all right-hand-side V slots. Note that, as is conventional in autosegmental treatment, the broken lines in [54] indicate a derived linkage.

[54]

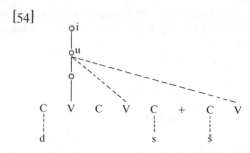

Again, by universal convention, lower nodes (in this case the node on the a-tier) would be filled in as a concomitant of a new association being created.

The same basic idea can be applied to Turkish (as indeed advocated by Archangeli 1985, within a standard feature framework). The vowel system of Turkish is classically analysed as in [55].

[55]

	−back		+back	
	−round	+round	−round	+round
+high	i	y	ɨ	u
−high	e	ø	a	o

Because of the presence of an unrounded back vowel (ɨ = IPA [ɯ]), it appears to present a serious problem for the unary system adopted in DP. But, if we appeal to underspecification, the system of Turkish, as noted in Schane (1984a: 139), can be analysed as in [56]:

[56] /i/   {i}   /y/ {i, u}   /ɨ/ { } /u/ {u}
     /e/   {i, a}   /ø/ {i, u, a} /a/ { a } /o/ {a, u}

On the basis of [56], all relevant classes can be defined as partially shown in [57]:

[57]   Front vowels: {i}   back vowels: ~{i}
       High vowels: ~{a}   low vowels: {a}
       Round vowels: {u}   front rounded: {i, u}, etc.

All the vowels of a word in Turkish agree in backness (*ie* frontness in the DP system). This will be represented by the presence or absence of the **i**-component throughout the word. Moreover, all high vowels agree in rounding with the preceding vowel, whether high or not. Consider the examples in [58] below, borrowed from Lyons (1968: 130), with morpheme boundaries

marked by a dash. (Note that [ö] and [ü] in [58] correspond
respectively to IPA [ø] and [y] used in this book.)

[58a] göz–ler–in–iz
'eye-*plur*-your-*plur*' = 'your eyes'
[58b] kol–lar–ım–ız
'arm-*plur*-my-*plur*' = 'our arms'
[58c] adam–lar–ın
'man-*plur*-of' = 'of (the) men'
[58d] ev–ler–in–de
'house-*plur*-his-in' = 'in their house'
[58e] kol–um
'arm–my' = 'my arm'
[58f] göz–üm–üz
'eye-my-*plur*' = 'our eyes'

Let us start, once again, from the universal stacking given in
[51]. To exemplify frontness agreement, consider the plural
morpheme which varies between [lar] and [ler] depending on the
front–back specification of the stem to which it is affixed. If we
assume its underlying form is /l{a}r/, we can derive the above
forms without any problem. For instance, *gözler* 'eyes' will be
derived as follows:

[59]

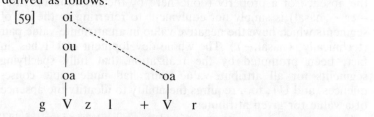

with spreading of the i-component to the last vowel. On the other
hand, the first person possessive marker has the following forms:
[im], [ym], [um] (as well as [im] not illustrated above). We assume
its underlying form is an unspecified vowel { } (which makes
it non-low since it lacks the a component). If we suppose that the
plural marker *-üz* in *gözümüz* also has an unspecified vowel, the
derivation of this word is as follows:

[60]

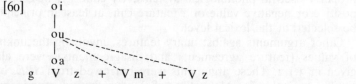

where the u-component automatically carries the front specification stacked on top of it.

This brief illustration shows how the formalism could be extended in a geometrical direction while preserving a grouping of the resonance components. It should be contrasted with recent studies where the same primitives have been used, but by assigning each component to a different plane (*eg* Goldsmith 1985), with a concomitant loss of the idea of gestures as sets of interactive features possibly related by dependency. The reader should nevertheless be aware that prosodic phenomena have been discussed in a somewhat different mode by J. M. Anderson, Ewen and Staun (1985) and J. M. Anderson (1987b) in particular.

8.3.4 Another look at binarism

In Chapter 3, some arguments in favour of binary features over unary features were mentioned. We have shown here how the unary system used in DP could be used to capture natural classes and function in rules. One argument, borrowed from Sommerstein (1977: 110), was that, since in a unary framework we have to refer to sets of segments which lack a given property (*eg* nonnasal), this is tantamount to reintroducing binarity by the back door. However, both syntactically and semantically, referring to the absence of a property (done here by the negation operator – *eg* ~ nasal) is simply not equivalent to referring to the set of segments which have the negative value in an attribute-value pair (technically, $\langle$nasal,$-\rangle$). The whole development of UT has, in fact, been prompted by the realization that fully specifying segments for all attribute-value pairs had undesirable consequences, and UT, too, requires the ability to identify the absence of a value for given attributes.

Unary systems can be conceived as radical versions of UT since, apart from default realizations of unspecified values, the whole apparatus of complement and default rules is argued to be unnecessary at the phonological level. While both 'pure' unary systems and UT claim that underlyingly all phonological contrasts are **privative** (in the sense of 3.1.1), unary systems claim that it is always the same pole of a feature which represents the positive property used in phonological systems. By contrast, in UT, the positive or negative value of a feature can, at least in principle, be selected at the lexical level.

Other arguments against unary features, involving the linking of values (feature agreements and disagreements), were also given in 3.1.2. These arguments were borrowed from *SPE*, but similar examples (*eg* McCarthy 1984) have figured prominently in the recent debate on unary and binary features. Another range of problems is posed by **opaque** segments. In 7.1.5, we saw that, when a given feature-value is spreading, we could account for segments which block the harmony, by specifying them for the opposite value to the value being spread. These various difficulties have been tackled most thoroughly by van der Hulst (1988b), van der Hulst and Smith (1986) and Ewen and Van der Hulst (1987). We should, nevertheless, note that the type of solution envisaged in 7.1.5 for opaque segments is also problematic for a thoroughgoing UT account, since it forces three values to be present lexically (+, − and Ø). Moreover, we have also shown above (cf the treatment of back unrounded vowels in Turkish and the height agreement requirement on rounding harmony in Yokuts), how problems which, at first sight, appeared intractable to the feature-system used in DP turned out to find an elegant treatment within this framework.

One difference between DP and classical systems of unary features is the possibility in DP of relating components in terms of dependency. This means that not all relations between segments are privative but also that **gradual** relations can be captured. The adoption of unary features and the assertion of the relevance of dependency are independent, but their link is obvious: it seems strange to postulate a relation of preponderance between attribute-value pairs in their standard interpretation.

8.4 Back unrounded vowels: epilogue and prologue

The above sections have shown how a variety of vowel systems and generalizations could be accounted for by recourse to the primitive components **i, a** and **u**. It was also argued that the presence of back unrounded vowels such as /ɨ/ and /a/ in Turkish were not as problematic for this type of account as might have appeared at first blush. But, systems with richer sets of back unrounded vowels do present a challenge for the notation adopted here. In order to examine this question more fully, it is necessary to mention the other vowel components which are universally available in DP.

In addition to the **i, a, u** components, two more components have been postulated in DP: ATR or expanded pharynx, symbolized here by **E** (cf J. M. Anderson and Ewen 1987: 244–5) and a component of centralization symbolized by schwa: **ə**. The E component is required to handle ATR-harmony in a variety of languages of the world (cf 7.2.5), one example of which is Kpokolo, further analysed below. But, it is important to point out that many languages alleged to involve ATR-harmony can

plausibly be interpreted as based on **a**-harmony – *eg* Nez Perce
as briefly discussed on p. 310 (*cf* J. M. Anderson and Durand
in press; van der Hulst 1988, in press; den Dikken and van der
Hulst in press). The component of centrality, ə, can be used to
characterize lax vowels such as [ɪ] (English *kick*) {i, ə} and [ʊ]
(English *cook*) {u, ə}. But, in so far as no language would appear
to make a contrast between back unrounded vowels and central
unrounded vowels, it is also plausible to suggest that the back
unrounded vowels of some languages might involve ə. Thus a
putative system such as the one in [61a] below might be analysed
as in [61b]:

[61a] i ɨ u [61b] {i}   {ə}   {u}
　　　e   ʌ o　　　　{i, a} {ə, a} {a, u}
　　　　　a　　　　　　　　　 {a}

To justify the recourse to the ə feature, it is worth pointing out
that, acoustically, back unrounded vowels appear to be more or
less intermediate between front and back vowels (in terms of
standard plottings based on F1 and F2 – *cf* 2.5.2). And, indeed,
J. M. Anderson and Ewen (1987: 221), on general phonetic
grounds, suggest {i, u, ə} as a characterization of [ɨ] (IPA [ɯ])
with the possibility of treating [ɤ] as {{i, u, ə}; a} and [ʌ] as {a;{i,
u, ə}} (*cf* too J. M. Anderson and Durand 1986: 28–9). Such
representations, however plausible, are not tested by these
authors against an existing system with a rich set of back
unrounded vowels.

On the other hand, Lass (1984) suggests that the **u** component,
which is a conflation of gravity and roundness in standard DP,
on the grounds of their unmarked co-occurrence, should be split
up into a component of roundness and a component of gravity.
Under this interpretation, **u** will be taken to denote 'roundness'
(flatness) only (whereas Lass uses ω) and the symbol **ɯ** will be
introduced to refer to gravity (or velar constriction). Thus, a
system such as /i, e, a, o, u, ɤ, ɨ/ could be represented as follows:

[62] /i/ {i}　　/ɨ/ {ɯ}　　/u/ {u, ɯ}
　　/e/ {i, a} /ɤ/ {ɯ, a} /o/ {a, u, ɯ}
　　　　　/a/ {a}

As pointed out by J. M. Anderson and Ewen (1987: 222) and
J. M. Anderson and Durand (1986: 29), such representations
raise a problem in that 'markedness' is no longer reflected by the
notation since back unrounded vowels come out as structurally
simpler than the more 'natural' back rounded ones. But this
objection should definitely be tempered in view of the impli-

cational markedness of the component ɯ. The fact is that **ɯ** is not needed for most systems and is only available in systems which already contain back rounded vowels. As Harry van der Hulst (in press) points out: 'It is not obvious that "system-complexity" should be reflected in the representation of the sounds which tend to only occur in more complex systems.' A further example of the relevance of this statement is provided by ATR-harmony. It is claimed by Kaye, Lowenstamm and Vergnaud (1985) that a [+ATR] realization is normal in the absence of a [+/−ATR] opposition. Thus, in a system such as /i, e, a, o, u/ the vowels would typically be realized with advanced tongue root. But in systems of the form /i, e, ə, o, u/ vs. /ɪ, ɛ, a, ɔ, ʊ/, [+ATR] vowels can be shown to possess a mark lacked by the [−ATR] vowels and therefore will be more complex in terms of componential make-up.

Be that as it may, it seems that an extra component in addition to **u** is indeed required to handle a system such as that of Kpokolo, as described in Kaye, Lowenstamm and Vergnaud (1985). The alternative to an extra component is to enrich the theory of representation, either as suggested by these authors within Charm and Government theory, or in the direction defended by van der Hulst (1988a, b) which is summarized pp. 309ff (but see note 10).

Kpokolo, an Eastern Kru language spoken in the Ivory Coast, has the following system according to Kaye, Lowenstamm and Vergnaud (KLV hereafter):

[63]   [−ATR]   [+ATR]
High   ɪ   ɨ   ʊ   i   ɨ   u
Mid   ɛ   з   ɔ   e   ə   o
Low   a

While the above diagrams and the symbols chosen by KLV predispose us to talk of central vowels in Kpokolo, it is argued by KLV that, structurally, /ɨ, ɨ, з/ behave as back unrounded vowels. As for /ə/, it is the [+ATR] partner of /a/, with a raising to a central position which is widely attested in ATR-systems. In terms of unary components, if Lass's suggestion is accepted, the Kpokolo vowels can be analysed as in [64]:

[64a] [−ATR]
/ɪ/ {i}   /ɨ/ {ɯ}   /ʊ/ {u, ɯ}
/ɛ/ {i, a}   /з/ {ɯ, a}   /ɔ/ {u, ɯ, a}
                  /a/ {a}

[64b] [+ATR]
/i/ {i, E]   /ɨ/ {ɯ, E}   /u/ {u, ɯ, E}
/e/ {i, a, E}   /o/ {u, ɯ, a, E}
              /ə/ {a, E}

The raising of the [+ATR] vowel /ə/ {a, E} to a central position can be interpreted as the result of a phonetic redundancy rule adding the **ɯ** component to its representation to produce {a, ɯ, E}. It will be noticed that the back unrounded vowels are marked for gravity (**ɯ**) only, whereas the back rounded vowels are marked for both gravity and rounding (**ɯ** and **u**). In [64b], if we maximized contrastivity, the vowels /u/ and /o/ should be specified as {u, E} and {u, a, E} respectively, the specifications in [64b] being the result of a redundancy rule: {u, E} → ɯ. And further simplifications could also be performed on [64a]. Since the alternations described below can be described by reference to the fuller representations of [64], the latter will form the basis of our argumentation here.

Granted that the componential analysis of [64] allows us to separate the Kpokolo vowels in a plausible way, it still behoves us to show how significant generalizations dealt with by KLV can be captured in a fairly direct manner.

The first observation made by KLV is that the vowel /ə/ behaves as the [+ATR] version of /a/. For instance, appending *-ji* (which contains the [+ATR] vowel /i/), to a mass or abstract noun, to give the meaning 'one of' or 'piece of' makes the previous vowel [+ATR], as in the alternation: *gla–gləji* 'teeth' (all glosses are borrowed from KLV). This is straightforward here since /a/ is {a} and /ə/ is {a, E} (triggered by /i/ = {i, E}).

More interesting is the phenomenon of unrounding in Kpokolo. Here, /ə/ in the [+ATR] set appears but now as the partner of /o/ as in [65] below. (Tones have been left out in all the examples for clarity.)

[65] singular   plural
     tolu   təli   'groin'
     kpolu   kpəli   'rat'

These alternations can be explained as cases of **u**-deletion: that is, if the component **u** is lost by /o/ {u, ɯ, a, E} when the plural suffix /i/ is added, we obtain {a, E, ɯ}, the phonetic realization of /ə/. The other example of **u**-loss within the [+ATR] set is provided by pairs such as:

[66] singular   plural
     susu   sɨsi   'charcoal'
     mudu   mɨdi   'claw'

which are equally unproblematic given that /u/ is {ɯ, u, E} while
/ɨ/ is {ɯ, E}.

Within the [−ATR] set, we observe alternations such as:

[67] singular   plural
     dɔbʊ   dɔbɩ   'duck'
     jʊlʊ   jɨlɩ   'sun'

Again, given the characterization of /ʊ/ as {ɯ, u} *vs* /ɨ/ as
{ɯ} and of /ɔ/ as {ɯ, u, a} vs. /ɜ/ as {ɯ, a}, unrounding can
be straightforwardly captured as **u**-loss.

Finally, KLV note that /a/ and /ɜ/ alternate in forms such as
[68]:

[68] singular   plural
     jaba   jɜbɩ   'shorts'
     gaga   gɜgɩ   'hill'

Forms of this type reveal that /a/ occurs whenever the final vowel
is /a/, otherwise we get /ɜ/. Although KLV put forward an
elegant analysis in terms of government reversal between
elements characterizing the singular and plural forms, another
possibility is that the underlying form of the above stems contains
/ɜ/ {a, ɯ} from which the ɯ component is deleted in singular
forms to give /a/ {a}. Such a rule could be seen as a way of
satisfying an /a . . . a#/ template which seems favoured in
Kpokolo.

A different route is taken by van der Hulst (1988, in press), who
suggests that only the three DP primitives **i, a, u** are required
provided we are ready to modify the notation in the following
way. As in DP and in KLV's Charm and Government theory,
components can function as governor (head) or dependant
(operator). But, firstly, the interpretation of a component will
vary according to its status as governor or dependant. The three
primitives have the following dual interpretation:

[69] Interpretation of

	i	**a**	**u**
Governor	Palatal constriction	Pharyngeal constriction	Velar constriction
Dependant	Advanced tongue root	Openness	Rounding

Secondly, the same feature can occur in both governor and
dependant positions. Thirdly, components in dependant position
(but not in governor position) may be combined as in DP. Thus,

Nez Perce, which has a system /i, æ, a, o, u/ can be represented as follows:

[70] /i/   /u/   /o/   /æ/   /a/
     I   U   U   A _   A
                   | |
                   a   a

where capital letters are used for a component in governing position to facilitate discussion. Since Nez Perce vowel harmony can be summarized as follows:

[71] /i/   /u/
                       ↓
                      /o/

     /æ/ →/a/

the structures in [70] allow an elegant analysis in terms of a-spreading in dependent position (*cf* too J. M. Anderson and Durand in press).

Van der Hulst shows how a number of systems can be adequately handled if this new framework is accepted. As far as Kpokolo is concerned, he puts forward the following representations (where **i** in dependent position characterizes [+ATR] segments):[11]

[72] /i/ /ɪ/ /ɨ/ /ɨ/ /u/ /ʊ/ /e/ /ɛ/ /ə/ /ʒ/ /o/ /ɔ/ /a/
     I   I   U   U   U   U   I   I   A   A   A   A   A
     | | | | | | | | | | | | |
     i   i   u,i u   a,i a   i   i   u,i u   a

All the Kpokolo alternations given above are adequately handled on the basis of [72]. As in our account, **u**-loss is at work in the examples of [66]/[67] – *eg susu-sisi* (compare the dependant representations of /u/ and /ɨ/). The /a/ – /ʒ/ alternation can be straightforwardly dealt with as an example of **a**-loss. And all assimilations to [+ATR] can be treated as the acquisition of a dependant **i** component by [−ATR] segments. To handle the fact that /ə/ functions as the [+ATR] partner of /a/, we can see that **i**-addition has the following effect:

[73] /a/
     A   A
     | — i-addition → |
     a   a,i

The resulting segment is not present in the Kpokolo system and is merged with /ə/, which is phonetically adjacent, by the following equivalence rule:

[74]
$$\begin{array}{ccc} A & & A \\ | & = & | \\ a,i & & i \end{array}$$

The future of the unary components of DP and their internal organization cannot be predicted. Nevertheless, it is interesting to observe that many researchers are now approaching vowel systems within closely related notations and offering simpler and more insightful analyses than in classical generative phonology. It is to be hoped that a convergence will ultimately take place or, at least, that there will result a greater understanding of the intrinsic content of phonological primitives. In so far as DP specialists can combine their approach with the ambitious universalist goals spelled out in 7.5, DP should remain an important source of insights on phonological structure.

Notes

1. For a recent evaluation of DP, cf Basbøll (1988).
2. Whether headship within syllable margins should be assigned to the most sonorous element is an open question. See J. M. Anderson (1986) for arguments in favour of counter-sonority so that in eg /fl/, the head would be /f/ and the dependant /l/.
3. See J. M. Anderson (1971, 1977, 1980b, 1984, 1986a, b, 1987a, in press) on dependency representations in syntax and morphology. For classical dependency systems, cf Robinson (1970) and the text-book presentation of Matthews (1981: Ch. 4).
4. Here /ai/ has been used instead of /aj/ to remind readers that the second element of the diphthong is actually a non-syllabic vowel.
5. Archangeli and Pulleyblank (in press) argue that a treatment of Yoruba in terms of unary features is problematic since it is [−ATR] which is spreading. Van der Hulst, using a framework closely related to the present one (cf 8.4), argues that it is the component a which spreads in Yoruba. Note too that the spread of [−ATR] could be dealt with in this framework by postulating a component of tongue-root retraction (cf 2.3.2.2 and Anderson and Ewen 1987: 6.7.3).
6. See Anderson and Ewen (1987: 32) on class inclusions between operators such as the comma, the semi-colon, etc.
7. See den Dikken and van der Hulst (in press) for a reconsideration of the DP categorial features.
8. From the point of view of contrastivity, however, /t, d/ in [48] are overspecified. Cf J. M. Anderson and Ewen (1987: 8.2), J. M. Anderson (1987b, to appear a, b), Durand (1988) for ways of eliminating redundancies in consonantal systems.

9. But *cf* J. M. Anderson and Durand (to appear) for· a different description of the phenomena described here. The feature-stacking advocated in van der Hulst (in press) is different in that it is **u** which is carried by **i**.

10. An even more elegant treatment of Kpokolo could be offered within DP if contrastivity in the [−ATR] set was maximized as follows: $/\iota/ = \{i\}$, $/i/ = \{\ \}$, $/\upsilon/ = \{u\}$, $/\varepsilon/ = \{i, a\}$, $/ɜ/ = \{a,\}$,$/ɔ/ = \{a, u\}$ and $/a/ = \{a\}$. Here $/i/$ is an unspecified vowel and $/ɜ/$ is **underspecified** being made up of the component **a** and of the combinator ",", indicating that some other (unspecified) component is present (see J. M. Anderson and Durand to appear for a defence of this distinction in Yokuts). All the alternations mentioned in the body of the text could be accounted for straightforwardly without any need to invoke an extra component of gravity **ɯ**. This solution has not been pursued here to keep the notational apparatus as simple as possible.

11. The representations adopted here are borrowed from the pre-final version of van der Hulst (in press). The published version presents a slightly different solution which reached me too late for modification of the text.

Appendix

Phonetic symbols

The phonetic symbols used in this book are the IPA symbols (given on the next page) unless otherwise indicated.

The main departures from IPA conventions are the following:

- č, ǰ, š and ž are respectively used for IPA tʃ, dʒ, ʃ and ʒ.
- ɨ is used for a high back unrounded vowel [ɯ].
- Stresses are marked by an accent over vowels: v́ (primary stress), v̀ (secondary stress), v̌ (tertiary stress), v (unstressed).

Note too that:

- Diphthongs are written here as vowel + semivowel sequences: *eg* [aj] and [aw] instead of [ai] and [au].
- ι is used for the vowel often transcribed [ɪ].
- ʊ is used for the vowel often transcribed [ɷ].

THE INTERNATIONAL PHONETIC ALPHABET

(Revised to 1979)

CONSONANTS (pulmonic air-stream mechanism)

	Bilabial	Labiodental	Dental, Alveolar, or Post-alveolar	Retroflex	Palato-alveolar	Palatal	Velar	Uvular	Labial-Palatal	Labial-Velar	Pharyngeal	Glottal
Nasal	m	ɱ	n	ɳ		ɲ	ŋ	ɴ				
Plosive	p b		t d	ʈ ɖ		c ɟ	k g	q ɢ		k͡p g͡b		ʔ
(Median) Fricative	ɸ β	f v	θ ð s z	ʂ ʐ	ʃ ʒ	ç ʝ	x ɣ	χ ʁ		ʍ	ħ ʕ	h ɦ
(Median) Approximant		ʋ	ɹ	ɻ		j	ɰ		ɥ	w		
Lateral Fricative			ɬ ɮ									
Lateral (Approximant)			l	ɭ		ʎ	ʟ					
Trill			r					ʀ				
Tap or Flap			ɾ	ɽ				ʀ				

CONSONANTS (non-pulmonic air-stream)

	Bilabial	Dental, Alveolar, or Post-alveolar	Palato-alveolar	Velar
Ejective	p'	t'		k'
Implosive	ɓ	ɗ		
(Median) Click	ʘ	ʇ		
Lateral Click		ʖ		

DIACRITICS

- ̥ or ̊ Voiceless ṇ ḍ
- ̬ Voiced ṣ ṭ
- ʰ Aspirated tʰ
- ̤ Breathy-voiced b̤ a̤
- ̪ Dental ṭ
- ̫ Labialized ṭ
- ̡ Palatalized ṭ
- Velarized or Pharyngealized ɫ
- ̩ Syllabic ṇ l̩
- ̑ or ̯ Simultaneous ʃf (but see also under the heading Affricates)

OTHER SYMBOLS

- ɕ, ʑ Alveolo-palatal fricatives
- ʄ, ʓ Palatalized ʃ, ʒ
- ɺ Alveolar lateral flap
- ɧ Simultaneous ʃ and x
- ʃ Variety of ʃ resembling s, etc.
- ɪ = i
- ʊ = u
- ɘ = Variety of ə
- ɚ = r-coloured ə

VOWELS

	Front		Back	Front	Back
				Front	Back
Close	i	ɨ	ɯ u	y ʉ u	
Half-close	e	ə	ɤ o	ø ɵ o	
Half-open	ɛ	ɜ	ʌ ɔ	œ ɞ ɔ	
Open	æ a	ɐ	a ɑ	ɶ ɒ	
	Unrounded			Rounded	

STRESS, TONE (PITCH)

ˈ stress, placed at beginning of stressed syllable : ˌ secondary stress : ˉ high level pitch, high tone : ˍ low level : ˊ high rising : ˏ low rising : ˆ high falling : ˎ low falling : ˇ rise-fall : ^ fall-rise.

AFFRICATES can be written as digraphs, as ligatures, or with slur marks; thus ts, tʃ, dʒ: ʦ t͡ʃ d͡ʒ. c, ɟ may occasionally be used for tʃ, dʒ.

Bibliography

ABERCROMBIE, D. (1964a) 'Syllable quantity and enclitics in English'. In D. Abercrombie *et al.* (eds) *In Honour of Daniel Jones*, London: Longman. Reprinted in Abercrombie (1965).

ABERCROMBIE, D. (1964b) 'A phonetician's view of verse structure', *Linguistics* 6, 5–13. Reprinted in Abercrombie (1965).

ABERCROMBIE, D. (1965) *Studies in Phonetics and Linguistics*, London: Oxford University Press.

ABERCROMBIE, D. (1967) *Elements of General Phonetics*, Edinburgh: Edinburgh University Press.

ABERCROMBIE, D. (1968) 'Paralanguage', *British Journal of Disorders of Communication* 3, 55–59.

ALLEN, W. S. (1969) 'The Latin accent: a restatement', *Journal of Linguistics* 5, 193–203.

ALLEN, W. S. (1970) *Vox Latina: A Guide to the Pronunciation of Classical Latin*, Cambridge: Cambridge University Press (1st edn, 1965).

ALONSO, D., VICENTE, A. Z. and CANELLADA, M. J. (1950) 'Vocales andaluzas. Contribución al estudio de la fonología peninsular', *Nueva Revista de Filología Hispánica* 4, 209–30.

ANDERSON, J. M. (1969) 'Syllabic or non-syllabic phonology', *Journal of Linguistics* 5, 136–42.

ANDERSON, J. M, (1971) *The Grammar of Case: Towards a Localistic Theory*, Cambridge: Cambridge University Press.

ANDERSON, J. M. (1977) *On Case Grammar*, London: Croom Helm.

ANDERSON, J. M. (1980a) 'On the internal structure of phonological segments: evidence from English and its history, *Folia Linguistica Historica* 1, 165–91.

ANDERSON, J. M. (1980b) 'Towards dependency morphology: the structure of the Basque verb'. In Anderson and Ewen (1980).

ANDERSON, J. M. (1984) *Case Grammar and the Lexicon. University of Ulster Occasional Papers in Linguistics and Language Learning* 10.

ANDERSON, J. M. (1986a) 'Structural analogy and case grammar', *Lingua* 70, 79–129.

ANDERSON, J. M. (1986b) 'Suprasegmental dependencies'. In Durand (1986a).

ANDERSON, J. M. (1987a) 'Structural analogy and dependency phonology'. In Anderson and Durand (eds).

ANDERSON, J. M. (1987b) 'The limits of linearity'. In Anderson and Durand (eds).

ANDERSON, J. M. (in press) *Structural Analogy in Language*, Ann Arbor: Karoma Press.

ANDERSON, J. M. (to appear a) 'System geometry and segment structure: a question of Scots economy', NELS.

ANDERSON, J. M. (to appear b) 'Contrastivity and non-specification in dependency phonology'.

ANDERSON, J. M. and J. DURAND (1986) 'Dependency phonology'. In Durand (1986a).

ANDERSON, J. M. and J. DURAND (eds) (1987) *Explorations in Dependency Phonology*, Dordrecht: Foris.

ANDERSON, J. M. and J. DURAND (1988) 'Underspecification in dependency phonology'. In P. M. Bertinetto and M. Loporcaro 1988.

ANDERSON, J. M. and J. DURAND (in press) 'Vowel harmony and non-specification in Nez Perce'. In van der Hulst and Smith

ANDERSON, J. M. and J. DURAND (to appear 'Unspecified and underspecified segments in Dependency Phonology: Yawelmani and other dialects of Yokuts'.

ANDERSON, J. M. and C. EWEN (eds) (1980) *Studies in Dependency Phonology*, Ludwigsburg Studies in Language and Linguistics 4.

ANDERSON, J. M. and C. EWEN (1987) *Principles of Dependency Phonology*, Cambridge: Cambridge University Press.

ANDERSON, J. M., C. EWEN and J. STAUN (1985) 'Phonological structure: segmental, suprasegmental and extrasegmental', *Phonology Yearbook* 2, 203–24.

ANDERSON, J. M. and C. JONES (1974) 'Three theses concerning phonological representations'. *Journal of Linguistics* 10: 1–26. First version in *Edinburgh Working Papers in Linguistics* 1, 1972.

ANDERSON, J. M. and C. JONES (1977) *Phonological Structure and the History of English*, Amsterdam: North-Holland.

ANDERSON, S. R. (1971) 'Nasal consonants and the internal structure of segments', *Language* 52, 326–44.

ANDERSON, S. R. (1975) 'On the interaction of phonological rules of various types', *Journal of Linguistics* 11, 39–62.

ANDERSON, S. R. (1982) 'The analysis of French schwas: or, how to get something for nothing', *Language* 58, 535–71.

ANDERSON, S. R. (1985) *Phonology in the Twentieth Century. Theories of Rules and Theories of Representation*, Chicago: University of Chicago Press.

ARCHANGELI, D. (1984) 'Underspecification in Yawelmani phonology and morphology', MIT PhD thesis.

ARCHANGELI, D. (1985) 'Yokuts harmony: evidence for coplanar representation in nonlinear phonology'. *Linguistic Inquiry* 16: 335–72.

ARCHANGELI, D. and D. PULLEYBLANK (in press) 'Yoruba vowel harmony', *Linguistic Inquiry*.

ARONOFF, M. (1976) *Word Formation in Generative Grammar*, Linguistic Inquiry Monograph 1, Cambridge Mass.: MIT Press.

ARONOFF, M. and R. T. OEHRLE (eds) (1984) *Language Sound Structure*. Cambridge, Mass.: MIT Press.

ARONOFF, M. and S. N. SRIDHAR (1983) 'Morphological levels in English and Kannada, or Atarizing Reagan', *Papers from the Parasession on the Interplay of Phonology, Morphology and Syntax*, Chicago Linguistic Society.

BASBØLL, H. (1968) 'The phoneme system of advanced standard Copenhagen', *ARIPUC* 3, 33–54.

BASBØLL, H. (1978) 'Boundaries and ranking of rules in French phonology'. In B. de Cornulier and F. Dell (eds) *Etudes de phonologie française*, Paris: Editions du CNRS.

BASBØLL, H. (1981) 'On the function of boundaries in phonological rules'. In D. Goyvaerts (ed.) *Phonology in the 1980s*, Ghent: E. Story-Scientia.

BASBØLL, H. (1984) 'On the relation between vowel height and frontback: a comment on Eli Fischer-Jørgensen's paper "Some basic vowel features, their articulatory correlates and their explanatory power in phonology"', *ARIPUC* 18, 277–84.

BASBØLL, H. (1988) Review of Durand (1986a), *Studies in Language* 12, 485–97.

BASBØLL, H. and J. WAGNER (1985) *Kontrastive Phonologie des Deutschen und Dänischen*, Tübingen: Niemeyer.

BAUER, L. (1983) *English Word-formation*, Cambridge: Cambridge University Press.

BENDOR-SAMUEL, J. T. (1960) 'Some problems of segmentation in the phonological analysis of Terena', *Word* 16, 348–55. Also in Palmer (1970).

BERTINETTO, P. M. and M. LOPORCARO (eds) (1988) *Certamen Phonologicum I*, Proceedings of the Cortona Phonology Meeting, 1987, Turin: Rosenberg and Sellier.

BLOOMFIELD, L. (1926) 'A set of postulates for the study of language', *Language* 1, 1–5.

BLOOMFIELD, L. (1933) *Language*. New York: Holt (13th edn, 1976), London: Allen & Unwin.

BLUMSTEIN, S.E. and K.N. STEVENS (1981) 'Phonetic features and acoustic invariance in speech', *Cognition* 10, 25–32.

BOOIJ, G. (1984) 'French C/Ø alternations, extrasyllabicity and Lexical Phonology', *The Linguistic Review* 3, 181–207.

BOOIJ, G. (1985) 'Coordination reduction in complex words: a case for prosodic phonology'. In van der Hulst and Smith (1985).

BOOIJ, G. (1988) 'On the relation between lexical and prosodic phonology'. In Bertinetto and Loporcaro (1988).

BOOIJ, G. and D. DE JONG (1987) 'The domain of liaison: theories and data', *Linguistics* 25, 1005–25.

BOOIJ, G. and J. RUBACH (1987) 'Postcyclic versus postlexical rules in Lexical Phonology', *Linguistic Inquiry* **18**, 1–44.

BRESNAN, J. (1971) 'Sentence stress and syntactic transformation', *Language* **47**, 257–81.

BRESNAN, J. (1972) 'Stress and syntax: a reply', *Language* **48**, 326–42.

BRESNAN, J. (ed.) (1982) *The Mental Representation of Grammatical Relations*, Cambridge, Mass.: MIT Press.

BROWMAN, C. P. and L. M. GOLDSTEIN (1986) 'Towards an articulatory phonology', *Phonology Yearbook* **3**, 219–52.

BROWN, G. (1970) 'Syllables and redundancy rules in generative phonology', *Journal of Linguistics* **6**, 1–17.

BROWN, G. (1972) *Phonological Rules and Dialect Variation*, Cambridge: Cambridge University Press.

BROWN, G. (1977) *Listening to Spoken English*, London: Longman.

BRUCK, A., R. A. FOX and M. W. LA GALY (eds) (1974) *Papers from the Parasession on Natural Phonology, April 18, 1974*, Chicago: Chicago Linguistic Society.

CAPRANICA, R. R. (1965) *The Evoked Vocal Response of the Bullfrog*, Cambridge, Mass.: MIT Press.

CARBONERO, P. (ed.) (1982) *Sociolinguistica Andaluza* (vols I and II), Seville: Publicaciones de la Universidad de Sevilla.

CATFORD, J. C. (1977) *Fundamental Problems in Phonetics*, Edinburgh: Edinburgh University Press.

CERDA-MASSO, R. (1984) 'Fonemas o prosodias, en el andaluz oriental?'. In A. Bernabé *et al.* (eds) *Athlon. Satura Grammatica in Honorem Francisci R. Adrados*, vol. I, Madrid: Gredos.

CHOMSKY, N. (1964) *Current Issues in Linguistic Theory*, The Hague: Mouton.

CHOMSKY, N. (1965) *Aspects of the Theory of Syntax*, Cambridge, Mass.: MIT Press.

CHOMSKY, N. (1981) *Lectures on Government and Binding*, Dordrecht: Foris.

CHOMSKY, N. (1986) *Knowledge of Language. Its Nature, Origin and Use*, New York: Praeger.

CHOMSKY, N. and M. HALLE (1968) *The Sound Pattern of English*, New York: Harper & Row.

CLEMENTS, G. N. (1976) 'Vowel harmony in non-linear generative phonology', Indiana University Linguistics Club.

CLEMENTS, G. N. (1981) 'Akan vowel harmony: a non-linear analysis'. In G. N. Clements (ed.) *Harvard Studies in Phonology*, vol. II, *pp* 108–77.

CLEMENTS, G. N. (1983) 'The hierarchical representation of tone features'. In I. R. Dihoff (ed.) *Current Approaches to African Linguistics*, vol. 1, Dordrecht: Foris.

CLEMENTS, G. N. (1985) 'The geometry of phonological features', *Phonology Yearbook* **2**, 225–52.

CLEMENTS, G. N. and K. FORD (1979) 'Kikuyu tone shift and its synchronic consequences', *Linguistic Inquiry* **10**, 179–210.

CLEMENTS, G. N. and S. J. KEYSER (1983) *CV Phonology: A Generative Theory of the Syllable*, Cambridge, Mass.: MIT Press.

COATES, R. (1979) 'Review of J. Foley, *Foundations of Theoretical Phonology*', *Journal of Linguistics* 15, 132–41.

COLMAN, F. (1987) 'The phonology and morphology of an Old English digraph *ie*' in Anderson and Durand (1987).

CONTEH, P. *et al.* (1983) 'A reanalysis of tone in Mende'. In J. Kaye *et al.* (eds) *Current Approaches to African Linguistics*, vol. 2, Foris: Dordrecht.

CONTRERAS, H. (1969) 'Simplicity, descriptive adequacy and binary features', *Language* 45, 1–8.

CREIDER, C.A. (1986) 'Binary vs. n-ary features' *Lingua* 70, 1–14.

DARWIN, C. J. (1987) 'Speech perception and recognition' in J. Lyons *et al.* (eds) *New Horizons in Linguistics* vol. 2, Harmondsworth: Penguin Books.

DAVENPORT, M. and J. STAUN (1986) 'Sequence, segment and configuration: two problems for dependency phonology'. In Durand (1986a).

DELATTRE, P. (1965) *Comparing the Phonetic Features of English, French, German and Spanish*, London: Harrap.

DELATTRE, P. (1967) 'Acoustic or articulatory invariance?', *Glossa* 1(1), 3–25.

DELL, F. (1970) 'Les règles phonologiques tardives et la morphologie derivationnelle du français', MIT PhD thesis.

DELL, F. (1973) *Les règles et les sons: introduction à la phonologie générative*, Paris: Hermann. (English translation, *Generative Phonology and French Phonology*, 1980, Cambridge: Cambridge University Press.)

DELL, F. (1979a) '*On French Phonology and Morphology* and some vowel alternations in French', *Studies in French Linguistics* 1 (3), 1–29.

DELL, F. (1979b) 'La morphologie dérivationnelle du français et l'organisation de la composante lexicale en grammaire générative', *Revue Romane* 14, 185–216.

DELL, F., D. HIRST and J.-R. VERGNAUD (eds) (1984) *Forme sonore du langage: Structure des représentations en phonologie*, Paris: Hermann.

DELL, F. and E. O SELKIRK (1978) 'On a morphologically governed vowel alternation in French'. In S. J. Keyser (ed.) *Recent Transformational Studies in European Languages*, Cambridge, Mass.: MIT Press.

DELL, F. and J. R. VERGNAUD (1984) 'Les développements récents en phonologie: quelques idées centrales'. In Dell, Hirst and Vergnaud (1984).

DEN DIKKEN, M. and H. VAN DER HULST (in press) 'Segmental hierarchitecture'. In van der Hulst and Smith, (in press).

[DONEGAN] MILLER, P. J. (1973) 'Bleaching and coloring', *Chicago Linguistic Society* 9, 386–97.

DRESHER, B. E. (1981) 'Abstractness and explanation in phonology'. In N. Hornstein and D. Lightfoot (eds) *Explanation in Linguistics*, London: Longman.

DRESSLER, W. (1985) *Morphonology*, Ann Arbor: Karoma Press.

DURAND, J. (1976) 'Generative phonology, dependency phonology and Southern French', *Lingua Stile* **XI**(i): 3–23.

DURAND, J. (1980) 'Esquisse d'une théorie de la syllabe en phonologie de dépendance', *Modèles linguistiques* **III.2**, 147–71.

DURAND, J. (ed.) (1986a) *Dependency and Non-linear Phonology*, London: Croom Helm.

DURAND, J. (1986b) 'French liaison, floating segments and other matters in a dependency framework'. In Durand (1986a).

DURAND, J. (1987) 'On the phonological status of glides: the evidence from Malay', in Anderson and Durand (1987).

DURAND, J. (1988) 'Phénomènes de nasalité en français du Midi: phonologie de dépendance et sous-spécification', *Recherches Linguistiques* **17**, 29–54. (English version in Slater, Durand and Bate (1988).)

DURAND, J. and C. LYCHE (1978) 'The s-Ø alternation in French: a morphological solution', *Journal of Linguistics* **14**, 259–76.

DURAND, J., C. SLATER and H. WISE (1987) 'Observations on schwa in Southern French', *Linguistics* **25**(5), 983–1004.

EIMAS, P. D., E. R. SIQUELAND, P. JUSCZYK and J. VIGORITO (1971) 'Speech perception in infants', *Science* **171**, 303–6.

ENCREVE, P. (1983) 'La liaison sans enchaînement', *Actes de la recherche en sciences sociales* **46**, 39–66.

ENCREVE, P. (1988) *La liaison avec et sans enchaînement. Phonologie tridimensionnelle et usages du français*, Paris: Seuil.

EWEN, C. (1980) *'Aspects of phonological structure with particular reference to English and Dutch'*, PhD thesis, University of Edinburgh.

EWEN, C. (1982) 'The internal structure of complex segments'. In van der Hulst and Smith (1982).

EWEN, C. (1986) 'Segmental and suprasegmental structure'. In Durand (1986a).

EWEN, C. and VAN DER HULST, H. (1985) 'Single-valued features and the non- linear analysis of vowel harmony'. In H. Bennis and F. Beukema (eds) *Linguistics in the Netherlands 1985*, Dordrecht: Foris.

EWEN, C. and VAN DER HULST, H. (1987) Single-valued features and the distinction between [−F] and [ØF]. In H. Bennis and F. Beukema (eds) *Linguistics in the Netherlands 1986*, Dordrecht: Foris.

FABB, N. (1988) 'English suffixation is constrained only by selectional restrictions', *Natural Language and Linguistic Theory* **6**: 4, 527–539.

FALLOWS, D. (1981) 'Experimental evidence for English syllabification and syllable structure', *Journal of Linguistics* **17**, 309–17.

FANT, G. (1971) 'Distinctive features and phonetic dimensions'. In G. E. Perren and J. L. M. Trim (eds) *Applications of Linguistics*, Cambridge: Cambridge University Press.

FERGUSON, C. A. (1963) 'Assumptions about nasals: a sample study in phonological universals'. In J. Greenberg (ed.) *Universals of Language*, Cambridge, Mass.: MIT Press.

FISCHER-JØRGENSEN, E. (1975) *Trends in Phonological Theory: a Historical Introduction*. Copenhagen: Akademisk Forlag.

FISCHER-JØRGENSEN, E. (1985) 'Some basic vowel features, their articulatory correlates, and their explanatory power in phonology'. In Fromkin (1985).

FOLEY. J. (1977) *Foundations of Theoretical Phonology*, Cambridge: Cambridge University Press.

FROMKIN, V. (1971) 'The non-anomalous nature of anomalous utterances', *Language* **47**, 27–54.

FROMKIN, V. (1972) 'Discussion paper on speech physiology', *UCLA Working Papers in Phonetics* **23**, 37–60.

FROMKIN, V. (ed.) (1973) *Speech Errors as Linguistic Evidence*. The Hague: Mouton.

FROMKIN, V. (ed.) (1978) *Tone: a Linguistic Survey*, New York: Academic Press.

FROMKIN, V. (ed.) (1985) *Phonetic Linguistics. Essays in Honor of Peter Ladefoged*, New York: Academic Press.

FUDGE, E. (1967) 'The nature of phonological primes', *Journal of Linguistics* **3**, 1–36.

FUDGE, E. (1969) 'Syllables', *Journal of Linguistics* **5**, 253–86.

FUDGE, E. (1987) 'Branching structure within the syllable', *Journal of Linguistics* **23**, 359–77.

FUJIMURA, O. (ed.) (1973) *Three Dimensions of Linguistics Theory*, Tokyo: TEC Corporation.

GAZDAR, G., E. KLEIN, G. PULLUM and I. SAG (1985) *Generalized Phrase Structure Grammar*, Oxford: Blackwell.

GIEGERICH, H. J. (1980) 'On stress-timing in English phonology', *Lingua* **51**, 187–221.

GIEGERICH, H. J. (1985) *Metrical Phonology and Phonological Structure*, Cambridge: Cambridge University Press.

GIEGERICH, H. J. (1986a) 'Relating to metrical structure'. In Durand (1986a).

GIEGERICH, H. J. (1986b) 'A relational model of German syllable structure', Duisburg: Linguistic Agency, University of Duisburg.

GIMSON, A. C. (1980) *An Introduction to the Pronunciation of English*, (3rd edn), London: Edward Arnold.

GOLDSMITH, J. (1976) 'Autosegmental phonology', Indiana University Linguistics Club. (Also published, 1979, by Garland Publishing, New York.)

GOLDSMITH, J. (1979) 'The aims of autosegmental phonology'. In D. A. Dinnsen (ed.) *Current Approaches to Phonological Theory*, Bloomington: Indiana University Press.

GOLDSMITH, J. (1985) 'Vowel harmony in Khalkha Mongolian, Yaka, Finnish and Hungarian', *Phonology Yearbook* **2**, 253–75.

GOLDSMITH, J. (1987) 'Vowel systems', in A. Bosch, B. Need and E. Schiller (eds.) *Papers from the Parasession on Autosegmental and Metrical Phonology*, Chicago: Chicago Linguistic Society.

GOYVAERTS, D. (1978) *Aspects of Post-SPE Phonology*, Ghent: Story-Scientia.

GOYVAERTS, D. and G. K. PULLUM (eds) (1975) *Essays on the Sound Pattern of English*, Ghent: E. Story-Scientia.

GRACE, E. C. (1975) 'In defence of *vocalic'*, *Language Sciences* **36**, 1–6.

GUIERRE, L. (1979) *Essai sur l'accentuation en anglais contemporain*, Département de Recherches Linguistiques, Université de Paris VII.

GUIERRE, L. (1984) *Drills in English Stress-Patterns*, Paris: Armand Colin-Longman

HALL, B. and HALL, R. M. R. (1980) 'Nez Perce vowel harmony: an Africanist explanation and some theoretical questions', in Vago (1980).

HALLE, M. (1959) *The Sound Pattern of Russian*, The Hague: Mouton.

HALLE, M. (1973) 'Prolegomena to a theory of word formation', *Linguistic Inquiry* **4**, 3–16.

HALLE, M. (1977) 'Tenseness, vowel shift, and the phonology of the back vowels in Modern English', *Linguistic Inquiry* **8**, 611–25.

HALLE, M. (1981) 'Knowledge unlearned and untaught: what speakers know about the sounds of their language'. In Halle, Bresnan and Miller (1981).

HALLE, M. (1983) 'On distinctive features and their articulatory implementation', *Natural Language and Linguistic Theory* **1**, 91–105.

HALLE, M., J. BRESNAN and G. A. MILLER (eds) (1981) *Linguistic Theory and Psychological Reality*, (3rd edn; 1st edn 1978), Cambridge, Mass.: MIT Press.

HALLE, M and G. N. CLEMENTS (1983) *Problem Book in Phonology*, Cambridge, Mass.: MIT Press.

HALLE, M. and K. P. MOHANAN (1985) 'The segmental phonology of Modern English', *Linguistic Inquiry* **16**, 57–116.

HALLE, M. and K. N. STEVENS (1969) 'On the feature "Advanced Tongue Root"', *MIT Quarterly Progress Report* **94**, 209–15.

HALLE, M. and K. N. STEVENS (1971) 'A note on laryngeal features', *MIT Quarterly Progress Report* **101**, 198–213.

HALLE, M. and J.-R. VERGNAUD (1980) 'Three dimensional phonology', *Journal of Linguistic Research* **1**, 83–105.

HALLE, M. and J.-R. VERGNAUD (1982a) 'Processus d'harmonie'. In J. Guéron and T. Sowley (eds) *Grammaire transformationnelle: théorie et méthodologie*, Université de Paris VIII: Encrages.

HALLE, M. and J.-R. VERGNAUD (1982b) 'On the framework of autosegmental phonology'. In van der Hulst and Smith (1982)

HALLE, M. and J.-R. VERGNAUD (1987a) 'Stress and the cycle', *Linguistic Inquiry* **18**, 45–84.

HALLE, M. and J.-R. VERGNAUD (1987b) *An Essay on Stress*, Cambridge, Mass.: MIT Press.

HAMMOND, R. M. (1980) 'Las realizaciones fonéticas del fonema /s/ an el español cubano rápido de Miami', in G. E. Scavnicky (ed.) *Dialectología hispano-americana. Estudios actuales*, Washington DC: Georgetown University Press.

HARAGUCHI, S. (1977) *The Tone Pattern of Japanese: an Autosegmental Theory of Tonology*, Tokyo: Kaitakusha.

HARRIS, J. W. (1983) *Syllable Structure and Stress in Spanish: A Non-*

linear Analysis, Linguistic Inquiry Monograph 8, Cambridge, Mass.: MIT Press.

HARRIS, Z. S. (1951) *Structural Linguistics*, Chicago: University of Chicago Press.

HASSAN, A. (1974) *The Morphology of Malay*, Kuala Lumpur: Dewan Bahasa dan Pustaka.

HAWKINS, P. (1984) *Introducing Phonology*, London: Hutchinson.

HAYES, B. (1981) 'A metrical theory of stress rules', Indiana University Linguistics Club.

HAYES. B. (1982) 'Extrametricality and English stress', *Linguistic Inquiry* 13, 227–76.

HAYES, B. (1983) 'A grid-based theory of English meter', *Linguistic Inquiry* 14, 357–94.

HAYES, B. (1984) 'The phonology of rhythm in English', *Linguistic Inquiry* 15, 33–74.

HAYES, B. and S. PUPPEL (1985) 'On the rhythm rule in Polish', in van der Hulst and Smith (1985).

HAYWARD, K. M. and R. J. MICKEY (1987) '"Guttural": arguments for a new distinctive feature'. Paper presented at the September meeting of the LAGB, Bradford.

HJELMSLEV, L. (1948) 'Le verbe et la phrase nominale'. In *Mélanges de philologie, de littérature et d'histoire ancienne offerts à J. Marouzeau*, pp 235–81. Reprinted in *Essais Linguistiques*, pp 165–91. (Travaux du cercle linguistique de Copenhague, XII).

HJELMSLEV, J. (1953) *Prolegomena to a Theory of Language*, Bloomington: Indiana University Press.

HOCKETT, C. F. (1942) 'A system of descriptive phonology', *Language* 18, 3–21.

HOFFMANN, C. (1963) *A Grammar of the Margi Language*, London: Oxford University Press.

HOGG, R. and C. B. MCCULLY (1987) *Metrical Phonology*, Cambridge: Cambridge University Press.

HOMBERT, J.-M. (1973) 'Speaking backwards in Bakwiri', *Studies in African Linguistics* 4(3), 227–35.

HOOPER, J. B. (1972) 'The syllable in phonological theory', *Language* 48, 525–40.

HOOPER, J. B. (1974) 'Rule morphologization in Natural Generative Grammar'. In Bruck *et al.* (1974).

HOOPER, J. B. (1975) 'The archi-segment in Natural Generative Phonology', *Language* 51, 536–60.

HOOPER, J. B. (1976) *An Introduction to Natural Generative Phonology*, New York: Academic Press.

HUDSON, G. (1974) 'The representation of non-productive alternation'. In J. M. Anderson and C. Jones (eds) *Historical Phonology*, vol. 2, Amsterdam: North-Holland.

HUGHES, A. and TRUDGILL, P. (1979) *English Accents and Dialects*, London: Edward Arnold.

HULST, H. VAN DER (1988) 'The dual interpretation of |i|, |u| and |a|', *NELS* **18**.

HULST, H. VAN DER (in press) 'The geometry of vocalic features'. In van der Hulst and Smith (1988).

HULST, H. VAN DER and N. SMITH (eds) (1982) *The Structure of Phonological Representations*, Parts I and II, Dordrecht: Foris.

HULST, H. VAN DER and N. SMITH (eds) (1985) *Advances in Non-linear Phonology*, Dordrecht: Foris.

HULST, H. VAN DER and N. SMITH (1986) 'On neutral vowels'. In K. Bogers, H. van der Hulst and M. Mous (eds) *The representation of suprasegmentals in African languages*, Dordrecht: Foris.

HULST, H. VAN DER and N. SMITH (eds) (in press) *Features, Segmental Structure and Harmony Processes*. Dordrecht: Foris.

HYMAN, L. M. (1972) *A Phonological Study of Fe2fe2-Bamileke*, Studies in African Linguistics, Supplement 4.

HYMAN, L. M. (1973) 'The feature [grave] in phonological theory', *Journal of Phonetics* **1**, 329–37.

HYMAN, L. M. (1975) *Phonology: Theory and Analysis*, New York: Holt, Rinehart and Winston.

HYMAN, L. M. (1985) *A Theory of Phonological Weight*, Dordrecht: Foris.

JAEGER, J. J. (1986) 'On the acquisition of abstract representations for English vowels', *Phonology Yearbook* **3**, 71–97.

JAKOBSON, R. (1968) *Child Language, Aphasia and Phonological Universals*, The Hague: Mouton.

JAKOBSON, R., G. FANT and M. HALLE (1952) *Preliminaries to Speech Analysis*, Cambridge, Mass.: MIT Press.

JAKOBSON, R. and M. HALLE (1956) *Fundamentals of Language*, The Hague: Mouton.

JAKOBSON, R. and M. HALLE (1968) 'Phonology in relation to phonetics'. In B. Malmberg (ed.) *Manual of Phonetics*, Amsterdam: North-Holland (1st edn, 1957, ed. Kaiser).

JAKOBSON, R. and L. R. WAUGH (1979) *The Sound Shape of Language*, Brighton: Harvester Press.

JOHNSON, W. (1987) 'Lexical levels in French phonology', *Linguistics* **25**, 889–913.

JONES, D. (1964) *An Outline of English Phonetics*, Cambridge: Heffer.

JONES, D. (1977) *English Pronouncing Dictionary* (13th edn), A. C. Gimson (ed.), London: Dent.

JONES, S. (1929) 'Radiography and pronunciation', *Brit. J. Radiol.* **2**, 149–50.

KAHN, D. (1976) 'Syllable-based generalizations in English phonology', Indiana University Linguistics Club.

KAISSE, E. M. (1985) *Connected Speech: The Interaction of Syntax and Phonology*, Orlando, Fl.: Academic Press.

KAISSE, E. M. and P. A. SHAW (1985) 'On the theory of Lexical Phonology', *Phonology Yearbook* **2**, 1–30.

KAYE, J. (1971) 'Nasal harmony in Desano', *Linguistic Inquiry* **2**, 37–56.

KAYE, J. (1981) 'Les diphtongues cachées du vata', *Studies in African Linguistics* **12**, 225–44.

KAYE, J. (1982) 'Harmony processes in Vata'. In van der Hulst and Smith (1982).

KAYE, J. (in press) *Phonology. A Cognitive View*, Hillsdale, New Jersey: Lawrence Erlbaum Associates.

KAYE, J. (to appear) 'Government in phonology: the case of Moroccan Arabic', *The Linguistic Review*.

KAYE, J. and J. LOWENSTAMM (1981) 'Syllable structure and markedness theory. In A. Belletti, L. Brandi and L. Rizzi (eds) *Theory of Markedness in Generative Grammar*, Pisa: Scuola Normale Superiore.

KAYE, J. and J. LOWENSTAMM (1984) 'De la syllabicité'. In Dell, Hirst and Vergnaud 1984.

KAYE, J. and J. LOWENSTAMM (1985) 'Compensatory lengthening in Tiberian Hebrew'. In L. Wetzels and E. Sezer (eds) *Studies in Compensatory Lengthening*, Dordrecht: Foris.

KAYE, J., J. LOWENSTAMM and J.-R. VERGNAUD (1985) 'The internal structure of phonological segments: a theory of charm and government', *Phonology Yearbook* **2**: 305–28.

KAYE, J., J. LOWENSTAMM and J.-R VERGNAUD (1988) 'Constituent structure and government in phonology'. To appear in German in *Linguistische Berichte*.

KEAN, M.-L. (1980) 'The theory of markedness in generative grammar', Indiana University Linguistics Club.

KEAN, M.-L. (1981) 'On the theory of markedness: some general considerations and a case in point'. In A. Belletti, L. Brandi and L. Rizzi (eds) *Theory of Markedness in Generative Grammar*, Pisa: Scuola Normale Superiore.

KENSTOWICZ, M. (1972) 'The morphophonemics of the Slovak noun', *Papers in Linguistics* **5**, 550–67.

KENSTOWICZ, M. (1982) 'Gemination and spirantization in Tigrinya', *Studies in the Linguistic Sciences* **12**(1).

KENSTOWICZ, M. and C. KISSEBERTH (1979) *Generative Phonology. Description and Theory*, New York: Academic Press.

KENSTOWICZ, M. and J. RUBACH (1987) 'The phonology of syllabic nuclei in Slovak', *Language* **63**, 463–97.

KENYON, J. S. and T. A. KNOTT (1944) *A Pronouncing Dictionary of American English*, Springfield, Mass.: Merriam.

KIPARSKY, P. (1968a) 'How abstract is phonology?', Indiana Linguistics Club. In Fujimura (1973).

KIPARSKY, P. (1968b) 'Linguistic universals and linguistic change'. In E. Bach and R. Harms (eds) *Universals in Linguistic Theory*, New York: Holt, Rinehart and Winston.

KIPARSKY, P. (1968c) 'Metrics and morphophonemics in the Kalevala'. In C. Gribble (ed.) *Studies Presented to Professor Roman Jakobson by his Students*, Cambridge, Mass.: Slavica Publishers.

KIPARSKY, P. (1973a) '"Elsewhere" in phonology', in S. R. Anderson and P. Kiparsky (eds) *Festschrift for Morris Halle*, New York: Holt, Rinehart & Winston.

KIPARSKY, P. (1973b) 'Abstractness, opacity and global rules'. In Fujimura (1973).

KIPARSKY, P. (1979) 'Metrical structure assignment is cyclic', *Linguistic Inquiry* **10**, 421–42.

KIPARSKY, P. (1981) 'Remarks on the metrical structure of the syllable'. In W. U. Dressler, O. E. Pfeiffer and J. R. Rennison (eds) *Phonologica 1980*, Innsbruck: Innsbrucker Beiträge zur Sprachwissenschaft.

KIPARSKY, P. (1982a) 'From cyclic phonology to lexical phonology'. In van der Hulst & Smith (1982).

KIPARSKY, P. (1982b) 'Lexical morphology and phonology'. In I.-S. Yang (ed.) *Linguistics in the Morning Calm*, Seoul: Hanshin.

KIPARSKY, P. (1983) 'Word formation and the lexicon'. In F. Ingemann (ed.) *Proceedings of the 1982 Mid-America Linguistics Conference*, Lawrence, Kans.: University of Kansas.

KIPARSKY, P. (1985) 'Some consequences of Lexical Phonology', *Phonology Yearbook* **2**, 85–138.

KIPARSKY, P. and L. MENN (1977) 'On the acquisition of phonology'. In J. Macnamara (ed.) *Language Learning and Thought*, New York: Academic Press.

KISSEBERTH, C. (1969) 'Theoretical implications of Yawelmani phonology', PhD thesis, University of Illinois.

KLAUSENBURGER, J. (1984) *French Liaison and Linguistic Theory*, Stuttgart: Steiner-Verlag-Wiesbaden.

KLOEKE, W. U. S. VAN LESSEN (1981) 'How strident is the raspberry?', in A. Belletti, L. Brandi and L. Rizzi (eds) *Theory of Markedness in Generative Grammar*, Pisa: Scuola Normale Superiore.

KOUTSOUDAS, A. (1980) 'The question of rule ordering: some common fallacies', *Journal of Linguistics* **16**, 19–35.

KOUTSOUDAS, A., G. SANDERS and C. NOLL (1974) 'On the application of phonological rules', *Language* **50**, 1–28.

KUHL, P. K. and J. D. MILLER (1978) 'Speech perception by the chinchilla: identification functions for synthetic VOT stimuli', *Journal of the Acoustical Society of America* **63**, 905–17.

KURODA, S.-Y. (1967) *Yawelmani Phonology*, Cambridge, Mass.: MIT Press.

KURYŁOWICZ, J. (1941) 'Contribution à la théorie de la syllabe', *Biuletin Polskiego Towarszistwa Jezyko-Znawaczego* **8**, 80–113.

KURYŁOWICZ, J. (1971) 'A problem of Germanic alliteration'. In M. Barahmer, S. Helsztyński and J. Kryżanowski (eds) *Studies in Language and Literature in Honour of Margaret Schlauch*, New York: Russell & Russell.

LADEFOGED, P. (1967) *Three Areas of Experimental Phonetics*, Oxford: Oxford University Press.

LADEFOGED, P. (1968) *A Phonetic Study of West African Languages* (1st edn, 1964) Cambridge: Cambridge University Press.

LADEFOGED, P. (1971) *Preliminaries to Linguistic Phonetics*, Chicago: University of Chicago Press.

LADEFOGED, P. (1972) 'The three glottal features', *UCLA Working Papers in Phonetics* **22**, 95–101.

LADEFOGED, P. (1977) 'The abyss between phonology and phonetics',

Papers from the Thirteenth Regional Meeting, Chicago Linguistic Society, *pp* 225–35.

LADEFOGED, P. (1980) 'What are linguistic sounds made of?', *Language* **56**(3), 485–502.

LADEFOGED, P. (1982) *A Course in Phonetics* (2nd edn), New York: Harcourt, Brace, Jovanovich.

LADEFOGED, P. and A. TRAILL (1984) 'Linguistic phonetic descriptions of clicks', *Language* **60**(1), 1–20.

LAKS, B. (1988) 'Des grilles et des arbres', *Recherches Linguistiques* **17**, 135–194.

LANGENDOEN, D. T. (1968) *The London School of Linguistics: A Study of the Linguistic Theories of B. Malinowski and J. R. Firth*, Cambridge, Mass.: MIT Press.

LARSEN, R. S. and E. V. PIKE (1949) 'Huasteco intonations and phonemes', *Language* **25**, 268–77.

LASS, R. (1975) 'How intrinsic is content? Markedness, sound change and "family universals"'. In Goyvaerts and Pullum (1975).

LASS, R. (1976) *English Phonology and Phonological Theory*, Cambridge: Cambridge University Press.

LASS, R. (1980) *On Explaining Language Change*, Cambridge: Cambridge University Press.

LASS, R. (1984) *Phonology*, Cambridge: Cambridge University Press.

LASS, R. and J. M. ANDERSON (1975) *Old English Phonology*, Cambridge: Cambridge University Press.

LAVER, J. (1979) *The Phonetic Description of Voice Quality*, Cambridge: Cambridge University Press.

LEBEN, W. (1973) 'Suprasegmental Phonology', MIT PhD thesis.

LEBEN, W. (1982) 'Metrical or autosegmental'. In van der Hulst and Smith 1982.

LEECH, G. (1981) *Semantics* (2nd edn), Harmondsworth: Penguin Books.

LEVIN, J. (1983) 'Dependent levels of representation: the skeletal tier and syllabic projections', paper delivered at the Glow meeting, York. Abstract in the Glow *Newsletter* **10**, 52–4.

LEVIN, L. S. (1981) 'A look at English vowels', unpublished manuscript, MIT.

LIBERMAN, A. M., F. S. COOPER, D. P. SHANKWEILER, and M. STUDDERT-KENNEDY (1967) 'Perception of the speech code', *Psychological Review* **74**, 431–61.

LIBERMAN, A. M. and I. G. MATTINGLY (1985) 'The motor theory of speech perception revised', *Cognition* **21**, 1–36.

LIBERMAN, M. (1975) *The Intonational System of English*, MIT PhD thesis, published (1979), New York: Garland.

LIBERMAN, M. and A. PRINCE (1977) 'On stress and linguistic rhythm', *Linguistic Inquiry* **8**, 249–336.

LIEBERMAN, P. (1975) *On the Origins of Language: An Introduction to the Evolution of Human Speech*, New York: Macmillan.

LIEBERMAN, P. (1977) *Speech Physiology and Acoustic Phonetics: An Introduction*, New York: Macmillan.

LIEBERMAN, P. (1984) *The Biology and Evolution of Language*, Cambridge, Mass.: Harvard University Press.

LIGHTNER, T. M. (1963) 'A note on the formulation of phonological rules', *Quarterly Report of the Research Laboratory of Electronics*, MIT, no. 68, 187–9.

LINDAU, M. (1975) 'Features for vowels', *UCLA Working Papers in Phonetics* 30.

LINDAU, M. (1978) 'Vowel features', *Language* 54, 541–63.

LOCAL, J. and A. SIMPSON (in press) *Doing phonology*, Manchester: Manchester University Press.

LOVE, N. (1981) *Generative Phonology. A Case-Study from French*, Amsterdam: Benjamins.

LOWENSTAMM, J. and J.-F. PRUNET (1986) 'Le tigrinya et le principe du contour obligatoire', *Revue Québecoise de Linguistique* 16, 181–207.

LYONS, J. (1968) *Introduction to Theoretical Linguistics*, Cambridge: Cambridge University Press.

LYONS, J. (1977) *Semantics*, Cambridge: Cambridge University Press.

MADDIESON, I. (1984) *Patterns of Sounds*, Cambridge: Cambridge University Press.

MALMBERG, B. (1971) *Les domaines de la phonétique*, Paris: Presses Universitaires de France.

MARTINET, A. (1937) 'La phonologie du mot en danois', *Bulletin de la Société Linguistique de Paris* 38, 169–266.

MARTINET, A. (1955) *Economie des changements phonétiques*. Berne: Editions A. Francke.

MASCARO, J. (1976) 'Catalan phonology and the phonological cycle', MIT PhD thesis, distributed by Indiana University Linguistics Club.

MATTHEWS, P. H. (1972) *Inflectional Morphology*, Cambridge: Cambridge University Press.

MATTHEWS, P. H. (1981) *Syntax*. Cambridge: Cambridge University Press.

MCCARTHY, J. (1979) 'Formal problems in Semitic phonology and morphology', MIT PhD thesis, distributed by Indiana University Linguistics Club.

MCCARTHY, J. (1981) 'A prosodic theory of nonconcatenative morphology', *Linguistic Inquiry* 12, 373–418.

MCCARTHY, J. (1984) 'Theoretical consequences of Montanes vowel harmony', *Linguistic Inquiry* 15, 291–318.

MCCARTHY, J. (1986) 'OCP effects: gemination and antigemination', *Linguistic Inquiry* 17, 207–63.

MCCAWLEY, J. D. (1986) 'Today the world, tomorrow phonology', *Phonology Yearbook* 3, 27–43.

MICHAELS, D. (1980) 'Spelling and the phonology of tense vowels', *Language and Speech* 23, 379–92.

MOHANAN, K. P. (1985) 'Syllable structure and lexical strata in English', *Phonology Yearbook* 2, 139–55.

MOHANAN, K. P. (1986) *The Theory of Lexical Phonology*, Dordrecht: Reidel.

MONSEN, R. B. and A. M. ENGEBRETSON, (1977) 'Study of variations in the male and female glottal wave', *Journal of the Acoustical Society of America* **62**, 981–93.

MORALES, H. L. (1984) 'Desdoblamiento fonológico de la vocales en el andaluz oriental: reexamen de la cuestión, *Revista Española de Lingüística* **14**(1), 85–97.

MORIN, Y.-C. (1983) 'Pour une histoire des voyelles longues en français: quelques problèmes', paper presented at the 7th annual meeting of the Linguistic Association of the Atlantic Provinces, University of Moncton.

MORIN, Y.- C. (1987) 'French data and phonological theory', *Linguistics* **25**, 815–43.

MORIN, Y.-C. and J. KAYE (1982) 'The syntactic bases for French liaison', *Journal of Linguistics* **18**, 291–330.

MOULTON, W. G. (1977) 'Unity and diversity in the phonology of standard American English'. In H. Walter (ed.) *Phonologie et société, Studia Phonetica*, vol. 13, Paris: Didier.

NESPOR, M. (1988) 'On the separation between prosodic phonology and rhythmic phonology', MS.

NESPOR, M. and I. VOGEL (1982) 'Prosodic domains of external sandhi rules'. In van der Hulst and Smith (1982).

NESPOR, M. and I. VOGEL (1986) *Prosodic Phonology*, Dordrecht: Foris.

NEWMAN, S. (1944) *Yokuts Language of California*, Viking Fund Publications in Anthropology, no. 2, New York.

NOSKE, R., J. SCHINKEL and N. SMITH (1982) 'The question of rule ordering: some counter fallacies', *Journal of Linguistics* **18**, 389–408.

OHALA, J. J. (1974) 'Experimental historical phonology'. In J. M. Anderson and C. Jones (eds) *Historical Phonology*, vol. 2, Amsterdam: North-Holland.

OHALA, J. J. (1985) 'Around *Flat*' in Fromkin (1985).

OHALA, J. J and H. KAWASAKI (1984) 'Prosodic phonology and phonetics', *Phonology Yearbook* **1**, 113–27.

ONN, F. M. (1980) *Aspects of Malay Phonology and Morphology. A Generative Approach*, Kuala Lumpur: Universiti kebangsaan Malaysia.

PAGLIUCA, W. and R. MOWREY (1980) 'On certain evidence for the feature [grave]', *Language* **56**(3), 503–14.

PALMER, F. R. (ed.) (1970). *Prosodic Analysis*, London: Oxford University Press.

PIKE, K. (1947) 'Grammatical prerequisites to phonemic analysis', *Word* **3**, 155–72.

PIKE, K. (1967) *Language in Relation to a Unified Theory of Human Behaviour*, The Hague: Mouton.

PIKE, K. and E. V. PIKE (1947) 'Immediate constituents of Mazateco syllables', *International Journal of American Linguistics* **13**, 78–91.

PLENAT, M. (1986) 'Lexique et phonologie', paper presented at a seminar GRECO-GALF, 'Lexique et traitement automatique du langage', Toulouse.

PLENAT, M. (1987) 'On the structure of rime in standard French', *Linguistics* **25**(5), 867–87.

POSTAL, P. M. (1968) *Aspects of Phonological Theory*, New York: Harper & Row.

PRINCE, A. (1983) 'Relating to the grid', *Linguistic Inquiry* 14, 19–100.

PULLEYBLANK, D. (1986) *Tones in Lexical Phonology*, Dordrecht: Foris.

PULLUM, G. K. and A. M. ZWICKY (1984) 'The syntax-phonology boundary and current syntactic theories', *Ohio State University Working Papers in Linguistics* 29, 105–16.

QUIRK, R., S. GREENBAUM, G. LEECH, and J. SVARTVIK (1985) *A Comprehensive Grammar of the English Language*, London: Longman.

REENEN, P. VAN (1982) *Phonetic Feature Definitions: Their Integration into Phonology and their Relation to Speech. A Case Study of the Feature NASAL*, Dordrecht: Foris.

RENNISON, J. (1986) 'On tridirectional feature systems for vowels', in Durand (1986a).

RIEMSDIJK, H. VAN and E. WILLIAMS (1986) *Introduction to the Theory of Grammar*, Cambridge, Mass.: MIT Press.

RISCHEL, J. (1964) 'Stress, juncture and syllabification in phonemic description', *Proceedings of the IXth International Congress of Linguistics*, 85–93.

RISCHEL, J. (1968) 'Notes on the Danish vowel pattern', *ARIPUC* 3, 177–205.

ROBINS, R. H. (1957) 'Vowel nasality in Sundanese: a phonological and grammatical study'. In *Studies in Linguistic Analysis*, Oxford: Basil Blackwell.

ROBINSON, J. J. (1970) 'Dependency structures and transformational rules', *Language* 46, 259–85.

ROCHET, B. (1982) 'The mid-vowels in Bordeaux French', *Orbis* 29 (1–2), 76–104.

ROTENBERG, J. (1975) 'French liaison, phrase structure and semi-cyclical rules', MS, MIT.

ROTENBERG, J. (1978) 'The syntax of phonology', MIT PhD thesis.

RUBACH, J. (1981) *Cyclic Phonology and Palatalization in Polish and English*, Warsaw: Wydawnictwa Uniwersytetu Warszawskiego.

RUBACH, J. (1984a) *Cyclic and Lexical Phonology: the Structure of Polish*, Dordrecht: Foris.

RUBACH, J. (1984b) 'Segmental rules of English and cyclic phonology', *Language* 60, 21–54.

RUDES, B. (1976) 'Lexical representation and variable rules in Natural Generative Phonology', *Glossa* 10, 111–50.

RUHLEN, M. (1978) 'Nasal vowels'. In J. Greenberg (ed.) *Universals of Human Language*, vol. 2: *Phonology*, Stanford: Stanford University Press.

SAGEY, E. C. (1986) 'The representation of features and relations in non-linear phonology', MIT PhD thesis.

SALVADOR, G. (1977) 'Unidades fonológicas vocálicas en andaluz oriental', *Revista Española de Lingüística* 7(1), 1–23.

SANDERS, G. (1974) 'The simplex-feature hypothesis', *Glossa* 8, 141–92.

SAPIR, E. (1933) 'La réalité psychologique des phonèmes', *Journal de Psychologie Normale et Pathologique* 30, 247–65. Translated as 'The psychological reality of phonemes' in Mandelbaum (ed.) (1949) *Selected Writings of Edward Sapir*, Berkeley: University of California Press.

SAPORTA, S. (1965) 'Ordered rules, dialect differences and historical processes', *Language* 41, 218–24.

SCALISE, S. (1984) *Generative Morphology*, Dordrecht: Foris.

SCHACHTER, P. (1969) 'Natural assimilation rules in Akan', *International Journal of American Linguistics* 35, 342–55.

SCHANE, S. A. (1968) *French Phonology and Morphology*, Cambridge, Mass.: MIT Press.

SCHANE, S. A. (1972) 'Non-cyclic word stress'. Mimeographed paper, La Jolla: California.

SCHANE, S. A. (1978) 'L'emploi des frontières de mot en français'. In B. de Cornulier and F. Dell (eds) *Etudes de phonologie française*, Paris: Editions du CNRS.

SCHANE, S. A. (1984a) 'The fundamentals of particle phonology', *Phonology Yearbook* 1, 129–55.

SCHANE, S. A. (1984b) 'Two English vowels movements: a particle analysis'. In Aronoff and Oehrle (1984).

SCHEIN, B. (1981) 'Spirantization in Tigrinya'. In H. Borer and Y. Aoun (eds) *Theoretical Issues in the Grammar of Semitic Languages*, MIT Working Papers in Linguistics 3, 32–43.

SEBEOK, T. A. and F. J. INGEMAN (1961) *An Eastern Cheremis Manual*, Indiana University.

SELKIRK, E. O. (1972) 'The phrase phonology of English and French', MIT PhD thesis. Indiana Linguistics Club, 1981.

SELKIRK, E. O. (1974) 'French liaison and the X̄ notation', *Linguistic Inquiry* 5, 573–90.

SELKIRK, E. O. (1980) 'The role of prosodic categories in English word stress', *Linguistic Inquiry* 11, 563–605.

SELKIRK, E. O. (1982a) 'The syllable'. In van der Hulst and Smith 1982.

SELKIRK, E. O. (1982b) *The Syntax of Words*, Linguistic Inquiry Monograph 7, Cambridge, Mass.: MIT Press.

SELKIRK, E. O. (1984a) *Phonology and Syntax: The Relation between Sound and Structure*, Cambridge, Mass.: MIT Press.

SELKIRK, E. O. (1984b) 'On the major class features and syllable theory'. In Aronoff and Oehrle (1984).

SIEGEL, D. (1974) 'Topics in English morphology', MIT PhD thesis.

SLATER, C., J. DURAND and M. BATE (eds) (1988) *French Sound Patterns: Changing Perspectives*, Occasional Papers no. 32 of the Department of Language and Linguistics of the University of Essex.

SOMMERSTEIN, A. H. (1977) *Modern Phonology*, London: Edward Arnold.

SPENCER, A. (1984) 'Eliminating the feature [lateral]', *Journal of Linguistics* 20, 23–43.

SPENCER, A. (1985) 'Towards a theory of phonological development', *Lingua* 68, 3–38.

SPENCER, A. (1988) 'Arguments for morpholexical rules', *Journal of Linguistics* 24, 1–29.

SPROAT, R. (1985) 'On deriving the lexicon', MIT PhD thesis.

STANLEY, R. (1967) 'Redundancy rules in phonology', *Language* **43**, 393–436.

STAUN, J. (1987) 'On the representation of stød'. In Anderson and Durand (1987).

STEINBERG, D. D. and R. K. KROHN (1975) 'The psychological reality of Chomsky and Halle's vowel shift rule'. In E.F.K. Koerner (ed.) *The Transformational-Generative Paradigm and Modern Linguistic Theory*, Amsterdam: Benjamins.

STEWART, J. M. (1967) 'Tongue root position in Akan vowel harmony', *Phonetica* **16**, 185–204.

SWEET, H. (1877) *A Handbook of Phonetics*, Oxford: Henry Frowde.

TRANEL, B. (1981) *Concreteness in Generative Phonology: Evidence from French*, Berkeley: University of California Press.

TRUBETZKOY, N. (1969) *Principles of Phonology*, Berkeley: University of California Press. (Translation of *Grundzüge der Phonologie, Travaux du cercle linguistique de Prague* **7**, 1939.)

TRUDGILL, P. (1974) *The Social Differentiation of English in Norwich*, Cambridge: Cambridge University Press.

VAGO, R. M. (ed.) (1980) *Issues in Vowel Harmony*, Amsterdam: Benjamins.

VAGO, R. M. (1985) 'The treatment of long vowels in word games', *Phonology Yearbook* **2**, 329–42.

VALDMAN, A. (1976) *Introduction to French Phonology and Morphology*, Rowley, Mass.: Newbury House.

VASQUEZ, W. (1953) 'El fonema /s/ en el español del Uruguay', *Revista de la facultad de humanidades y ciencias* **10**, 87–94.

VENNEMANN, T. (1972a) 'Sound change and markedness theory'. In R. Stockwell and A. Macaulay (eds) *Historical Linguistics in Generative Grammar*, Bloomington: Indiana University Press.

VENNEMANN, T. (1972b) 'On the theory of syllabic phonology', *Linguistische Berichte* **18**, 1–18.

VENNEMANN, T. (1974) 'Words and syllables in Natural Generative Grammar', in Bruck *et. al.* (1974).

VENNEMANN, T. and LADEFOGED, P. (1971) 'Phonetic features and phonological features', *UCLA Working Papers in Phonetics* **21**, 13–24.

VICENTE, A. Z. (1967) *Dialectología española*, Madrid: Editorial Gredos.

VINCENT, N. (1976) 'Three queries concerning one thesis concerning phonological representations', *Journal of Linguistics* **12**, 75–82.

VINCENT, N. (1986) 'Constituency and syllable structure'. In Durand (1986a).

VINCENT, N. (1988) 'Non-linear phonology in a diachronic perspective: stress and word-structure in Latin and Italian'. In Bertinetto and Loporcaro (1988).

WALL, R. (1973) *Introduction to Mathematical Linguistics*, Englewood Cliffs: Prentice-Hall.

WALTER, H. (1976) *La dynamique des phonèmes dans le lexique français contemporain*, Paris: France-Expansion.

WANG, H. S. and B. DERWING (1986) 'More on English vowel shift: the back vowel question', *Phonology Yearbook* **3**, 99–116.

WANG, S.-Y. (1967) 'Phonological features of tone', *International Journal of American Linguistics* **33**, 93–105.

WELLS, J. C. (1982) *Accents of English*, 3 vols, Cambridge: Cambridge University Press.

WILLIAMS, E. S. (1976) 'Underlying tone in Margi and Igbo', *Linguistic Inquiry* **7**, 463–84.

WILLIAMSON, K. (1977) 'Multivalued features for consonants', *Language* **53**, 843–71.

WILSON, R. D. (1966) 'A criticism of distinctive features', *Journal of Linguistics* **2**, 195–206.

WOO, N. (1969) 'Prosodic Phonology', MIT doctoral dissertation, Circulated by Indiana University Linguistics Club.

WOOD, S. (1982) *X-Ray and Model Studies of Vowel Articulations, Working Papers* **23**, Department of Linguistics, Lund University.

YIP, M. (1980) 'Why Scanian is not a case for multivalued features'. *Linguistic Inquiry* **11**, 432–6.

YIP, M. (1988) 'The obligatory contour principle and phonological rules: a loss of identity', *Linguistic Inquiry* **19**, 65–100.

ZWICKY, A. M. (1975) 'Settling on an underlying form: the English inflectional ending'. In D. Cohen and J. R. Wirth (eds) *Testing Linguistic Hypotheses*, New York: Wiley.

ZWICKY, A. M. and E. M. KAISSE (eds) (1987) *Syntactic Conditions on Phonological Rules, Phonology Yearbook* **4**.

ZWICKY, A. M. and G. K. PULLUM (1986) 'The principle of phonology-free syntax: introductory remarks', *Ohio State University Working Papers in Linguistics* **32**, 63–91.

Index